The Truth About
Human Origins

Brad Harrub, Ph.D.
Bert Thompson, Ph.D.

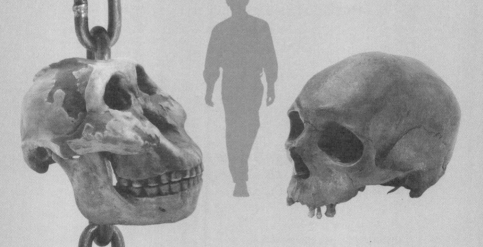

APOLOGETICS PRESS

Apologetics Press, Inc.
230 Landmark Drive
Montgomery, Alabama 36117-2752

© Copyright 2003
ISBN 10: 0-932859-58-5
ISBN 13: 978-0-932859-58-7
Printed in China

Library of Congress Cataloging-in-Publication

Brad Harrub (1970 -) and Bert Thompson (1949 -)
The Truth About Human Origins
Includes bibliographic references, and subject and name indices.
ISBN10 0-932859-58-5
ISBN13 978-0-932859-58-7
1. Creation. 2. Science and religion. 3. Apologetics and Polemics
I. Title

213—dc21   2003111100

DEDICATION

On occasion, there are certain individuals who quietly step into our lives—and who leave such an indelible imprint that we find our existence changed forever.

This book is dedicated to four such individuals, whom we never will be able to repay for their unwavering moral and financial support of our work, and who expect nothing in return for their incredible generosity—except our continued pledge to teach and defend the Truth.

This book (and numerous others like it) never could have come to fruition without the ongoing support of these two Christian couples who, although separated by many miles, walk side by side in their combined efforts to ensure the success of Apologetics Press.

This side of heaven, few will know the full impact of their sacrifices. Fortunately, God does.

TABLE OF CONTENTS

FOREWORD

Ever since Copernicus decided to put the Sun at the center of the solar system, various scientists and philosophers have worked overtime in their efforts to diminish the role of humankind in the Universe. As a result, we have gone from being the crowning glory of God's creation, to a hairless ape stuck on a small planet circling a mediocre sun in the distant reaches of one arm of a single galaxy that is one among billions of others. Some of the most widely read authors in the evolutionary camp (such as Carl Sagan, Stephen Jay Gould, Steven Weinberg, and Richard Dawkins) have repeatedly emphasized the lack of our uniqueness, and the "luck" supposedly related to our very existence (mundane as it may be).

Thus, man is viewed as occupying neither the center of the Universe, nor any sort of preeminent place in the living world; rather, we are nothing more, nor less, than the product of the same natural, evolutionary processes that created all of the "other animals" around us. In short, we are at best a "cosmological accident." Or, to express the idea in the words of the late, eminent evolutionist of Harvard, George Gaylord Simpson: "Man is the result of a purposeless and natural process that did not have him in mind. He was not planned. He is a state of matter, a form of life, a sort of animal, and a species of the Order Primates, akin nearly or remotely to all of life and indeed to all that is material" (1967, p. 345).

According to the most extreme version of this view, it is the utmost arrogance on man's part to identify **any** characteristic that distinguishes him from members of the animal kingdom. Any differences we might think we perceive are merely a matter of degree, and for all the things we may do better, there are other things we certainly do worse. Other primates, in particular, are worthy of coequality because they are supposed to be our nearest living relatives. Some even have gone so far as to suggest that this kinship puts a burden on us to make laws granting special rights to apes (Cavalieri and Singer, 1993; cf. Maddox, 1993).

The problem with such extreme positions is that they provide no reasonable stopping point. If we include other primates in a "global community of equals," then why not include all mammals, all animals, all living things? If apes' rights advocates can devise criteria that divide humans and apes from the other animals, then is it not equally legitimate for humans to devise criteria that separate us from the apes? In other words, can we say that there are no essential differences between humans and, say, chimpanzees? To put it another way, are there enough similarities to make us treat all primates on the same level (or almost on the same level) as members of our own species? Or is man truly unique in his own right?

In this book, we affirm the unqualified uniqueness of humankind. The fact is, there are numerous different aspects that man possesses—which animals do not. And each of those aspects not only is significant, but also serves to separate man from the animal kingdom in a most impressive fashion. Consider, for example, the following few examples among many that could be offered (and will be, later in this volume).

- First, man is capable of **speaking and communicating his thoughts via language**.
- Second, man can i**mprove his education, accumulate knowledge, and build on past achievements.**
- Third, man is **creative**, and can express himself via art, music, writing, etc.
- Fourth, closely related to man's creative ability is his gift of **reasoning**.
- Fifth, included in man's uniqueness is his **free-will** capacity to make rational choices.
- Sixth, **only man lives by a standard of morality, and has the ability to choose between right and wrong**.

- Seventh, only man possesses a **conscience**.
- Eighth, only man can experience heart-felt **emotions**.
- Ninth, man alone possesses a unique, inherent **religious inclination**; i.e., he has the ability to worship.
- Finally, and very likely most important, is the fact that man bears the spiritual imprint of God due to the fact that he possesses an **immortal soul**.

Knowing "the truth about human origins" centers on these (and other related) factors. It is our goal in this book to examine a number of these issues, and to provide what renowned American news commentator Paul Harvey might call "the rest of the story." We invite you to join us on a fascinating journey examining the origin and uniqueness of humanity—a journey that, we promise, will be anything but dull, and one that may even change the way you think about yourself and your fellow travelers in this pilgrimage we call "life."

Brad Harrub
Bert Thompson
December 2003

INTRODUCTION

It begins very early in a child's life, and never recedes—the constant barrage of speculation suggesting that men evolved from ape-like creatures over millions of years of geologic time. By early adolescence, many children already have a subconscious image of early man as a club-carrying, long-armed, hair-covered creature who lived in a cave. High school science books reinforce this notion with pictures of creatures like Lucy and Neanderthal Man, and by the end of their college careers, students frequently have accepted this evolutionary progression of man as a scientific fact. As such, man's existence, and his status in the Universe, are placed on a level just slightly above that of the animals.

Many in the current generation view man as little more than an educated ape that is the end result of fortuitous (and completely natural) circumstances. All of our actions and behaviors thus are viewed simply as "carry-overs" from our ape-like ancestry. With fragmentary skulls of our alleged ancestors in hand, evolutionists strive diligently to remove any vestige of a supernatural Creator.

But what is the real truth about human origins? What do those fossilized skulls **really** tell us about early man and his appearance on the Earth? This book begins by examining the "record of the rocks" in exacting detail, and in so doing, reveals the paucity of evidence for evolutionary theory. It documents that on more than one occasion, evolutionary scientists have paraded a "missing link" before the world, only to discover that it was not even close to being human (and, in some cases, actually was fraudulent!).

This volume also addresses DNA similarities, as well as the frequently parroted claim that chimpanzees are "98% human." While such announcements make for good headlines, the scientific data portend something entirely different.

In uncovering the truth about human origins, we also examine three critically important problems that evolutionists have struggled mightily to explain—or, at times, have simply avoided altogether: (1) the origin of language and communication; (2) the origin of gender and sexual reproduction; and (3) the origin of consciousness. These physiological differences represent vast chasms between humans and animals—chasms that evolutionists have not been able to span with either the available scientific evidence or fanciful hypothetical constructs.

We invite you to examine the data presented here—and then decide for yourself **the truth about human origins**. Personally, we believe that there is a far better explanation for the origin of mankind than organic evolution—to wit, a divine Creator. By the time you have finished reading this book, see if you don't agree.

1

THE "RECORD OF THE ROCKS" [PART I]

Homo sapiens, the genus and species classification for humans, means literally "wise man"—a designation that at times appears almost comical in light of the contentious claims of evolutionists that humans descended from ape-like ancestors. The pictures of our putative predecessors adorn the walls of science classrooms all over the world. Most of us, in fact, are familiar with the charts that show an ape on one end, a human at the other, and a whole host of ape-like intermediates in between. In an effort to bolster their theory of common descent for all living creatures, evolutionists have worked feverishly to demonstrate a convincing continuity between humans and our alleged ape-like ancestors. And, admittedly, at times they appear to have done their job so well that the ape-like intermediates they depict attain such fame that children immediately recognize their names and can easily recite their traits. For instance, while many individuals may not recognize the scientific name of *Australopithecus afarensis,* they very likely have heard of "Lucy" (the popular name for a famous set of fossils). Pictures of her fossilized remains have been paraded before us as an example of what is arguably the most famous, and the most widely known, of all the so-called "missing links."

Using a handful of bone fragments, a piece of a skull, or a few teeth, evolutionary artists portray what they want us to believe these hairy, ape-like creatures must have looked like. Frequently, we see them carrying primitive clubs, living in caves, or huddled around a fire with others of their kind. And so, from a very young age, children deposit deep within the recesses of their minds the images of these creatures crawling down out of the trees in Africa, learning to walk uprightly, and eventually evolving larger brains, advanced intelligence, and language. This image, however, is completely fictitious—as we will document in this chapter, and as some evolutionists themselves have been willing to admit publicly. Paleontologist Douglas Palmer, for example, stated in the March 16, 2002 issue of *New Scientist:* "The trouble is we probably know more about the evolution of extinct trilobites than we do about human evolution" (173[2334]:50).

In this book, we would like to critically examine the actual evidence of human origins found within the fossil record. Additionally, we would like to offer an updated, "corrected" interpretation of that evidence, because the current evolution-based interpretation simply does not fit the available facts.

BIOLOGICAL TAXONOMY AND HUMAN EVOLUTION

As we begin to assemble, disassemble, and then reassemble the puzzle of the "record of the rocks" in regard to human evolution, we first need to understand the terminology currently in use in evolutionary circles regarding what frequently is called "fossil man." A brief refresher course in biological nomenclature seems appropriate at this juncture.

Scientists employ what is commonly referred to as the **binomial nomenclature** system, first devised by the Swedish botanist Carolus Linnaeus (1707-1778), and revised somewhat down through the years. Biologists today group all living organisms into specific hierarchical assemblages, in which each category is "nested" within the next higher category. Depicted in a graphic format, the assemblages would appear something similar to the chart as seen on the next page (after Mayr, 2001, p. 23).

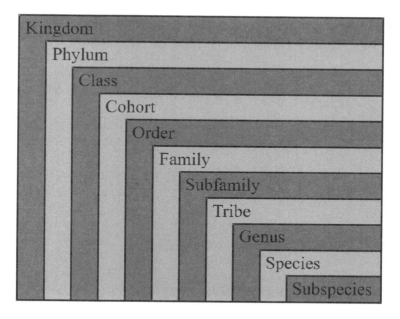

The earliest scientist to attempt to divide organisms into recognizable groups (which he called "kingdoms") was Linnaeus. He recognized only two distinct groups: Animalia (animals) and Plantae (plants). Later modifications to the two-kingdom concept were made by the German embryologist, Ernst Haeckel (1834-1919), who suggested the addition of a third kingdom (which he referred to as the Protista) that included two groups: (1) Protozoans (like, for example, the amoeba); and (2) Monera.

Later, American biologist Herbert F. Copeland (1902-1968) of Sacramento City College in Sacramento, California, split Haeckel's Monera into two groups. He retained the original Monera designation, but used it to refer only to prokaryotes (i.e., bacteria in the traditional sense). He placed the eukaryotes (plus various algae) into a new kingdom, the Protoctista. [Eukaryotes are cells that are characterized by membrane-bound organelles (such as the nucleus, ribosomes, et al.). Animals, plants, fungi, and protoctists are eukaryotes. Prokaryotes are cells that possess a plasma membrane themselves, yet lack a true nucleus and membrane-bound organelles within their cytoplasm. In prokaryotes, the DNA normally is found in a single, naked, circular chromosome (known as a genophore) that lies free in the cytoplasm. Archaebacteria and eubacteria are prokaryotes.]

Then, in 1959, American Robert H. Whittaker of Cornell University proposed his now-famous "five-kingdom concept," which included Animalia, Plantae, Fungi, Protoctista, and Monera (see Whittaker, 1959). Of the five kingdoms, one (Monera) is prokaryotic, and four (Animalia, Plantae, Fungi, and Protoctista) are eukaryotic. It is the five-kingdom concept that still is used widely by most scientists and that was, in fact, the basis for the classic 1998 atlas of the living world, *Five Kingdoms: An Illustrated Guide to the Phyla of Life on Earth*, by Lynn Margulis and Karleve V. Schwartz that has become practically the taxonomists' "Bible."

However, as molecular biology began to come into its own, and as scientists were able to examine the DNA of various organisms, it became apparent to them that the five-kingdom concept no longer provided enough accuracy. Carl Woese, a biologist from the University of Illinois, proposed two radical changes in the taxonomic system then in place. First, he divided the bacteria (Whittaker's Monera) into two distinct groups that, at the time, he labeled: (1) Archaebacteria and; (2) Eubacteria. [Archaebacteria (from the Greek *archae*, meaning ancient) are organisms that exist in a variety of "hostile" environments such as hot-water springs, or even within solid rock, frequently are thermophilic (heat-loving), produce methane, and are anaerobic (live only in the absence of free oxygen). For an excellent discussion of the Archaea, see Ward and Brownlee, 2000, pp. 6-10.] Second, Woese proposed an entirely new category, the "domain," which he boldly placed above kingdoms. In his scheme, the five kingdoms were spread over three domains: (1) Archaea (which Woese subdivided into two kingdoms—Crenarchaeota (heat-loving forms) and

Euryarchaeota (mainly methane-producing forms); (2) Bacteria; and (3) Eucarya (which includes the plants, animals, protests, and fungi). [For an up-to-date treatment of the history of the taxonomic matters discussed here, see Tudge, 2000, pp. 95-106.]

Today, the current status in taxonomy acknowledges Woese's "domain" proposal. However, the five-kingdom concept still remains extremely popular, and likely will until such a time at some point in the distant future when it is overtaken by the domain concept. [Identification of an organism usually is given by listing only the genus and species. For example, the common pine tree is known as *Pinus ponderosus.* The common rat is *Rattus rattus.* The common housecat is referred to as *Felis domesticus.* And so throughout this book whenever you see two Latinized names being used (e.g.: *Australopithecus africanus* or *Homo erectus*), that simply represents the genus and species of the particular creature under discussion.]

At this point, we would like to call attention to three specific terms that are used when man or man's alleged ancestors are being discussed since they currently are the source of some controversy within the taxonomic branch of science. These terms are: (1) hominoid; (2) hominid; and (3) hominin. An explanation is in order.

Briefly stated, under the broad outlines of the Linnaean system, humans would be classified as follows: Animalia (since man is considered as an animal); Chordata (because humans have backbones); Mammalia (since humans have hair and suckle their young); Primates (because humans share certain morphological traits with apes, monkeys, and lemurs); *Hominidae* (since humans are separated from "other apes" by, among other traits, bipedalism); *Homo* (mankind's generic classification as human); and *sapiens* (the species name designating "wise"). In chart form, then, man's exact scientific classification would be rendered as at appears in the listing on the next page.

Kingdom	Animalia
Phylum	Chordata
Subphylum	Vertebrata
Superclass	Tetrapoda
Class	Mammalia
Order	Primates
Suborder	Anthropoidea
Tribe	Catarrhina
Superfamily	Hominoidea
Family	*Hominidae*
Subfamily	Homininae
Tribe	Hominini
Genus	*Homo*
Species	*sapiens*
Subspecies	*sapiens*

As the chart above indicates, the Linnaean system also recognizes groupings such as superfamilies, subfamilies, tribes, etc. In the case of humans, the most frequently recognized superfamily is the Hominoidea (from which the term "hominoids" is derived). The term hominoid includes all of the living apes. In fact, under the superfamily Hominoidea, three families are included: (1) the *Hylobatidae* (which includes the so-called lesser apes of Asia, the gibbons, and the siamangs); (2) the *Hominidae* (which includes living humans and fossil apes that allegedly possess a suite of characteristics such as bipedalism, reduced canine tooth size, increasing brain size, etc.); and (3) the *Pongidae* (which includes the remaining African great apes such as gorillas, chimpanzees, and the Asian orangutan). It is from the level of the superfamily onward that most of the present debate over the classification of humans begins. In a December 4, 2001 article titled "Is It Time to Revise the System of Scientific Naming?" on *National Geographic's* Web site, Lee R. Berger, a paleoanthropologist at the University of Witwatersrand in Johannesburg, South Africa, discussed the controversy from an evolutionary viewpoint (which explains the evolution-based dates, which we do not accept).

Modern-day genetic research is providing evidence that morphological distinctions are not necessarily proof of evolutionary relatedness. Recent evidence suggests that humans are in fact more closely related to the chimpanzee and bonobo than either species is to the gorilla. Chimps and humans share something like 98 percent of genes, indicating that we share a common ape ancestor.

Divergence times between the two groups based on a molecular clock suggest that the chimpanzee/human split occurred between five and seven million years ago. In turn, the African apes, including humans, are more closely related to each other than any are to the orangutan.

In recognition of these and other genetic relationships, some argue that we must overhaul the present morphologically based classification system for one that is more representative of our true evolutionary relationships as evinced by our genes.

This is where the term **hominin** comes into play. Under the new classification model, hominoids would remain a primate superfamily, as has always been the case. Under this hominoid umbrella would fall orangutans, gorillas, chimps, and humans, all in the family *Hominidae.*

In recognition of their genetic divergence some 11 to 13 million years ago, the orangutans would be placed in the sub-family Ponginae and the African apes, including humans, would all be lumped together in the sub-family Homininae. The bipedal apes—all of the fossil species as well as living humans—would fall into the tribe Hominini (thus hominin). All of the fossil genera, such as *Australopithecus, Ardipithecus, Kenyanthropus,* and *Homo,* would fall into this tribe.

A few evolutionary biologists want a more extreme classification, which would include humans and chimpanzees within the same genus, the genus *Homo* (2001, emp. added).

The taxonomic controversy, therefore, turns out to be a matter of "old" versus "new." Under the old, morphologically based system, the term "hominid" refers to the **bipedal ape lineage** (which would include humans). Under the new, molecular-based system, hominid refers not just to bipedal apes, but rather to the broader grouping of **all the great apes**. Thus, under the new system, "hominin" (as opposed to "hominid") would refer to all (living or dead) species of bipedal apes (which, again, would include humans). It is likely that the newer term will "win out" in the end (as Berger noted in his article). Until it does, however, we may expect to continue to see both terms appear in the scientific literature concerning human classification and/or evolution.

There is one part of the evolutionary classification scheme, however, where there is no controversy. Every man, woman, and child living today is classified as *Homo sapiens sapiens*.

DID MAN EVOLVE FROM THE APES?

Evolutionists today, of course, do not contend that man descended from the **apes**. Instead, they contend that both men and apes descended from a **common ancestor**. We, however, agree with the late evolutionary paleontologist of Harvard University, George Gaylord Simpson, who summed up such an idea quite succinctly when he wrote:

> On this subject, by the way, there has been way too much pussyfooting. Apologists emphasize that man cannot be descendant of any **living** ape–a statement that is obvious to the verge of imbecility–and go on to state or imply that man is not really descended from an ape or monkey at all, but from an earlier common ancestor. In fact, that earlier ancestor would certainly be called an ape or monkey in popular speech by anyone who saw it. Since the terms **ape** and **monkey** are defined by popular usage, man's ancestors were apes or monkeys (or successively both). It is pusillanimous [cowardly–BH/BT] if not dishonest for an informed investigator to say otherwise (1964, p. 12, emp. in orig).

Ironically, some evolutionists have even gone so far as to suggest—albeit incorrectly—that Charles Darwin himself never claimed that man came from the apes. Yet he most certainly did. In *The Descent of Man*, Darwin wrote:

> But a naturalist would undoubtedly have ranked as an ape or a monkey, an ancient form which possesses many characters common to the Catarhine and Platyrhine monkeys, other characters in an intermediate condition, and some few, perhaps, distinct from those now found in either group. **And as man from a genealogical point of view belongs to the Catarhine or Old World stock, we must conclude, however, much the conclusion may revolt our pride, that our early progenitors would have been properly designated.** But we must not fall into the error of supposing that the early progenitors of the whole Simian stock, including man, was identical with, or even closely resembled, any **existing** ape or monkey (1871, pp. 519-520, emp. added).

Since the time of Darwin, evolutionists have struggled to devise plausible theories about why those ancient apes decided to leave the confines of the treetops in favor of bipedal locomotion on the plains. Marcel-Paul Schutzenberger defined the problem well when he lamented:

> Gradualists [those who believe in slower rates of evolution—BH/BT] and saltationists [those who believe in a more rapid rate of evolution—BH/BT] alike are completely incapable of giving a convincing explanation of the quasi-simultaneous emergence of a number of biological systems that distinguish human beings from the higher primates: bipedalism, with the concomitant modification of the pelvis, and, without a doubt, the cerebellum, a much more dexterous hand, with fingerprints conferring an especially fine tactile sense; the modifications of the pharynx which permits phonation; the modification of the central nervous system, notably at the level of the temporal lobes, permitting the specific recognition of speech. From the point of view of embryogenesis, these anatomi-

cal systems are completely different from one another. Each modification constitutes a gift, a bequest from a primate family to its descendants. It is astonishing that these gifts should have developed simultaneously (1996, pp. 10-15).

It is indeed "astonishing" that these apes (or, to be more politically correct, "ape-like creatures") could have experienced the "simultaneous emergence of a number of biological systems" that distinguish them from human beings. It is equally "astonishing" to see how evolutionists have interpreted the evidence of the fossil record that they insist establishes such an event as actually having occurred. We invite you to join us on this fascinating journey while we investigate "the record of the rocks" as it applies to human evolution.

AN EXAMINATION OF THE
"RECORD OF THE ROCKS"

As we begin an examination of the fossil record as it allegedly relates to human evolution, let's be blunt about one thing. Of all the branches to be found on that infamous "evolutionary tree of life," the one leading to man should be the best documented. After all, as the most recent evolutionary arrival, pre-human fossils supposedly would have been exposed to natural decay processes for the shortest length of time, and thus should be better preserved and easier to find than any others. [Consider, for example, how many dinosaur fossils we possess, and those animals were supposed to have existed over sixty-five million years before man!] In addition, since hominid fossils are of the greatest interest to man (because they are supposed to represent his past), it is safe to say that more people have been searching for them longer than for any other type of fossils. If there are any real transitional forms anywhere in the world, they should be documented most abundantly in the line leading from the first primate to modern man. Certainly, the fossils in this field have received more publicity than in any other. But exactly what does the human fossil record reveal?

Not much, as it turns out. First, there is the problem caused by the paucity of physical evidence. In their book, *People of the Lake*, Richard Leakey and Roger Lewin addressed this point when they wrote:

> What the fossils tell us directly, of course, is what our ancestors and their close relatives look like. Or rather, to be more accurate, they give us some clues about the physical appearance of early hominids, because until someone is lucky enough to come across a complete skeleton of one of our ancestors, **much of what we can say about them is pure inference, guesswork** (1978, p. 19, emp. added).

And more often than not, that "guesswork" is based on an appalling lack of evidence, as the evolutionists themselves have been known to admit. John Reader, author of the book, *Missing Links*, wrote in *New Scientist:*

> The entire hominid collection known today would barely cover a billiard table, but it has spawned a science because it is distinguished by two factors which inflate its apparent relevance far beyond its merits. First, the fossils hint at the ancestry of a supremely self-important animal—ourselves. Secondly, the collection is so tantalisingly incomplete, and the specimens themselves often so fragmented and inconclusive, that more can be said about what is missing than about what is present. Hence the amazing quantity of literature on the subject. ...[B]ut ever since Darwin's work inspired the notion that fossils linking modern man and extinct ancestor would provide the most convincing proof of human evolution, preconceptions have led evidence by the nose in the study of fossil man (1981, 89:802).

Lyall Watson, writing in *Science Digest*, put it even more bluntly: "The fossils that decorate our family tree are so scarce that there are still more scientists than specimens. The remarkable fact is that all the physical evidence we have for human evolution can still be placed, with room to spare, inside a single coffin" (1982, 90[5]:44). And, as you will see in the pages that follow, even though numerous hominid fossils have been discovered since Reader and Watson offered such assessments, none qualifies as a legitimate "human ancestor."

The public, of course, continues to be misled into thinking that some sort of "documented evolutionary progression" from an ape-like creature to modern man has been found within the fossil record. That, as it turns out, is "wishful thinking," to use the words of paleontologist David Raup:

> A large number of well-trained scientists outside of evolutionary biology have unfortunately gotten the idea that the fossil record is far more Darwinian than it is. This probably comes from the over-simplification inevitable in secondary sources: low-level textbooks, semi-popular articles, and so on. Also, there is probably some wishful thinking involved. **In the years after Darwin, his advocates hoped to find predictable progressions. In general, these have not been found**—yet the optimist has died hard, and some pure fantasy has crept into textbooks (1981, 213: 289, emp. added).

As we make our way in this book through the alleged evidence for human evolution, you will witness firsthand some of that "pure fantasy."

Furthermore, the public at large generally has no idea just how paltry, and how fragmentary (literally!), the "evidence" for human evolution actually is. Harvard professor Richard Lewontin lamented this very fact when he stated:

> When we consider the remote past, before the origin of the actual species *Homo sapiens*, we are faced with a fragmentary and disconnected fossil record. Despite the excited and optimistic claims that have been made by some paleontologists, no fossil hominid species can be established as our direct ancestor…. The earliest forms that are recognized as being hominid are the famous fossils, associated with primitive stone tools, that were found by Mary and Louis Leakey in the Olduvai gorge and elsewhere in Africa. These fossil hominids lived more than 1.5 million years ago

and had brains half the size of ours. They were certainly not members of our own species, and we have no idea whether they were even in our direct ancestral line or only in a parallel line of descent resembling our direct ancestor (1995, p. 163).

Second, it is practically impossible to determine which "family tree" one should accept. Richard Leakey (of the famed fossil-hunting family in Africa) has proposed one. His late mother, Mary Leakey, proposed another. Donald Johanson, former president of the Institute of Human Origins in Berkeley, California, has proposed yet another. And as late as 2001, Meave Leakey (Richard's wife) has proposed still another. At an annual meeting of the American Association for the Advancement of Science some years ago, anthropologists from all over the world descended on New York City to view hominid fossils exhibited by the American Museum of Natural History. Reporting on this exhibit, *Science News* had this to say:

> One sometimes wonders whether orangutans, chimps and gorillas ever sit around the tree, contemplating which is the closest relative of man. (And would they want to be?) Maybe they even chuckle at human scientists' machinations as they race to draw the definitive map of evolution on earth. If placed on top of one another, all these competing versions of our evolutionary highways would make the Los Angeles freeway system look like County Road 41 in Elkhart, Indiana (see "Whose Ape Is It, Anyway?," 1984, p. 361 parenthetical item in orig.).

How, in light of such admissions, can evolutionary scientists possibly defend the idea of ape/human evolution as a "scientifically proven fact"?

The evolutionary tree that has been presented to demonstrate the origin of humans has two main branches (and assorted twigs) within the primate family (*Hominidae*). One consists of the genus *Australopithecus*, while the other is composed of the genus *Homo*. The categories to which various fossils have been assigned may be more telling than we first thought, for evidence now exists which demonstrates that all fossils in the *Australopithecus* group share a common trait—one buried deep within the ear—while all those in the genus *Homo* share a completely different physiology, likewise related to the ear. Richard Leakey commented:

> Part of the anatomy of the inner ear are three C-shaped tubes, the semicircular canals. Arranged mutually perpendicular to each other, with two of the canals oriented vertically, the structure plays a key role in the maintenance of body balance. At a meeting of anthropologists in April 1994, Fred Spoor, of the University of Liverpool, described the semicircular canals in humans and apes. The two vertical canals are significantly enlarged in humans compared with those in apes, a difference Spoor interprets as an adaptation to the extra demands of upright balance in a bipedal species. What of early human species? Spoor's observations are truly startling. In **all** species of the genus *Homo*, the inner ear structure is indistinguishable from that of modern humans. Similarly, in **all** species of *Australopithecus*, the semicircular canals look like those of apes.... [I]f the structure of the inner ear is at all indicative of habitual posture and mode of locomotion, it suggests that the australopithecines were not just like you and me, as Lovejoy suggested and continues to suggest (1994, pp. 34-36, emp. added).

Thus it appears that, as creationists have contended, all fossils can be placed into one of two groups: apes or humans.

While it is impossible to present **any** scenario of human evolution upon which even the evolutionists themselves would agree, the schematic on the next page (gleaned from the latest scientific literature) represents the most up-to-date assessment available on the subject (see Figure 1). [NOTE: We do not accept the evolution-based dates attached to the finds, but have left them intact for reference purposes.]

In the search for man's alleged ancestors, evolutionists claim that some 28 millions years ago there existed a monkey-like creature by the name of *Aegyptopithecus zeuxis* that occupies

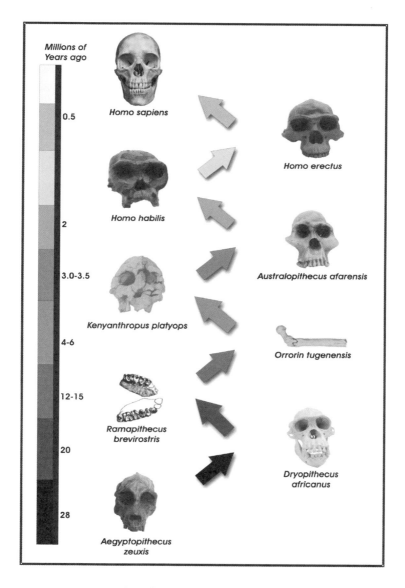

Figure 1 — The alleged evolutionary timeline of man

the exalted status of the first animal on the long road toward humankind. It is, then, with *Aegyptopithecus zeuxis* that we begin our investigation.

Aegyptopithecus zeuxis

According to Richard Leakey and Roger Lewin (in their book *Origins*), the ancestor that humans share with all living apes is *Aegyptopithecus zeuxis* (linking Egyptian ape)–a creature that they suggest lived 28 million years ago, and that they have identified specifically as "the first ape to emerge from the Old World monkey stock" (1978, p. 52). A 12-year-old child, however, could look at the fossil remains of *Aegyptopithecus,* and be able to identify them as having come from an ape. There is no controversy here; evolutionists acknowledge that *Aegyptopithecus* is merely an ape.

Figure 2 — Artist's concept of *Aegyptopithecus zeuxis*

Dryopithecus africanus

The next creature in the search for man's alleged evolutionary ancestor is *Dryopithecus africanus.* [*Dryopithecus* means "woodland ape"; the creature also goes by the name *Proconsul.*] *D. africanus,* according to Leakey and Lewin, was "the ancestor to both apes and humans," and, according to evolutionary theory, "is the stock from which all modern apes evolved" (1977, p. 56).

The first fossil of *D. africanus* (which supposedly lived in Africa some 20 million years ago) was discovered by Louis and Mary Leakey (Richard's parents) in 1948 at Rusinga Island, Lake Victoria, Africa. Standard evolutionary theory suggests that "earlier members of *Dryopithecus* may well have given rise to the ancestors of both the human and the ape lines" (Leakey and Lewin, p. 56). And so the next creature in the evolutionary chart will be *D. africanus,* at about 20 million years.

But based on what evidence? Paleontologist David Pilbeam answered that when he wrote: "It has come to be rather generally assumed, albeit in a rather vague fashion, the pre-Pleistocene hominid ancestry was rooted in the Dryopithecinae" (1968, 24:368). Upon reading that statement, creation scientist Duane Gish noted somewhat dryly:

> When a scientist is forced to "assume" something in a rather "vague fashion," it should be obvious that he is resorting to wholly unscientific methods to establish what he cannot do by a valid scientific method. What strange qualities could paleoanthropologists detect in an animal that allows them to decide on one hand that it was the progenitor of the chimpanzee, the gorilla, and the orangutan, and yet on the other hand was the progenitor of the human race? (1995, p. 223).

Figure 3 — Artist's representation of *Dryopithecus africanus*

In the end, however, as Pilbeam and Elwyn Simons pointed out, *Dryopithecus* already was "too committed to ape-dom" to be the progenitor of man (1971, 173:23). Again, no controversy here; the animal is admittedly an ape.

Ramapithecus brevirostris

G. Edward Lewis, a student at Yale University, was the first to discover *Ramapithecus*, and it was he who named it. The species name assigned to the creature was *brevirostris*, meaning "short-snouted." Mr. Lewis found his specimen (a single upper jaw) in 1932 around Haritalyangar, a cluster of villages in the Siwalik Hills about a hundred miles north of New Delhi, India. *Ramapithecus* was dated at approximately 12-15 million years ago. At the time, Lewis designated the find the first true hominid. In their book, *The Monkey Puzzle*, evolutionists John Gribbin and Jeremy Cherfas observed:

> …[W]e now come to the interesting bit, the beginning of our own ancestral line. It starts with a creature called *Ramapithecus*, found first in India and named after a prince in Indian mythology. *Ramapithecus* is known to us as a handful of jaw scraps and teeth and a bit of skull; there is none of his body skeleton, though in keeping with his status as man's ancestor he is usually drawn upright. The oldest ramapithecine fossils are about 14 million years old, and the conventional wisdom has it that some time during the long gap between *Aegyptopithecus* and *Dryopithecus* there lived a common ancestor of *Dryopithecus* and *Ramapithecus*. **This missing link, probably around 25 million years old, would be the youngest common ancestor of man and the African apes, for by the time we find *Dryopithecus* in the fossils, according to the traditional picture, the line of *Ramapithecus* and man has already split off and become distinct**. That all the ramapithecine fossils are younger than the dryopithecine fossils is just the luck of the draw; some day, the paleontologists hope, a very old *Ramapithecus* will turn up (1982, p. 74, emp. added).

According to Leakey and Lewin, *Ramapithecus* fossil finds currently consist of a few fragments of upper and lower jaws and a collection of teeth from some 30 or so creatures. In 1961, Louis Leakey found a *Ramapithecus* specimen (an upper jaw and, later, a lower jaw) at Fort Ternan in southern Kenya. Even

Figure 4 — Artist's representation of *Ramapithecus brevirostris*. Jaw fragment at lower left represents actual fossils found.

though *Ramapithecus* fossils have been found in Greece, India, Pakistan, Turkey, Hungary, and China, Leakey and Lewin believe that the only species to give rise to the hominids was the one from Africa (1977, p. 30). Perhaps this would be a good place to insert some of their candid admissions.

> Now if we are absolutely honest, we have to admit that we know nothing about *Ramapithecus*; we don't know what it looked like; we don't know what it did; and naturally, we don't know how it did it! But with the aid of jaw and tooth fragments and one or two bits and pieces from arms and legs, all of which represents a couple of dozen individuals, we can make some guesses, more or less inspired.

> Before we slip into a mood of total speculation, it is worth trying to squeeze out of the miserable fragments of petrified limb bones some clues about how *Ramapithecus* got around.... We cannot be certain, but it must have happened some time because by the time reasonable hominid fossils appear (at about three millions years ago) our ancestors were walking about with a respectable upright gait (p. 27, parenthetical item in orig.).

> Why did *Ramapithecus* take to eating tough fibrous foods—a life-style that must have demanded more and more time on the ground rather than in the trees? Why did its canines shrink? Why did it start to walk around on two legs, when, by all accounts, walking on four is much less expensive, energetically? And what kind of social life was it having? These are the sort of questions to which we would like the answers, but to which, for the moment, we have only guesses (pp. 31-32).

> What can we say about the sexual selection of *Ramapithecus*? Nothing. At least nothing that comes from direct evidence (p. 35).

> Did *Ramapithecus* live in harems? Were the males much bigger than the females? And did the males have a thick coat so as to make them look even bigger, just like the geladas? It is possible, but we simply don't know (p. 36).

How bright was *Ramapithecus*? With little more than a fossil teeth and jaws for evidence, it is not easy to say, of course (p. 37).

The most dramatic thing to have happened to *Ramapithecus* during that frustrating fossil void is that it learned how to walk upright. We don't know how it got around the place before it adopted this highly unusual method of locomotion; maybe it moved smoothly on all fours, much as olive baboons do today. We don't know (p. 39).

We are talking here of **habitual** upright walking, rather than **occasional** bipedalism, something that all apes are capable of, inelegant though it looks. That it happened we know. That there are considerable advantages to be had once an ape has stood up is incontrovertible. But **why** it should happen in the first place is a mystery because most of the advantages are apparent only when upright walking is very well advanced.... We have to admit to being baffled about the origins of upright walking (pp. 40,42, emp. in orig.).

A number of years ago, Robert Eckhardt, a paleoanthropologist at Penn State University, published an article in *Scientific American* headlined by the statement: "Amid the bewildering array of early fossil hominids, is there one whose morphology marks it as man's hominid ancestor? If the factor of genetic variability is considered, the answer appears to be no" (1972, 226[1]:94). In other words, according to Eckhardt, at that time, nowhere among the fossil apes or ape-like creatures could be found what might be judged to be a proper ancestor for man. Simons, Pilbeam, and others consider *Ramapithecus* to have been a hominid—a judgment made solely on the basis of a few teeth and jaw fragments. Eckhardt made twenty-four different measurements on a collection of fossil teeth from two species of *Dryopithecus* and one species of *Ramapithecus*, and compared the range of variation found for these fossil species to similar measurements made on a population of domesticated chimpanzees from a research center and on a sample of wild chimpanzees in Liberia.

The range of variation in the living chimpanzee populations actually was greater than those in the fossil samples for fourteen of the twenty-four measurements, the same for one, and less for nine of the measurements. Even in the minority of cases where the range of variation of the fossil samples exceeded those in living chimpanzees, the differences were very small. Thus, in tooth measurements, there was greater variation among living chimpanzees, or a single group of apes, than there was between *Dryopithecus*, an admitted ape, and *Ramapithecus*, an alleged hominid. And remember, *Ramapithecus* was judged to be a hominid solely on the basis of its dental characteristics!

Eckhardt extended his calculations to five other species of *Dryopithecus* and to *Kenyapithecus* (which, according to Pilbeam and Simons, is the equivalent of *Ramapithecus*). After stating that on the basis of tooth-size calculations there appears to be little basis for classifying the dryopithecines in more than a single species, Dr. Eckhardt went on to say: "Neither is there compelling evidence for the existence of any distinct hominid species during this interval unless the designation 'hominid' means simply any individual ape that happens to have small teeth and a corresponding small face" (226[1]:101). Eckhardt's conclusion was that *Ramapithecus* seems to have been an ape—morphologically, ecologically, and behaviorally.

Even more devastating evidence against the assumption of a hominid status for *Ramapithecus* have been recent revelations concerning the living, high-altitude baboon *Theropithecus galada* found in Ethiopia. This baboon has incisors and canines that are small (relative to those of extant African apes), closely packed and heavily worn cheek teeth, powerful masticatory muscles, and a short, deep face, plus other man-like features allegedly possessed by *Ramapithecus* (and *Australopithecus*, a creature we will discuss later). Since this animal is nothing but a baboon in all respects, and is living today, it is certain that it has no genetic relationship to man. Yet it has many of the facial, dental, and mandibular characteristics used to classify *Ramapithecus* as a hominid.

While it is true that the possession of such features by monkeys or apes is highly exceptional, to include these facial, dental, and mandibular characteristics among those considered to be diagnostic of hominids, since they are possessed at least in one case by a monkey, is both unwarranted and invalid. These facts would render highly uncertain, if not impossible, the classification of any fossil as a hominid solely on the basis of dental and associated characteristics.

These considerations, plus the information compiled by Eckhardt, offer compelling evidence that *Ramapithecus* was no hominid at all, but was simply an ape or monkey with a diet and habitat similar to that of galada baboons. Thus, there is no real evidence for a hominid of any kind in the huge 20-million-year gap between the supposed branching point of apes, australopithecines, and man. Many evolutionists believe that man's ancestors branched off from the apes roughly 20 million years ago; thus, they date the australopithecine fossils from 2-4 million years ago or thereabouts. Based on evolutionary dating methods, this would mean that there was a period of about 20-24 million years during which hominids supposedly were evolving, yet not a single undisputed hominid fossil from that period has been discovered.

Remember that evolutionists believe that *Ramapithecus* was in man's lineage because the incisors and canine teeth (the front teeth) of this animal were relatively small in relation to the cheek teeth (as is the case in man). They believe the shape of the jaw was parabolic, as in humans, rather than U-shaped, as in most apes. And because of some other subtle anatomical distinctions found relating to the jaw fragments, the creature's face is believed to have been shortened (although no bones of the face or skull have yet been recovered).

Thus, all of the evidence linking *Ramapithecus* to man is based solely upon extremely fragmentary dental and mandibular (jaw) evidence. But, of course, as Duane Gish has aptly observed: "With less evidence, broader speculations are allowed" (no date).

In the end, what shall we say about *Ramapithecus*? While it is true that in the past some anthropologists considered this creature to be the first true hominid, that no longer is the case. Thanks to additional work by Pilbeam, we now know that *Ramapithecus* was not a hominid at all, but merely another ape (1982, 295:232). Anthropologist Jonathan Marks summed up the evidence regarding *Ramapithecus* by observing simply: "Looks, as we all know, can be deceiving, and *Ramapithecus* has since been shown not to have been a human ancestor. Details of its face show it to have been more closely related to the orangutan" (2002, p. 12). Gish, therefore, was correct in stating: "He is no longer considered to have been a creature in the line leading to man" (1985, p. 140). Once again, no controversy here; the animal is admittedly an ape.

What, then, shall we say of these three "ancestors" that form the taproot of man's family tree? We simply will say the same things the evolutionists themselves have admitted: all three were nothing but apes. Period.

Orrorin tugenensis

The 13 fossil fragments that form *Orrorin tugenensis* (broken femurs, bits of lower jaw, and several teeth) were found in the Tugen Hills of Kenya in the fall of 2000 by Martin Pickford and Brigitte Senut of France, and have been controversial ever since. If *Orrorin* were considered to be a human ancestor, it would predate other candidates by around 2 million years. Pickford and Senut, however, in an even more drastic scenario, have suggested that **all** the australopithecines–even those considered to be our direct ancestors–should be relegated to a dead-end side branch in favor of *Orrorin*. Yet paleontologist David Begun of the University of Toronto conceded that evolutionists have been

Figure 5 — Broken femur from *Orrorin tugenensis*

completely unable to tell whether *Orrorin* was "on the line to humans, on the line to chimps, a common ancestor to both, or just an extinct side branch" (2001). **Lots** of controversy here–but no evidence of a creature on its way to becoming human.

Australopithecus (Ardipithecus) ramidus

In 1994, Tim White and his coworkers described a new species known as *Australopithecus ramidus* (White, et al., 371: 306-312. [*Australopithecus* means "southern ape"; "*Ardi*" means "ground" or "floor" in the Afar language of Africa; *ramidus* means "root."] The initial fossil find in 1993 included seventeen fossils (mainly dental) found within volcanic strata covering about 1.5 kilometers west of the Awash River within the Afar Depression at Aramis, Ethiopia. Eleven of the fossils were comprised of a single tooth, a piece of a tooth, or in one case, a piece of bone. The strata in which the fossils were found were dated by evolutionists as being 4.4 million years old. Later, in 1994, a mandible and partial postcranial skeleton of a single individual also was found. The authors of the paper in *Nature* described the cranial fossils as "**strikingly chimpanzee-like in morphology**" (1994: 371:310, emp. added). The pieces of arm bone were described as exhibiting "a host of characters usually associated with modern apes" (371:311). The August 23, 1999 issue of *Time* magazine contained a feature article, "Up from the Apes," about the creature (Lemonick and Dorfman, 1999). Morphologically speaking, this was the earliest, most ape-like australopithecine to date, and appeared to be a good candidate for the most distant common ancestor of the hominids. [For an excellent discussion of *A. ramidus*, see Wise, 1994.]

In 1995, however, White completely reclassified the creature as *Ardipithecus ramidus* (1995, 375:88). And one year after that, Donald Johanson (the discoverer of "Lucy") admitted in the March 1996 issue of *National Geographic* that *A. ramidus* possessed "many chimp-like features" and that "its position on the human family tree is in question" (189[3]:117).

Australopithecus anamensis

In 1965, a research team from Harvard University discovered a small piece of a left humerus in the Kanapoi region of East Lake, Turkana in Africa. It would be thirty years before that single bone would be assigned to its appropriate place in human paleoanthropology—as a member of the *Australopithecus anamensis* group of fossils (see Johanson and Edgar, 1996). Except for the discovery of a single molar in 1982, no further *A. anamensis* fossils were found until the early 1990s, when Meave Leakey and her coworkers from the National Museums of Kenya began their work in the Kanapoi region. Initially, the finds were classified tentatively as *Australopithecus afarensis* (see Coffing, et al., 1994). In 1995, Meave Leakey and colleagues reclassified the finds as *Australopithecus anamensis* (Leakey, et al., 1995). [*Anamensis* means "lake" in the Turkana language.] The latest fossils—which contain no postcranial material, and consist almost exclusively of teeth—are dated at 3.8-4.2 million years old.

All of the fossils found by Leakey and her coworkers were found within a single region east of Lake Turkana. And what do those fossils tell us? The respected Archaeologyinfo.com Web site explained: "The dental apparatus of *A. anamensis* is markedly ape-like," and "in general, the dentition of *A. anamensis* is very primitive for a hominid." Yet Leakey, et al., believe that *A. anamensis* was bipedal—a belief based on the examination of postcranial fragments, specifically a single piece of a tibia. And what is it about the tibia that has caused the researchers to suggest that *A. anamensis* may have walked in an upright fashion? The distal portion of the tibia is thick in areas that are subjected to high forces of stress during bipedal locomotion, and the condyles (which join with the femur to form the knee joint) are concave and equal in size—two conditions present in modern humans (Johanson and Edgar, 1996).

Yet the meager numbers of fossils that have been found are admitted by evolutionists to bear striking similarities to both *Ardipithecus* and *Pan* (the actual genus of the chimpanzees). In fact, as the Archaeologyinfo.com Web site went on to state:

Though specific comparisons between *A. anamensis* and *Ardipithecus ramidus* would be difficult, due to the small skeletal collections that have been obtained for both fossil hominids, a general similarity seems to be clear. Both species have retained ape-like crania and dentition, while also exhibiting rather advanced postcrania, more or less typically hominid-like in form (see "*Australopithecus anamensis,*" 2003, emp. added).

The conclusion? *A. anamensis* is "more or less" a hominid, even though it is similar to *Ardipithecus ramidus* (which, as Donald Johanson admitted, possesses "many chimp-like features"). Its dentition is "markedly ape-like." And it is "very primitive" for a hominid. Enough said.

Ardipithecus ramidus kadabba

The bright yellow and white wording on the front cover of the July 23, 2001 issue of *Time* announced somewhat authoritatively, "How Apes Became Humans," and claimed that a new hominid discovery of a creature known as *Ardipithecus ramidus kadabba* (kadabba–taken from the Afar language –means "basal family ancestor") tells "scientists about how our oldest ancestors stood on two legs and made an evolutionary leap." Yet those empty cover-story words became almost secondary as *Time* readers found themselves utterly enthralled by the "ape-man" drawing that filled the whole cover.

Time cover courtesy of TIMEPIX. Copyright © 2001. Used by permission.

- 29 -

Unfortunately, many readers may never make it to page 57, where staff writers Michael Lemonick and Andrea Dorfman admitted that the discoverers of the fossils under discussion, Yohannes Haile-Selassie and his colleagues, "haven't collected enough bones yet to reconstruct with great precision what *kadabba* looked like." That seemingly insignificant fact, however, did not prevent the magazine's editors from putting an intimidating, full-color "reconstruction" of this new fossil find on the cover—an image, if we may kindly say so, that becomes somewhat less than forthright in light of the actual facts of the matter. A thorough investigation of this "scientific discovery" reveals that this creature was "reconstructed" from only 6 bone fragments and a few teeth—of which, the only one that might provide the artist with any structural information of the head was a portion of the right mandible.

In their article, "One Giant Step for Mankind," Lemonick and Dorfman invited readers to meet their "newfound ancestor, a chimplike forest creature that stood up and walked 5.8 million years ago" (2001, 158:54). According to evolutionists, *Ardipithecus ramidus kadabba* lived between 5.2 and 5.8 million years ago, which beats the previous record holder by nearly a million-and-a-half years and, according to evolutionists' estimates, places *A. kadabba* "very close to the time when humans and chimps first went their separate ways" (158:56). Lemonick and Dorfman went on to comment:

> ...[N]o one has yet been able to say precisely when that first evolutionary step on the road to humanity happened, nor what might have triggered it. But a discovery reported last week [July 12–BH/BT] in the journal *Nature* has brought paleontologists tantalizingly close to answering both these questions (158[3]: 56; for the original *Nature* article, see Haile-Selassie, 2001).

That's a pretty bold statement, considering the fact that researchers had only the following bone fragments from which to glean all of this information: a fragment of the right mandible, one intermediate hand phalanx, the left humerus and ulna, a distal humerus, a proximal hand phalanx fragment, a left clavicle fragment, a proximal foot phalanx, and a few teeth. In addition, these bones were not laid out neatly in typical skeletal format, all grouped together and just waiting for researchers to dig them up. No indeed! These few bones took researchers **5 years** to collect, and came from **5 different locations!** And so, from a fossilized toe, a piece of jawbone, a finger, arm bones, a clavicle, and a few teeth we have this incredible "ape-man" to prove "how apes became human."

Prominently displayed in the center of page 59 of the *Time* article is a single unimpressive toe bone, about which Lemonick and Dorfman wrote: "This toe bone proves the creature walked on two legs." **Amazing, is it not, what one can discern from a single toe bone!** The human foot contains 26 individual bones (see Netter, 1994, p. 492), yet evolutionists claim that they can distinguish walking characteristics from an examination of just one? That bold caption also failed to inform the reader that this toe bone (found in 1990) is "chronologically younger" than the other bone fragments, and was found in a separate location from the rest of the fossils. In fact, the bone fragments that make up this new specimen came from five localities of the Middle Awash in Ethiopia: Saitune Dora, Alaya, Asa Koma, Digiba Dora, and Amba East (Haile-Selassie, 2001, 412:181). Lemonick and Dorfman conceded: "Exactly how this hominid walked is still something of a mystery, though with a different skeletal structure, its gait would have been unlike ours" (158:57). But that did not stop the authors from speculating that "*kadabba* almost certainly walked upright much of the time," and that "many of its behaviors undoubtedly resembled those of chimpanzees today" (158:57). Interesting speculation—especially in view of the fact that the ages of the fossilized bone fragments composing *kadabba* vary by hundreds of thousands of years according to the evolutionists' own dating schemes. What was it that convinced evolutionists that *kadabba* walked upright and was on the road to becoming man? A single toe bone!

In contemplating the origin of "two-leggedness," the authors of the *Time* article suggested that these animals were rewarded with additional food for their bipedal mobility. The writers then went into painstaking detail to describe the environment in which researchers believe these creatures lived—an environment that, in their view, necessitated that the animals walked upright. Meave Leakey, head of paleontology at the National Museums of Kenya, wife of Richard Leakey, a well-known member of the world's most famous fossil-hunting family, stated: "And if you're moving into more open country with grasslands and bushes and things like this, and eating a lot of fruits and berries coming off low bushes, there is a [expletive deleted] of an advantage to be able to reach higher. That's why the gerenuk [a type of antelope—BH/BT] evolved its long neck and stands on its hind legs, and why the giraffe evolved its long neck" (as quoted in Lemonick and Dorfman, p. 59). Yet even staunch evolutionists (such as the late Stephen Gould) cringe at statements like that. In fact, in an article titled "The Tallest Tale" that he penned for the May 1996 issue of *Natural History*, Dr. Gould began by stating: "The tallest tale is the textbook version of giraffe evolution—a bit of a stretch." Gould then went on to state:

> Giraffes, we are told, got long necks in order to browse the leaves at the tops of acacia trees, thereby winning access to a steady source of food available to no other mammal. Lamarck, the texts continue, explained the evolution of long necks by arguing that giraffes stretched and stretched during life, elongated their necks in the process and then passed the benefits along to their offspring by altered heredity. This lovely idea may embody the cardinal virtue of effort rewarded, but heredity, alas, does not operate in such a manner. A neck stretched during life cannot alter the genes that influence neck length and offspring cannot reap any genetic reward from parental striving (1999b, 105[5]: 19-20).

In commenting on why this example of evolution with the giraffe's neck is bad science, Dr. Gould wrote:

If we choose a weak and foolish speculation as a primary textbook illustration (falsely assuming that the tale possesses weight of history and a sanction in evidence), then we are in for trouble as critics properly nail the particular weakness and then assume that the whole theory must be in danger if supporters choose such a fatuous case as a primary illustration (105[5]:56, parenthetical item in orig.).

Creationist Luther D. Sunderland further reiterated the foolishness of this line of thinking when he stated:

Evolutionists cannot explain why the giraffe is the only four-legged creature with a really long neck and yet everything else in the world [without that long neck —BH/BT] survived. Many short-necked animals, of course, existed side by side in the same locale as the giraffe (1988, pp. 83-84).

And so, as Leakey herself pointed out, the evolutionists' theories regarding bipedalism "are all fairy tales really because you can't prove anything" (as quoted in Lemonick and Dorfman, p. 60). Fairy tales?

While *Ardipithecus ramidus kadabba* undoubtedly will stir controversy among evolutionists as to exactly where it fits into the "evolutionary family tree," it does little to answer the questions of "how apes became human," or when and why these creatures became bipedal. Given the small measurements of the fossilized bones collected, *kadabba* is very likely to find itself relegated to the same branch as the infamous Lucy (*Australopithecus afarensis*)—simply a fossilized ape.

Kenyanthropus platyops

In the March 22, 2001 issue of *Nature,* a new hominid genus named *Kenyanthropus platyops* (from eastern Africa) was described (Leakey, et al., 2001). Using their new specimen to rework humanity's pedigree, paleoanthropologist Meave Leakey and her colleagues at the National Museums of Kenya in Nairobi argued that the small-brained creature is so unusual it belongs not just to a new species, but rather to an entirely new genus! This new species now is nestled in the roots of the human family tree at a time when scientists thought only one ancestral species existed, leaving it unclear just which (if either!) was the direct forebear of modern humankind.

The authors named this new find *Kenyanthropus platyops,* which means flat-faced man of Kenya, "in recognition of Kenya's contribution to the understanding of human evolution through the many specimens recovered from its fossil sites" (410:433). However, an exhaustive study of the article reveals a list of 36 cranio-dental fossils from this site, of which only 5 contain bone fragments. The remaining 31 are fragments of teeth. Only two of these specimens, the skull and a partial upper jaw, are intact enough to be assigned to this new taxon. The authors described their new finds as "a well-preserved temporal bone, two partial maxillae, isolated teeth, and most importantly a largely complete, although distorted, cranium" (410:433). Distorted indeed! Even an untrained eye can look at the figures provided in the article and see the extensive damage to this newly found fossil. The flat face of *platyops* adds another wrinkle in the evolutionary timeline—a wrinkle that is no small problem because creatures younger than *K. platyops* (and therefore closer to *Homo sapiens*) have much more pronounced, ape-like facial features. *K. platyops* was dated at 3.5 million years, and yet has a much flatter face than any other hominid that old. Thus, the evolutionary scenario seems to be moving in the wrong direction!

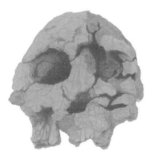

Figure 6 — *Kenyanthropus platyops*

Additionally, the authors provided a table in which the derived cranial features of this new species were compared to other finds (410:434). Out of the 21 characteristics listed, *Kenyanthropus platyops* differs from *Homo rudolfensis* (considered the most primitive species in our own genus, which also includes *Homo erectus* and *Homo habilis*) in only one area: the upper molar size. *H. rudolfensis* is listed as having a moderate upper molar, whereas *K. platyops* is listed as small. So, as a result of a very fragmented and "distorted" cranium that possesses "small" upper molars, we now have been graced with a new genus.

Scattered throughout the text of the March 22, 2001 *Nature* article were hidden reminders that everything about this recent discovery is speculative and indefinite. Below are a few statements that the authors used to describe this new find (also referred to as KNM-WT 40000):

> Most of the [cranial] vault is heavily distorted, both through post-mortem diploic expansion and compression from an inferoposterior direction (p. 434).

> The original shape of the severely distorted mastoids cannot be reconstructed, but other parts of the left temporal are well preserved (p. 435).

> It is preserved in two main parts, the neurocranium with the superior and lateral orbital margins, but lacking most of the cranial base; and the face, lacking the premolar and anterior tooth crowns and the right incisor roots (p. 433).

> Only the right M^2 crown is sufficiently preserved to allow reliable metric dental comparisons. It is particularly small, falling below the known ranges of other early hominin species (p. 434).

> Inability to distinguish between first and second molars makes meaningful intertaxon comparisons of these elements difficult (p. 437).

> The sex of KNM-WT 40000 is difficult to infer. The small M^2 crown size could suggest that the specimen is female (p. 436).

One quick and easy way for a paleontologist to get the public's attention is to announce a find that is either: (1) very old; or (2) directly related to the ancestry of humans. With *K. platyops,* Leakey does both. And so the race for claim on the oldest "common" ancestor is on—again! In 1994, Tim White and colleagues described the new species *Australopithecus ramidus,* dated at 4.4 million years old. Morphologically, this was the most ape-like australopithecine yet discovered (as well as the earliest), and seemed a good candidate for the most distant common ancestor of the hominids. A year later, Meave Leakey and her colleagues described the 3.9-4.2 million year old *Australopithecus anamensis.* This taxon is slightly more similar to *Ardipithecus* and *Pan* (the chimpanzees) than the better known and slightly later *A. afarensis,* and stood for a while as the ancestor of the later hominids (or a close cousin to some unknown, ancestral taxon).

Some have argued that part or all of the material regarding *K. platyops* belongs more properly in the genus *Australopithecus.* If Leakey, et al., are right in their assertion that facial flatness connects *K. platyops* and *H. rudolfensis* in a significant manner, then that implies that their lineage had an evolutionary history distinct from the australopithecines. Therefore, evolutionists would conclude that we are descended from *Kenyanthropus* by way of *H.* (or *K.*) *rudolfensis,* or that the latter species is completely distinct from us and does not belong in our genus.

Aside from the obvious concerns over the extrapolations made from this fossil find, there are two other issues with which the authors conveniently chose not to deal. (1) No postcranial remains have been recovered from the site in which the cranium was found, and as a result, we know nothing about *K. platyops'* locomotory adaptation, particularly its degree of bipedality. Was this creature even able to walk upright as humans do? (2) Leakey placed a tremendous amount of importance on the flatness of the facial features of this fossil, due to the widely acknowledged fact that more modern creatures would possess an admittedly flatter facial structure than their older, more ape-like alleged ancestors.

Tim White, the renowned anthropologist from the University of California at Berkeley, recognized immediately the serious nature of the problem that *K. platyops* presented to the standard evolutionary scenario, and was not afraid to discuss the problem in a quite public fashion (in fact, he has been one of the most vocal critics of *K. platyops*). He wrote: "If you think of a family tree with a trunk, **we're talking about two trunks**, if they're right" (as quoted in McCall, 2001, p. 4-A, emp. added). A tree with—two trunks?

Apparently, however, they are not "right." Two years after Meave Leakey and her coworkers announced the discovery of *K. platyops*, no less of an evolutionary anthropologist than Tim White himself called into question the legitimacy of Leakey's decision to create a completely new genus and species to "house" her find. White's discussion centered on the issue of whether paleontologists take into consideration skeletal variations when they report the latest "missing link." His point is a legitimate one, and, truth be told, is one that should be made much more frequently than it is. After all, anyone who has ever sat in a room full of 200 individuals of various ages and from various cultures, realizes that skulls (and body sizes) come in a variety of shapes and forms. But, on occasion, impatient paleontologists are all too eager to be the ones to identify the next branch on the family tree. Thus, they rush to judgment—only later to discover they were "not right." In an article he authored for the March 28, 2003 issue of *Science* ("Early Hominids—Diversity or Distortion?"), White rebuked some of his overzealous paleontologist colleagues as he attempted to "rein in" the tendency of fossil hunters to classify every new find as a different genus or species.

In his article, he quoted two former Harvard professors—Ernst Mayr, who once described hominid taxonomy as a "bewildering diversity of names," and George Gaylord Simpson, who lamented "the chaos of anthropological nomenclature" (White, 2003, 299:1994). White then commented that many paleoanthropologists herald each new fossil as evidence for biodiversity, thus pointing to a "bushy" hominid tree. But, as White noted: "Whether judged from fossil evidence or zoological considerations, the metaphor of an early hominid bush seems seriously misplaced" (p. 1994). He then offered as an example the 2002 announcement of the African "Toumaï" hominid cranium from Chad, which, he noted,

> was enthusiastically greeted as "the tip of an iceberg of taxonomic diversity during hominid evolution 5-7 million years ago." The same author even predicted

a Late Miocene "African ape equivalent of the Burgess Shale." **How could a single fossil from a previously unknown period warrant such claims?** (p. 1994, emp. added).

How indeed? How can scientists make bold claims with just a single specimen, especially when they consider the normal variation found in that room of 200 people? White inquired:

> New hominid fossils are routinely given new species names such as *Ardipithecus ramidus, Australopithecus anamensis, Australopithecus garhi,* and *Homo antecessor.* At the same time, long-abandoned names such as *H. heidelbergensis* and *H. rhodesiensis* have recently been resurrected. Textbook authors and publishers eagerly adopt these taxa. But does the resultant nomenclature accurately reflect early hominid species diversity? (p. 1994).

He then went on to make a statement that should (but probably will not) echo throughout the halls of academia.

> To evaluate the biological importance of such taxonomic claims, **we must consider normal variation within biological species. Humans** (and presumably their ancestors and close relatives) **vary considerably in their skeletal and dental anatomy.** Such variation is well documented, and stems from ontogenetic, sexual, geographic, and idiosyncratic (individual) sources (p. 1994, parenthetical items in orig., emp. added).

The fact is, even within our own families, we find huge variations.

In his article in *Science,* White launched an all-out attack on those who are so quick to name new species. One of the first bombs he dropped was aimed at Meave Leakey because of her (mis)naming of *Kenyanthropus platyops.* White believes this is just one more example of scientists being too quick to give us a "bushy family tree."

In an article titled "Flat-faced Man in Family Feud" that was posted on the Nature Science Update portion of *Nature's* Web site on March 28, 2003, Rex Dalton noted that White believes it was "geology, not genes" that "gave the Flat-faced Man his distinctive looks" (2003). In other words, White has suggested that, over time, fine-grained rock invaded tiny cracks in the skull, and distorted its shape in an irregular way (White was granted access to the *Kenyanthropus* fossil). His explanation for the unusually flat face is based on skulls of pigs that, he noted, were "flattened and narrowed by geological deformation, not natural selection." And White is not alone in his assessment. Elwyn Simons, who studies primate evolution at Duke University, concurred: "The evidence may not support the description of a new genus" (as quoted in Dalton, 2003).

Dalton noted that Bernard Wood, a hominid specialist at George Washington University in Washington, D.C., agrees that geological processes very likely altered the skull. Dalton also pointed out that Leakey's team knew that. Wood noted: "What is at issue is whether that alteration materially affects if this is a new genus" (as quoted in Dalton). White went on to say:

> There are two questions to be asked in considering whether the fossil constitutes evidence of early hominid species diversity. First, are the described morphological differences from the *A. anamensis* to *A. afarensis* lineage real, or are they merely artifacts of postmortem fossilization processes? Second, does the putatively new morphology lie outside the expected range of phenotypic variation of this lineage? (p. 1995).

His first point was illustrated in the *Science* article by an intricate sequence of pictures of pig skulls that almost anyone would consider to be separate species. Yet experts know the skulls are all from the **same** species. Geological processes, as it turns out, distorted the skulls. After burial, these skulls were crushed, extruded, and otherwise modified, sometimes in nonlinear and asymmetric ways. In illustrating his second point, White showed two very different-looking skulls of modern female chimpanzees. One skull was narrow, the other broad; one profile had a pronounced slant, while the other was compressed. The teeth, brow ridges, skullcap, and eye sockets were vastly different—yet both these specimens belonged to the same species—and are even the same sex! White remarked: "This variation is normal in a single sex of an extant species; even more variation is present in other extant ape species" (p. 1995).

The phrase, "a picture speaks a thousand words," comes to mind as one reads Dr. White's *Science* article. The pig skulls are grossly distorted, and the two chimpanzee skulls show incredible variation. Entire cranial regions are different between the two. Given the fact that we know geological conditions distort fossils, and given the fact that we see so much variation within species, one cannot help but wonder how many "missing links" have been "created" using only **one** skull—a skull that was either damaged by geological conditions, or simply was a variation of a human?

In the "acknowledgments" section of her *Nature* article, Leakey thanked the National Geographic Society for funding her fieldwork and laboratory studies. This simple "thank-you" likely indicates that the editors of *National Geographic* soon will be mailing a full-color, slick-paper, professionally produced, eye-catching magazine into our homes so that we, our children, and our grandchildren can read articles about this new species. *National Geographic* and others are quick to run cover stories featuring world-famous evolutionists such as Donald C. Johanson (discoverer of our alleged hominid ancestor, "Lucy") or the late Louis and Mary Leakey (in-laws of Meave, both of whom spent their entire professional careers on the African continent searching for the ever-elusive "missing link" between humans and ape-like ancestors). However, when the issue hits newsstands near you, remember what Greg Kirby, senior lecturer in population biology at Flinders University, Adelaide, said in an address on the case for evolution in South Australia in 1976: "…not being a paleontologist, I don't want to pour too much scorn on paleontologists, but if you were to spend your life picking up bones and finding little fragments of head and little fragments of jaw, there's a very strong desire to exaggerate the importance of those fragments…" (as quoted in Snelling, 1990, p. 16).

2

THE "RECORD OF THE ROCKS" [PART II]

Australopithecus afarensis

Donald Johanson's account of the discovery of the creature now known popularly as "Lucy" reads like a Hollywood script—filled with mystery, excitement, and emotion. In Johanson's own words, "Lucy was utterly mind-boggling" (Johanson and Edey, 1981, p. 180). He tells of feeling a strong, subconscious "urge" to go with American graduate student Tom Gray to locality 162. The superstitious paleontologist even recalls writing in his daily diary that he was "feeling good" about the day. So, on November 30, 1974, Johanson (who was serving at the time as the director of the Cleveland, Ohio, Museum of Natural History) and Gray loaded up in a Land Rover and headed out to plot an area of Hadar, Ethiopia, known as "locality 162." After several hours of surveying in 100+ degree heat, the two decided to head back. However, on returning to their vehicle, Johanson suggested they take an alternate route in order to survey the bottom of a nearby gully. In Johanson's words: "It had been thoroughly checked out at least twice before by other workers, who had found nothing interesting. Nevertheless, conscious of the 'lucky' feeling that had been with me since I woke, I decided to make that small final detour."

Buried in the sandy hillside of the slope was an arm bone—the single bone that eventually led to the unearthing of a skeleton that was nearly **40% complete.** While the description of this famous find may read like some serendipitous treasure unearthed in a movie script, the truth is far from it. It soon would become one of the most famous (and most controversial) fossils of all time, and would shake every limb on the famous hominid family tree, completely upsetting then-current theories about how man came to be bipedal. Richard Leakey and Roger Lewin stated of the find: "Johanson had stumbled on a skeleton that was about 40% complete, **something that is unheard of in human prehistory farther back than about a hundred thousand years**. Johanson's hominid had died at least 3 million years ago" (1978, p. 67, emp. added). But as additional studies were carried out, it soon became obvious that this "missing link" was, in fact, "too good to be true."

Dr. Johanson named his find *Australopithecus afarensis*–thus designating it as the southern ape from the Afar depression of northeastern Ethiopia (Johanson, et al., 1978, 28:8). The creature quickly earned the nickname "Lucy," after the Beatles' song, "Lucy in the Sky with Diamonds," which played through the celebratory night at Johanson's camp. The fossil, officially designated as AL 288-1, consisted of skull fragments, a lower jaw, ribs, an arm bone, a part of a pelvis, a thighbone, and fragments of shinbones. It was said to be an adult, and was dated at 3.5 million years. [Johanson also found at Hadar the remains of some 34 adults and 10

Figure 1 — Reconstruction of skull of *Australopithecus afarensis*

infants, all of which are dated at 3.5 million years.] In their assessment of exactly where this new species fit in, Johanson and colleague Tim White took pride in noting: "These new hominid fossils, recovered since 1973, constitute the earliest definitive evidence of the family *Hominidae*" (1979, 203:321). Not only was this fossil find unusually complete, but it also was believed to have been from an animal that walked in an upright fashion, as well as being the oldest human ancestor–the equivalent of a grand slam in baseball.

Figure 2 — Artist's concept of *Australopithecus afarensis*

Having collected the fossils, Johanson and White were responsible for publishing their descriptions, as well as providing an interpretation of how they fit into the hominid family tree. Not wanting to waste valuable space on the description of *A. afarensis* in one of the major science journals, they ultimately decided to publish it in *Kirtlandia,* a relatively obscure publication of the Cleveland Museum of Natural History. Then, in what was either an extremely naïve (albeit zealous) move, or a calculated, ambitious one, Johanson and White decided to bump the Leakey's prized *Australopithecus africanus* off the main hominid tree and replace it with *A. afarensis* (for their full assessment, see Johanson and White, 1979). Leaky's *A. africanus* was relegated to a tangential side branch that went—literally—nowhere. This decision eventually would weigh heavily on Lucy as she fell under attack from scientists who felt she was nothing more than another example of *A. africanus*—or worse yet, an animal with a great deal of chimp-like qualities.

One of the ironic discoveries regarding Lucy had to do with the size of her skull. Prior to her discovery, evolutionists had assumed that these ape-like species had evolved larger brains, which then allowed them to crawl down out of the trees and begin foraging for food on the ground. According to evolutionary timelines, the creatures adopted bipedalism as their primary form of transportation, and once on the ground, began to use tools. Lucy took this nice, neat little story and flipped it upside down. Her brain case was not enlarged. In fact, from all appearances, it was comparable in size to the common chimpanzee. And yet, Johanson and White were absolutely convinced this creature walked uprightly like man. They noted:

> Bipedalism appears to have been the dominant form of terrestrial locomotion employed by the Hadar and Laetolil hominids. Morphological features associated with this locomotor mode are clearly manifested in these hominids, and for this reason the Laetoli and Hadar hominid remains are **unequivocally assigned to the family *Hominidae*** (1979, 203:325, emp. added).

Johanson insisted that *afarensis* was the direct ancestor of man (see Johanson and Edey, 1981). In fact, the words "the dramatic discovery of our oldest human ancestor" can be found emblazoned on the cover of his book, *Lucy: The Beginnings of Humankind.* Numerous evolutionists, however, strongly disagree. Lord Solly Zuckerman, the famous British anatomist, published his views in his book, *Beyond the Ivory Tower.* He studied the australopithecines for more than 15 years, and concluded that if man descended from an apelike ancestor, he did so without leaving a single trace in the fossil record (1970, p. 64). Some might complain, "But Zuckerman's work was done before Lucy was even discovered." True, but that misses the point. Zuckerman's research—which established conclusively that the australopithecines were nothing but knuckle-walking apes—was performed on fossils **younger** (i.e., closer to man) than Lucy!

And therein lies the controversy. If Lucy and her descendants were discovered to be nothing more than an ape, then all of Johanson's fame and fortune would instantly vanish like an early morning fog hit by a hot noonday Sun. Remember—this single discovery **made** Johanson's career. Upon returning the entire Hadar hominid fossil collection to the National Museum in Ethiopia (as he had previously agreed he would), Johanson recounted:

> Lucy had been mine for five years. The most beautiful, the most nearly complete, the most extraordinary hominid fossil in the world, she had slept in my office safe all that time. I had written papers about her, appeared on television, made speeches. I had shown her proudly to a stream of scientists from all over the world. **She had—I knew it—hauled me up from total obscurity into the scientific limelight** (Johanson and Edey, 1981, p. 374, emp. added).

Thus, one can understand why he would have such a vested interest in keeping this fossil upright and walking on two feet. If others were to discover that Lucy was not a biped, then her hominid status would be relegated to that of nothing but an ape—something far less rewarding for Dr. Johanson, professionally speaking.

Did Johanson examine the evidence prior to making his decision about Lucy's ability to walk uprightly? Or was Lucy "upright" and "walking" even before all of her fossils were uncovered—i.e., from the moment that single **arm bone** buried in the sand was discovered? By his own admission, Johanson noted: "This time I knew at once I was looking at a hominid elbow. **I had to convince Tom, whose first reaction was that it was a monkey's.** But that wasn't hard to do" (Johanson, et al., 1994, p. 60, emp. added). However, as more and more individuals gained access to the fossils (or replicas thereof), Johanson's "hominid" began to be called into question.

We would like for you to examine the evidence regarding this famous hominid fossil, and then determine for yourself whether Lucy and her kin were, in fact, our human ancestors —or merely ancient apes. Consider the following anatomical discoveries that have been made since Johanson's initial declaration of Lucy as a entirely new hominid species.

Lucy's Rib Cage

Due to the impossibility of reconstructing Lucy's skull from the few fragments that were available, the determination that Lucy walked uprightly like a human had to be derived from her hips and ribs. Peter Schmid, a paleontologist at the Anthropological Institute in Zurich, Switzerland, studied Lucy extensively, and then summarized his efforts as follows.

> When I started to put the skeleton together, I expected it to look human. Everyone had talked about Lucy as being very modern, very human, so I was surprised by what I saw. I noticed that the ribs were more round in cross-section, more like what you see in apes. Human ribs are flatter in cross-section. But the shape of the rib cage itself was the biggest surprise of all. The human rib cage is barrel shaped, and I just couldn't get Lucy's ribs to fit this kind of shape. But I could get

them to make a conical-shaped rib cage, like what you see in apes (as quoted in Leakey and Lewin, 1992, pp. 193-194). Schmid went on to note:

> The shoulders were high, and, combined with the funnel-shaped chest, would have made arm swinging improbable in the human sense. It wouldn't have been able to lift its thorax for the kind of deep breathing that we do when we run. The abdomen was pot-bellied, and there was no waist, so that would have restricted the flexibility that's essential for human running (as quoted in Leakey and Lewin, p. 194).

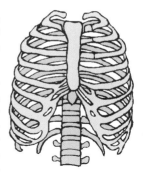

Figure 3 — Lucy's rib cage was conical shaped, unlike the barrel-shaped rib cage of a human (above).

True, ribs can be "tweaked" and rotated so that they appear more "barrel like" or conical, but the best (and correct) arrangement always will be the original morphology. The facets from the ribs that line up on the vertebrae provide a tighter fit when aligned correctly In Lucy's case, her ribs are conical, like those found in apes.

Lucy's Pelvis and Gender

A great deal of the "hype" regarding Lucy has been pure speculation from the very beginning. In fact, incredible though it may seem, even the gender of this creature is now being called into question. Johanson's original assessment stated: "The most complete **adult** skeleton is that of AL 288-1 ('Lucy'). The small body size of this evidently **female** individual (about 3.5 to 4.0 feet in height) is matched by some other postcranial remains…" (Johanson and White, 1979, 203:324). And yet, in his original review, Johanson's description of postcranial [below the skull—BH/BT] data was both speculative and deficient. Johanson and colleagues noted: "Strong dimorphism in body size; all skeletal elements with high level of robusticity in muscle and tendon insertion; pelvic region and lower limbs indicate adaptation to bipedal locomotion…" (Johanson, et al., 1978, 28:7-8). From the beginning, it was considered an adult female. It would be from the shattered fragments of the pelvis that Donald Johanson and others would interpret the AL 288-1 fossils as being a female—primarily due to the diminutive size. But these bones were far from being problematic. As Hausler and Schmid discovered: "The sacrum and the auricular region of the ilium are shattered into numerous small fragments, such that the original form is difficult to elucidate. Hence it is not surprising that the reconstructions by Lovejoy and Schmid show marked differences" (1995, 29:363).

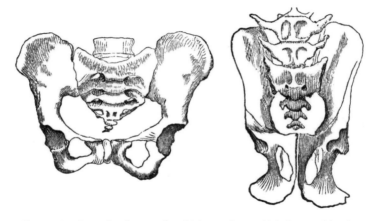

Figure 4 — Lucy had a smaller, kidney-shaped birth canal (as in the illustration at the right), as opposed to that found in a human (left).

In regard to Lucy's pelvis, Johanson affirmed: "Lucy's wider sacrum and shallower pelvis gave her a smaller, kidney-shaped birth canal, compared to that of modern females. She didn't need a large one because her newborn infant's brain wouldn't have been any larger than a chimpanzee infant's brain" (Johanson, et al., 1994, p. 66). That admission begs the question as to why this fossil was not categorized from the outset as simply a chimpanzee. But this gender declaration poses additional problems for Lucy. As Hausler and Schmid noted: "If AL 288-1 was female, then one can exclude this species from the ancestors of *Homo* because its pelvis is certainly less primitive than the pelvis of Sts 14 [designation for a specific *A. africanus* fossil–BH/BT]" (29:378). Both of the pelvises mentioned display some degree of damage, and both are missing critical parts, but it should be noted that in regard to the Lucy fossil, **more than one attempt was made at reconstruction**.

After various reconstructions of the inlet and midplane of Lucy's pelvis, along with comparisons to other fossils and modern humans, it became evident that the shape of Lucy's pelvis was not structured correctly for the eventuality of a birth process. The pelvis was just too narrow to accommodate an australopithecine fetus. Hausler and Schmid noted that Lucy's pelvis was ridgeless and heart-shaped—which means that "she" was more likely a "he." They noted:

> Contrary to Sts 14 [designation for a specific *A. africanus* fossil–BH/BT], delivery [of a baby–BH/BT] in AL 288-1 would have been more complicated than in modern humans, if not impossible, due to the protruding promontorium.... Consequently, there is more evidence to suggest that AL 288-1 was male rather than female. A female of the same species as AL 288-1 would have had a pelvis with a larger sagittal diameter and a less protruding sacral promontorium. ...Overall, the broader pelvis and the more laterally oriented iliac blades of AL 288-1 would produce more favourable insertion sites for the climbing muscles in more heavily built males.... **It would perhaps be better to change the trivial name to "Lucifer" according to the old roman god who brings light after the dark night because with such a pelvis "Lucy" would apparently have been the last of her species** (29:380, emp. added).

This declaration produced an immediate reaction from the evolutionist community, as many scientists worked diligently to try to defend Lucy. If Hausler and Schmid's conclusion is correct, then this implies that the equivalent female of this species would be even smaller—something unheard of in trying to compare this creature to modern-day humans! Lucy's pelvis is not what it should be for an upright-walking hominid —but the dimensions easily fall within primates found among the family *Pongidae* (apes).

Lucy's Appendages—Made for Bipedalism, or Swinging from Trees?

But what do Lucy's arms and legs tell us in regard to her locomotion? If she were a biped, surely her upper and lower extremities would point toward an upright stance. After all, the bone that led to Johanson's discovery of Lucy was that of an arm. Yet the bony framework that composes Lucy's wrists may be the most telling factor of all. Brian Richmond and David Strait of George Washington University experienced what many might call a "eureka!" moment while going through some old papers on primate physiology at the Smithsonian Institute in Washington, D.C.

> "We saw something that talked about special knuckle walking adaptations in modern African apes," Dr. Richmond said. "I could not remember ever seeing anything about wrists in fossil hominids…. Across the hall was a cast of the famous fossil Lucy. We ran across and looked at it and bingo, it was clear as night and day" (see BBC News, 2000).

The March 29, 2000 *San Diego Union Tribune* reported:

> A chance discovery made by looking at a cast of the bones of "Lucy," the most famous fossil of *Australopithecus afarensis,* shows her wrist is stiff, like a chimpanzee's, Brian Richmond and David Strait of George Washington University in Washington, D.C., reported. This suggests that her ancestors walked on their knuckles (Fox, 2000).

Richmond and Strait discovered that knuckle-walking apes have a mechanism that locks the wrist into place in order to stabilize this joint. In their report, they noted: "Here we present evidence that fossils attributed to *Australopithecus anamensis* (KNM-ER-20419) and *A. afarensis* (AL 288-1) retain specialized wrist morphology associated with knuckle-walking" (2000, 404:382, parenthetical item in orig.). They went on to note:

> Pre-bipedal locomotion is probably best characterized as a repertoire consisting of terrestrial knuckle-walking, arboreal climbing and occasional suspensory activities, not unlike that observed in chimpanzees today. This raises the question of why bipedalism would evolve from an ancient ancestor already adapted to terrestrial locomotion, and is consistent with models relating the evolution of bipedalism to a change in feeding strategies and novel non-locomotor uses of the hands (404:384, emp. added).

Moreover, additional evidence has come to light which suggests that Lucy is little more than a chimpanzee. Johanson and his coworkers admitted in an article in the March 31, 1994 issue of *Nature* that Lucy possessed chimp-proportioned arm bones (see Kimbel, et al., 1994) and that her alleged descendants (e.g., *A. africanus* and *H. habilis*) had ape-like limb proportions as well—which is a clear indication that she did not evolve into something "more human."

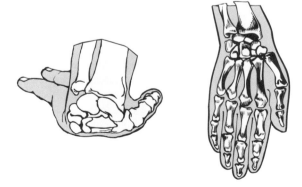

Figure 5 — Illustration depicting non-locking hand joint of human, which contrasts with locking-type joint possessed by Lucy

Not only have Lucy's wrists and arm-bones been called into question, but there also is a mountain of evidence that demonstrates this creature was better adapted for swinging through the trees, like modern-day chimps. After thoroughly examining *A. afarensis* fossils, Stern and Susman noted: "It is demonstrated that *A. afarensis* possessed anatomic characteristics that indicate a significant adaptation for movement in the trees" (1983, 60:280). They went on to comment: "The AL 333-91 [designation for specific *A. afarensis* fossil—BH/BT] pisiform [bone of the hand—BH/BT] is 'elongate and rod shaped' and thus resembles the long, projecting pisiform of apes and monkeys" (60:281).

Stern and Susman's research detailed the fact that the hands and feet of *Australopithecus afarensis* are devoid of the normal human qualities assigned to hands and feet. Instead, their research demonstrated that these creatures had long, curved fingers and toes typical of arboreal primates. [In reading through the following descriptions of the fossils, bear in mind that the St. Louis, Missouri zoo proudly displays a life-size replica of Lucy—with perfectly formed human hands and feet.]

Stern and Susman noted: "The overall morphology of metacarpals II-V [bones that comprise the hand—BH/BT] is similar to that of chimpanzees and, therefore, might be interpreted as evidence of developed grasping capabilities to be used in suspensory behavior" (60:283). In looking at the morphology of the fingers, they affirmed:

> The markedly curved proximal phalanges [bones of the fingers—BH/BT] indicate adaptation for suspensory and climbing activities which require powerful grasping abilities.... The trapezium [bone at the base of the first digit—BH/BT] and first metacarpal are very chimpanzee-like in relative size and shape.... Enlarged metacarpal heads and the mildly curved, parallel-sided shafts are two such features of the Hadar metacarpals not seen in human fingers. The distal phalanges, too, retain ape-like features in *A. afarensis.* ...On the other hand, the Hadar fossil falls within the

range of each ape and less than 1 SD [standard deviation–BH/BT] unit away from the means of gorilla and orangutan (60:284).

In their concluding remarks, Stern and Susman remarked:

> It will not have escaped the reader's attention that the great bulk of evidence supporting the view that the Hadar hominid was to a significant degree arboreal. ...We discovered a substantial body of evidence indicating that arboreal activities were so important to *A. afarensis* that morphologic adaptations permitting adept movement in the trees were maintained (60:313).

In the September 9, 1994 issue of *Science*, Randall Susman reported that the chimp-like thumbs in *A. afarensis* were far better suited for tree climbing than tool making (Susman, 1994). Lucy also possessed a nonhuman gait, based on ratio of leg size to foot size (see Oliwenstein, 1995, 16[1]:42). One researcher even went so far as to suggest that *A. afarensis* was little more than a failed experiment in ape bipedalism, and as such should be consigned to a side branch of the human evolutionary tree (as reported by Shreeve, 1996). So not only were Lucy's ribs and pelvis wrong, but her limbs also were physiologically more conducive to swinging around in treetops.

Australopithecine Teeth:
More Evidence that Lucy was Arboreal

One of Donald Johanson's specialties is identifying differences within the teeth of alleged hominids. In fact, in his original description, he gave a great deal of attention to the dentition of *A. afarensis*. By measuring the various differences in molars and canines, he systematically assigned various fossils to predetermined groups. However, even his highly trained eyes may have missed some important microscopic data. Anthropologist Alan Walker has been working on ways of possibly determining behavior based on evidence from the fossil record. One of his methods includes quantitative analysis of tooth microwear. Using image enhancement and optical diffraction methods of scanning, Walker believes he might be able to reconstruct ancient diets from paleontological samples. In speaking of Walker's material, Johanson noted:

> Dr. Alan Walker of Johns Hopkins has recently concluded that the polishing effect he finds on the teeth of robust australopithecines and modern chimpanzees indicates that australopithecines, like chimps, were fruit eaters.... If they were primarily fruit eaters, as Walker's examination of their teeth suggests they were, then our picture of them, and of the evolutionary path they took, is wrong (Johanson and Edey, 1981, p. 358).

So rather than foraging on the ground for food, we have microscopic evidence that australopithecines were fruit eaters.

Australopithecine Ears: Human-like or Ape-like?

Knowing that modern human bipedalism is unique among primates (and other mammals), Fred Spoor and his colleagues decided to evaluate the vestibular apparatus of the inner ear—an area designed to help coordinate body movements. Modern human locomotor activity requires that the vestibular apparatus of the inner ear be able to maintain body posture, even though we constantly are balancing all of our weight on very small areas of support. Anyone who has ever suffered vertigo knows firsthand just how crucial this area is for balance and everyday activities.

Using high-resolution computed tomography, these researchers were able to generate cross-sectional images of the bony labyrinth that comprised the inner ear. They noted: "Among the fossil hominids, the earliest species to demonstrate the modern human morphology is *Homo erectus*. In contrast, the semicircular canal dimensions in crania from southern Africa attributed to *Australopithecus* and *Paranthropus* resemble those of the extant great apes" (Spoor, et al., 1994, 369: 645). With that single declaration, Spoor and his colleagues have drawn a line which unequivocally states that all fossils prior to *Homo erectus* possessed ape-like morphology, allowing them to climb trees, swing from branches, or walk hunched over on their knuckles.

Their measurements led to the following observation: "Among the fossil hominids, the australopithecines show great-ape-like proportions and *H. erectus* shows modern-human-like proportions" (369:646). So, not only were the ribs, pelvis, limbs, hands, and feet of this "fruit eater" chimp-like, but there also is evidence which suggests that the organ required for balance in *Australopithecus afarensis* was chimp-like as well.

 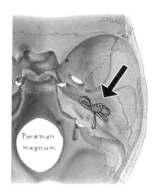

Figure 6 — Size and orientation of semi-circular canals in the ears of humans (pictured above) are significantly different from those discovered in creatures identified as australopithecines.

Lucy: Hominid or Chimp?

When Lucy first arrived on the scene, newsmagazines such as *Time* and *National Geographic* noted that she had a head shaped like an ape, with a brain capacity the size of a large chimp's—about one-third the size of a modern man's. In an article that appeared in *New Scientist*, evolutionist Jeremy Cherfas noted: "Lucy, alias *Australopithecus afarensis*, had a skull very like a chimpanzee's, and a brain to match" (1983, 93:172). Adrienne Zihlman observed: "Lucy's fossil remains match up remarkably well with the bones of a pygmy chimp" (1984, 104:39). It should be no surprise then, that in Stern and Susman's 1983 analysis of *A. afarensis*, they pointed out:

> These findings of ours, in conjunction with Christie's (1977) observation on enhanced rotation at the tibio-talar joint in AL 288-1, Tardieu's (1979) deductions about greater voluntary rotation at the knee in AL 288-1, Senut's (1981) and Feldesman's (1982a) claims that the humerus of AL 2881 is pongid in certain of its features, and Feldesman's (1982b) demonstration that the ulna of AL 288-1 is most similar to that of *Pan paniscus* [a chimp—BH/BT], all seem to lead ineluctably to the conclusion that the Hadar hominid was vitally dependent on the trees for protection and/or sustenance (60:311).

All of these characteristics led inevitably to the conclusion that Lucy was simply a chimp-like creature. And yet, more than a decade earlier, Charles Oxnard, while at the University of Chicago, already had passed judgment on these creatures. His multivariate computer analyses indicated that the australopithecines were nothing but knuckle-walking apes (1975).

You might be asking yourself why this charade has been allowed to go on this long. The answer—woven around power, fame, and money—can be found in Johanson's own words.

> There is no such thing as a total lack of bias. I have it; everybody has it. The fossil hunter in the field has it…. In everybody who is looking for hominids there is a strong urge to learn more about where the human line started. If you are working back at around three million, as I was, that is very seductive, because you begin to get an idea that that is where *Homo* did start. You begin straining your eyes to find *Homo* traits in fossils of that age…. Logical, maybe, but also biased. **I was trying to jam evidence of dates into a pattern that would support conclusions about fossils which, on closer inspection, the fossils themselves would not sustain** (Johanson and Edey, 1981, pp. 257,258, emp. added).

He went on to admit: "It is hard for me now to admit how tangled in that thicket I was. But the insidious thing about bias is that it does make one deaf to the cries of other evidence" (p. 277). Questions are being raised as to whether or not *afarensis* is more primitive than *africanus*, or whether they are one and the same. Others point to the all the chimp-like features, and question whether this creature ever really walked uprightly. Finally, in the March 1996 issue of *National Geographic*, Donald Johanson himself admitted: "Lucy has recently been dethroned" (189[3]:117). His (and Lucy's) fifteen minutes of fame are history. As Lee Berger declared: "One might say we are kicking Lucy out of the family tree" (as quoted in Shreeve, 1996). [For an extensive discussion and refutation of *Australopithecus afarensis*, see Gish, 1995, pp. 241-262.] Isn't it fascinating to see how often the "hominid family tree" gets pruned?

Australopithecus africanus/Australopithecus boisei

At this point, we need to discuss briefly two creatures that, although not as important in the lineage of man as they once were, nevertheless have become so popular and well known that they at least bear mentioning here. In 1924, Raymond Dart (professor of anatomy at the University of Witwatersrand, South Africa) had presented to him a skull that had been uncovered at the lime mines at Taung, South Africa (Taung means "place of the lion" in the Bantu Language). He described his find in *Nature* magazine in 1925, and labeled it *Australopithecus africanus*. [The word *Australopithecus* means "southern ape."] He further indicated that it was the direct ancestor of humans. It was the skull, professor Dart said, of an infant creature, 4-5 years old (see Dart, 1925). Other investigators, such as John T. Robinson and Robert Broom (as well as Dart himself) uncovered additional finds of *Australopithecus africanus* in later years, but none ever received the acclaim that Dart's original skull did. In fact, in commenting on this fact in his book, *Bones of Contention*, Marvin Lubenow noted:

By 1960, it would have been difficult to find any public-school book that touched on human origins that did not have a picture of the Taung skull. That popularity has remained. The fossil received much publicity in 1984, the sixtieth anniversary of its discovery. Pictures of Taung are still found in most books dealing with human origins (1992, p. 50).

It is because of "that popularity" that we felt compelled to discuss *Australopithecus africanus* here. But it is not **just** because of the creature's popularity. As it turns out, *Australopithecus africanus* has become the subject of some controversy over the past several years. Here, by way of summary, is what happened.

In 1973, a geologist from South Africa, T.C. Partridge, used thermoluminescence analysis of calcite, as well as uranium dating methods, to date the cave from which the Taung skull had come (1973, 246:75-79; see also Tattersall, et al., 1988, p. 571; Klein, 1989, p. 113). Whereas the Taung child had been dated at somewhere between two and three millions years old, Dr. Partridge's data indicated that the cave could not have been any older than about 0.87 million years old—which meant that the age of the Taung discovery would have to be **decreased** to no older than 0.87 million years. And therein is the controversy.

As anatomist Phillip Tobias (also of the University of Witwatersrand at the time) admitted: "…[T]he fact remains that less than one million years is a discrepant age for a supposed

Figure 7 — *Australopithecus africanus*

gracile australopithecine in the gradually emerging picture of African hominid evolution" (see Butzer, 1974, 15[4]:411). That is to say, if *Australopithecus africanus* was the direct ancestor of humans, and was dated at only 0.87 million years, that became problematic, since no one would believe that it was possible to go from *Australopithecus africanus* to

Figure 8 — Artist's rendition of *Australopithecus africanus*

modern humans in the "short" time span of just a little over three-quarters of a million years. Further compounding the problem was the fact that modern humans already had been documented as being on the scene in Africa 0.75 million years ago. Karl W. Butzer of the University of Chicago recognized the problem immediately, and wrote in *Current Anthropology*:

> If the Taung specimen is indeed no older than the youngest robust australopithecines of the Transvaal, then such a late, local survival of the gracile [a term used to describe *Australopithecus africanus*–BH/BT] lineage would seem to pose new evolutionary…problems (1974, 15[4]:382).

Problems—to be sure. But, as it turned out, those "problems" never were addressed, since just a year after Partridge offered up the "young" dates of 0.87 million years for the cave in which the Taung fossil had been found, Donald Johanson discovered Lucy, and the problem of the obviously incorrect dates that had been assigned to the Taung skull faded into the background. In the meantime, Johanson and his collaborator, Tim White, revised the human family tree, and *Australopithecus afarensis* (Lucy) replaced *Australopithecus africanus* (Taung) as our direct nonhuman evolutionary ancestor. Thus, the dating of *A. africanus* became a non-issue, and *africanus* was moved off to the australopithecine branch of the family tree, becoming the link between Lucy and the robust australopithecines (discussed below).

All of this would have worked just fine—from an evolutionary viewpoint—were it not for the discovery in 1985 of the now-famous "black skull," KNM-WT 17000 (see Walker, et al., 1986). Dated at 2.5 million years, the black skull appears to have more in common with *Australopithecus afarensis* and the robust australopithecines. Where, then, does *Australopithecus africanus* fit? As Lubenow noted: "Australopithecine phylogeny is now in disarray…. *Africanus* became odd man out. Many evolutionists are now moving *africanus* (including Taung) back into the human line, between Lucy and *Homo habilis*" (1992, p. 52).

But that makes Partridge's re-dating of the cave (in which the Taung skull was found) relevant again. How can *A. africanus* be "only" 0.87 million years old and be moved back into the phylogenetic line leading to humans? As Lubenow went on to note: "His work has not even been addressed, let alone answered.... [T]he full analysis and description of the Taung skull still has not been published, and the dating problem raised by Partridge continues to be ignored" (p. 52). The attitude of some evolutionists seems to be: if the data do not conform to the theory, then simply ignore the data.

Fourteen years after Raymond Dart found the Taung skull, on June 8, 1938, Robert Broom bought from a lime-quarry worker a maxillary fragment containing a single first molar. After examining the material, Broom was convinced that this was a different species from *A. africanus*. Broom learned from the quarry worker that a young boy by the name of Gert Terblanche (who worked as a local guide) had found the bones. Terblanche led Dr. Broom to Kromdraai, the place of the specimen's discovery, where Broom found several more cranial and mandibular fragments associated with the original maxillary specimen. Eventually, this partial cranium (designed as TM 1517) became the type specimen for the creature that came to be known as *Australopithecus robustus*. Broom's efforts were instrumental in altering the view that the South African specimens were not simply apes, but hominids. After he published a scientific monograph on the finds in 1946, the South African australopithecines were taken seriously as human ancestors.

A. robustus remains have been discovered mainly at three different sites in South Africa: Swartkrans, Dreimulen, and Kromdraai, and are dated at approximately 2 million years old. However, almost all of the *A. robustus* cranial specimens are extremely fragmentary; only one, SK 1585, has been complete enough to obtain a brain size (530 cc). The main issue regarding *A. robustus* is whether or not it should remain a separate species from *A. boisei* (discovered by Louis and Mary Leakey, discussed below). Some evolutionists insist upon placing the creatures into separate lineages, while others suggest that *A. africanus, A. robustus* and *A. boisei* should be included in a monophyletic lineage (under the genus name *Paranthropus*), since postcranial evidence shows little difference among the three. Before we discuss that point further, let us introduce *Australopithecus boisei*.

On July 17, 1959, while her husband Louis was ill at their work site at Olduvai Gorge in Tanzania, Mary Leakey ventured out on yet another fossil hunt and discovered some teeth (attached to a skull, as it turns out) sticking out of the ground. She and her husband Louis later named it *Zinjanthropus boisei*. [*Zinjanthropus* means "East Africa Man"; *boisei* derives from Charles Boise, a philanthropist who had funded some of the Leakey's research through the National Geographic Society.] The Leakey's gave the creature the nickname "Nutcracker Man" because of its massive jaws, and dated it at 1.8 million years.

At first, even though *Zinjanthropus* appeared to share a suite of traits with Broom's *Australopithecus robustus*, the Leakeys were convinced that they had discovered the first toolmaker. And since fashioned tools are associated only with man, they were certain that they had in their possession the skull of the direct ancestor of humans. Louis discussed the find in the feature article—"Finding the World's Earliest Man"—that he authored for the September 1960 issue of *National Geographic*, and in which he boldly proclaimed that the fossils were **"obviously human"** (118[3]:421, emp. added). On page 435, underneath the artist's concept of what *Zinjanthropus boisei* was supposed to have looked like, was the following caption: "This **earliest man yet found** lived beside the shore of a long-vanished lake" (emp. added).

But, the "obviously human" and "earliest man" designations were not to stick. In 1960 and 1961, the Leakeys discovered additional fossils, to which they gave colorful nicknames such as Cinderella (Olduvai Hominid 13), George (O.H. 16),

Twiggy (O.H. 24—yes, named after the British model by the same name), and Johnny's Child (O.H. 7, named after Louis' son Jonathan). Eventually, these fossil finds were placed into the genus and species of *Homo habilis*. Since the fossils were dated at 1.8 million years, and since they were more "modern" than *Zinjanthropus*, Louis and Mary realized that *Zinjanthropus*, their "obviously human, earliest man," wasn't either, but instead was a "super-robust australopithecine." They thus renamed the creature *Australopithecus boisei*, because it was similar to the specimen Raymond Dart found 35 years earlier.

To complicate matters even more, some researchers believe that there should be only **two** different species. The suggestion is that *A. boisei* and *A. robustus* are one and the same (and should be referred to as the robust australopithecines because of their larger size), while *A. africanus,* the smaller of the bunch (and thus referred to as the gracile form) is a separate species entirely. Still other evolutionists believe that all three creatures should be placed into the genus *Paranthropus,* since, as we pointed out above, postcranial evidence shows little difference among the three.

What should we make of all of this? Very little, truth be told. Most of it is a completely moot point nowadays. As we noted earlier, Lord Solly Zuckerman, the famous British anatomist, studied the australopithecines for more than 15 years, and concluded that if man did descend from an ape-like ancestor, he did so without leaving a single trace in the fossil record (1970, p. 64).

In his volume, *Man: His First Million Years*, the late evolutionist Ashley Montagu remarked that "...the skull form of **all** australopithecines shows too many specialized and ape-like characters to be either the direct

Figure 9 — *Australopithecus robustus*

ancestor of man or of the line that led to man" (1957, pp. 51-52, emp. added). One of the world's foremost experts on the australopithecines, Charles Oxnard (of the departments of anatomy and anthropology at the University of Chicago), performed computerized multivariate analysis of *Australopithecus*, and compared them to similar analyses of man and modern apes. According to Dr. Oxnard, his studies show that *Australopithecus* was **not** an intermediate between man and ape. In an article in *Nature*, he wrote:

> Multivariate studies of several anatomical regions, shoulder, pelvis, ankle, foot, elbow, and hand are now available for the australopithecines. These suggest that the common view, that these fossils are similar to modern man or that on those occasions when they depart from a similarity to man they resemble the African great apes, may be incorrect. Most of the fossil fragments are in fact uniquely different from both man and man's nearest living genetic relatives, the chimpanzee and gorilla. To the extent that resemblances exist with living forms, they tend to be with the orangutan… (1975, 258:389).

Writing on the australopithecines in the journal *Homo*, Oxnard concluded:

> Finally, the quite independent information from the fossil finds of more recent years seems to indicate absolutely that these australopithecines, of half to 2 million years and from sites such as Olduvai and Sterkfontein, **are not on a human pathway** (1981, 30: 243).

They most certainly are not. As we will document later in the section on *Homo habilis*, Louis Leakey eventually reported the **contemporaneous existence** of *Australopithecus, Homo habilis*, and *Homo erectus* fossils at Olduvai Gorge (see Mary Leakey, 1971, 3:272). If *Australopithecus, Homo habilis*, and *Homo erectus* existed as contemporaries, it should be plainly obvious that one could not have been ancestral to another. The australopithecines are an evolutionary dead-end.

The Laetoli Footprints

In the April 1979 issue of *National Geographic*, Mary Leakey reported finding fossil footprint trails at Laetoli, Tanzania. The strata above the footprints were dated at 3.6 million years, while the strata below them were dated at 3.8 (Leakey, 1979, 155:450). Lubenow remarked: "These footprint trails rank as one of the great fossil discoveries of the twentieth century" (1992, p. 173). Why is this the case? Not only did Dr. Leakey discover three distinct trails containing sixty-nine prints, but **she also found footprints that depicted one individual actually walking in the steps of another!–something that only humans have the intelligence (or inclination) to do**. Dr. Leakey was forced to admit that the footprints were "remarkably similar to those of modern man" (155:446). In her autobiography, *Disclosing the Past*, she wrote:

> The Laetoli Beds might not have included any foot bones among the hominid remains they had yielded to our search, but they had given us instead one of the most graphic alternative kinds of evidence for bipedalism one could dream of discovering. **The essentially human nature and the modern appearance of the footprints were quite extraordinary**.
>
> As the 1978 excavations proceeded, we noted a curious feature. In one of the two trails, some of the individual prints seemed unusually large, and **it looked to several of us as if these might be double prints**, though by no amount of practical experiment in the modern dust could we find a way in which one individual could create such a double print....
>
> **The prints in one of the trails did indeed turn out to be double**, as Louise [Robbins, an anthropologist–BH/BT] and I and several others had expected, and at last we understood the reason, namely that *three* hominids had been present....
>
> I will simply summarize here by saying that we appear to have prints left three and a half million years ago, by three individuals of different stature: **it is tempting to see them as a man, a woman and a child** (1984, pp. 177,178, italics in orig., emp. added).

Tempting indeed! In an article titled "The Scientific Evidence for the Origin of Man," David Menton discussed Dr. Leakey's self-proclaimed views on this matter.

> In a recent lecture in St. Louis, Mary Leaky pointed out one additional feature of her footprints that one does not often see mentioned in the literature; all of the larger foot prints of the trail have a smaller footprint superimposed on them! **Mary Leaky herself conceded that it appears that a child was intentionally lengthening its stride to step in an elder's footprints**! It shouldn't be necessary to emphasize that this is a far more sophisticated behaviour than one expects from apes. In addition there were thousands of tracks of a wide variety of animals that are similar or identical to animals living in the area today including antelopes, hares, giraffes, rhinoceroses, hyenas, horses, pigs and two kinds of elephants. Even several birds' eggs were found and many of these could be easily correlated with eggs of living species (1988, emp. added).

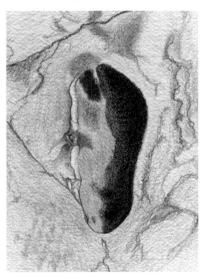

Figure 10 — Laetoli footprint
©2005 A.P./Thomas A. Tarply

Yet most evolutionists insist upon ascribing the footprints to *A. afarensis*–on the assumption that humans simply could not have lived as far back as 3.7 million years. The specialist who carried out the most extensive study to date of the Laetoli footprints, however–and who did so at the personal invitation of Mary Leakey herself–is Russell Tuttle of the University of Chicago. He noted in his research reports that the individuals who made the tracks were barefoot and probably walked habitually unshod. As part of his investigation, he observed seventy Machiguenga Indians in the rugged mountains of Peru—people who habitually walk unshod. After analyzing the Indians' footprints and examining the available Laetoli fossilized toe bones, Tuttle concluded that the ape-like feet of *A. afarensis* simply could not have made the Laetoli tracks (see Bower, 1989, 135:251). In fact, he even went so far as to state:

> **A barefoot *Homo sapiens* could have made them. ...In all discernible morphological features, the feet of the individuals that made the trails are indistinguishable from those of modern humans** (as quoted in Anderson, 1983, 98:373, emp. added).

Several years later, in an article on the Laetoli footprints in the February 1989 issue of the *American Journal of Physical Anthropology*, Dr. Tuttle wrote: "In discernible features, **the Laetoli G prints are indistinguishable from those of habitually barefoot *Homo sapiens***" (78[2]:316, emp. added). One year later, he then went on to admit in the March 1990 issue of *Natural History:*

> In sum, the 3.5 million-year-old footprint traits at Laetoli site G resemble those of habitually unshod modern humans. None of their features suggests that the Laetoli hominids were less capable bipeds than we are. **If the G footprints were not known to be so old, we would readily conclude that they were made by a member of our genus, *Homo*.** In any case, we should shelve the loose assumption that the Laetoli footprints were made by Lucy's kind, *Australopithecus afarensis* (p. 64, emp. added).

Louise Robbins, the anthropologist who worked closely with Mary Leakey on the Laetoli project, commented: "The arch is raised—the smaller individual had a higher arch than I do —and the big toe is large and aligned with the second toe.... **The toes grip the ground like human toes. You do not see this in other animal forms**" (1979, 115:196-197, emp. added).

Interestingly, Mary Leakey originally labeled the Laetoli footprints as "*Homo* sp. indeterminate," indicating that she was **willing** to place them into the genus of man, but was **unwilling** to designate them as *Homo sapiens*–which they clearly were. It is obvious, of course, why she was unwilling to call them *Homo sapiens*. Since the tracks (3.7 million years old) are dated as being **older** than Lucy (3.5 million years old), and since Lucy is supposed to have given rise to humans, how could humans have existed **prior to Lucy** in order to make such footprints? [See Lubenow, 1992, pp. 45-58 for a more detailed refutation of Lucy, and pp. 173-176 for a discussion of the Laetoli footprints.]

Homo habilis/Homo rudolfensis

The specimens that eventually would be designated as *Homo habilis* were discovered in 1960 and 1961 by Louis Leakey at Olduvai Gorge in Tanzania, Africa (Leakey, et al., 1964). [The name *Homo habilis* means literally "able man" or "handy man."] The actual designation of the fossils to the genus and species of *Homo habilis* took place three years later in 1964, however, when Dr. Leakey and his coworker, Phillip Tobias of the University of Witwatersrand in South Africa, authored an article titled "A New Species of the Genus *Homo* from Olduvai Gorge" for the April 4, 1964 issue of *Nature* (Leakey, 1964). From the very moment of their initial discovery, the *Homo habilis* fossils were the subject of an intense controversy. Many evolutionists voiced their opinion that the fossils represented nothing more than a mixture of australopithecine and *Homo erectus* fossils, and thus did not merit being placed into a new taxon. Furthermore, scientists who examined the fossils admitted that the finds included both adult and juvenile forms, and therefore were skeptical of creating a new species designation since juveniles are notoriously difficult to evaluate.

But there was much more to the controversy than that. In his book, *Bones of Contention*, Marvin Lubenow explained why.

However, a philosophical problem was also at the center of the controversy. At that time, the accepted scenario for human evolution went from *Australopithecus africanus* (including Taung) to *Homo erectus* and then on to *Homo sapiens*. Many evolutionists felt that there was not "room" between *africanus* and *erectus* for another species, nor was there need for one. But Louis was marching to the tune of a different drummer. Louis believed in "old *Homo*." Louis did not believe that humans had evolved from the australopithecines, at least not from the ones that had been discovered thus far. He believed that the transition from primates to humans took place much farther back in time. In Louis's evolutionary scheme, there was not only room for a new taxon, there was a desperate need for one. In fact, Louis felt that he had discovered the true ancestor of modern humans (1992, p. 159).

And that was only half of the problem. There was something else that was equally as serious, or perhaps more so. As Lubenow went on to clarify:

> Louis Leakey was at least consistent. He recognized that for evolution to go from *africanus* to *erectus* to *sapiens* represented a problem. The cranium of *africanus*, although very small, is thin, high domed, and gracile. The *erectus* cranium is thick, low domed, and robust. The *sapiens* cranium is thin, high domes, and gracile. Thus, to go from *africanus* to *erectus* to *sapiens* represents a reversal in morphology. And a reversal is an evolutionary "no-no." It was for this reason that Louis believed that neither *Homo erectus* nor the Neanderthals were in the mainstream of evolution. Both these robust groups, he felt, were evolutionary cul-de-sacs that led to extinction. The *Homo habilis* cranium, on the other hand, was thin, high domed, and gracile. By going from *habilis* directly to *sapiens*, Louis avoided the reversal problem. Although most evolutionists have accepted *habilis* into the hominid family, they have also retained *erectus*. Hence, they still have a reversal problem in going from *habilis* to *erectus* to *sapiens*.

The concept of reversals in the fossil record is intriguing. A rule in evolution, "Dollo's Law," says that reversals in morphology are not supposed to happen....

Evolutionists have a logical reason for holding to this "you-can't-go-back" idea. Mutations are, they say, the raw material for evolutionary change. When mutations occur in an organism, those mutations represent permanent changes in the genetic structure of the organism. Whether the mutational events are for better or for worse, the genes that had programmed the former condition are gone. Through mutations, those genes are permanently changed and have become different genes which program for something a bit different. To believe that chance mutations could occur that would exactly restore the former genes would be like believing in the tooth fairy. Hence, reversals have not been considered a part of evolutionary theory.

This lack of reversals gives to evolution a one-way directionality which is basic to the system.... However, in spite of the many references in today's literature to reversals, seldom is there any hint that evolutionists understand the serious implications these reversals have for their theory (pp. 159-160,161).

In 1972, at East Turkana, Kenya, Richard Leakey discovered the famous skull KNM-ER 1470 (KNM standing for Kenya National Museum; ER is for East Rudolf, where the fossils were found). Leakey classified the skull as *H. habilis*, and originally dated it at 2.9 million years (a date later revised downward to 1.9 million years; for an in-depth discussion of the evolutionary presuppositions and politics behind the KNM-ER 1470 "re-dating scenario," see Lubenow, pp. 247-266).

Figure 11 — *Homo habilis*

KNM-ER 1470 was a shocking find, since it was dated so old, yet had a very large cranium (800 cc) and an extremely modern cranial morphology, including high doming and thin

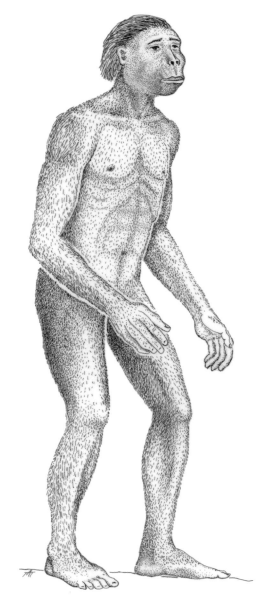

Figure 12 — Artist's rendition of *Homo habilis*

walls. The skull was so much at odds with what evolutionary theory would have predicted that Richard Leakey himself commented: "Either we toss out this skull or we toss out our theories of early man. It simply fits no previous model of human beginnings" (1973b, 143[6]:819). *Science News,* in discussing the new fossil discovery, commented: "Leakey further describes the whole shape of the brain case as **remarkably reminiscent of modern man**, lacking the heavy and protruding eyebrow ridges and thick bone characteristics of *Homo erectus*" (see "Leakey's New...," 1972, 102:324, emp. added). In a report that he wrote for *Nature,* Richard Leakey commented: "The 1470 cranium is quite distinctive from *H. erectus...*" (1973a, 242:450). Yes, it certainly is! Comparisons have documented that skull 1470 is much more modern than any of the known *Homo erectus* fossils. Furthermore, not only does 1470 qualify for true human status based on cranial shape, size, and thickness of the cranial wall, but there also is evidence from the inside of the skull that Broca's area (the part of the brain that controls the muscles for producing articulate speech in humans) was present. An article from the Leakey Foundation in the spring of 1991 reported the find as follows:

> The two foremost American experts on human brain evolution—Dean Falk of the State University of New York at Albany and Ralph Holloway of Columbia University—usually disagree, but even they agree that Broca's area is present in a skull from East Turkana known as 1470. Philip [sic] Tobias,...renowned brain expert from South Africa, concurs.... So, if having the brains to speak is the issue, apparently *Homo* has had it from the beginning (see *AnthroQuest,* 1991, 43: 13).

Even though all the available evidence points to skull 1470 being from a true human, evolutionists have continued to suggest that it was from a "hominid" on the way to "becoming" human. Examine the way famed anthropological artist Jay Matternes put "flesh on the bones" of 1470 for the June 1973 issue of *National Geographic.* The being from whom skull 1470 was supposed to have come was drawn as a young black woman who looks quite human—except for the fact that she has a very apelike nose. [Human noses are composed of cartilage, which generally does not fossilize, and the nose was missing on 1470.] Thus, it is obvious that there was a singular purpose behind giving the woman an apelike nose—to make her look as "primitive" as possible. Had she been given a human nose, no one would have questioned the fact that this particular specimen of *Homo habilis* was, in fact, *Homo sapiens*. As Louis Leakey himself stated: "I submit that morphologically it is almost impossible to regard *Homo habilis* as representing a stage between *Australopithecus africanus* and *Homo erectus*" (1966, 209:1280-1281).

Today, the "problem" of *Homo habilis* has been resolved, thanks to two incredibly important finds. First, in 1986, Tim White, working with Donald Johanson at Olduvai Gorge, found a partial adult skeleton that has been designed as Olduvai Hominid 62 and dated at approximately 1.8 million years old. This was the first time that postcranial material had been found in association with a *Homo habilis* skull. The surprise was that the body of this *H. habilis* adult was not large, as *H. habilis* was thought to be, but actually was smaller (just a little more than three feet tall) than the famed australopithecine, Lucy (discussed earlier). As Lubenow noted:

> Thus, we have strong evidence that the category known as *Homo habilis* is not a legitimate taxon but is composed of a mixture of material from at least two separate taxa—one large and one small. This new discovery also seems to remove the taxon *Homo habilis* as a legitimate transition between *afarensis* (or *africanus*) and *Homo erectus* (1992, p. 165).

[Some evolutionists, in an attempt to salvage *Homo habilis* as a form ancestral to man, have suggested that the smaller, gracile forms should continue to be considered as *H. habilis*, while the larger forms should be renamed as *Homo rudolfensis*.] Perhaps this is why Duane Gish, in his book, *Evolution: The Fossils Still Say No!*, remarked about *Homo habilis*:

No paleoanthropologist has succeeded in sorting out all the creatures that are put into the taxon *Homo habilis* by some and taken out by others. Some insist that *H. habilis* is a bona fide taxon, including creatures intermediate between the australopithecines, either *afarensis* or *africanus,* and *Homo erectus.* Others argue just as strenuously that those creatures classified as *H. habilis* are no more than variants of the australopithecines (1995, p. 265).

In fact, evolutionist Ian Tattersall wrote under the title of "The Many Faces of *Homo habilis*" in the journal *Evolutionary Anthropology*: "...[I]t is increasingly clear that **Homo habilis has become a wastebasket taxon**, little more than a convenient recipient for a motley assortment of hominid fossils from the latest Pliocene and earliest Pleistocene" (1992,[1]:34-36, emp. added). In speaking of *H. habilis,* geologist Trevor Major summarized the situation as follows:

> In fact, the whole issue of its place among *Homo* is highly contentious, and **the species has become a dumping ground for strange and out-of-place fossils**. Some paleontologists have tried to impose some order by reassigning australopithecine-like specimens to *Homo rudolfensis,* and the most modern-looking specimens to "early African *erectus*" or *Homo ergaster* (to which some would assign the Turkana boy). Apart from a small difference in brain size between australopithecines (less than 550 ml) and habilines (around 500-650 ml), there are no other compelling reasons to divide them between two genera (1996, 16:76, parenthetical items in orig., emp. added).

Second, and even more damaging to the evolutionary scenario, was the fact that Louis Leakey later reported the contemporaneous existence of *Australopithecus, Homo habilis,* and *Homo erectus* fossils at Olduvai Gorge (see Mary Leakey, 1971, 3:272). And even more startling was Mary Leakey's discovery of the remains of a **circular stone hut** at the bottom of Bed I at Olduvai Gorge–**beneath** fossils of *H. habilis*! Evolutionists have long attributed the deliberate manufacture of shelter only to *Homo sapiens,* yet Dr. Leakey discovered the australo-pithecines and *H. habilis* together with manufactured housing. As Gish asked:

> If *Australopithecus, Homo habilis,* and *Homo erectus* ex-isted contemporaneously, how could one have been ancestral to another? And how could any of these crea-tures be ancestral to Man, when Man's artifacts are found at a lower stratigraphic level, directly under-neath, and thus earlier in time to these supposed an-cestors of Man? (1995, p. 271).

Good questions. Lubenow was forced by all the available ev-idence to conclude that, as a possible fossil ancestral form of man, "*Homo habilis* is dead" (p. 166). We agree.

Homo erectus/Homo ergaster

And what about *Homo erectus?* Until March 2002, most evo-lutionary anthropologists and paleontologists believed that **two** creatures belonged in the *H. erectus* niche: *Homo ergaster* and *Homo erectus. H. ergaster* was believed to have emerged in Africa and then spread to Europe. *H. erectus* was believed to have existed mainly in Asia. But an article in the March 21, 2002 issue of *Nature* has challenged the traditional thinking about these two species. Writing under the title of "Remains of *Homo erectus* from Bouri, Middle Awash, Ethiopia," Berhane Asfaw (of the Rift Valley Research Service in Addis Ababa, Ethiopia) and his co-authors discussed their discovery of a partial skull (referred to as a calvaria), which they have labeled as *H. erectus.* The skull, discovered on December 27, 1997 in the Afar Rift of Ethiopia known as the Middle Awash, in a sedimentary section of the Bouri formation known as the Dakanihylo ("Daka"), has been dated at approximately 1 million years old (Asfaw, et al., 2002). The significance in the evolutionary debate of what is now being called the Daka skull is this:

> The skull is almost identical to *Homo erectus* fossils found in Asia…. It is so similar, the team believes that it cannot possibly be that of another species. The Daka specimen suggests that *Homo erectus* was not limited to

Asia, separated from its contemporary, *Homo ergaster.*
Homo erectus instead was a robust, far-flung species that
lived in Asia, Africa, and Europe (McKee, 2002).

Tim White, one of the co-authors of the *Nature* paper, put it
this way:

> This fossil is a crucial piece of evidence showing that
> the splitting of *Homo erectus* into two species is not jus-
> tified…. What we are saying in this paper is that the
> anthropological splitting common today is giving the
> wrong impression about the biology of these early hu-
> man ancestors. The different names indicate an ap-
> parent diversity that is not real. *Homo erectus* is a bio-
> logically successful organism, not a whole series of dif-
> ferent human ancestors, all but one of which went ex-
> tinct (as quoted in "Ethiopian Fossil Skull…," 2002).

Asfaw, et al., wrote:

> To recognize the basal fossils representing this ap-
> parently evolving lineage with the separate species
> name "*H. ergaster*" is therefore doubtfully necessary
> or useful. At most, the basal members of the *H. erectus*
> lineage should be recognized taxonomically as a
> chrono-subspecies (*H. erectus ergaster*) [2002, 416:
> 318-319, parenthetical item in orig.].

The graduate student who actually found the skull (and who is
a co-author of the *Nature* paper), Henry Gilbert, probably said
it best when he commented: "One of the biggest impacts this
calvaria will have on the field is in making *Homo erectus* look
more like a single species again" (as quoted in "Ethiopian Fossil Skull…," 2002).

Now that evolutionists have wiped out one-half of the *Homo
erectus* niche by eliminating *Homo ergaster*, what shall we say
about the single remaining member of the *H. erectus* category?
Examine a copy of the November 1985 issue of *National Geographic* and see if you can detect any differences between the
pictures of *Homo erectus* and *Homo sapiens* (Weaver, 168:576-
577). The fact is, there are no recognizable differences. Almost
forty years ago, Ernst Mayr, the famed evolutionary taxono-

mist of Harvard, remarked: "The *Homo erectus* stage is characterized by a body skeleton which, so far as we know, does not differ from that of modern man in any essential point" (1965, p. 632). His statement is as true today as when he originally made it. Furthermore, the skull of *H. erectus* shares many features with the Neanderthals, but with flatter brow ridges and a less prominent mid-facial region. Some *H. erectus* skeletons were short and stocky like the Neanderthals, but one specimen –a nine to eleven-year-old boy from West Turkana, Kenya–was quite tall and slender (Andrews and Stringer, 1993, p. 242). Cranial volume varied from 850 to over 1100 milliliters (ml) for *H. erectus*, and 1250 to over 1740 ml for Neanderthals. The average for modern humans is 1350 ml, but we exhibit a broad range of 700 to 2200 ml (Lubenow, 1992, p. 138).

In general, such things as skeletal proportions, the angularity of the face, and the shape of the brain case vary considerably among fossil humans. Yet such differences–which are every bit as dramatic–occur just as frequently among modern humans. A Watusi today could not fail to miss a Mbuti pygmy who strolled into his village, and an Inuit certainly would stand out at a gathering of Australian aborigines. Despite obvious facial features, both *H. erectus* and *H. sapiens neanderthalensis* appear to fit within a distinct human kind. Although some specimens do exhibit a mixture of traits, there is no clear lineage from, say, *H. erectus* to *H. sapiens.*

In fact, the evidence of the fossil record suggests that they not only were contemporaries, but also in some cases were even neighbors (Stringer and Gamble, 1993, p. 137). Remarkable confirmation of that very scenario was presented in two different articles in the December 13, 1996 issue of *Science* (Gibbons, 1996; Swisher, et al., 1996). Creationist Marvin

Figure 13 – *Homo erectus*

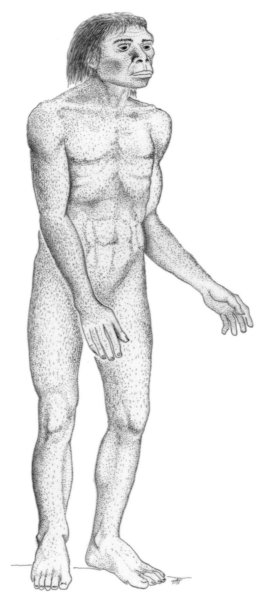

Figure 14 — Artist's reconstruction of *Homo erectus*

Lubenow, in his text on the alleged fossil evidence for human evolution, *Bones of Contention*, summarized the imaginary *Homo erectus* to *Homo habilis* to *Homo sapiens* lineage as follows:

> …*Homo erectus* individuals have lived side by side with other categories of humans for the past two million years (according to evolutionist chronology). This fact eliminates the possibility that *Homo erectus* evolved into *Homo sapiens*…. On the far end of the *Homo erectus* time continuum, *Homo erectus* is contemporary with *Homo habilis* for 500,000 years. In fact, *Homo erectus* overlaps the entire *Homo habilis* population…. Thus, the almost universally accepted view that *Homo habilis* evolved into *Homo erectus* becomes impossible…. *Homo habilis* could not be the evolutionary ancestor of *Homo erectus* because the two groups lived at the same time as contemporaries….

> When a creationist emphasizes that according to evolution, descendants can't be living as contemporaries with their ancestors, the evolutionist declares in a rather surprised tone, "Why, that's like saying that a parent has to die just because a child is born!" Many times I have seen audiences apparently satisfied with that analogy. But it is a very false one. In evolution, one species (or a portion of it) allegedly turns into a second, better-adapted species through mutation and natural selection. However, in the context of human reproduction, I do not turn into my children; I continue on as a totally independent entity. Furthermore, in evolution, a certain portion of a species turns into a more advanced species because that portion of the species allegedly possesses certain favorable mutations which the rest of the species does not possess. Thus the newer, more advanced group comes into direct competition with the older unchanged group and eventually eliminates it through death…. The analogy used by evolutionists is without logic, and the problem of contemporaneousness remains.

> Although the most recent date usually given for the disappearance of *Homo erectus* is about 300,000 y.a., at least 106 fossil individuals having *Homo erectus* morphology

are dated by evolutionists themselves as being **more recent** than 300,000 y.a. Of those 106 fossils individuals at least sixty-two are dated **more recently than 12,000 y.a.** This incontrovertible fact of the fossil record effectively falsifies the concept that *Homo erectus* evolved into *Homo sapiens* and that *Homo erectus* is our evolutionary ancestor. In reality, it falsifies the entire concept of human evolution (1992, pp. 121,127,129, 131, parenthetical items and emp. in orig.).

Lubenow therefore has suggested that all these forms should be included within a highly variable, created humankind (pp. 120-143). The fossil evidence for evolution (human or otherwise) simply is not there. Apes always have been apes, and humans always have been humans.

Furthermore, in examining the evidence regarding the origins of humans, we need to keep in mind the condition of the original fossils. The skeletons and skulls often are extremely fragmented or crushed (as in the case of the Daka skull and *Kenyanthropus platyops*), and do not look anything like the skeletons you see in science classrooms. The skeletons often are crushed by the weight of the dirt and rocks on top of them, and rarely are they complete. Rather than simply digging up a complete skeleton, researchers often find small pieces of bones scattered over large areas (some as large as a football field!). Often these fossilized bone fragments are put together like a jigsaw puzzle with missing pieces. Occasionally, however, pieces get put together that really belong to **two or three different puzzles**! For, you see, it is not just a few links out of the chain that are missing. It is the entire chain!

Homo sapiens idaltu

In our discussion of *Kenyanthropus platyops* in chapter one, we mentioned a specific criticism of the creature that appeared in an article ("Early Hominids–Diversity or Distortion?") authored by University of California (Berkeley) anthropologist Tim White in the March 28, 2003 issue of *Science* (2003). White publicly disparaged Meave Leakey and her colleagues for "overinterpreting" the alleged diversity seen in hominid fossils, and for "rushing to judgment" to name a new species (which, White suggested, very likely belonged in a genus and species that already existed).

Three months must represent a very long time in the evolutionary community–time enough to conveniently "forget" the chastisement you unsparingly heaped on your erring colleagues, and **time enough to make exactly the same mistake yourself!** Three short months was the amount of time that passed between White's cautioning of his fellow evolutionists, and his own announcement of a new species!

The June 12, 2003 issue of *Nature* carried a striking series of photos announcing White's latest find. There–emblazoned on the cover under the title "African Origins"–was a subtitle that boldly announced: "Ethiopian fossils are the earliest *Homo sapiens.*" Headlines that screamed, "Oldest *Homo sapiens* fossils found," appeared in almost every major media outlet. In fact, MSNBC even sent out "news bites" that showed up on cellular phones and pagers, stating:

> **OLDEST HUMAN FOSSILS DISCOVERED**: *Homo sapiens* fossils found in Ethiopia are the oldest known found, making them a key link between pre-human and modern humans.

White and his colleagues designated this "latest and greatest" find as *Homo sapiens idaltu*–the new sub-species name "idaltu" (which means elder) having come from the African Afar language.

While the names of the paleoanthropologists, the locations of the fossils, or the name given to a new fossil discovery may change, the story remains the same: Evolutionists claim to have made a "landmark discovery" that will "change the way people think about their own history." Or, the suggestion is offered that such-and-such a find "documents beyond doubt that evolution occurred in the past, and will shake up the evolutionary tree of life." While some admit that "these fossils raise more questions and contradict some of the previous data," the bottom line always is something like this: "Our find sets a new age record, making **it** the most important (oh, by the way, we would appreciate more funding in the future)." OK, so that last little bit usually is not included in the media clips. But it is true all the same. These researchers are dependent on grants, and those grants commonly are awarded based on past achievement(s). Thus, the researcher who can grab the most spotlight, pound his or her chest the loudest, and claim an appropriate "fifteen minutes of fame," likely will be rewarded in the end (including making a considerable sum on the side for writing a book on the "most important find" in human history!)

So what did Tim White and his colleagues **really** find? The very first sentence in an on-line *National Geographic* report stated: "Three fossil skulls recovered from the windswept scrabble of Ethiopia's dry and barren Afar rift valley lend archaeological credence to the theory that modern humans evolved in Africa before spreading around the world" (Roach, 2003). **Three** fossilized skulls? Well, not exactly. In commenting on the find, Chris Stringer noted: "Three individuals are represented by separate fossils: a nearly complete adult cranium (skull parts excluding lower jaw), a less complete juvenile cranium, and some robust cranial fragments from another adult" (2003, 423: 692, parenthetical item in orig.). The fact of the matter is, the third "skull" is so fragmented that White and his colleagues decided not to even include a photo of it in their report in *Nature*. They found some bone fragments, and from those they composed an adult skull and part of a juvenile skull (with some leftovers remaining unused).

The *Nature* article contained some good science, in that the researchers did uncover some fossils. They put them together (as they thought they best fit). They took them back to the lab, made measurements, and compared them with other anthropometric data. But that was where the good science stopped, and speculation began. In an effort to help fill in some gaps in evolutionary theory, White and his colleagues painted a "before" picture that was intended to help explain away and fill such gaps. Over the past several years, evolutionists have had a hard time explaining just how man evolved "out of Africa," when researchers were finding Neanderthal fossils in Europe. How could this occur, when previously, evolutionists asserted that *Homo sapiens* had evolved from Neanderthals, and then left Africa? Enter the "side-by-side" theory. This latest twist in evolution has both modern humans and Neanderthals co-existing in many of the same regions, including Europe. That helped explain the Neanderthal fossils in Europe, but evolutionists still needed evidence in Africa to back up their claims. Then, Tim White, and his coworkers arrived to save the day. They not only speculated about how their new find fits into the "out of Africa" theory, but also went on to note: "When considered with the evidence from other sites, this shows that modern human morphology emerged in Africa long before the Neanderthals vanished from Eurasia" (2003, 423:746-747).

Truth be told, this latest find is nothing more than a modern human that has been dated (using evolutionary methods) at 154,000-160,000 years old. When you disregard the dating (due to the inherent evolutionary assumptions), you will see that White and his colleagues found nothing more than bone fragments from two human adults and a child (*Homo sapiens*) who once lived in Africa. That's it. End of story. Tim White would do well to reread his own cautionary advice to his evolutionary colleagues, regarding hastily assigning new names for every bone fragment discovered. As the old adage suggests, "the sauce that's good for the goose, is good for the gander."

WHAT DOES THE "RECORD OF THE ROCKS" REALLY SHOW?

While artists' depictions of ape-like ancestors strive to provide us with missing links, we now know that fossils indistinguishable from modern humans can be traced all the way back to 4.5 million years ago (using evolutionary dating methods).

This suggests that true humans were on the scene **before** australopithecines appeared in the fossil record. Additionally, we now know that anatomically modern *Homo sapiens*, Neanderthals, archaic *Homo sapiens*, and *Homo erectus* all lived as contemporaries at one time or another. None of these creatures evolved from a more robust form to a more gracile condition. Additionally, all the fossils ascribed to the *Homo habilis* category are contemporary with *Homo erectus*. Thus *Homo habilis* not only did not evolve **into** *Homo erectus*, but it could not have evolved **from** *Homo erectus*.

More than 6,000 human-like fossils exist. Some are partial skulls, while others may be only a few teeth. Most of these fossils can be placed into one of two groups: apes or humans. A few fossils do have odd characteristics or show abnormal bone structure. But does that mean humans evolved? No. It simply means that we have variations in bone structure—variations you probably can see all around you. Some heads are big; others are small. Some noses are pointed, and some are flat. Some jawbones look angled, while some look square. Does that mean some of us still are "evolving"? Or does it mean that there are occasional differences in humans?

Remember this simple exercise the next time you see a picture of one of those ape-like creatures displayed prominently across the front cover of a national news magazine. Look at a skeleton (any one will do) and try to draw the person that used to live with that bony framework. What color was the hair? Was it curly, or straight? Was the person a male or a female? Did he or she have chubby cheeks, or thin? These are difficult (if not impossible!) questions to answer when we are presented only a few bones with which to work. The reconstructions you see in pictures are not based **merely on the fossil evidence**, but also are based on **what evolutionists believe these creatures "should" have looked like**. The fossil evidence itself, however, is clear. Man always has been man; he did not evolve over millions of years. Rather, God, the Giver of life, created mankind on the sixth day of creation, just as the Bible states (Genesis 1:26-27).

THE PARADE OF FOSSIL ERRORS

We all have seen pictures of our alleged animal ancestors. Artists draw these creatures as hairy animals that shared both human and ape-like characteristics, often carrying clubs and living in caves. Most of us even recognize their names: Neanderthal Man, Rhodesian Man, Lucy, Java Man. But what is the truth about the origin of humankind? Did we evolve from ape-like ancestors as many would have us believe, or were we made in the image and likeness of God as Genesis 1:26-27 teaches? Examine the evidence that follows, and then you be the judge. We think you will see that man did not evolve from ape-like creatures, but was created by God.

In looking at the evidence regarding the origins of humans, we first need to dig deeply into the ground. Buried under layers of dirt and rocks we find fossilized skeletons–many of which, once they are uncovered, are stored in vaults where they are better protected than gold. However, these skeletons do not look anything like the skeletons you see in science classrooms or those that are taped to the wall at Halloween. These skeletons often are crushed by the weight of the materials on top of them, and rarely are they complete. Rather than simply digging up a complete skeleton, researchers frequently find small pieces of bones scattered over large areas (some as large as a football field!). Often, these fossilized bone fragments are put together like a jigsaw puzzle–with missing pieces. Occasionally, however, pieces get put together that belong to two or three different puzzles! But what about all the pictures you've seen on the covers of magazines–those complete ape-like skulls? Many times, such images are simply pictures of casts that were created using whatever bone fragments were available. From the casts, researchers try to imagine what the creature (a hairy "proto-human" frequently shown living in a cave) might have looked like. Actually, these alleged ape-like creatures that are supposed to be the "missing links" between humans and apes are far from it. Consider the evidence.

NEANDERTHAL MAN

For many years, evolutionists taught that Neanderthals (sometimes spelled Neandertals) were brawny, prehistoric creatures that used primitive stone tools, whereas "modern" humans' descendants were more sophisticated. If we were to spot a Neanderthal walking the streets of a modern city, we likely would recognize him by his prominent brow ridges, low forehead, flat skull, weak chin, jutting mid-facial region, very large nose, forward-sloping face, and short, muscular limbs—to name some of the more visible characteristics (see Stringer and Gamble, 1993, pp. 76-77). *The American Heritage Dictionary of the English Language* uses words such as crude, boorish, and slow-witted to describe this species. However, as the facts slowly are becoming known, they are requiring a renovation of that definition.

After discovering the first Neanderthal skullcap in 1856 in the Neander Valley near Dusseldorf, Germany, German anatomist Ruldolph Virchow said in essence that the fossil was the remains of a modern man afflicted with rickets and osteoporosis. In 1958, at the International Congress of Zoology, A.J.E. Cave stated that his examination of the famous Neanderthal skeleton established that it was simply an old man who had suffered from arthritis. Francis Ivanhoe authored an article that appeared in *Nature,* titled "Was Virchow Right About Neanderthal?" (1970). Virchow had reported that the Neander-

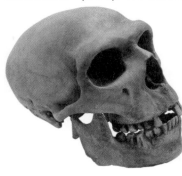

thal man's ape-like appearance was due to a condition known as rickets, which is a vitamin D deficiency characterized by overproduction and deficient calcification of bone tissue. The disease results in skeletal deformities, enlargement of the liver and spleen, and tenderness throughout all the body. Dr. Cave noted that every Neanderthal child's skull that had

Figure 15—Neanderthal skull

been studied to that point in time apparently was affected by severe rickets, which in children commonly produces a large head due to late closure of the epiphysis and fontanels.

Even though Ivanhoe was an evolutionist, he nevertheless went on to note that the wide distribution of Neanderthal finds in various parts of the world explained the differences seen in bone configuration. The extreme variation in locations of these Neanderthal discoveries probably played a role in the diversity of fossils assigned to the Neanderthal group. The differences likely were the result of different amounts of sunlight for a given area, which prevented or retarded vitamin D production (vitamin D is manufactured in the skin upon exposure to sunlight). In adults, a lack of vitamin D causes osteomalacia, a softening of the bones that results in longer bones "bowing" (a condition reported in many Neanderthal fossils).

Scientists have debated long and hard concerning whether there exists any difference between modern humans and Neanderthal specimens. One of the world's foremost authorities on the Neanderthals, Erik Trinkaus concluded:

> Detailed comparisons of Neanderthal skeletal remains with those of modern humans have shown that there is nothing in Neanderthal anatomy that conclusively indicates locomotor, manipulative, intellectual or linguistic abilities inferior to those of modern humans (1978, p. 10).

In the March 2, 2001 issue of *Science,* Ann Gibbons authored an article titled *The Riddle of Coexistence* (Gibbons, 2001). She began with a dramatic opening, asking the reader to imagine forty thousand years ago when "our ancestors wandered into Europe and met another type of human already living there, the brawny, big-brained Neandertals." She then went on to state that "such a collision between groups of humans must have happened many times" (291:1725). Can't you just picture that introduction? "Hi, I'm Neandertal Man." Reply, "Nice to meet you Mr. Neandertal, I'm Modern Man."

This "collision" of two groups was necessitated by recent fossil findings that place Neanderthals and modern humans in the same place at the same time. Scientists dated the remains of anatomically modern humans from caves at Qafzeh and Skhul in Israel, and found them to be 92,000 to 100,000 years old (according to their measuring techniques). **However, this is 40,000 years before the fossil record has Neanderthals inhabiting the neighboring cave of Kebara, only 100 meters away from Skhul!** No missing link here.

NEBRASKA MAN

The June 24, 1922 *Illustrated London News* presented on its front cover a man and a woman who had been reconstructed from a **single tooth** found in the state of Nebraska. The artist even incorporated clothing and imaginary surroundings into the drawings of this alleged "missing link." When Henry Fairfield Osborn, head of the department of vertebrate paleontology at New York's American Museum of Natural History, received the fossil tooth in February of that year, he would have thought it a gift from the gods—had he believed in any god at all. Marxist in his views, and a prominent member in good standing of the American Civil Liberties Union, he was aware that plans were being made by the ACLU to challenge legislation that would forbid the teaching of evolution in American schools. He saw in the tooth precious evidence for the test case, which eventually was held in 1925 at Dayton, Tennessee (the famous Scopes "Monkey Trial").

Figure 16 — Artist's depiction of Nebraska Man

The trial, as it turns out, was an arranged affair, but the tooth was not brought in as evidence because dissension occurred among those who knew of its existence. The truth leaked out slowly and obscurely at first, but eventually was thrust into the public eye in the January 6, 1923 issue of the *American Museum Novitiates*, where nine authorities cited numerous objections to the claim that the tooth was even distantly related to the primate. A further search was made at Snake Creek (the site of the original discovery), and by 1927 it was concluded (albeit begrudgingly) that the tooth was that of a species of *Prosthennops,* an extinct genus related to the modern peccary (a wild pig). These facts were not considered generally newsworthy, but did appear in *Science* (see Gregory, 1927, 66:579). The fourteenth edition of the *Encyclopaedia Britannica* (1929, 14:767) coyly admitted that a mistake had been made and that the tooth belonged to a "being of another order." Creationist Duane Gish observed: "This is a case in which a scientist made a man out of a pig, and the pig made a monkey out of the scientist" (1995, p. 328).

PILTDOWN MAN

Piltdown was an archaeological site in England where, in 1908 and 1912, fossil remains of humans, apes, and other mammals were found. In 1913, at a nearby site, researchers found an ape's jaw with a canine tooth worn down like a human's. And thus another missing link was put forth—one that possessed the skull of a human and the jawbone of an ape. Piltdown was proclaimed genuine by several of the most brilliant British evolutionists of the day—Sir Arthur Smith-Woodward, Sir Arthur Keith, and Grafton Elliot Smith. How did these faked fragments of bone fool the best scientific minds of the time? Perhaps the desire to be part of a great discovery blinded those charged with authenticating it. Many English scientists felt left out by other discoveries on the Continent. Neanderthal had been found in Germany in 1856, and Cro-Magnon in France in 1868. Perhaps national (or professional) pride had kept the researchers from noticing the scratch marks made by the filing of the jaw and teeth—items that were apparent to investigators after the hoax was exposed.

Of course, the deception did far more than dupe a few evolutionists. The whole world was taken in. Museums worldwide proudly displayed copies and photographs of the Piltdown remains. Books and periodicals also spread the news across the globe. Thus, the fraud had many convinced that mankind did, indeed, come from an evolutionary ancestry—which shows how gullible people can be at times. In 1953, Piltdown Man was exposed as a forgery. The skull was modern, and the teeth on the ape's jaw had been filed down and treated biochemically to make them appear "old." No missing link here.

JAVA MAN

This "missing link" was classified as *Homo erectus*, the creature that supposedly gave rise to *Homo sapiens* (humans). Eugene Dubois went to the former Dutch Indies as a health officer in 1887. Because he had had an interest in geology and paleontology since his youth, he immediately began searching for fossils. First he worked on Sumatra, and then went to Java where he supervised the collection of more than twelve thousand fossils from the area around the mountain of Lawu. The fossils varied from fish to elephants to hippopotami, but fossils of anthropoids or early humans were conspicuously absent. In 1890, the Dutch anatomist focused his attention on the banks of Solo near the village Trinil. In a bend of this river, he found eroded layers of sandstone and volcanic ash—which seemed to him the perfect place to search for fossils. Excavators discovered a human-like fossilized tooth in September 1891. A month later, they uncovered the upper part of a skull. The bone of the skull was thick and had such a curve that its brains could be only half as big as the brain of a modern human. In the front of the skull, above the missing orbits, were clear eyebrow bags. Initially, Dubois believed that the fossils belonged to a large, extinct chimpanzee.

Figure 17 — Java Man's skull cap

The team kept digging in the riverbank, however, and one year later discovered a thighbone in the same sandstone layers, about fifteen meters upstream from the spot where the tooth and the skull had been discovered. In contrast to the ape-like skull, the thighbone looked like a modern human thighbone. It was clear that it belonged to an upright-walking creature. Dubois' first reaction was to attribute these discoveries to one individual—an upright-walking specimen of an extinct species of chimpanzee. He dubbed it *Anthropopithecus erectus* (i.e., the erect-walking, human-like anthropoid). Despite further excavations, the team did not discover more than one other tooth. The teeth and femur were, in fact, human. However, the skullcap eventually was shown to be from a giant gibbon (monkey). No missing link here.

Figure 17 — Artist's depiction of Java Man

RHODESIAN MAN

This famous skeleton was found in a zinc mine in 1921 in what was then British Rhodesia in southern Africa. The find consisted of the bones of three or four family members: a man, a woman, and one or two children. The bones were dug out by workers at a mining company, not by an experienced scientist, and so there is much that still remains unknown about the exact circumstances surrounding their owners. Only the skull of the man survived, and it was this skull that ended up causing evolutionists headaches. Once the fossil reached the British Museum of Natural History, the first staff member to examine the bones was Sir Arthur Smith-Woodward. [This was the same scientist who previously had achieved worldwide acclaim as the co-discoverer of what has since become known as one of the most blatant scientific frauds of modern times—Piltdown Man.] The facial bones forced Smith-Wood-ward to admit, in his paper written in 1921 for *Nature,* their "very human characteristics." He still alleged certain ape-like qualities, and no underling was going to challenge his authority while he remained in office. Smith-Woodward retired in 1928, and events took a still darker turn. Before he retired, he placed W.P. Pycraft, one of the Museum's professional ornithologists (a specialist in birds) and "assistant keeper" of the Museum's department of zoology, in charge of the reconstruction of Rhodesian Man's bones. Why a **bird** specialist should be assigned to reconstruct **human** remains, no one is quite sure. What specialized knowledge would an ornithologist have regarding the finer points of human anatomy that would qualify him for such a task? Nevertheless, rather than have an expert in human anatomy reconstruct the crushed hip, Pycraft reconstructed it—with an entirely false orientation. This then gave poor Rhodesian Man a rather ridiculous posture—that of having the knees bowed outwards, while the feet (which

were not available) were turned inwards. Rhodesian Man thus was nicknamed "stooping man" as a result of the posture given to him by these "bird men." It was not until many years later—when scientists trained in human anatomy examined the skeleton—that the find was determined to be nothing more than modern man. No missing link here.

Figure 18 — Rhodesian Man skull

CONCLUSION

In the July 2002 issue of *Scientific American,* editor in chief John Rennie published what he intended to be a stinging rebuke of creationism, titled "15 Answers to Creationist Nonsense." Amidst all the derogatory things he had to say, he nevertheless admitted that "the historical nature of macroevolutionary study involves **inference** from fossils and DNA **rather than direct observation**" (2002, 287[1]:80, emp. added). Thank you, Mr. Rennie, for pointing out the obvious. Twenty-five years earlier, Stephen Jay Gould had tried to get across the same point when he wrote:

> Paleontologists have paid an exorbitant price for Darwin's argument. We fancy ourselves as the only true students of life's history, yet to preserve our favored account of evolution by natural selection, we view our data as so bad that we never see the very process we profess to study (1977b, 86[5]:14, emp. added).

Just how bad are the data? Consider the following real-life scenario. The July 11, 2002 issue of *Nature* announced the discovery by French scientist Michel Brunet of a fossil hominid that he designated as *Sahelanthropus tchadensis*–a creature purported to show a mixture of "primitive" and "evolved" characteristics such as an ape-like brain size and skull shape, combined with a more human-like face and teeth. The authors of the article also reported that the creature had a remarkably large brow ridge—more like that of younger human species—and they dated it at between six and seven million years old (i.e., 3.5 million years older than any other fossil hominid; see Brunet, et al., 2002).

In an article ("New Face in the Family") that she authored for the July 10, 2002 on-line edition of ABCNews.com, science writer Amanda Onion reported the find as follows:

> A team of French and Chadian researchers announced today they have found the skull, jaw fragments and teeth of a six million to seven million-year-old relative of the human family. The find, which is the oldest human relative ever found, suggests humans may have begun evolving from chimpanzees sooner than researchers realized.
>
> The skull's human-like face and teeth are surprising since they come from a period when researchers believed human ancestors just began evolving. Many expected a specimen as old as this one—named Toumaï—to appear more chimp-like.

An international team led by French paleontologist Michel Brunet found the unusually complete skull, two lower jaw fragments, and three teeth last year in Chad, Central Africa.

The skull shows both chimp and human-like features, but is clearly a member of the hominid family—the family including species more closely related to humans than chimpanzees. Brunet called the find *Sahelanthropus tchadensis*—referring to the discovery site in Chad, in Africa's Sahel region, and nicknamed it "Toumaï," "hope of life" in Africa's Goran language.

He may have walked on two feet but researchers say it's difficult, if not impossible, to know if this ancient hominid was a direct ancestral link to humans or possibly a false start within the apparently complex "bush" of life (2002).

The vaunted *New York Times* reported the find in its August 6, 2002 on-line edition, under the heading of "Skulls Found in Africa and Europe Challenge Theories of Human Origins":

Two ancient skulls, one from central Africa and the other from the Black Sea republic of George, have shaken the family tree to its roots, sending scientists scrambling to see if their favorite theories are among the fallen fruit. Probably so, according to paleontologists, who may have to make major revisions in the human genealogy and rethink some of their ideas.... At each turn, the family tree, once drawn straight as a ponderosa pine, has had to be reconfigured with more branches leading here and there and, in some cases, apparently nowhere....

In announcing the discovery in the July 11 [2002] issue of the journal *Nature*, Dr. Brunet's group said the fossils—a cranium, two lower jaw fragments, and several teeth—promised to "illuminate the earliest chapter in human evolutionary history." The age, face, and geography of the new specimen were all surprises.... The most puzzling aspect of the new skull is that it seems to belong to two widely separated periods.... "A hominid of this age," Dr. [Bernard] Wood [a pale-

ontologist of George Washington University–BH/BT]
wrote in *Nature*, "should certainly not have the face of
a hominid less than one-third of its geological age"
(see Wilford, 2002).

So are we **now** to believe that some fossil hominids experienced "devolution"? Truth be told, we can believe pretty much whatever we want about *Sahelanthropus tchadensis*–since, as it turned out, it was manufactured from the skull of a gorilla. Read the following assessment, made after further study of the skull.

A prehistoric skull touted as the oldest human remains ever found is probably not the head of the earliest member of the human family, but of an ancient female gorilla, according to a French scientist.

Dr. Brigitte Senut of the Natural History Museum in Paris, said yesterday that aspects of the skull, whose discovery in Chad was announced on Wednesday, **were sexual characteristics of female gorillas rather than indications of a human**. Dr. Senut, a self-confessed heretic amid the hoopla over the skull, which dates back six or seven million years, said its short face and small canines merely indicated a female and were not conclusive evidence that it was a hominid.

"I tend towards thinking this is the skull of a female gorilla," she said. "The characteristics taken to conclude that this new skull is a hominid are sexual characteristics. Moreover, other characteristics such as the occipital crest [the back of the skull where the neck muscles attach–BH/BT]...remind me much more of the gorilla."

...The skull's braincase is ape-like, the face is short, and the teeth, especially the canines, are small and more like those of a human. But Dr. Senut said these features were characteristic in female gorillas. She cited the case of a skull that was discovered in the 1960s, and accepted for 20 years as that of a hominid before everyone agreed it was a female gorilla.

Dr. Senut was not the only French scientist to raise questions about the hominid theory. Yves Coppens, of the College of France, told the daily *Le Figaro* that the skull had an ambiguous shape, with a back like that of a monkey. "The exact status of this new primate is not yet certain," he said (Chalmers, 2002, emp. added).

One scientist assessed *S. tchadensis* as follows:

> The discovery consisted of a single, partial skull, albeit distorted, broken and recemented after burial, with no bones below the neck. It has excessively heavy brow ridges, a sagittal crest, and an ape-sized brain. The living creature would have been chimp size, but its (now distorted) face was (probably) flatter than most chimps and its teeth showed wear patterns more typical of hominids than chimps....
>
> Unfortunately there is no direct way to date the new specimen. The six-seven million year age came from nearby mammal, reptile, and fish fossils, similar specimens of which are found in Kenya, several hundred miles to the south, and have been dated to six-seven million years old....
>
> Summarizing the facts, we have one partial, broken, distorted, and recemented skull and a few teeth, which at best, point to a transition between chimp and the chimp-like *Australopithecus*, coupled with a poorly established date (Morris, 2002, 31[9]:1,2, parenthetical items in orig.).

So what is the point of all of this? The point is this: The **evidence** is one thing; the **inferences** drawn from that evidence are entirely another. David Hull, the well-known philosopher of science, wrote as early as 1965:

> [S]cience is not as empirical as many scientists seem to think it is. Unobserved and even unobservable entities play an important part in it. Science is not just the making of observations. It is the making of inferences on the basis of observations within the framework of a theory (16[61]:1-18).

Data (a.k.a., "the facts") do not explain themselves; rather, they must be explained. And therein lies an important point that all too often is overlooked in the creation/evolution controversy. Rarely is it the **data** that are in dispute; it is the **interpretation** placed on the data that is in dispute. Sady, in today's scientific paradigm (especially where evolution is concerned), **theories sometimes overrule the data**. In his 2000 book, *Science and Its Limits*, philosopher Del Ratzsch noted that this primacy of "theories over data" has had enormous implications for the practice of science, the end result being that the ultimate "court of appeal" has effectively moved away from the actual data and toward the "informed consensus" of scientists. As he put it:

> Pieces of observational data are extremely important. ...[T]here is still room for disagreement among scientists over relative weights of values, over exactly when to deal with recalcitrant data, and over theory and evidence. But such disagreements often take place within the context of a broad background agreement concerning the major presuppositions of the discipline in question. **This broad background of agreement is usually neither at issue nor at risk. It has a protected status**.... Thus, objective empirical data have substantial and sometimes decisive influence on individual theories, but they have a more muted impact on the larger-scale structure of the scientific picture of reality (p. 71, emp. added).

In other words, when it comes to the "large-scale structure of the scientific picture of reality" (as, for example, when the paradigm of evolution is under discussion), do not look for the data themselves to make much of a difference. In such an instance, the actual data have a "more muted impact." Or, as Mark Twain remarked in *Life on the Mississippi:* "There is something fascinating about science. One gets such wholesale returns of conjecture out of such a trifling investment of fact" (1883, p. 156).

The proposed timeline and fossil lineage for our alleged descent is so muddled and contorted that evolutionists themselves frequently have difficultly knowing which branches are viable versus which are merely dead-ends. Jeremy Rifkin summed it up quite well when he wrote:

> What the "record" shows is nearly a century of fudging and finagling by scientists attempting to force various fossil morsels and fragments to conform with Darwin's notions, all to no avail. **Today the millions of fossils stand as very visible, ever-present reminders of the paltriness of the arguments and the overall shabbiness of the theory that marches under the banner of evolution** (1983, p. 125, emp. added).

Once again, we find ourselves in agreement.

3

MOLECULAR EVIDENCE OF HUMAN ORIGINS

While many evolutionists proclaim that human DNA is 98% identical to chimpanzee DNA, few would lie by idly and allow themselves to receive a transplant using chimpanzee organs. As a matter of fact, American doctors tried using chimp organs in the 1960s, but in all cases the organs were totally unsuitable. The claim of 98% similarity between chimpanzees and humans is not only deceptive and misleading, but also is scientifically incorrect. Today, scientists are finding more and more differences in DNA from humans and chimps. For instance, a 2002 research study proved that human DNA was at least 5% different from chimpanzees—and that number will probably continue to grow as we learn all of the details about human DNA (Britten, 2002).

In 1962, James Watson and Francis Crick received the Nobel Prize in Physiology or Medicine for their discovery concerning the molecular structure of DNA. Just nine years earlier, in 1953, these two men had proposed the double helical structure of DNA—the genetic material responsible for life. By demonstrating the molecular arrangement of four nucleotide base acids (adenosine, guanidine, cytosine, and thymine—usually designated A, G, C, and T) and how they join together, Watson and Crick opened the door for determining the genetic makeup of humans and animals. The field of molecular biology became invigorated with scientists who wanted to compare the proteins and nucleic acids of one species with those of another. Just thir-

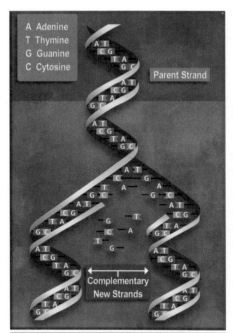

A Adenine
T Thymine
G Guanine
C Cytosine

Parent Strand

Complementary
New Strands

Figure 1 — DNA shown in double-helix, parent-strand form (top), and during replication of two new complementary strands (bottom). Courtesy U.S. Department of Energy Human Genome Program [on-line], http://www.ornl.gov/hgmis.

teen short years after Watson and Crick were awarded their Nobel Prize, the declaration was made that "the average human polypeptide is more than 99 percent identical to its chimpanzee counterpart" (King and Wilson, 1975, pp. 114-115). This genetic similarity in the proteins and nucleic acids, however, left a great paradox—why do we not look or act like chimpanzees if our genetic material is so similar? King and Wilson realized this quandary, and wrote: "The molecular similarity between chimpanzees and humans is extraordinary because they differ far more than many other sibling species in both anatomy and life" (p. 113). Nevertheless, the results matched what evolutionists had hoped to find, and as such, the claim has reverberated through the halls of science for decades as evidence that humans evolved from an ape-like ancestor.

One year following Watson and Crick's Nobel ceremony, chemist Emile Zuckerkandl observed that the protein sequence of hemoglobin in humans and the gorilla differed by only 1 out of 287 amino acids. Zuckerkandl noted: "From the point of view of hemoglobin structure, it appears that gorilla is just an abnormal human, or man an abnormal gorilla, and the two species form actually one continuous population" (1963, p. 247). The molecular and genetic evidence only strengthened the evolutionary foundation for those who alleged that humans had emerged from primate ancestors. Professor of physiology Jared Diamond even titled one of his books *The Third Chimpanzee*, thereby viewing the human species as just another big mammal. From all appearances, it appeared that evolutionists had indeed won a battle—humans were at least 98% identical to chimpanzees. However, after spending his professional career looking for evolutionary evidence in molecular structures, biochemist Christian Schwabe was forced to admit:

> Molecular evolution is about to be accepted as a method superior to paleontology for the discovery of evolutionary relationships. As a molecular evolutionist I should be elated. **Instead it seems disconcerting that many exceptions exist to the orderly progression of species as determined by molecular homologies;** so many in fact that I think the exception, the quirks, may carry the more important message (1986, p. 280, emp. added).

On April 14, 2003, the International Human Genome Sequencing Consortium (headed up in the United States by the National Human Genome Research Institute and the Department of Energy) announced the successful completion of the Human Genome Project. The Consortium had completed its task a full two years ahead of schedule, and sequenced the entire human genome of 3.1 billion base pairs (see "Human Genome Report...," 2003; Pearson, 2003b). Before this massive project was created, scientists estimated that humans possessed 80,000 to 100,000 genes (a gene is a section of DNA that is a basic unit of heredity, while the genome constitutes the total genetic composition of an organism). As preliminary data from the genome project began to stream in, a special issue of *Science*, published on February 16, 2001, set the number of genes in a human at between 35,000 and 40,000 (see Pennisi, 2001, 291: 1178; Malakoff, 2001, 291:1194). One year later almost to the day, *Science* reported the revised number—70,000

(Shouse, 2002, 295:1457; Haney, 2002). Currently, it appears that approximately 1.5% of the human genome consists of genes that code for proteins. These genes are clustered in small regions, with large amounts of "non-coding" DNA (often referred to as "junk DNA") between the clusters. The function of these non-coding regions is only now being determined. These findings indicate that even if **all** of the human genes were different from those of a chimpanzee, the DNA still could be 98.5 percent similar if the non-coding DNA of humans and chimpanzees was identical.

Jonathan Marks, professor of anthropology at the University of California in Berkeley, pointed out an oft'-overlooked problem with this "similarity" line of thinking.

> Because DNA is a linear array of those four bases—A, G, C, and T—only four possibilities exist at any specific point in a DNA sequence. The laws of chance tell us that two random sequences from species that have no ancestry in common will match at about one in every four sites. Thus even two unrelated DNA sequences will be 25 percent identical, not 0 percent identical (2000, p. B-7).

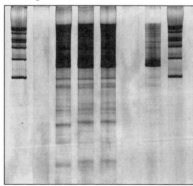

Figure 2 — Electrophoresis results, documenting what are referred to as non-coding ("junk") portions of DNA strands

Therefore a human and **any** earthly DNA-based life form must be at least 25% identical. Would it be correct, then, to suggest that daffodils are one-quarter human? The idea that daffodils are one-quarter human is neither profound nor enlightening, but outright ridiculous! There is hardly any biological comparison—except perhaps the DNA—that would make daffodils appear similar to humans. As Marks went on to concede:

[M]oreover, the genetic comparison is misleading because it ignores qualitative differences among genomes…. Thus, even among such close relatives as human and chimpanzee, we find that the chimp's genome is estimated to be about 10 percent larger than the human's; that one human chromosome contains a fusion of two small chimpanzee chromosomes; and that the tips of each chimpanzee chromosome contain a DNA sequence that is not present in human (p. B-7).

The truth is, if we took all of the DNA from every cell, and then compared the DNA in monkeys and humans, the 4-5% difference in DNA would represent approximately **200 million differences in a human body, compared to that of an ape!** To help make this number understandable, consider the fact that if evolutionists were forced to pay you one penny for every one of those differences, you would walk away with $2,000,000. Given those proportions, a 5% difference does not sound quite so small.

CHROMOSOMAL COUNTS

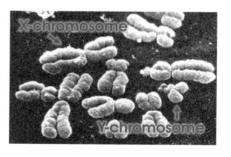

It would seem to make sense that if humans and chimpanzees were genetically identical, then the manner by which they store DNA also would be similar. Yet it is not. DNA, the fundamental blueprint of life, is tightly compacted into chromosomes. All cells that possess a nucleus contain a specific number of chromosomes. Common sense would necessitate that organisms that share a common ancestry would possess the same number of chromosomes. However, chromosome numbers in living organisms vary from 308 in the black mulberry (*Morus nigra*) to six in animals such as the mosquito (*Culex pipiens*) or nematode worm (*Caenorhabditis elegans*) [see Sinnot, et al., 1958]. In addition, complexity does not appear to affect chromosomal number. The radiolaria, a simple protozoon, has over 800, while humans possess 46. Chimpanzees, on the other hand, possess 48 chromosomes. A strict comparison of chromosome number would indicate that we are more closely related to the Chinese muntjac (a small deer found in Taiwan's mountainous regions), which also possesses 46 chromosomes.

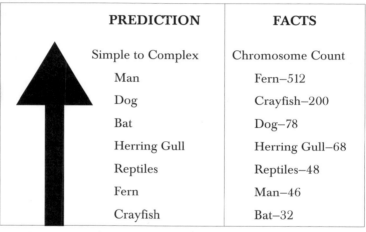

PREDICTION	FACTS
Simple to Complex	Chromosome Count
Man	Fern—512
Dog	Crayfish—200
Bat	Dog—78
Herring Gull	Herring Gull—68
Reptiles	Reptiles—48
Fern	Man—46
Crayfish	Bat—32

Figure 3 — Chromosome numbers in various organisms

This hurdle of differing numbers of chromosomes may appear trivial, but we must remember that chromosomes contain genes, which themselves are composed of DNA spirals. If the blueprint of DNA locked inside those chromosomes codes for only 46 chromosomes, then how can evolution account for the loss of two entire chromosomes? The job of DNA is to continually reproduce itself, and if we infer that this change in chromosome number occurred through evolution, then we are asserting that the DNA locked in the original number of chromosomes did not do its job correctly or efficiently. Considering that each chromosome carries many genes, losing chromosomes does not make physiological sense, and probably would prove deadly for new species. No respectable biologist would suggest that by **removing** one (or several) chromosomes, a new species would likely be produced. To remove even one chromosome could potentially remove the DNA codes for millions of vital body factors. Eldon J. Gardner summed it up this way: "Chromosome number is probably more constant, however, than any other single morphological characteristic that is available for species identification" (1968, p. 211). Humans always have had 46 chromosomes, whereas chimps always have had 48.

REAL GENOMIC DIFFERENCES

One of the downfalls of previous molecular genetic studies has been the limit at which chimpanzees and humans could be compared accurately. Scientists often would use only 30 or 40 known proteins or nucleic acid sequences, and then from those extrapolate their results for the entire genome. Today, however, we have the majority of the human genome sequences, almost all of which have been released and made public. **This allows scientists to compare every single nucleotide base pair between humans and primates—something that was not possible prior to the Human Genome Project**. In January 2002, a study was published in which scientists had constructed and analyzed a first-generation human/chimpanzee comparative genomic map. This study compared the alignments of 77,461 chimpanzee bacterial artificial chromosome [BAC] end sequences to human genomic sequences. Fujiyama and colleagues "detected candidate positions, including two clusters on human chromosome 21 that suggest large, nonrandom regions of differences between the two genomes" (2002, 295:131). In other words, the comparison revealed some "large" differences between the genomes of chimps and humans.

Amazingly, the authors found that, of the entire human genome, only 48.6% matched chimpanzee nucleotide sequences. The human Y chromosome was only 4.8% covered by chimpanzee sequences! This study analyzed the alignments of 77,461 chimpanzee sequences to human genomic sequences obtained from public databases. Of these, 36,940 end sequences were unable to be mapped to the human genome (295:131). Almost 15,000 of those sequences that did not match with human sequences were speculated to "correspond to unsequenced human regions or are from chimpanzee regions that have diverged substantially from humans or did not match for other unknown reasons" (295:132). While the authors noted that the quality and usefulness of the map should "increasingly improve as the finishing of the human genome sequence proceeds" (295:134), the data already support what creationists have stated for years–the 98% equivalency figure between chimps and humans is grossly misleading, as Britten's study revealed (Britten, 2002).

Arrangement 1:

Humans:	CCTCCGCGCG	CCG	CTCCGCGCCGCCGGGC**A**CGGCC
Chimps:	CCTCCGCCGCGCGCCG		C**T**CCGCGCCACCGGGC**A**CGGCC
Gorillas:	CCGCCGCCGC	CGCCGTCGTCGCCTC	CGCCGCGCCACCGGGACCGGCC
Orangutans:	C		CGTCGCCTCCGCCACGCCGCGCCACCGGGCCGGGCC

Arrangement 2:

Humans:	CCTCCGCCGCGCCGCT	CCGCGCCGCCGGGC**A**CGGCCCCGC
Chimps:	CCTCCGCCGCGC**G**CCGCT	CCGCGCC**A**CCGGGC**A**CGGCCCCGC
Gorillas:	CCGCCGCCGCCGCCGT C**G**TCGCCTCCG	CCGCGCC**A**CCGGGACCGGCCCCGC
Orangutans:	CCGTCGCCTCCGCCACGCCGCGCCACCGGGCCGGGCCGGCCCGGCCCGCCCCGC	

Figure 4 — Comparison of human and ape DNA sequences © = cytosine, G = guanine, A = adenine, T = thymine). Arrangement 1 shows more similarity between chimps and humans (consistent with evolutionary consensus). Arrangement 2 shows more similarity between chimps and gorillas than between chimps and humans. Both arrangements try to find the greatest number of matches by inserting artificial gaps. The letters bolded show key points of agreement.

Exactly **how** misleading came to light in an article–"Jumbled DNA Separates Chimps and Humans"–published in the October 25, 2002 issue of *Science*, shortly before this book went to press. The first three sentences of the article, written by Elizabeth Pennisi (a staff writer for *Science*), represented a "that was then, this is now" type of admission of defeat. She wrote:

> For almost 30 years, researchers have asserted that the DNA of humans and chimps is at least 98.5% identical. Now research reported here last week at the American Society for Human Genetics meeting suggests that **the two primate genomes might not be quite as similar after all**. A closer look has uncovered nips and tucks of homologous sections of DNA that weren't noticed in previous studies (298:719, emp. added).

Genomicists Kelly Frazer and David Cox of Perlegen Sciences in Mountain View, California, along with geneticists Evan Eichler and Devin Locke of Case Western University in Cleveland, Ohio, compared human and chimp DNA, and discovered a wide range of insertions and deletions (anywhere from between 200 bases to 10,000 bases). Cox commented: "The implications could be profound, because such genetic hiccups could disable entire genes, possibly explaining why our closest cousin seems so distant" (as quoted in Pennisi, 298:721).

Roy Britten, of the California Institute of Technology in Pasadena, analyzed chimp and human genomes with a customized computer program. To quote Pennisi's article:

> He compared 779,000 bases of chimp DNA with the sequences of the human genome, both found in the public repository GenBank. Single-base changes accounted for 1.4% of the differences between the human and chimp genomes, and insertions and deletions accounted for an additional 3.4%, he reported in the 15 October [2002] *Proceedings of the National Academy of Sciences*. Locke's and Frazer's groups didn't commit to any new estimates of the similarity between the species, but **both agree that the previously accepted 98.5% mark is too high** (298:721, emp. added).

While Locke's and Frazer's team was unwilling to commit to any new estimate of the similarity between chimps and humans, Britten was not. In fact, he titled his article in the October 15, 2002 *Proceedings of the National Academy of Sciences,* "Divergence between Samples of Chimpanzee and Human DNA Sequences is 5%" (Britten, 99:13633-13635). In the abstract accompanying the article, he wrote: **"The conclusion is that the old saw that we share 98.5% of our DNA sequence with chimpanzee is probably in error**. For this sample, a better estimate would be that 95% of the base pairs are exactly shared between chimpanzee and human DNA" (99:13633, emp. added). The news service at NewScientist.com reported the event as follows:

> It has long been held that we share 98.5 per cent of our genetic material with our closest relatives. That now appears to be wrong. In fact, we share less than 95 per cent of our genetic material, **a three-fold increase in the variation between us and chimps**.
>
> The new value came to light when Roy Britten of the California Institute of Technology became suspicious about the 98.5 per cent figure. Ironically, that number was originally derived from a technique that Britten himself developed decades ago at Caltech with colleague Dave Kohne. By measuring the temperature at which matching DNA of two species comes apart, you can work out how different they are.
>
> But the technique only picks up a particular type of variation, called a single base substitution. These occur whenever a single "letter" differs in corresponding strands of DNA from the two species.
>
> But there are two other major types of variation that the previous analyses ignored. "Insertions" occur whenever a whole section of DNA appears in one species but not in the corresponding strand of the other. Likewise, "deletions" mean that a piece of DNA is missing from one species.
>
> Together, they are termed "indels," and Britten seized his chance to evaluate the true variation between the two species when stretches of chimp DNA were re-

cently published on the internet by teams from the Baylor College of Medicine in Houston, Texas, and from the University of Oklahoma.

When Britten compared five stretches of chimp DNA with the corresponding pieces of human DNA, he found that single base substitutions accounted for a difference of 1.4 per cent, very close to the expected figure.

But he also found that the DNA of both species was littered with indels. His comparisons revealed that they add around another 4.0 per cent to the genetic differences (see Coghlan, 2002, emp. added).

It seems that, as time passes and scientific studies increase, humans appear to be less like chimps after all. In a separate study, Barbulescu and colleagues also uncovered another major difference in the genomes of primates and humans. In their article "A HERV-K Provirus in Chimpanzees, Bonobos, and Gorillas, but not Humans," the authors wrote: "**These observations provide very strong evidence that, for some fraction of the genome, chimpanzees, bonobos, and gorillas are more closely related to each other than they are to humans**" (2001, 11:779, emp. added). The data from these results go squarely against what evolutionists have contended for decades–that chimpanzees are closer genetically to humans than they are to gorillas. Another study using interspecies representational difference analysis (RDA) between humans and gorillas revealed **gorilla-specific** DNA sequences (Toder, et al., 2001)–that is, gorillas possess sequences of DNA that are not found in humans. The authors of this study suggested that sequences found in gorillas but not humans "could represent either ancient sequences that got lost in other species, such as human and orang-utan, or, more likely, recent sequences which evolved or originated specifically in the gorilla genome" (9:431).

The differences between chimpanzees and humans are not limited to genomic variances. In 1998, a structural difference between the cell surfaces of humans and apes was detected. After studying tissues and blood samples from the great apes, and sixty humans from various ethnic groups, Muchmore and colleagues discovered that human cells are missing a particular form of sialic acid (a type of sugar) found in all other mammals (1998, 107[2]:187). This sialic acid molecule is found on the surface of every cell in the body, and is thought to carry out multiple cellular tasks. This seemingly "minuscule" difference can have far-reaching effects, and might explain why surgeons were unable to transplant chimp organs into humans in the 1960s. With this in mind, we never should declare, with a simple wave of the hand, "chimps are almost identical to us" simply because of a large genetic overlap.

Homology (i.e., similarity) does not prove common ancestry. The entire genome of the tiny nematode (*Caenorhabditis elegans*) also has been sequenced as a tangential study from the Human Genome Project. Of the 5,000 best-known human genes, 75% have matches in the worm (see "A Tiny Worm Challenges Evolution"). Does this mean that we are 75% identical to a nematode? Just because living creatures share some genes with humans does not mean there is a linear ancestry. Biologist John Randall admitted this when he wrote:

> The older textbooks on evolution make much of the idea of homology, pointing out the obvious resemblances between the skeletons of the limbs of different animals. Thus the "pentadactyl" [five bone—BH/BT] limb pattern is found in the arm of a man, the wing of a bird, and flipper of a whale, and this is held to indicate their common origin. Now if these various structures were transmitted by the same gene couples, varied from time to time by mutations and acted upon by environmental selection, the theory would make good sense. Unfortunately this is not the case. Homologous organs are now known to be produced by totally different gene complexes in the different species. The concept of homology in terms of similar genes handed on from a common ancestor has broken down... (as quoted in Fix, 1984, p. 189).

Yet textbooks and teachers still proclaim that humans and chimps are 98% genetically identical. The evidence clearly demonstrates vast molecular differences—differences that can be attributed to the fact that humans, unlike animals, were created in the image and likeness of God (Genesis 1:26-27; see Lyons and Thompson, 2002a, 2002b). Elaine Morgan commented on this difference when she observed:

> Considering the very close genetic relationship that has been established by comparison of biochemical properties of blood proteins, protein structure and DNA and immunological responses, the differences between a man and a chimpanzee are more astonishing than the resemblances. They include structural differences in the skeleton, the muscles, the skin, and the brain; differences in posture associated with a unique method of locomotion; differences in social organization; and finally the acquisition of speech and tool-using, together with the dramatic increase in intellectual ability which has led scientists to name their own species *Homo sapiens sapiens*—wise wise man. During the period when these remarkable evolutionary changes were taking place, other closely related ape-like species changed only very slowly, and with far less remarkable results. **It is hard to resist the conclusion that something must have happened to the ancestors of *Homo sapiens* which did not happen to the ancestors of gorillas and chimpanzees** (1989, pp. 17-18, emp. added).

That "something" actually is "Someone"—the Creator.

"MITOCHONDRIAL EVE"

On the first day of 1987, a scientific "discovery" seized the attention of the popular press. The original scientific article that caused all the commotion—"Mitochondrial DNA and Human Evolution"—appeared in the January 1, 1987 issue of *Nature*, and was authored by Rebecca Cann, Mark Stoneking, and Allan C. Wilson (see Cann, et al., 1987). These three scientists announced that they had "proven" that all modern human beings can trace their ancestry back to a single woman who lived 200,000 years ago in Africa. This one woman was nicknamed "Eve" (a.k.a., "mitochondrial Eve")—much to the media's delight. An article in the January 26, 1987 issue of *Time* magazine bore the headline, "Everyone's Genealogical Mother: Biologists Speculate that 'Eve' Lived in Sub-Saharan Africa" (Lemonick, 1987). A year later, that "speculation" became a major *Newsweek* production titled, "The Search for Adam and Eve" (Tierney, et al., 1988). The provocative front cover presented a snake, tree, and a nude African couple in a "Garden of Eden" type setting. The biblical-story imagery was reinforced as the woman offered an apple to the man.

A word of explanation is in order. For decades, evolutionists had been trying to determine the specific geographical origin of humans—whether we all came from one specific locale, or whether there were numerous small pockets of people placed around the globe. When they set out to determine the specific geographical origin of humans, a curious piece of data came to light. As they considered various human populations, Africans seemed to show much more genetic variation than non-Africans (i.e., Asians, Europeans, Native Americans, Pacific Islanders, et al.). According to molecular biologists, this increased variability is the result of African populations being older, thus, having had more time to accumulate mutations and diverge from one another. This assumption led some researchers to postulate that Africa was the ancient "cradle of civilization" from which all of humanity had emerged.

The genetic material (DNA) in a cell's nucleus controls the functions of the cell, bringing in nutrients from the body and making hormones, proteins, and other chemicals. Outside the nucleus is an area known as the cytoplasmic matrix (generally referred to simply as the cytoplasm), which contains, among other things, tiny bean-shaped organelles known as mitochondria. These often are described as the "energy factories" of the cell.

Mitochondria contain their own DNA, which they use to make certain proteins; the DNA in the nucleus oversees production of the rest of the proteins necessary for life and its functions. However, mitochondrial DNA (mtDNA) was thought to be special for two reasons. First, it is short and relatively simple in comparison to the DNA found within the nucleus, containing only thirty-seven genes instead of the 35,000+ genes located in the nuclear DNA. This makes it relatively easy to analyze. Second, unlike nuclear DNA, which each person inherits in a jumbled form from both parents, mitochondrial DNA was thought to be passed on only through the mother's line (more about this later). Working from the assumption that mtDNA is passed to the progeny only by the mother, Dr. Cann and her coworkers believed that each new cell should contain copies of only the egg's mitochondria. In trying to draw the human family tree, therefore, researchers took a special interest in these minute strands of genetic code. What they **really** were interested in, of course, was the variations in mitochondrial DNA from one group of people to another.

Although our mtDNA should be, in theory at least, the same as our mother's mtDNA, small changes (or mutations) in the genetic code can, and do, arise. On rare occasions, mutations are serious enough to do harm. More frequently, however, the mutations have no effect on the proper functioning of either the DNA or the mitochondria. In such cases, the mutational changes will be preserved and carried on to succeeding generations.

Theoretically, if scientists could look farther and farther into the past, they would find that the number of women who contributed the modern varieties of mitochondrial DNA gets less and less until, finally, we arrive at one "original" mother. She, then, would be the only woman out of all the women living in her day to have a daughter in every generation till the present. Coming forward in time, we would see that the mtDNA varieties found within her female contemporaries were gradually eliminated as their daughters did not have children, had only sons, or had daughters who did not have daughters. This does not mean, of course, that we would **look like** this putative ancestral mother; rather, it means only that we would have received our mitochondrial DNA from her.

To find this woman, researchers compared the different varieties of mtDNA in the human family. Since mtDNA occurs in fairly small quantities, and since the researchers wanted as large a sample as possible from each person, they decided to use human placentas as their source of the mtDNA. So, Rebecca Cann and her colleagues selected 145 pregnant women and two cell lines representing the five major geographic regions: 20 Africans, 34 Asians, 46 Caucasians, 21 aboriginal Australians, and 26 aboriginal New Guineans (Cann, et al., 1987, 325: 32). All placentas from the first three groups came from babies born in American hospitals. Only two of the 20 Africans were born in Africa.

After analyzing a portion of the mtDNA in the cells of each placenta, they found that the differences "grouped" the samples by region. In other words, Asians were more like each other than they were like Europeans, people from New Guinea were more like each other than they were like people from Australia, and so on.

Next, they saw two major branches form in their computer-generated tree of recent human evolution. Seven African individuals formed one distinct branch, which started lower on the trunk than the other four. This was because the differences among these individuals were much greater than the differences between other individuals and other groups. More differences mean more mutations, and hence more time to accumulate those changes. If the Africans have more differences, then their lineage must be older than all the others. The second major branch bore the non-African groups and, significantly, a scattering of the remaining thirteen Africans in the sample. To the researchers, the presence of Africans among non-Africans meant an African common ancestor for the non-African branches, which, likewise, meant an African common ancestor for both branches. The nickname "Eve" stuck to this hypothetical common ancestral mother, and later, then, fired the media's imagination.

Having concluded that the African group was the oldest, Dr. Cann and her colleagues wanted to find out just **how** old the group might be. To do this, they used what is known as a "molecular clock" that, in this case, was based on mutations in the mtDNA. The rate at which the clock ticked was determined from the accumulation of changes over a given period of time. As we note below in our discussion of the so-called molecular clock, if the assumption was made that there was one mutation every 1,000 years, and if scientists found a difference of 10 mutations between us and our ancient hypothetical ancestor, they then could infer that that ancestor lived 10,000 years ago.

The researchers looked in two places for their figures. First, they compared mtDNA from humans with that from chimpanzees, and then used paleontology and additional molecular data to determine the age of the supposed common ancestor. This (and similar calculations on other species) revealed a mutation rate in the range of 2% to 4% per million years. Second, they compared the groups in their study that were close geographically, and took the age of the common ancestor from estimated times of settlement as indicated by anthropology and archaeology. Again, 2% to 4% every million years seemed reasonable to them.

Since the common mitochondrial ancestor diverged from all others by 0.57%, she must have lived sometime between approximately 140,000 $(0.57 \div 4 \times 1,000,000)$ and 290,000 $(0.57 \div 2 \times 1,000,000)$ years ago. The figure of 200,000 was chosen as a suitable round number.

The results obtained from analysis of mitochondrial DNA eventually led to what is known in evolutionary circles as the "Out of Africa" theory. This is the idea that the descendants of mitochondrial Eve were the only ones to colonize Africa and the rest of the world, supplanting all other hominid pop-

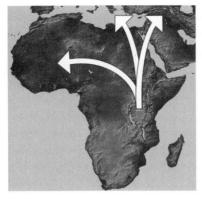

ulations in the process. Some (though not all) evolutionists claim that such an interpretation is in agreement with archaeological, paleontological, and other genetic data (see Stringer and Andrews, 1988; for an opposing viewpoint, see the written debate in the April 1992 issue of *Scientific American*).

While many evolutionists have accepted the mitochondrial DNA tree, they differ widely in their views regarding both the source of the nuclear DNA and the "humanity" of Eve. Some believe that Eve contributed **all** the nuclear DNA, in addition to the mitochondrial DNA. Some believe she was an "archaic" *Homo sapiens*, while others believe she was fully human. The exact interpretation is hotly debated because mitochondrial DNA is "something of a passenger in the genetic processes that led to the formation of new species: it therefore neither contributes to the formation of a new species nor reveals anything about what actually happened" (Lewin, 1987, 238:24).

THE DEMISE OF MITOCHONDRIAL EVE

Things change rapidly in science. What is popular one day, is not the next. Theories come, and theories go. And so it is with mitochondrial Eve. She once was in vogue as the evolutionary equivalent of "wonder woman." Now, she has become virtually the "crazy aunt in the attic" who no one wants to admit even exists.

But it was not forbidden fruit that caused her demise this time around. The "passing" of one of evolution's most familiar icons is due to two groups of new scientific facts that have surfaced since her introduction in 1987. **If** humans received mitochondrial DNA only from their mothers, then researchers could "map" a family tree using that information. And, **if** the mutations affecting mtDNA had occurred at constant rates, then the mtDNA could serve as a molecular clock for timing evolutionary events and reconstructing the evolutionary history of extant species. It is the "ifs" in these two sentences that are the problem.

Mitochondrial Eve is alleged to have lived in Africa at the beginning of the Upper Pleistocene period (between 100,000 and 200,000 years ago). She has been described as the most-recent common ancestor of all humans on Earth today, with respect to matrilineal descent. The validity of these assertions, however, is dependent upon two critically important assumptions: (1) that mtDNA is, in fact, derived exclusively from the mother; and (2) that the mutation rates associated with mtDNA have remained constant over time. However, **we now know that both of these assumptions are wrong!**

First, let us examine the assumption that mtDNA is derived solely from the mother. In response to a paper that appeared in *Science* in 1999, anthropologist Henry Harpending of the University of Utah lamented: "There is a cottage industry of making gene trees in anthropology and then interpreting them. This paper will invalidate most of that" (as quoted in Strauss, 1999b, 286:2436). Just as women thought they were getting their fair shake in science, the tables turned. As one study noted:

> Women have struggled to gain equality in society, but biologists have long thought that females wield absolute power in a sphere far from the public eye: in the mitochondria, cellular organelles whose DNA is thought to pass intact from mother to child with no paternal influence. On page 2524, however, a study by Philip Awadalla of the University of Edinburgh and Adam Eyre-Walker and John Maynard Smith of the University of Sussex in Brighton, U.K., finds signs of mixing between maternal and paternal mitochondrial DNA (mtDNA) in humans and chimpanzees. **Because biologists have used mtDNA as a tool to trace hu-**

man ancestry and relationships, the finding has implications for everything from the identification of bodies to the existence of a "mitochondrial Eve" 200,000 years ago (Strauss, 1999b, 286: 2436, emp. added).

Earlier that same year, Strauss had written another article in *Science*, titled "Can Mitochondrial Clocks Keep Time?," in which she remarked:

> New information about the complexities of mitochondrial biology is also raising new questions about the mtDNA clock. Conventional wisdom has it that mitochondrial DNA comes only from the mother's egg. But electron microscopy and DNA detection studies have revealed that **the sperm's mitochondria can enter the egg** (1999a, 283:1438, emp. added).

Strauss went on to note:

> Recombination could also be bad news for use of mtDNA in other questions of human ancestry…. Recombination could also cause problems for mitochondrial Eve. Studies of mtDNA from living people on various continents show a surprising homogeneity, suggesting that we are all descended from a woman who lived a mere 200,000 years ago in Africa. **But such homogeneity might be due to recombination rather than a common recent ancestor** (283: 1438).

Svante Pääbo of the Max Planck Institute for Evolutionary Anthropology opined: "Mitochondrial Eve is the one woman who carried the ancestral mitochondrial DNA. **There was no woman, if there was recombination**" (as quoted in Strauss, 1999a, 283:1438, emp. added).

One year after Strauss' articles, researchers made this startling admission:

> Mitochondrial DNA (mtDNA) is generally assumed to be inherited exclusively from the mother…. Several recent papers, however, have suggested that elements of mtDNA may sometimes be inherited from the father. This hypothesis is based on evidence that

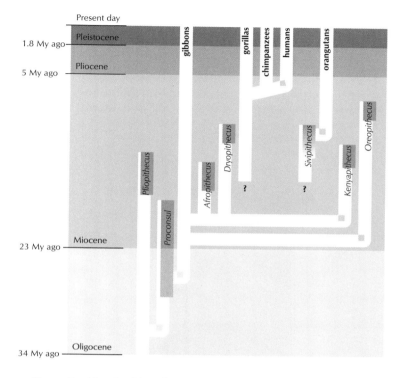

Figure 5 — Hominoid evolution according to Andrews and Stringer (1993, p. 220). Rectangles with italicized names represent the occurrence of extinct ape species. Note the almost complete absence of suggested fossil ancestors leading up to humans and modern apes (bold text). "My" = millions of years.

mtDNA may undergo recombination. If this does occur, maternal mtDNA in the egg must cross over with homologous sequences in a different DNA molecule; paternal mtDNA seems the most likely candidate…. **If mtDNA can recombine, irrespective of the mechanism, there are important implications for mtDNA evolution and for phylogenetic studies that use mtDNA** (Morris and Lightowlers, 2000, 355:1290, emp. added).

In 2002, a study was conducted that concluded:

> Nevertheless, even a single validated example of paternal mtDNA transmission suggests that the interpretation of inheritance patterns in other kindreds thought to have mitochondrial disease should not be based on the dogmatic assumption of absolute maternal inheritance of mtDNA.... The unusual case described by Schwartz and Vissing **is more than a mere curiosity** (Williams, 347:611, emp. added).

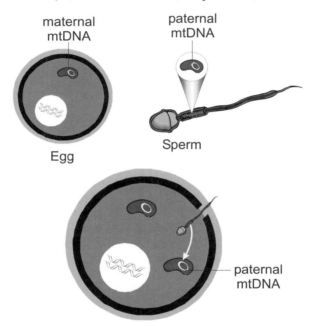

Figure 6 — Illustration of how paternal mtDNA in the sperm can cross over with homologous sequences in a different DNA molecule, specifically the maternal mtDNA contained within the egg

And now we know that these are more than small "fractional" amounts of mtDNA coming from fathers. The August 2002 issue of the *New England Journal of Medicine* contained the results of one study, whose authors remarked:

> Mammalian mitochondrial DNA (mtDNA) is thought to be strictly maternally inherited.... Very small amounts of paternally inherited mtDNA have been detected by the polymerase chain reaction (PCR) in mice after several generations of interspecific back-crosses.... We report the case of a 28-year-old man with mitochondrial myopathy due to a novel 2-bp mtDNA deletion.... We determined that the mtDNA harboring the mutation was paternal in origin and accounted for **90 percent** of the patient's muscle mtDNA (Schwartz and Vissing, 347:576, emp. added).

Ninety percent! And all this time, evolutionists have been selectively shaping our family tree using what was alleged to be only **maternal** mtDNA!

As scientists have begun to comprehend the fact, and significance, of the "death" of mitochondrial Eve, many have found themselves searching for an alternative. But this recombination ability in mtDNA makes the entire discussion a moot point. As Strauss noted:

> Such recombination could be a blow for researchers who have used mtDNA to trace human evolutionary history and migrations. They have assumed that the mtDNA descends only through the mother, so they could draw a single evolutionary tree of maternal descent—all the way back to an African "mitochondrial Eve," for example. But "with recombination there is no single tree," notes Harpending. Instead, different parts of the molecule have different histories. Thus, **"there's not one woman to whom we can trace our mitochondria,"** says Eyre-Walker (1999b, 286: 2436, emp. added).

Our thoughts on the matter exactly.

THE MOLECULAR CLOCK– DATING MITOCHONDRIAL ANCESTORS

Second, let us examine the assumption that the mutations affecting mtDNA did actually occur at constant rates. The researchers who made the initial announcement about Eve not only gave a location for this amazing female, but also proposed the time period during which she was supposed to have lived. However, in order for the mtDNA theory to be of any practical use, those scientists had to assume that random mutations in the DNA occurred at documented, steady rates. For example, if they speculated that there was one mutation every 1,000 years, and they found a difference of 10 mutations between us and our ancient hypothetical ancestor, they then could infer that that ancestor lived 10,000 years ago. Scientists—who use this concept to determine the age of mitochondrial Eve—refer to this proposed mutation rate as a "molecular clock." One group of researchers described the process as follows:

> The hypothesis of the molecular clock of evolution emerged from early observations that the number of amino acid replacements in a given protein appeared to change linearly with time. Indeed, if proteins (and genes) evolve at constant rates they could serve as molecular clocks for timing evolutionary events and reconstructing the evolutionary history of extant species (Rodriguez-Trelles, et al., 2001, 98:11405, parenthetical item in orig.).

It sounds good in theory, but the actual facts tell an entirely different story. As these same researchers went on to admit:

> The neutrality theory predicts that the rate of neutral molecular evolution is constant over time, and thus that there is a molecular clock for timing evolutionary events. It has been observed that **the variance of the rate of evolution is generally larger than expected** according to the neutrality theory, **which has raised the question of how reliable the molecular clock is or, indeed, whether there is a molecular clock at all**.... The observations are inconsistent with the predictions made by various subsidiary hypotheses proposed to account for the overdispersion of the molecular clock (98:11405, emp. added).

Another study that was published in 2002 pointed out a built-in, natural bias for older ages that result from use of the molecular clock. The researchers who carried out the study noted:

> There is presently a conflict between fossil- and molecular-based evolutionary time scales. Molecular approaches for dating the branches of the tree of life frequently lead to substantially deeper times of divergence than those inferred by paleontologists.... Here we show that molecular time estimates suffer from a methodological handicap, namely that they are asymmetrically bounded random variables, constrained by a nonelastic boundary at the lower end, but not at the higher end of the distribution. **This introduces a bias toward an overestimation of time** since divergence, which becomes greater as the length of the molecular sequence and the rate of evolution decrease. ...Despite the booming amount of sequence information, molecular timing of evolutionary events has continued to yield conspicuously deeper dates than indicated by the stratigraphic data. Increasingly, the discrepancies between molecular and paleontological estimates are ascribed to deficiencies of the fossil record, while sequence-based time tables gain credit. **Yet, we have identified a fundamental flaw of molecular dating methods, which leads to dates that are systematically biased towards substantial overestimation of evolutionary times** (Rodriguez-Trelles, et al., 2002, 98:8112,8114, emp. added).

Until approximately 1997, we did not have good empirical measures of mutation rates in humans. However, that situation greatly improved when geneticists were able to analyze DNA from individuals with well-established family trees going back several generations. One study revealed that mutation rates in mitochondrial DNA were **eighteen times higher than previous estimates** (see Parsons, et al., 1997).

Ann Gibbons authored an article for the January 2, 1998 issue of *Science* titled "Calibrating the Mitochondrial Clock," the subheading of which read as follows: "Mitochondrial DNA appears to mutate much faster than expected, prompting new DNA forensics procedures and raising troubling questions about the dating of evolutionary events." In that article, she discussed new data which showed that the mutation rates used to obtain mitochondrial Eve's age no longer could be considered valid.

> Evolutionists have assumed that the clock is constant, ticking off mutations every 6,000 to 12,000 years or so. But if the clock ticks faster or at different rates at different times, some of the spectacular results—such as dating our ancestors' first journeys into Europe at about 40,000 years ago—may be in question (1998a, 279:28).

Gibbons then quoted Neil Howell, a geneticist at the University of Texas Medical Branch in Galveston, who stated: "We've been treating this like a stopwatch, and I'm concerned that it's as precise as a sun dial. I don't mean to be inflammatory, but I'm concerned that we're pushing this system more than we should" (279:28). Gibbons concluded:

> Regardless of the cause, evolutionists are most concerned about the effect of a faster mutation rate. For example, researchers have calculated that "mitochondrial Eve"—the woman whose mtDNA was ancestral to that in all living people—lived 100,000 to 200,000 years ago in Africa. **Using the new clock, she would be a mere 6,000 years old** (279:29, emp. added).

"Mitochondrial Eve" a mere 6,000 years old—instead of 200,000?! Gibbons quickly went on to note, of course, that "no one thinks that's the case," (279:29). She ended her article by discussing the fact that many test results are (to use her exact word) "inconclusive," and lamented that "for now, so are some of the evolutionary results gained by using the mtDNA clock" (279:29).

We now know that the two key assumptions behind the data used to establish the existence of "mitochondrial Eve" are **not just flawed, but wrong**. The assumption that mitochondrial DNA is passed down only by the mother is completely incorrect (it also can be passed on by the father). And, the mutation rates used to calibrate the so-called "molecular clock" are now known to have been in error. (To use the words of Rodriguez-Trelles and his coworkers, the method contains a "fundamental flaw.")

Philip Awadalla and his coworkers noted in *Science:* "Many inferences about the pattern and tempo of human evolution and mtDNA evolution have been based on the assumption of clonal inheritance. These inferences will now have to be reconsidered" (1999, 286:2525). Yes, they will. The same year that Awadalla, et al., published their paper on recombination in mitochondrial DNA, Evelyn Strauss published a paper in *Science* ("Can Mitochondrial Clocks Keep Time?)" in which she noted:

> The DNA sequences pouring in from sequencing projects have fueled the effort and extended the clock approach to many genes in the cell nucleus. But the wash of data has uncovered some troubling facts. **It's now clear that in many cases, the main assumption underlying molecular clocks doesn't hold up**: Clocks tick at different rates in different lineages and at different times…. For the clock to work with either sort of DNA [nuclear or mitochondrial—BH/BT], nucleotide changes must tick away steadily so scientists can convert the number of nucleotide differences seen between two organisms into the number of years since they diverged. Different genes evolve at different rates, depending on the selective forces upon them, but the model requires only that each gene's clock maintains its own rate. **Early work hinted that this might not always be true, and now a plethora of data shows that many genes don't conform to this model** (1999a, 283:1435,1436, emp. added).

John Avise, an evolutionary geneticist at the University of Georgia in Athens, went so far as to remark: "There's an emerging consensus that there are significant rate heterogeneities across different lineages. How big they are and how to deal with them is very much a matter of concern" (as quoted in Strauss, 283:1435).

SERIOUS ERRORS IN
MITOCHONDRIAL DNA DATA
IN THE SCIENTIFIC LITERATURE

Avise commented that the problems with the molecular clock are a "matter of concern." Philip Awadalla suggested that the inferences that have been drawn from those clocks "will now have to be reconsidered." Ann Gibbons reported that the "evolutionary results gained by using the mtDNA clock" are "inconclusive." When each of these writers made those statements, they had no idea about the "bomb" that was about be dropped on the evolutionary community regarding the inaccuracy of huge sections of the reported mitochondrial DNA data. Just when evolutionists thought it could not possibly get any worse —it did!

The "evolutionary results gained by using the mtDNA clock" are not just "inconclusive." They are **wrong**! In the January 2003 edition of the *Annals of Human Genetics*, geneticist Peter Forster of Cambridge published an article ("To Err is Human") in which he documented that, to use his words, **"more than half of the mtDNA sequencing studies ever published contain obvious errors**." He then asked: "Does it matter? Unfortunately, in many cases it does." Then came the crushing blow for "Mitochondrial Eve": "...**fundamental research papers, such as those claiming a recent African origin for mankind** (Cann, et al., 1987; Vigilant, et al., 1991)...**have been criticized, and rejected due to the extent of primary data errors**" (67[1]:2, emp. added). Then, as if to add salt to an already open and bleeding wound, Dr. Forster acknowledged that the errors discovered thus far are "only the tip of the iceberg...," and that "there is no reason to suppose that DNA sequencing errors are restricted to mtDNA" (2003, 67[1]:2,3).

One month later, *Nature* weighed in with an exposé of its own. In the February 20, 2003 issue, Carina Dennis authored a commentary on Forster's work titled "Error Reports Threaten to Unravel Databases of Mitochondrial DNA." Dennis reiterated the findings that "more than half of all published studies of human mitochondrial DNA (mtDNA) sequences contain mistakes." Then, after admitting that "published mtDNA sequences are popular tools for investigating the evolution and demography of human populations," she lamented: "[T]he **problem is far bigger than researchers had imagined. The mistakes may be so extensive that geneticists could be drawing incorrect conclusions to studies of human populations and evolution**" (2003, 421:773, emp. added).

In her report, Dennis quoted Eric Shoubridge, a geneticist ·a McGill University's Montreal Neurological Institute in Canada, who investigates human diseases that result from problems with mtDNA. His response was: "I was surprised by the number of errors. What concerns me most is that these errors could be compounded in the databases" (421:773). In 1981, the complete sequence of human mtDNA–known as the "Cambridge Reference Sequence"–was published in a database format for scientists to use in their research (see Anderson, et al., 1981). It is from that initial database that many of the mtDNA sequences have been taken and used to predict, among other things, the Neolithic origin of Europeans (Simoni, et al., 2000) and the "factuality" of the creature known as "Mitochondrial Eve." Yet Dr. Forster has been busily engaged in making corrections to that 1981 database almost since its inception, and has compiled his own database of corrected mitochondrial sequences.

Eric Shoubridge (quoted above) isn't the only one who is "concerned" about Peter Forster's findings. Neil Howell, vice president for research at MitoKor, a San Diego-based biotech company that specializes in mitochondrial diseases, suggested that Forster's error-detection method "may even **underestimate** the extent of the errors"(as quoted in Dennis, 421:773-774, emp. added).

What has been the response of the scientific community? Let Forster answer: "Antagonism would be an understatement in some cases" (as quoted in Dennis, 421:773). He did note, however, that, at times, some of the scientists whose published papers have been found to contain the errors were "forthcoming in resolving discrepancies in sequences." That is nice—since "truth" and "knowledge" are what science is supposedly all about (our English word "science" derives from the Latin *scientia*, meaning knowledge).

In the end, where does all of this leave "Mitochondrial Eve"? Could we put it any plainer than Dr. Forster did when he said that "fundamental research papers, such as those claiming a recent African origin for mankind have been criticized, and rejected due to the extent of primary data errors"? Criticized— **and rejected**?!

Poor Eve. How many times, we wonder, will she have to die before she finally can be buried—permanently—and left to "rest in peace"? We suggest that, rather than merely "reconsidering" their theory and attempting to revamp it accordingly, evolutionists need to admit, honestly and forthrightly, that the clock is "broken," and that mitochondrial Eve, as it turns out, has existed only in their minds, not in the facts of the real world. Science works by analyzing the data and forming hypotheses based on those data. Science is not supposed to "massage" the data until they fit a certain preconceived hypothesis. All of the conclusions that have been drawn from research on mitochondrial Eve via the molecular clock must now be discarded as unreliable. A funeral and interment are in order for mitochondrial Eve.

NEANDERTHAL VS. HUMAN DNA– IS IT A MATCH?

Creationists accept the "Neanderthal" species as nothing more than modern man. Evolutionists disagree, based mainly on studies regarding Neanderthal DNA. The July 11, 1997 issue of the journal *Cell* contained an article by Krings, et al., titled "Neanderthal DNA sequences and the Origin of Modern Humans" (Krings, et al., 1997). In that article, Dr. Krings and his coworkers explained how they successfully extracted mitochondrial DNA (mtDNA—which resides in the cell's mitochondria or "energy factories") from the humerus (right arm bone) of the original Neanderthal fossil discovered in 1856. The scientific team doing the research, led by Svante Pääbo of the University of Munich, chose to search for mtDNA rather than nuclear DNA, due in large part to the fact that whereas there are only two copies of DNA in the nucleus of each cell (one from each parent), there are 500 to 1,000 copies per cell of mtDNA. Hence, the possibility was much greater that some of the ancient mtDNA might have been preserved. Unlike nuclear DNA, mtDNA can be passed on in an unchanged form from a mother to her offspring. [And, as noted earlier, we now know that mtDNA from the father can be passed on in a similar fashion.] Thus, since changes in mtDNA are the result of mutations rather than genetic mixing, evolutionists believe that mtDNA is a more accurate reflection of evolutionary history.

At the conclusion of their research, the scientists who were involved suggested that fewer differences in the mtDNA exist between modern humans, than exist between modern humans and the Neanderthal specimen. Therefore, based upon those differences, evolutionists have suggested that the Neanderthal line diverged from the line leading to modern humans about 550,000 to 690,000 years ago, and that Neanderthals became extinct without contributing any genetic material to modern humans through intermarriage. As Marvin Lubenow explained:

> The implications are that the Neandertals did not evolve into fully modern humans, that they were a different species from modern humans, and that they were just one of many proto-human types that were failed evolutionary experiments. We alone evolved to full humanity (1998, 12[1]:87).

When the first Neanderthal fossil was discovered, the creature was classified as *Homo neanderthalensis*, and as such was considered a separate species within the genus *Homo*. However, when additional evidence became available (in 1964) to suggest that Neanderthals were, in fact, humans, Neanderthals were re-classified as *Homo sapiens neanderthalensis* (i.e., a sub-species of humans), and modern humans were given a sub-species designation as well—*Homo sapiens sapiens*. Now, there is a clamoring among evolutionists—based on mtDNA evidence—to return to the original *H. neanderthalensis* designation. In his 1999 book, *The Human Inheritance*, Bryan Sykes of the Institute of Molecular Medicine at Oxford University, wrote:

> The mitochondrial DNA pattern of the Neanderthal does indeed show that human mtDNA diversity was much greater in the past, and allows a calibration of the divergence time of the Neanderthal pattern from that characterising modern humans of about 600 ka [thousand years ago—BH/BT]. Gene divergence precedes population and species divergence, but this figure is certainly compatible with interpretations from the fossil record that the Neanderthal lineage separated from our own at about 300 ka. Equally, it is incompatible with suggestions that Neanderthals were either uniquely ancestral to recent Europeans through evolution, or were partly ancestral through hybridisation (pp. 43-44).

In his 2000 book, *Genes, People, and Languages*, Luigi Cavalli-Sforza, who is professor emeritus of genetics at Stanford University and the director of the International Human Genome Project, commented:

> There is a considerable difference between the mtDNA of this Neandertal and that of practically any modern human. From a quantitative evaluation of this difference it was estimated that the last common ancestor of Neandertal and modern humans lived about half a million years ago. It is not quite clear where those common ancestors lived, but modern humans and Neandertal must have separated early and developed separately, modern humans in Africa and Neandertals in Europe. The results of mitochondrial DNA show clearly that Neandertal was not our direct ancestor, unlike earlier hypotheses made by some paleoanthropologists (p. 35).

We beg to differ! The results of mtDNA research **do not** "show clearly that Neandertal was not our direct ancestor." A closer examination of the mtDNA research shows that it is not all it has been cracked up to be. The Krings study compared DNA sequences from **1669** modern humans with **one** Neanderthal. Statistically, this not only is insignificant, but also incorrect. As Lubenow wrote in regard to this mtDNA research:

> Statistics has been used to cloud the relationship between Neandertals and modern humans. It is improper to use statistical "averages" in situations where many entities are being compared with only one entity. In this case, 994 sequences from 1669 modern humans are compared with one sequence from one Neandertal. Thus, there is no Neandertal "average," and the comparison is not valid (1998, 12[1]:92).

The original study showed that the Neanderthal individual had a minimum of 22 mtDNA substitution differences when compared to modern humans. Yet the mtDNA substitution differences among modern humans range from 1 to 24. As Lubenow correctly noted:

> That means that there are a few modern humans who differ by 24 substitutions from a few other modern humans—two substitutions more than the Neandertal individual. Would not logic demand that those few modern humans living today should also be placed in a separate species? To state the question is to reveal the absurdity of using such differences as a measure of species distinctions (12[1]:92).

Furthermore, as Maryellen Ruvolo of Harvard has pointed out, the genetic variation between the modern and Neanderthal sequences is within the range of substitutions within other single species of primates. She concluded: "...[T]here isn't a yardstick for genetic difference upon which you can define a species" (as quoted in Kahn and Gibbons, 1997, 277:177). Geneticist Simon Easteal of Australian National University, noting that chimpanzees, gorillas, and other primates have much more intra-species mtDNA diversity than modern humans, wrote: "The amount of diversity between Neanderthals and living humans is not exceptional" (as quoted in Wong, 1998, 278[1]:32). In an article in *Scientific American* titled "Ancestral Quandary: Neanderthals Not Our Ancestors? Not So Fast," Kate Wong observed: "The evolutionary history of mtDNA, a lone gene, is only so informative." She then went on to quote geneticist Alan R. Templeton of Washington University, who admitted: "You can always construct a gene tree for any set of genetic variation. But there's a big distinction between gene trees and population trees" since a population tree comprises the histories of many genes (1998, 278[1]:30). D. Melnick and G. Hoelzer of Columbia University even went so far as to state: "Our results suggest serious problems with use of mtDNA to estimate 'true' population genetic structure..." (1992, p. 122). Why is this the case? Luigi Cavalli-Sforza admitted that "..the mitochondrial genome represents only a small fraction of an individual's genetic material and may not be representative of the whole" (as quoted in Mountain, et al., 1993, p. 69).

In an article titled "Recovery of Neandertal DNA: An Evaluation," Marvin Lubenow (1998, 12[1]:95) offered several different alternative interpretations for the mtDNA data which have been used to suggest that Neanderthals and humans are not the same species. Among those were the following.

1. Perhaps the single individual from whom the mtDNA was extracted was from a small, isolated group of Neanderthals. After all, the Neander Valley in Germany (where the fossil was discovered in 1856) is one of the northernmost Neanderthal sites, close to ice-age glaciers. Of the 345 Neanderthal individuals discovered thus far, only 14 are from Germany, and 12 of them were far to the south of where this individual was found.

2. Perhaps Neanderthals did, in fact, contribute to the modern gene pool, but their sequences disappeared through random genetic loss, selection, or both. Biochemist John Marcus has suggested that the human race might well have had much greater mtDNA sequence variation in the past but, being genetically stronger, ancient humans were able to cope with in-

creased genetic variation. Today, because our genome contains many more harmful mutations, we are somewhat "weaker." Perhaps greater mtDNA variation was deleterious to health, and selective pressure therefore has reduced the amount of variation in present populations.

3. Perhaps the single Neanderthal from whom the mtDNA sequences were derived was at one extreme of a diverse spectrum in Neanderthals that included other more modern-like sequences. Future recovery of mtDNA from other Neanderthals (if that is possible) could help confirm whether or not this is true.

4. Perhaps our Neanderthal ancestors underwent a population "bottleneck" that wiped out a great deal of the original genetic variation. In support of such a concept, Kahn and Gibbons wrote in *Science:* "Living humans are strangely homogeneous genetically, presumably because...their ancestors underwent a population bottleneck that wiped out variations" (1997, 277:175).

Over the past several years, the scientific community has witnessed (not always to its liking, we might add) a serious "redefining" of the Neanderthal people. Some anthropologists of the past depicted them as culturally stagnant, if not outright stupid, individuals. In 1996, however, researchers were forced to reevaluate their long-held views on Neanderthals, due to the discovery of five different types of musical instruments, items of personal ornamentation (similar to our jewelry), and even the first example of a Neanderthal cave painting (see: Hublin, et al., 1996; "Neanderthal Noisemaker," 1996; Folger and Menon, 1997; "Human Origins," 1997). Furthermore, almost all anthropologists recognize burial rituals as being not just strictly associated with humans, but as a distinctly religious act as well. That being the case, the strongest evidence to date that the Neanderthals were, in fact, human, is that at four different sites where Neanderthal fossils were found, **Neanderthals and modern humans were buried together**! As Lubenow noted:

> That Neandertals and anatomically modern humans were buried together constitutes strong evidence that they lived together, worked together, intermarried, and were accepted as members of the same family, clan, and community.... If genuine mtDNA was recovered from the fossil from the Neander Valley, the results have been misinterpreted (1998, 12[1]:89).

Yes, they have. In his 2001 book, *The Evolution Wars*, Michael Ruse noted:

> Modern humans, that is *Homo sapiens* like us, were at one point thought all to come after Neanderthals, but now the thinking is that our remains date back almost as far, and **there is evidence in some places that modern humans lived together with Neanderthals**.... A new skeleton, apparently **a modern human/Neanderthal hybrid**, has just been discovered (Duarte, 1999) [2001b, pp. 187-188, emp. added].

As archaeologist Randall White of New York University said regarding the Neanderthals: "The more this kind of evidence accumulates, the more they look like us" (as quoted in Folger and Menon, 18[1]:33). Yes, they do. And so they should!

4

THE PROBLEM OF
GENDER AND SEXUAL
REPRODUCTION

The advertisement indicates that this particular ovulation predictor kit "is the only technology based solely on hormone monitoring that provides you with personalized daily fertility information for pregnancy planning." For around fifty dollars, a person can purchase this product, which is intended as an aid in determining the optimum moment for a human female to conceive. Viewing this scenario through a baboon's eyes, the ad would seem to indicate that baboons are a somewhat more superior species when compared to humans. The female baboon, for example, does not need a "hormonal monitoring kit" to detect her period of ovulation. Instead, she gives off a distinctive smell, and the skin around her genitalia swells and turns a bright red color that is visible from some distance. Most other female animals are equally aware of their own ovulation, and often will "advertise" it to males using visual signals, odors, or behaviors. The question becomes: Whence did these differences in physiology and behavior originate? Or, to put it more bluntly: How did sex evolve?

Take a look around. The world surrounding you is literally teeming with living organisms ranging in size from microscopic bacteria to giant California redwoods. But how did it all get here? One of the first thoughtful questions children often ask is, "Where did I come from?" If we were to allow evolutionists to answer this question, they would point to fragments from the fossil record and declare that humans have descended from an ancient ape-like ancestor. Evolutionists have spent many decades trying to iron out a seamless sequence of descendants in their so-called "evolutionary tree of life." However, one of the most glaring failures of this alleged lineage is its inability to account for the origin of sexual (as opposed to asexual) reproduction and the existence of a male and female within each species that reproduces sexually.

Biology textbooks are quick to illustrate amoebas evolving into intermediate organisms, which then conveniently give rise to amphibians, reptiles, mammals, and, eventually, humans. Yet, interestingly, we never learn exactly when (or how!) independent male and female species developed. Somewhere along this evolutionary path, both males and females were required to permit the procreation that was necessary to further the existence of a particular species. But how do evolutionists explain this? When pressed to answer questions like, "Where did males and females actually come from?," or "What is the evolutionary origin of sex?," evolutionists become as silent as the tomb in which they have laid this problem. How is it that at one point in time, "nature" was able to evolve a female member of a species that produces eggs and is internally equipped to nourish a growing embryo, while at the same time evolving a male member that produces motile sperm cells? And, further, how is it that these gametes (eggs and sperm) "conveniently" evolved so that they each contain **half** the normal chromosome number of somatic (body) cells? [Somatic cells reproduce via the process of **mitosis**, which maintains the species' standard chromosome number; gametes are produced via the process of **meiosis**, which halves that number. We will have more to say about both later.]

The evolution of sex (and its accompanying reproductive capability) is not always a favorite topic of discussion in many evolutionary circles, because no matter how many theories and proposals evolutionists conjure up (and there are several!), they still must surmount the enormous hurdle of explaining the origin of the first fully functional female and the first fully functional male necessary to begin the process. In his book, *The Masterpiece of Nature: The Evolution of Genetics and Sexuality*, Graham Bell admitted that the whole problem of sexual reproduction "represents the most important challenge to the modern theory of evolution" (1982, book jacket). He then went on to describe the dilemma in the following manner:

> **Sex is the queen of problems in evolutionary biology**. Perhaps no other natural phenomenon has aroused so much interest; certainly none has sowed as much confusion. The insights of Darwin and Mendel, which have illuminated so many mysteries, have so far failed to shed more than a dim and wavering light on the central mystery of sexuality, emphasizing its obscurity by its very isolation (p. 19, emp. added).

The same year that Bell published his book, evolutionist Philip Kitcher noted: "Despite some ingenious suggestions by orthodox Darwinians, there is no convincing Darwinian history for the emergence of sexual reproduction" (1982, p. 54). Evolutionists since have freely admitted that the origin of gender and sexual reproduction still remains one of the most difficult problems in biology (see, for example, Maynard-Smith, 1986, p. 35). In his 2001 book, *The Cooperative Gene*, evolutionist Mark Ridley wrote (under the chapter title of "The Ultimate Existential Absurdity"): "Evolutionary biologists are much teased for their obsession with why sex exists. People like to ask, in an amused way, 'isn't it obvious?' Joking apart, **it is far from obvious.... Sex is a puzzle that has not yet been solved; no one knows why it exists**" (pp. 108,111, emp. added). In an article in *Bioscience* on "How Did Sex Come About?," Julie Schecter remarked:

> Sex is ubiquitous.... Yet sex remains a mystery to researchers, to say nothing of the rest of the population. Why sex? At first blush, its disadvantages seem to outweigh its benefits. After all, a parent that reproduces sexually gives only one-half its genes to its off-

spring, whereas an organism that reproduces by dividing passes on all its genes. Sex also takes much longer and requires more energy than simple division. Why did a process so blatantly unprofitable to its earliest practitioners become so widespread? (1984, 34: 680).

Why sex? Why indeed?! We invite you to read further as we survey several issues concerning the origin of gender and sexual reproduction.

"INTELLECTUAL MISCHIEF AND CONFUSION"–OR INTELLIGENT DESIGN?

The distinguished microbiologist of the University of Massachusetts at Amherst, Lynn Margulis, and her son Dorion Sagan (Ms. Margulis is one of the late Carl Sagan's former wives; Dorion is their son) have gone on record as stating: "Many theories of sex are clearly fallacious.... Putting these ideas of sexual origins together, our hypothesis is quite different from the accepted wisdom about the role of sex in evolution" (1997, pp. 290,293). Yes, it is. To quote them directly: "...complex microscopic beings and their descendants developed the first male and female genders, and our kind of cell-fusing sexuality involving penetration of an egg by a sperm" (p. 78). In his 2001 book, *Liaisons of Life*, Tom Wakeford addressed this unorthodox idea and concluded:

> Margulis's hypothesis for the origin of sexuality is radical. She believes that the ecological relations of ancient microbes drove a process that ultimately led to our way or reproducing. She bases this ambitious idea on a theory she published in 1967. Now classic, the theory attempted to explain the biggest missing link in evolution–the jump from bacteria (often called prokaryotes), all of which lack nuclei, to modern cells, or eukaryotes, whose cells contain nuclei.
>
> The differences between prokaryotes and eukaryotes are so profound that they make the distinction between dinosaurs and dogs or birds and bees look neg-

ligible. Eukaryotes include animals, plants, protists, and fungi, each cell of which generally contains hundreds of times more DNA than a prokaryote.

Unlike many other transitions in evolution, there are no intermediates between eukaryotes and prokaryotes. It is as if honeybees mutated into humans without any evidence of rats, cats, or chimpanzees in between. The evolutionary processes behind this great revolution have had to be discerned without the help of one of the evolutionist's most trusted sources of evidence—the fossil record (pp. 147-148, parenthetical item in orig.).

Perhaps it is this complete lack of evidence that has caused Margulis and Sagan to suggest that since sex is basically a historical mishap of sorts—a kind of "accidental holdover" from the era of single-celled organisms—then the maintenance of sex becomes a "nonscientific" question that "leads to intellectual mischief and confusion" (as quoted in Crow, 1988, pp. 59-60).

While there may well be many "clearly fallacious" theories regarding the **origin** of sex, and while the fact that sex exists may indeed represent to evolutionists a matter of "intellectual mischief and confusion," the **fact** of both the ubiquity and the complexity of sexual reproduction has not eluded Darwinists. Niles Eldredge, a staunch evolutionist at the American Museum of Natural History, has admitted that "sex occurs in all major groups of life" (Eldredge and Cracraft, 1980, p. 102). Or as Jennifer Ackerman wrote somewhat emphatically in her 2001 book, *Chance in the House of Fate:* "Now, it seems, nature **hurls** the sexes at each other" (p. 49, emp. added).

But **why** is this the case? Evolutionists are forced to concede that there must be "some advantage" to a system as physiologically and energetically complex as sex, as Mark Ridley admitted when he wrote: "...[I]t is highly likely that sex has **some advantage**, and that the advantage is **big**. Sex would not have evolved, and been retained, unless it had some advantage" (2001, p. 254, emp. added). Yet locating and explaining that advantage seems to have eluded our evolutionary colleagues. Sir John Maddox, who served for over twenty-five years as the editor of *Nature*, the prestigious journal published by the British Association for the Advancement of Science (and who was knighted by Queen Elizabeth II in 1994 for his "multiple contributions to science"), authored an amazing book titled *What Remains to be Discovered* in which he addressed the topic of the origin of sex, and stated forthrightly:

> The overriding question is when (and then how) sexual reproduction itself evolved. **Despite decades of speculation, we do not know**. The difficulty is that sexual reproduction creates complexity of the genome and the need for a separate mechanism for producing gametes. The metabolic cost of maintaining this system is huge, as is that of providing the organs specialized for sexual reproduction (the uterus of mammalian females, for example). What are the offsetting benefits? **The advantages of sexual reproduction are not obvious** (1998, p. 252, parenthetical items in orig., emp. added).

The fact that the advantages of sex are "not obvious" is well known (though perhaps not often discussed) within the hallowed halls of academia. J.C. Crow lamented:

> Sexual reproduction seems like a lot of baggage to carry along if it is functionless. Evolutionary conservatism perpetuates relics, but does it do so on such a grand scale as this?… It is difficult to see how a process as elaborate, ubiquitous, and expensive as sexual reproduction has been maintained without serving some important purpose of its own (1988, p. 60).

What is that "purpose"? And how can evolution via natural selection explain it? Would "Nature" (notice the capital "N") "select for" sexual reproduction? As it turns out, the common "survival of the fittest" mentality cannot begin to explain the high cost of first evolving, and then maintaining, the sexual apparatus. Sexual reproduction requires organisms to first produce, and then maintain, gametes (reproductive cells–i.e., sperm and eggs). Additionally, various kinds of incompatibility factors (like the blood Rh factor between mother and child) can pass along additional "costs" (some of which can be life threatening) that are inherent in this "expensive" means of reproduction. In sexual organisms, problems also can arise in regard to tissue rejection between the mother and the newly formed embryo. The human immune system

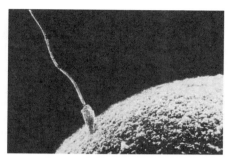

Figure 1 — Photomicrograph of male sperm cell attempting penetration of female egg cell

is vigilant in identifying foreign tissue (such as an embryo that carries half of the male's genetic information), yet evolutionists contend that the human reproductive system has "selectively evolved" this "elaborate, ubiquitous, and expensive" method of reproduction. In trying to reconcile the logic behind what causes such things to occur via naturalistic evolution, vitalist philosopher Arthur Koestler observed:

> Once upon a time it all looked so simple. Nature regarded the fit with the carrot of survival and punished the unfit with the stick of extinction. The trouble only started when it came to defining "fitness." ...Thus natural selection looks after the survival and reproduction of the fittest, and the fittest are those which have the highest rate of reproduction—we are caught in a circular argument which completely begs the question of what makes evolution evolve? (1978, p. 170).

The question of "what makes evolution evolve" is especially critical when it comes to the origin of sex and sexual reproduction. As Dr. Maddox went on to say: "Much more must be learned of the course of evolution before it is known how (rather than why) sexual reproduction evolved.... That task will require intricate work by future generations of biologists" (pp. 253,254, parenthetical item in orig.). It is our contention, based on the evidence at hand, that the intricacy, complexity, and informational content associated with sexual reproduction demand the conclusion that sex is neither a "historical accident" resulting in evolutionary baggage nor a product of organic evolution itself, but rather is the product of an intelligent Creator.

FROM ASEXUAL TO SEXUAL REPRODUCTION–THE ORIGIN OF SEX

Many single-celled organisms reproduce asexually. If we all descended from these single-celled creatures, as Margulis and Sagan have suggested, then why was the simple-yet-efficient method of asexual reproduction set aside in favor of sexual reproduction? In an intriguing article titled "The Enigma of Sex and Evolution," biologist Jerry Bergman wrote:

> Evolution requires sexual reproduction to have evolved from asexual reproduction via natural selection.... The lack of evidence of any biological systems that can bridge the chasm between sexual and asexual reproduction either today or in the past is also a major difficulty with evolution theory. Actually, the complete lack of any transitional forms for all sexual traits is a huge major fossil gap. The same problem also exists here as with any transitional form: structures are useless or worse until they are at least marginally functional. This is **especially** true regarding reproduction, and would result in rapid extinction if the features produced by mutations were less than fully functional (1996, 33: 230, emp. in orig.).

Dobzhansky and his co-authors commented on this "enigma" in their book, *Evolution*:

> With respect to the origin of sexual reproduction, two challenging questions present themselves. First, in what kinds of organisms did sex first arise? And second, what was the adaptive advantage that caused sexual reproduction to become predominant in higher organisms? (1977, p. 391)

Asexual reproduction is the formation of new individuals from cells of only one parent, without gamete formation or fertilization by another member of the species. Asexual reproduction thus does not require one egg-producing parent and one sperm-producing parent. A single parent is all that is required. In addressing this point, evolutionist George C. Williams admitted that the "immediate advantage of asexual reproduction is generally conceded by all those who have seriously concerned themselves with the problem" (1977, p. 8). In fact, he went on to note that "the masculine-feminine contrast is a *prima facie* difficulty for evolutionary theory" (p. 124).

Sporulation (spore formation) is one method of asexual reproduction among protozoa and certain plants. A spore is a reproductive cell that produces a new organism without fertilization. In some lower forms of animals (e.g., hydra), and in yeasts, **budding** is a common form of asexual reproduction as a small protuberance on the surface of the parent cell increases in size until a wall forms to separate the new individual (the bud) from the parent. **Regeneration** is another specialized form of asexual reproduction that allows some organisms (e.g. starfish and salamanders) to replace injured or lost parts. All of these processes require only one "parent," and work quite well in stable environments.

As they have struggled to explain the existence of **sexual** reproduction in nature, evolutionists have suggested four different (and sometimes contradictory) theories, known in the literature as: (1) the Lottery Principle; (2) the Tangled Bank Hypothesis; (3) the Red Queen Hypothesis; and (4) the DNA Repair Hypothesis. We would like to discuss each briefly.

The Lottery Principle

The Lottery Principle was first suggested by American biologist George C. Williams in his monograph, *Sex and Evolution* (1975). Williams' idea was that sexual reproduction introduced genetic variety in order to enable genes to survive in changing or novel environments. He used the lottery analogy to get across the concept that breeding **asexually** would be like buying a large number of tickets for a national lottery but giving them all the same number; **sexual** reproduction would be like purchasing few tickets, but giving each of them a different number. The essential idea behind the Lottery Principle is that since sex introduces variability, organisms would have a much better chance of producing offspring that will survive if they produced a **range** of types rather than just more of the same.

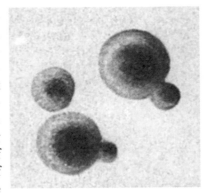

Figure 2 — An example of the asexual reproduction process known as budding

The point being made by those who hold to the Lottery Principle is that asexual reproduction is, in fact, poorly equipped to adapt to rapidly changing environmental conditions, due to the fact that the offspring are exact copies (i.e., clones) of their parents, and thus inherently possess less genetic variation, which ultimately could lead to improved adaptability and a greater likelihood of survival. As Carl Zimmer wrote under the chapter title of "Evolution from Within" in his 2000 book, *Parasite Rex*: "A line of clones might do well enough in a forest, but what if that forest changed over a few centuries to a prairie? Sex brought the variations that could allow organisms to survive change" (p. 163). Matt Ridley added:

> ...[A] sexual form of life will reproduce at only half the rate of an equivalent clonal form. The halved reproductive rate of sexual forms is probably made up for by a **difference in quality: the average sexual offspring is probably twice as good as an equivalent cloned offspring** (1993, p. 254, emp. added).

It would be "twice as good," of course, because it had twice the genetic endowment (having received half from each of the two parents). Reichenbach and Anderson summarized the issue as follows:

For example, why do most animals reproduce sexually rather than asexually, when asexual reproduction seems to conform best to the current theory that in natural selection the fittest are those that preserve their genes by passing them on to their progeny? One theory is that sexual reproduction provides the best defense against the rapidly reproducing, infectious species that threaten the existence of organisms. The **diversity in the species** that results from combining different gene pools favors the survival of those that are sexually reproduced over those that by cloning inherit repetitive genetic similarity (1995, p. 18, emp. added).

It is that "diversity in the species," according to the principle, which helps an organism maintain its competitive edge in nature's struggle of "survival of the fittest." But the Lottery Principle has fallen on hard times of late. It suggests that sex would be favored by a **variable** environment, yet a close inspection of the global distribution of sex reveals that where environments are **stable** (such as in the tropics), **sexual** reproduction is most common. In contrast, in areas where the environment is **unstable** (such as at high altitudes or in small bodies of water), **asexual** reproduction is rife.

The Tangled Bank Hypothesis

The Tangled Bank Hypothesis suggests that sex evolved in order to prepare offspring for the complicated world around them. The "tangled bank" phraseology comes from the last paragraph of Darwin's *Origin of Species* in which he referred to a wide assortment of creatures all competing for light and food on a "tangled bank." According to this concept, in any environment where there is intense competition for space, food, and other resources, a premium is placed on diversification. As Zimmer described it:

In any environment—a tidal flat, a forest canopy, a deep-sea hydrothermal vent—the space is divided into different niches where different skills are needed for survival. A clone specialized for one niche can give birth only to offspring that can also handle the same niche. But sex shuffles the genetic deck and deals the offspring different hands. It's basically spreading out progeny so that they're using different resources (2000, p. 163).

The Tangled Bank Hypothesis, however, also has fallen on hard times. In his book, *Evolution and Human Behavior*, John Cartwright concluded:

> Although once popular, the tangled bank hypothesis now seems to face many problems, and former adherents are falling away. The theory would predict a greater interest in sex among animals that produce lots of small offspring that compete with each other. In fact, sex is invariably associated with organisms that produce a few large offspring, whereas organisms producing small offspring frequently engage in parthenogenesis [asexual reproduction—BH/BT]. In addition, **the evidence from fossils suggests that species go for vast periods of time without changing much** (2000, p. 96, emp. added).

Indeed, the evidence **does** suggest "that species go for vast periods of time without changing much." Consider the following admission in light of that point. According to Margulis and Sagan, bacteria "evolved" in such a fashion as to ultimately be responsible for sexual reproduction. Yet if that is the case, why, then, have the bacteria themselves remained virtually unchanged—from an evolutionary viewpoint—for billions of years of Earth history? In his classic text, *Evolution of Living Organisms*, the eminent French zoologist, Pierre-Paul Grassé, raised this very point.

> [B]acteria, despite their great production of intraspecific varieties, **exhibit a great fidelity to their species**. The bacillus *Escherichia coli*, whose mutants have been studied very carefully, is the best example. **The reader will agree that it is surprising, to say the least, to want to prove evolution and to discover its mechanisms, and then to choose as a material for this study a being which practically stabilized a billion years ago** (1977, p. 87, emp. added).

Additionally, it should be noted that today we still see organisms that reproduce asexually, as well as organisms that reproduce sexually—which raises the obvious question: Why do some organisms continue to reproduce asexually, while others have "evolved" the ability to reproduce sexually? Don't the asexual organisms ever "need" genetic variety in order to enable genes to survive in changing or novel environments (the Lottery Principle)? Don't they ever "need" to prepare their offspring for the complicated world around them (the Tangled Bank Hypothesis)?

The Red Queen Hypothesis

The Red Queen Hypothesis was first suggested by Leigh Van Valen in an article titled "A New Evolutionary Law" in *Evolutionary Theory* (1973). His research suggested that the probability of organisms becoming extinct bears no relationship to how long they already may have survived. In other words, as Cartwright put it: "It is a sobering thought that the struggle for existence never gets any easier; however well adapted an animal may become, it still has the same chance of extinction as a newly formed species" (p. 97). Biologists came to refer to the concept as the Red Queen Hypothesis, named after the character in Lewis Carroll's *Through the Looking Glass* who took Alice on a long run that actually went nowhere. As the queen said to poor Alice, "Now, **here**, you see, it takes all the running **you** can do, to keep in the same place." Think of it as a "genetics arms race" in which an animal constantly must run the genetic gauntlet of being able to chase its prey, elude predators, and resist infection from disease-causing organisms. In the world of the Red Queen, organisms have to run fast—just to stay still! That is to say, they constantly have to "run to try to improve" (and the development of sex would be one way of accomplishing that). Yet doing so provides no automatic guarantee of winning the struggle known as "survival of the fittest." "Nature," said the eminent British poet Lord Tennyson, is indeed "red in tooth and claw." Currently, the Red

Queen Hypothesis seems to be the favorite of evolutionists worldwide in attempting to explain the reason as to the "why" of sex.

The DNA Repair Hypothesis

Think about it. Why are babies born young? Stupid question—with a self-evident answer, right? Evolutionists suggest otherwise. The point of the question is this. Our somatic (body) cells age. Yet cells of a newborn have had their clocks "set back." Somatic cells die, but the germ line seems to be practically immortal. Why is this the case? How can "old" people produce "young" babies? In a landmark article published in 1989, Bernstein, Hopf, and Michod suggested that they had discovered the answer: "We argue that the lack of ageing of the germ line results mainly from repair of the genetic material by meiotic recombination during the formation of germ cells. Thus our basic hypothesis is that the primary function of sex is to repair the genetic material of the germ line" (p. 4).

DNA can be damaged in at least two ways. First, ionizing radiation or mutagenic chemicals can alter the genetic code. Or, second, a mutation can occur via errors during the replication process itself. Most mutations are deleterious (see Cartwright, 2000, p. 98). In an asexual organism, by definition, any mutation that occurs in one generation will automatically be passed on to the next. In his book, *The Red Queen* (1993), Matt Ridley compared it to what occurs when you photocopy a document, then photocopy the photocopy, and then photocopy that photocopy, etc. Eventually, the quality deteriorates severely. Asexual organisms, as they continue to accumulate mutations, face the unpleasant prospect of eventually becoming both unable to reproduce and unviable—neither of which would be at all helpful to evolution.

But if sex "evolved," it would help solve this problem, since mutations, although they might still be passed on from one generation to the next, would not necessarily be **expressed** in the next generation (a mutation has to appear in the genes of **both** parents before it is expressed in the offspring). As Cartwright put it:

> In sexually reproducing species on the other hand, some individuals will be "unlucky" and have a greater share than average of deleterious mutations in their genome, and some will be "lucky," with a smaller share. The unlucky ones will be selected out. This in the long term has the effect of constantly weeding out harmful mutations through the death of those that bear them. Deleterious mutations…would have devastating consequences if it were not for sexual reproduction (p. 99).

In his book, *The Language of Genes*, Steve Jones claimed that sex exists because

> …if a sexless organism has a harmful change to the DNA, it will be carried by all her descendants. None of them can ever get rid of it, however destructive it might be, unless it is reversed by another change in the same gene—which is unlikely to happen. In time, another damaging error will occur in a different gene in the family line. A decay of the genetic message will set in as one generation succeeds another, just like the decay that takes place within our aging bodies as our cells divide without benefit of sex. In a sexual creature the new mutation can be purged as it passes to some descendant but not others (1993, p. 86).

But, as Bergman correctly pointed out:

> The problem with this conclusion is that a harmful or lethal mutation causes the entire line to die out, purging it forever form the population while millions of other lines carry on. With sex, because most mutations are recessive, many mutations that are not lethal are spread to the race in general. Problems result **only** if the same defect is inherited from both parents; thus, the harmful traits can accumulate in the race. With asexual animals the weaker lines are rapidly selected out, often in one generation (1996, 33:221, emp. in orig.).

It is clear, therefore, as Cartwright admitted in regard to the DNA repair hypothesis: "This theory is not without its problems and critics" (p. 99). One of those problems, expressed by Mark Ridley (no kin to Matt), is: "We do not know for sure that sex exists to purge bad genes" (2001, p. 254). No, we certainly do not. And, in fact, evidence is beginning to mount that perhaps the DNA Repair Hypothesis is itself in need of "repair." As Sir John Maddox noted:

> One view is that sexual reproduction makes it easier for an evolving organism to get rid of deleterious changes. That should certainly be the case if there is more than one genetic change and if their combined effect on the fitness of the evolving organisms is greater than the sum of their individual changes acting separately. **But there is no direct evidence to show that this rule is generally applicable.** Indeed, a recent experiment with the bacterium *E. coli* suggests otherwise (1998, p. 252, emp. added).

We should not overlook an important fact throughout all of this: These theories valiantly attempt to explain why sex **exists now**, but they do not explain **the origin** of sex. How, exactly, did nature accomplish the "invention" of the marvelous process we know as sex? In addressing this very issue, Maddox asked quizzically: "How did this process (and its complexities) evolve?... The dilemma is that **natural selection cannot anticipate changes in the environment**, and so arrange for the development of specialized sexual organs as a safeguard against environmental change" (p. 253, parenthetical item in orig., emp. added). Exactly our point! It is one thing to develop a theory or hypothesis to explain something that **already exists**, but entirely another to develop a theory of hypothesis to explain **why** that something (in this case, sex) **does exist**. As Mark Ridley begrudgingly admitted:

> Sex is not used simply for want of an alternative. Nothing, in an evolutionary sense, **forces** organisms to reproduce sexually. Indeed, the majority of live repro-

duction on Earth is probably not sexual. Microbes, such as bacteria, do most of the reproduction on this planet, and they usually do it by doubling their cellular contents and then dividing from one cell to two, without any genetic input from another cell (2001, p. 109, emp. added).

Perhaps Cartwright summarized the issue well when he said: "There is perhaps no single explanation for the maintenance of sex in the face of severe cost" (p. 99). Since he is speaking of a strictly naturalistic explanation, we would agree wholeheartedly. But we would go even farther to state that there is no purely naturalistic explanation **at all** for the origin **or** the maintenance of sex.

WHY SEX?

Why does sex exist at all? In his 2001 book, *Evolution: The Triumph of an Idea*, Carl Zimmer admitted:

> Sex is not only unnecessary, but **it ought to be a recipe for evolutionary disaster**. For one thing, it is an inefficient way to reproduce…. And sex carries other costs as well…. By all rights, any group of animals that evolves sexual reproduction should be promptly outcompeted by nonsexual ones. **And yet sex reigns**. …Why is sex a success, despite all its disadvantages? (pp. 230,231, emp. added).

From an evolutionary viewpoint, sex is indeed "an inefficient way to reproduce." As Williams noted, the task of determining why sexual reproduction evolved seems "immensely difficult…because we can immediately see an enormous disadvantage in sexual reproduction" (1977, pp. 155,169). The brief reproduction period involved with, and few offspring produced by, sexual reproduction produce such clear disadvantages that Princeton's eminent biologist, John Tyler Bonner, asked, "What use is sex" to evolution, and why would it evolve? (1958, p. 193; cf. also Maynard-Smith, 1971).

Think for a moment about some of the events that had to occur before sexual reproduction could "evolve." First, two physically distinct sexes, male and female, had to materialize (Crook, 1972, pp. 233-235). Second, the male and female had to "appear at the same time and in the same breeding community" (Sheppard, 1963, p. 239). Third, sperm production in the male, and egg production in the female, had to evolve. Fourth, the female had to evolve a structure (e.g., a uterus) capable of carrying the unborn until birth. Fifth, nature had to come up with a process by which the information carried within the DNA could be reproduced faithfully time and time again. It is the complexity of this process, and the manner in which it is copied from generation to generation, which drove Mark Ridley practically to distraction in *The Cooperative Gene*.

> The purpose of life is to copy DNA or, to be more exact, information in the form of DNA. Information copying, or information transfer, is a familiar enough activity to us in human culture. We do it all the time.... Human beings have invented an extraordinary range of media for transmitting, or copying, information. But I can tell you one thing about all these media. When humans set themselves to the task of copying information, they do just that: they copy it. In biological terms, clonal reproduction (or virgin birth) is the analogy for the way humans transmit information. No one in human culture would try the trick of first making two copies of a message, then breaking each into short bits at random, combining equal amounts from the two to form the version to be transmitted, and throwing the unused half away. **You only have to think of sex to see how absurd it is.** The "sexual" method of reading a book would be to buy two copies, rip the pages out, and make a new copy by combining half the pages from one and half from the other, tossing a coin at each page to decide which original to take the page from and which to throw away. To watch a play, you would go twice, pre-programmed to pay attention to the first performance at one random set of times, amounting to half the total length, and to pay attention to the second performance at the complementary other half set of times (2001, pp. 108-109, emp. added).

Again, from an evolutionary viewpoint, sex would be considered "absurd." But from a **design** viewpoint, it is nothing short of incredible!

Yet there is an even more important question than **why** sex exists. That question is this: **How** did sex come to exist? Evolution is dependent on change (our English word "evolution" derives from the Latin *evolvere*, meaning "to unroll; to change"). Quite obviously, if everything remained the same, there would be no evolution. Evolutionists believe that the driving forces behind evolution are genetic mutations and natural selection occurring over lengthy spans of geologic time (as Peter Ward put it in his 2001 book, *Future Evolution*, "Evolution takes time," p. 153). Mutations are primarily the result of **mistakes** that occur during DNA replication. There are three different types of mutations: beneficial, deleterious, and neutral (see Mayr, 2001, p. 98). Neutral mutations, while admittedly frequent, are, as their name implies, "neutral." They do not "propel" evolution forward in any significant fashion. Deleterious mutations "will be selected against and will be eliminated in due time" (Mayr, p. 98). That, then, leaves beneficial mutations, which, according to evolutionists, are incorporated into the species by natural selection, eventually resulting in new and different organisms.

But what does all of this have to do with the origin of sex? Evolutionists adhere to the view that the first organisms on Earth were **asexual**, and thus they believe that, during billions of years of Earth history, asexual organisms experienced numerous beneficial mutations that caused them to evolve into **sexual** organisms. But the change of a single-celled, asexual prokaryote (like a bacterium) into a multi-celled, sexual eukaryote would not be a "magical" process carried out by just a few, well-chosen beneficial mutations (as if nature had the power to "choose" anything!). In fact, quite the opposite would be true. Why so? Ernst Mayr, who probably ranks as the most eminent evolutionary taxonomist in the world, commented in his book, *What Evolution Is:* "Any mutation that induces changes in the phenotype [the outward, physical make-up of an organism—BH/BT] will either be favored or discriminated against by natural selection…. **[T]he occurrence of new beneficial mutations is rather rare**" (p. 98, emp. added). Beneficial mutations (viz., those that provide additional information for, and instructions to, the organism) are indeed "rather rare." Furthermore, as evolutionists candidly admit, mutations that affect the phenotype almost always are **harmful** (Crow, 1997; Cartwright, 2000, p. 98). Famed Stanford University geneticist Luigi Cavalli-Sforza addressed this fact when he wrote:

> Evolution also results from the accumulation of new information. In the case of a biological mutation, new information is provided by an error of genetic transmission (i.e., a change in the DNA during its transmission from parent to child). **Genetic mutations are spontaneous, chance changes, which are rarely beneficial, and more often have no effect, or a deleterious one** (2000, p. 176, parenthetical item in orig., emp. added).

In addressing the complete ineffectiveness of mutations as an alleged evolutionary mechanism, Grassé observed:

> Some contemporary biologists, as soon as they observe a mutation, talk about evolution. They are implicitly supporting the following syllogism (argument): mutations are the only evolutionary variations, all living beings undergo mutations, therefore all living beings evolve. This logical scheme is, however unacceptable: first, because its major premise is neither obvious nor general; second, because its conclusion does not agree with the facts. **No matter how numerous they may be, mutations do not produce any kind of evolution**…. The opportune appearance of mutations permitting animals and plants to meet their needs seems hard to believe. Yet the Darwinian theory is even more demanding: a single plant, a single animal would require thousands and thousands of lucky, appropriate events. Thus, miracles would become the rule: events

with an infinitesimal probability could not fail to occur…. There is no law against daydreaming, but science must not indulge in it (1977, pp. 88,103,107, parenthetical item in orig., emp. added).

Grassé is not the only prominent evolutionist to take such a view in regard to mutations as an ineffectual driving force for evolution. In a speech that he presented at Hobart College several years ago, the late Harvard paleontologist Stephen Jay Gould spoke out in a somewhat militant fashion about the subject when he said: "A mutation doesn't produce major new raw material. You don't make a new species by mutating the species…. That's a common idea people have; that evolution is due to random mutations. A mutation is not the cause of evolutionary change" (1984b, p. 106). [All of this raises the question: If mutations are **not** the cause of evolutionary change, then what is?]

There is more to the problem of the origin of sex, however, than "just" the fact of rare, beneficial mutations and their much-more-frequent cousins, the harmful, deleterious mutations. There is the added problem related to the two different types of cell division we mentioned earlier—mitosis and meiosis. During mitosis, **all** of the chromosomes are copied and passed on from the parent cell to the daughter cells. Meiosis (from the Greek meaning to split), on the other hand, occurs only in sex cells (eggs and sperm); during this type of replication, **only half** of the chromosomal material is copied and passed on. [For an excellent, up-to-date description of the intricate, complicated, two-part process by which meiosis occurs, see Mayr, 2001, p. 103.] Once meiosis takes place, "the result is the production of completely new combinations of the parental genes, all of them uniquely different genotypes [the genetic identity of an individual that does not show as outward characteristics—BH/BT]. These, in turn, produce unique phenotypes, **providing unlimited new material** for the process of natural selection" (Mayr, p. 104, emp. added).

It is those very facts—that meiosis allegedly has "evolved" the ability to halve the chromosome number (but only for gametes), **and** that it actually can provide "unlimited new material"—which make the meiotic process so incredible. And the critical importance of meiosis to life as we know it has been acknowledged (albeit perhaps begrudgingly) even by evolutionists. Margulis and Sagan, for example, wrote:

> We think that **meiosis** became tied to two-parent sex and that meiosis as a cell process, rather than two-parent sex, **was a prerequisite for evolution of many aspects of animals**.... **[M]eiosis seems intimately connected with complex cell and tissue differentiation**. After all, animals and plants return every generation to a single nucleated cell. We believe that meiosis, especially the chromosomal DNA-alignment process in prophase, is sort of like a roll call, ensuring that sets of genes, including mitochondrial and plastid genes, are in order before the multicellular unfolding that is the development of the embryo (1997, p. 291, emp. added).

Margulis and Sagan have admitted that meiosis is critical for sexual reproduction. Yet in their book, *Slanted Truths*, they stated unequivocally that "meiotic sex" evolved approximately "520 million years ago" (1997, p. 293). How, pray tell, could the bacteria that are supposed to be responsible for the evolution of sex have "stabilized a billion years ago" (as Dr. Grassé plainly stated that they did), and then 500 million years **after** that stabilization, mutate enough to "evolve" the painstaking process of meiosis? Is anyone actually listening to what evolutionists are saying? Read carefully the following scenario, as laid out in Jennifer Ackerman's 2001 book, *Chance in the House of Fate*, and as you do, concentrate on the items we have placed in bold print that are intended to draw the reader's attention to the "just-so" nature of the account being proffered.

> The first sex cells **may** have been interchangeable and of roughly the same size. **By chance**, some **may have been** slightly bigger than others and stuffed with nutrients, an advantage in getting progeny off

to a good start. **Perhaps** some were smaller, faster, good at finding mates. As organisms continued to meld and join their genetic material, the pairs of a larger cell with a smaller one proved an efficient system. **Over time**, the little rift between the sexes widened, as did the strategies of male and female for propagating their own genes (pp. 48-49, emp. added).

The first sex cells **may** have been.... **By chance**, some **may have been**.... **Perhaps** some were.... **Over time**, the.... It is little wonder then, that in their more candid moments, evolutionists admit, as Ackerman eventually did, that "when it comes to sex, we inhabit a mystery" (p. 115).

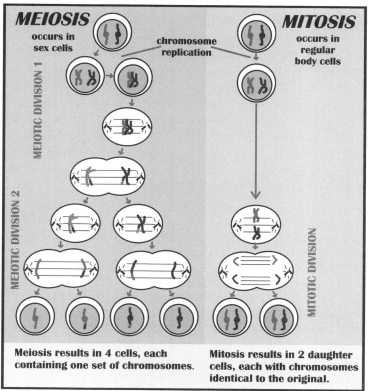

Figure 3 — Graphic depiction of meiosis and mitosis

Notice, however, the admission by Margulis and Sagan that "meiosis seems connected with complex cell and tissue differentiation." Yes, it certainly does—**now**! But how did a process as incredibly complex as meiosis ever get started in the first place? What (or, better yet, **Who**) "intricately connected it with complex cell and tissue differentiation"? With all due respect, there is not an evolutionist on the planet who has been able to come up with an adequate (much less believable) explanation as to how somatic cells reproduce by mitosis (thereby maintaining the species' standard chromosome number in each cell), while gametes are produced by meiosis, wherein that chromosome number is halved so that, at the union of the male and female gametes during reproduction, the standard number is reinstated.

Lewis Thomas, the highly regarded medical doctor who served for many years as president of the prestigious Sloan-Kettering Cancer Center in New York City, was unable to contain either his enthusiasm or his praise for the system that we know as "sexual reproduction." In his book, *The Medusa and the Snail,* he wrote about the "miracle" of how one sperm cell forms with one egg cell to produce the cell we know as a zygote, which, nine months later, will become a completely new human being. His conclusion?

> The mere existence of that cell should be one of the greatest astonishments of the earth. People ought to be walking around all day, all through their waking hours, calling to each other in endless wonderment, talking of nothing except that cell.... If anyone does succeed in explaining it, within my lifetime, I will charter a skywriting airplane, maybe a whole fleet of them, and send them aloft to write one great exclamation point after another around the whole sky, until all my money runs out (1979, pp. 155-157).

Dr. Thomas' money is perfectly safe. No one has been able to explain—from an evolutionary viewpoint—the origin of sex, the origin of the incredibly complex meiotic process that makes sex possible, or the amazingly intricate development of the embryo (which is itself a marvel of design). At conception, the chromosomes inherited from the sperm are paired with the chromosomes inherited from the egg to give the new organism its full chromosomal complement. Evolutionary theorists ask us to believe that random, chance occurrences brought about this marvelously interdependent process of, first, splitting the genetic information into equal halves, and, second, recombining it through sexual reproduction. Not only is an intricate process required to produce a sperm or egg cell in the first place via meiosis, but another equally intricate mechanism also is required to rejoin the genetic information during fertilization in order to produce the zygote, which will become the embryo, which will become the fetus, which eventually will become the newborn. The idea that all of this "just evolved" is unworthy of acceptance, especially in light of the evidence now at hand.

THE 50% DISADVANTAGE

While sexual reproduction requires two parents (and therefore is neither as rapid nor as efficient as asexual reproduction), it does possess certain advantages, not the least of which is that species can benefit from the variability of mixing genetic material from two different parents. During sexual reproduction, organisms are required to produce haploid gametes (sperm or egg cells) in which meiotic division has occurred, in order to remove half of the genes. Then, when the gametes fuse (i.e., when the sperm fertilizes the egg), they produce a zygote—a process that restores the full diploid complement of chromosomes, with half coming from each parent. In the end, sexual reproduction causes only half of a parent's genes to be sent to each of its progeny. British evolutionist Richard Dawkins of Oxford University described the process as follows: "Sexual reproduction is analogous to a roulette game in which the player throws away half his chips at each spin. The existence of sexual reproduction really is a huge paradox" (1986, p. 130). Ask yourself this question: If organisms benefit by passing along their own genetic material, then why would these organisms "evolve" into a situation in which the reproduction process not only poses an enormous risk for genetic errors through mistakes in DNA replication, but also replaces half of their genetic material with that from another parental unit?

Sexual reproduction has a "selective disadvantage" of at least 50%—a disadvantage that will not budge! At conception, the zygote **receives** 50% of its genetic material from the father and 50% from the mother. However, by reproducing sexually, both the mother and father are required to **give up** 50% of their own genetic material. This leaves both parents at a disadvantage, because a full 50% of their own genetic material will not be passed on. But, as Harvard's Mayr has admitted: "No matter what the selective advantage of sexual reproduction may be, **that it does have such an advantage in animals is clearly indicated by the consistent failure of all attempts to return to asexuality**" (2001, p. 104, emp. added). The conundrum of sexual reproduction leaves evolutionists completely baffled because the terms are permanently fixed and completely unyielding. Considering the possibility of potential mechanisms for reproduction, it remains to be determined why nature ever would "evolve" sexual reproduction at all. In his book, *Sex and Evolution*, George C. Williams commented on this "50% disadvantage":

> The primary task for anyone wishing to show favorable selection of sex is to find a previously unsuspected 50% advantage to balance the 50% cost of meiosis. Anyone familiar with accepted evolutionary thought would realize what an unlikely sort of quest this is. We know that a net selective disadvantage of 1% would cause a gene to be lost rapidly in most populations, and [yet] sex has a known disadvantage of 50%. The problem has been examined by some of the most distinguished of evolutionary theorists, but they have either failed to find any reproductive advantage in

sexual reproduction, or have merely showed the for-mal possibility of weak advantages that would prob-ably not be adequate to balance even modest recom-binational load. **Nothing remotely approaching an advantage that could balance the cost of mei-osis has been suggested. The impossibility of sex being an immediate reproductive adaptation in higher organisms would seem to be as firmly es-tablished a conclusion as can be found in current evolutionary thought. Yet this conclusion must surely be wrong. All around us are plant and an-imal populations with both asexual and sexual reproduction** (1975, p. 11, emp. added).

While evolutionists admit that sex is **dis**advantageous to an individual (at a whopping 50% rate!), they nevertheless claim that it has some "evolutionary advantage" to the entire species. Therefore, they classify sex as an "altruistic" trait because it operates at an expense to the individual, yet is beneficial to the entire community. Evolutionists commonly refer to this "benefit" as "diversity."

Early in the twentieth century, geneticists August Weismann, R.A. Fisher, and H.J. Muller elucidated the importance of di-versity, stating: "Sex increases diversity, enabling a species to more rapidly adapt to changing environments and thereby avoid extinction" (as quoted in ReMine, 1993, p. 200) They believed this diversity allowed evolution to occur much more rapidly. At first, their idea appeared plausible and reason-able, and, in fact, was taught in an unchallenged fashion for several decades. Commenting on the altruism theory about the origin of sex, M.T. Ghiselin stated:

> Weismann explicitly stated that sex exists for the good of the species, and even though Lloyd Morgan pointed out the fallacy [as early as 1890], this view remained the dominant one for nearly 80 years. Why this should have happened is something of a puzzle. The view does have certain intuitive appeal, but that does not explain why it was not subjected to more critical scru-tiny (1988, p. 11, bracketed item in orig.).

However, by the mid 1960s this explanation had been "subjected to a more critical scrutiny," and eventually the idea of group selection overriding individual selection was shown to be false and was discarded.

It also was believed that sexual reproduction might "speed up" evolution. However, theorists soon realized that—from an evolutionary viewpoint—an organism's "fitness" was damaged, not improved, as a result of sexual reproduction. Graham Bell pointed out:

> Sex...does not merely reduce fitness, but halves it. If a reduction in fitness of a fraction of one percent can cripple a genotype, what will be the consequence of a reduction of 50 percent? There can be only one answer: **sex will be powerfully selected against and rapidly eliminated wherever it appears. And yet this has not happened** (1982, pp. 77-78, emp. added).

Additional scientific findings have caused researchers to do a 180-degree turn-around in their explanation of the evolutionary purpose of sex. It now is claimed that sex is advantageous, **not because it hastens evolution, but rather, because it slows it down**. The necessity in this change in direction was lamented by Bell:

> To save the situation, then we must perform a complete volte-face [about-face—BH/BT]: just as it was self-evident to Weismann, Fisher and Muller that a faster rate of evolution would benefit a population, so we must now contrive to believe in the self-evident desirability of evolving slowly (p. 100).

This 180-degree about-face often is explained in the following manner. An asexual species is both too specialized and too dependent on its particular niche. As the niche vanishes, the species goes extinct. Asexual species thus inadvertently "adapt themselves out of existence" by refining a mode of life that is so restricted, it eventually disappears. Meanwhile, sexual species lag behind. Sex blunts the precision with which a species can adapt to a particular niche. Thus, according to evolutionists, sexual reproduction has slowed down evolution in

order to prevent extinction. Considering the incredible difficulty involved in inventing a coherent theory about the origin
of sex in the first place, and the vast smorgasbord of possible
explanations available to try to explain sex, it is no wonder
that we often find evolutionists disposing of one theory, only
to replace it instantaneously with another.

MARS AND VENUS, OR X AND Y?

Modern self-help books would have us believe that men
and women hail from "different planets," so to speak. But
what really separates them, we are told, are radically different
chromosomes. These chromosomes contain the genetic material that differentiates males and females. In order for a change
to occur from asexual reproduction to sexual reproduction,
two things had to occur at the very least: (1) a **single sex** first
had to "evolve" (so that it then could evolve into a second sex
—all the while retaining the first); and (2) double homologous
chromosomes also had to evolve.

But by what known method could an asexual organism produce a **sexual** organism? And did you ever wonder: Which
of the two sexes (male and female) evolved first? Well, wonder no more. Evolutionists somehow have divined the answer.
As Jennifer Ackerman boldly put it: "**The female was the
ancestral sex**, the first self-replicating organism; it gave rise
to the male, a variant, and the two still share many characteristics " (2001, pp. 113-114, emp. added). Of course, Ms. Ackerman offered not a shred of scientific evidence for her auda-
cious assertion—because there isn't any! Upon hearing her statement, we cannot help but be reminded of the now-famous comment made by R.E. Dickerson several years ago in a special
issue of *Scientific American* on evolution. Dr. Dickerson (who
was addressing specifically the evolution of the intricate "genetic machinery" of the cell) boasted that since "there are no
laboratory models, one can speculate endlessly, **unfettered
by inconvenient facts**" (1978, 239[3]:85, emp. added). That

also applies to the subject of the origin of sex. There are no adequate laboratory models; hence, Ms. Ackerman is free to "speculate endlessly, unfettered by inconvenient facts," and to claim without any proof whatsoever that "the female was the ancestral sex."

The second issue—the sudden appearance of double homologous chromosomes—presents no less of a problem. Why is this the case? Of the 46 human chromosomes, 44 are members of identical pairs, but two, the X and Y (generally referred to as the "sex chromosomes"), stand apart. Evolutionists thus are faced with the daunting challenge of explaining not only the origin of sex chromosomes themselves, but also the evolution of **two totally different sex chromosomes** (X and Y).

Human females possess two X chromosomes, while men possess one X and one Y. Some evolutionists (like Ackerman, quoted above) argue that the male Y chromosome somehow evolved from the female X chromosome. We know today that the X chromosome is the "home" for thousands of genes, while the Y has only a few dozen. Of those, only 19 are known to be shared by both X and Y. If, as evolutionists argue, the Y chromosome originally was identical to the X, then researchers have a great deal of work ahead of them in order to explain the fact that of the 19 shared genes, the X chromosomes possesses all 19 on the tip of the short arm of the chromosome, whereas they are scattered across the entire length of the Y. Thus while both chromosomes do share certain genes, those genes are found in totally different places, indicating that the male Y chromosome is not simply an "evolved" X chromosome.

DIFFERENCES AMONG VARIOUS SPECIES

In his book titled *Why Is Sex Fun?*, evolutionist Jared Diamond posed the question as to why men do not breast-feed babies. This problem caused Diamond to speculate:

Yes, it's true that no male mammal has ever become pregnant, and that the great majority of male mammals normally don't lactate. But one has to go further and ask why mammals evolved genes specifying that only females, not males, would develop the necessary anatomical equipment, the priming experience of pregnancy, and the necessary hormones. Both male and female pigeons secrete crop "milk" to nurse their squab; why not men as well as women? Among seahorses it's the male rather than the female that becomes pregnant; why is that not also true for humans? (1997, p. 42).

We also do not question that fact that most humans prefer to participate in sexual relations in private, whereas animals are indifferent to the presence of other animals or humans. Also of interest is the fact that most human women experience a complete shutdown of fertility somewhere between the ages of forty and fifty-five, whereas men do not. [Most animals do not experience a shutdown of their reproductive facilities at a similar time period in their lives.] We frequently do not question certain practices—simply because they are commonplace and because we are accustomed to seeing things performed a certain way. But we must learn to ask ourselves two questions: (1) "**How** did something get that way in the first place?"; and (2) "**Why** is it that way?"

What causes some animals to breed, and then spend years caring for their young, while others leave their young to fend for themselves almost immediately after birth? The method and nature of reproduction, and the degree of parental care, varies widely among living organisms. With the stroke of their pen, scientists have grouped pollination, asexual budding, sexual reproduction, and viral replication under the same "reproductive" umbrella, all the while giving scant attention to the complexity and intricacy involved in these various forms of reproduction. Consider, for example, the dizzying array of samaras, pomes, nuts, pips, and just plain fluff produced by trees. Some of the seed designs are absolutely ingenious, and, truth be told, dwarf mankind's attempts at engineering. Considering the odds of actual germination, it is no wonder that we find that in a bumper-crop year, the average oak can produce thousands of acorns, while an elm tree can produce tens of thousands of winged samaras (a dry, "winged" seed). Among the plant species, however, problems occur that cannot be explained by normal evolutionary theory. While most of the higher plants are hermaphrodites (i.e., they bear both pollen and eggs), there are those species in which pollen and eggs exist in separate plants. Indeed, the suggestion that dioecy [where female and male flowers are borne on separate plants] allegedly has "evolved" from hermaphroditism [where both female and male reproductive organs are found on the same flower] is a central problem in evolutionary biology (Ashman, 2000, p. 147).

Probably the most elaborate and showy courtship rituals belong to the bird family. Before mating season, many male birds grow colorful plumage that they use to "show-off" while trying to attract a mate. Courtship among reptiles often involves frequent fighting among rival males during breeding season. Many often display vivid colors, produce loud noises, or secrete pheromones (special scents) in an effort to communicate with and attract members of the opposite sex. Salmon, on the other hand, migrate to special spawning grounds during the breeding season. Often, these spawning grounds are located a great distance from normal feeding grounds because young fish have different feeding requirements compared to the adults. During their breeding periods, European eels also are known to travel great distances to special spawning grounds in the Sargasso Sea. The reproductive habits of social insects revolve around a tightly knit colony that centers on a queen.

Other "sexual oddities" can be observed amidst the animal kingdom. Take, for example, two types of seals. Using the lineage provided by evolutionists, it would appear that these two species are quite similar, and thus could be expected to reproduce in a comparable fashion. However, harbor seals are monogamous, whereas male elephant seals may inseminate as many as 100 females during their lifetimes. But this is only the tip of the proverbial iceberg. The following chart demonstrates only a few of the reproductive differences observed in just four common farm animals.

	Cow	Ewe	Sow	Mare
Age at Puberty	12 months	6 months	7 months	15 months
Length of Estrus Cycle	20-21 days	17 days	20-21 days	21 days
Duration of Estrus	18 hours	30 hours	2-3 days	5-6 days
Time of Ovulation	12-16 hours after end of estrus	end of estrus	40-44 hours after beginning of estrus	24-48 hours before the end of estrus
Gestation Length	283 days	148 days	114 days	336 days

The evolutionary "tree of life" does not demonstrate how these animals came to have gestation periods of different lengths, or varying estrus cycles, even though they allegedly have descended from the same "branch" (i.e., the mammals). Add to this mix the marsupials (from the Latin *marsupium*, meaning "pouch," since most, like the kangaroo, have some sort of pouch in which their young develop, thereby shortening the gestation period), and evolutionists find themselves with a bewildering hodgepodge of complexity so puzzling that simple lines and branches cannot even come close to explaining the history of sexual reproduction.

DIFFERENCES IN ANIMAL AND HUMAN SEXUALITY

Humans, unlike animals, do not copulate merely for reproductive purposes. Human females ovulate at only one point during their monthly cycle, but their bodies remain receptive throughout the month. This indicates that mating at all other times (i.e., outside of the ovulation period) has no procreative function. Thus, sexual relations in humans often are performed not for reproduction, but rather for enjoyment and pleasure. During sexual activity, the bodies of human males and females experience certain modifications and physiological changes that are not found in animals. Many of these represent modifications that account for the heightened stimulation and pleasure that occurs during copulation. If humans are a product of evolution, why, then, are females receptive to copulation almost all of the time, whereas animals utilizing an estrus cycle are not? Additionally, why do female humans experience menopause (the cessation of fertility via ovulation) as a regular phenomenon, which is not the norm for most wild animals? These are questions that evolutionists generally leave unasked, much less unanswered.

Genesis 31:35 indicates that menstrual bleeding of females has been with humanity since at least the time of Jacob and Rachel (cf. also Leviticus 20:18). The human female's menstrual cycle is divided into two main phases—the follicular, (or proliferative) phase, and the luteal (or secretory) phase. The follicular phase (during which estrogen levels rise) is characterized first by menstruation, and then by proliferation of the endometrial tissue. The ovarian cycle in female primates, however, consists of four stages: proestrus, estrus, matestrus, and diestrus. It is only in the second stage (estrus) that the female animal experiences a swelling of the vulva, during which various uterine processes occur that result in receptivity to copulation. Physically, a female primate is not able to receive a male unless she is in estrus. [The term "estrus" comes from the Greek meaning mad or frenetic desire, and generally is observed when female animals are "in heat."] Thus, the period of sexual receptivity of the female monkey or ape is much more restricted than that of a human female.

The differences that have been documented between estrus and menstrual cycles have caused evolutionists to formulate an attempted explanation for the human menstrual cycle. In 1993, Margie Profet, a self-taught evolutionary biologist, wrote a paper titled "Menstruation as a Defense Against Pathogens Transported by Sperm." Profet claimed that various microbial infections—caused by pathogen-toting spermatozoa—applied the adaptive pressure needed to cause menstruation. Simply put, she believed human sperm were carrying disease-causing organisms that necessitated the female to slough off the walls of the uterus as a means of self-defense. While other theories had existed prior to Profet's work, hers was the first to gain widespread scientific and public recognition. Three years later, Beverly Strassmann, an anthropologist at the University of Michigan in Ann Arbor, submitted a critical review of Profet's anti-pathogen hypothesis, and then proposed an alternative theory. She claimed that the reason the uterine endometrium is shed/reabsorbed in the cycle of regression and renewal is because it is energetically less costly than maintenance of the endometrium in an implantation state. We will leave it up to our readers to determine whether these scientists are "serious" or "seriously grasping." Suffice it to say that neither of these theories explains how or why the human female normally ovulates a single egg cell, instead of, say, five, six, seven, or more. They also do little to explain why human females routinely are sexually receptive, while animals are not. Anatomically speaking, how did humans "evolve" an anatomy that receives pleasure from sexual activity? **And why haven't we "evolved" enjoyment from other activities that evolutionists say were passed down from our ape-like ancestors?**

While God placed sexual relations only inside the marriage relationship (Hebrews 13:4), society has concluded that marriage and love are not prerequisites for sexual activity in humans. However, it should be noted when comparing human reproduction to that of animals, humans—married or unmarried–spend vast amounts of time, money, and energy in courtship and bonding prior to sexual relations. Can we observe various animals courting members of the opposite sex for months or years prior to having sexual relations? Commenting on the multiple facets that sex takes among humans, John Langone wrote:

> Sex is normal human behavior, a powerful drive that we are all born with, as natural as hunger and thirst. It enables us to bring new life into the world, and at the same time it is pleasurable. One cannot deny that we are often first attracted sexually to the one we decide to spend a good deal of time with, even our entire lifetime. Sex, also, is closely tied to our very vitality, our physical and mental vigor, our capacity to grow and create and act (1980).

Are we to believe, as many evolutionists espouse, that the differences observed in human sexual relations are merely a product of culture and upbringing? If this is true, then why do we find similar courting rituals in so-called "lost" civilizations that are protected from outside contact? Did humans "evolve" the ability to date, fall in love, and desire to be married to one individual for life?

THE COMPLEXITY OF THE HUMAN REPRODUCTIVE SYSTEM

Consider just how sophisticated the human reproductive cycle must be in order to function correctly. During early juvenile years, humans experience a delayed sexual development phase in which reproduction does not occur. Is it by mere chance that our bodies are not able to reproduce at such a young age? Once this juvenile period is over, changes occur throughout the body, requiring simultaneous coordination of further development in many different types of tissues. Additionally, the production and regulation of gametes must be timed just right. Females also must endure a previously unknown monthly ovulation cycle, which allows for fertilization.

Once fertilization takes place, the female body then must prepare itself for the many changes that occur during pregnancy. Are these carefully orchestrated processes mere happenstance?

While the male reproductive system may appear fairly simple, the true mechanics actually are quite complex. Unlike with other cells in the body, the production of sperm cells [spermatogenesis] does not occur at 98.6°F/37°C (normal body temperature). Instead, it occurs at a somewhat reduced temperature. To facilitate this, the sperm-producing organs, or testes, are located outside the body cavity in the scrotum, allowing them to remain about 3°C cooler than the rest of the body. This special location allows for the production of millions of sperm cells, which are stored according to maturity and then delivered during sexual intercourse. Additionally, males possess a cremaster muscle, which involuntarily raises or lowers the scrotal sac (depending on environmental conditions) in order to maintain a constant testicular temperature. Are such things as the precise location and temperature regulation of the male testes just a fortuitous occurrence—or the product of an intelligent Creator?

Likewise, the female body has been designed in such a manner as to be receptive to sperm, while at the same time being able to protect the abdominal area from bacteria in the environment. In addition, after producing eggs, the female reproductive system provides an environment in which a fertilized embryo can grow (keep in mind that the embryo does not possess its own blood supply, and therefore must obtain oxygen and nutrients from the mother's uterine wall). The uterus itself must be able to expand and hold the weight of an infant, plus the placenta and amniotic fluid—roughly 15 pounds—which is no small task (imagine a structure about the size of an orange able to expand and carry 3 five-pound bags of sugar!) After the child is born, the uterus returns to its normal size, and then, amazingly, is able to repeat this entire process again in future pregnancies. The female body also must orchestrate the production of milk for an infant, in conjunction with the baby's arrival.

While we take many of these feats for granted, science has yet to design a machine that even comes close to mimicking biological reproduction.

Reproductive hormones also play a critical role in the orchestrated process of sexual development and reproduction. While certain hormones can be found in both males and females, their actions and target organs are completely different between the two sexes. Additionally, females possess reproductive hormones that are not found in males. Did these reproductive hormones also just "evolve?" The following is a summary of the hormones (found in males or females) that are required for humans to be able to reproduce.

Males

1. Follicle-stimulating hormone—stimulates spermatogenesis
2. Luteinizing hormone—stimulates the secretion of testosterone
3. Testosterone—stimulates the development and maintenance of male secondary sexual characteristics

Females

1. Follicle-stimulating hormone—stimulates the growth of ovarian follicle
2. Luteinizing hormone—stimulates conversion of ovarian follicles into corpus luteum; stimulates secretion of estrogen
3. Estrogen—stimulates development and maintenance of female secondary sexual characteristics; prompts monthly preparation of uterus for pregnancy.
4. Progesterone—completes preparation of uterus for pregnancy; helps maintain female secondary sexual characteristics
5. Oxytocin—stimulates contraction of uterus; initiates milk release
6. Prolactin—stimulates milk production

The levels and production of these various hormones must be maintained carefully and regulated on a daily basis. Is this complex internal feedback mechanism—which is carried out primarily by the brain—purely a trait that was passed on from our alleged original sea-dwelling ancestors? If it is, why, then, don't those sea-dwelling organisms possess the same hormones? The complexity of the human reproductive system is practically incomprehensible. While scientists try to "play God" in their attempts to create living humans in laboratory settings, they still are light-years away from creating actual egg and sperm cells and all of the necessary components associated with them.

ANATOMICAL DIFFERENCES BETWEEN HUMAN MALES AND FEMALES

Any second-grade child easily could identify anatomical differences between the male and female species. However, these represent only **external** features. There also exist numerous **internal** differences. If we are to believe that sexual reproduction evolved from asexual reproduction, this means that the gametes also evolved. Anatomically speaking, what are the "chances" of a female evolving an egg large enough to accept the genetic material from the male (so that the conceived embryo has a chance to grow), yet small enough that it can fit through her own fallopian tubes? Furthermore, the egg also must possess the capability of creating a special barrier once that single sperm has penetrated the egg's cell wall, so that no other sperm can penetrate and add still more genetic material. And exactly how long in the evolutionary scheme of things did it take for a sperm cell to become small enough to be able to fertilize the egg, yet motile enough so that it could reach the egg?

With all of these anatomical differences, we must consider that each one also represents an entirely different type of cell that may or may not be present in the opposite sex. Yet evolutionists suggest that all of this is merely a "historical accident." Furthermore, the expense of producing two separate genders via such an accident is extremely costly for the species. Consider, for example, the fact that we have males and females in approximately equal numbers. Scientifically speaking, it requires only a few males to keep a species alive and thriving. From an evolutionary point of view, the expense of producing so many males would appear not only unnecessary, but also counterproductive. Jones noted:

> Biologists have an adolescent fascination with sex. Like teenagers, they are embarrassed by the subject because of their ignorance. What sex is, why it evolved and how it works are the biggest unsolved problems in biology. Sex must be important, as it is so expensive. If some creatures can manage with just females so that every individual produces copies of herself, why do so many bother with males? A female who gave them up might be able to produce twice as many daughters as before; and they would carry all of her genes. Instead, a sexual female wastes time, first in finding a mate and then in producing sons who carry only half of her inheritance. We are still not certain why males exist; and why, if we must have them at all, nature needs so many. Surely, one or two would be enough to impregnate all the females but, with few exceptions, the ratio of males to females remains stubbornly equal throughout the living world (1993, p. 84).

But what is this great expense to which biologists continually refer? The anatomical differences observed in males and females go far beyond the external differences observed by the second grader mentioned above. Yet scientists admittedly are reluctant to examine these differences in light of evolutionary theory. [A chart comparing some of the anatomical structures of males and females, and their primary functions, can be found on page 177.]

Realize that each one of these anatomical structures requires its own arterial and venous blood supply, as well as processes of nerve innervation that are not always apparent in the opposite sex. Additionally, many of these structures have their own specific lymphatic drainage. **How could the vascular and nervous tissue that supports the male prostate have evolved from a female equivalent, since females do not even possess a prostate?** Did humans continue to evolve to accommodate **all** the sexual and reproductive organs?

CELLULAR DIFFERENCES BETWEEN HUMAN MALES AND FEMALES

The human sperm cell and egg cell have been optimized in totally different ways. The egg is nonmotile, covered by a protective coating, and carries a large nutrient supply for growth and development. Sperm cells, by contrast, are extremely motile, built solely for fertilization, and have been streamlined for delivering DNA to the egg. Evolutionists would have us believe that these differences resulted from millions of years of trial and error. However, in the case of reproduction, **sperm and egg cells that are not fully functional do not result in fertilization–thus the species would not be able to reproduce, and therefore would become extinct.** How many generations of "error" would it take in this trial-and-error period before all sexually reproducing animals would die out? Are we to believe that these two totally different types of cells happened practically overnight by chance? Take a closer look at these two cells to determine if they are the products of chance—or the product of intelligent design.

Sperm cells are unlike any other cells in the body. They have been "stripped down" of everything unnecessary for fertilization–thus they are not encumbered with things like ribosomes, an endoplasmic reticulum, or a Golgi apparatus. However, the mitochondria (the powerhouses of the cell) have been arranged strategically in the center of the sperm cell where they can most efficiently propel the flagellum. This long, motile flagellum is driven by dynein motor proteins that use the energy of ATP (provided by all those mitochondria) to slide the microtubules inside the flagellum, thus bending certain portions of it. The head (or cap) of the sperm contains a specialized acrosomal vesicle, which contains hydrolytic enzymes that allow the sperm to penetrate the egg's outer layer. Without this special vesicle, the sperm cell would be unable to penetrate the coating of the egg cell. Upon contact with the egg, the contents of the acrosomal vesicle are released and the sperm cell then is bound tightly to the egg so that the genetic material can be transferred (Alberts, et al., 1994, p. 1026). Production of these incredible cells occurs throughout life. In a man, it takes about 24 days for a spermatocyte to complete meiosis in order to become a spermatid, and then another 5 weeks for a spermatid to develop into a mature motile sperm. Does this sound like something that occurred randomly overnight?

Egg cells, on the other hand, proliferate only in the fetus. These special cells undergo meiosis well before birth, but then can remain in a "suspended" state for up to 50 years. So while sperm cells are produced continually over a man's lifetime, egg cells are produced only during fetal development (i.e., no more are made after the female baby is born). During this fetal production stage, enough eggs are produced to last an adult woman throughout her life. The yolk, or egg cytoplasm, in these egg cells is rich in lipids, proteins, and polysaccharides. Egg cells also contain specialized secretory vesicles (located under the plasma membrane) that possess cortical granules. These granules alter the egg coat upon fertilization in order to prevent more than one sperm from fusing with the egg (Alberts, et al., p. 1022). Additionally, egg cell development (a developing egg is called an oocyte) occurs in timed stages after mensus begins. Interestingly, while the general stages of oocyte development are similar, we know today that this process actually varies from species to species. How does the randomness concept associated with evolution explain these extremely complex cellular characteristics, or the differences seen among species? Homer Jacobson addressed such problems when he stated:

MALE	
Organ	**Primary Function**
Penis	Erectile organ of copulation and urinary excretion
Testicle	Production of male sex hormones and sperm
Seminal Vesicles	Provide an alkaline fluid containing nutrients and prostaglandins
Ductus Deferens	Convey sperm to ejaculatory ducts
Prostate	Secretes alkaline fluid that helps neutralize acidic seminal fluid, and enhances motility of sperm
Epididymis	Storage and maturation of spermatozoa
Scrotum	Encloses and protects the testes
FEMALE	
Organ	**Primary Function**
Vagina	Organ of copulation, and passageway for fetus during parturition
Labia Major and Minor	Elongate vaginal canal and protect external genitalia
Clitoris	Erectile organ associated with feelings of pleasure during sexual stimulation
Ovary	Egg production and female sex hormones
Uterus	(Womb)–site of implantation; sustains life of the embryo
Uterine Tube	Convey egg or embryo toward uterus; common site of fertilization
Mammary Glands	Produce and secrete milk for nourishment of infant

Directions for the reproduction of plans, for energy and the extraction of parts from the current environment, for the growth sequence, and for the effector mechanism translating instructions into growth—all had to be simultaneously present at that moment. **This combination of events has seemed an incredibly unlikely happenstance, and has often been ascribed to divine intervention** (1955, 43:121, emp. added).

THE FUTURE OF HUMAN REPRODUCTION

During their investigation of the complexity of sexual reproduction at the cellular level, Bruce Alberts and his colleagues commented: "Whatever the origins of sex may be, it is striking that practically all complex present-day organisms have evolved largely through generations of sexual, rather than asexual reproduction. Asexual organisms, although plentiful, seem mostly to have remained simple and primitive" (1994, p. 1013). Striking indeed! Yet we as humans currently find ourselves on the verge of a reproductive shift—one that will place evolutionists in the position of playing God, while simultaneously eluding many of these tough questions.

Within our lifetimes, there can be little doubt that we will see serious scientific attempts at human cloning (by "serious" we mean experiments intended to carry a clone from its formation in the laboratory to birth via a surrogate mother). Cloning already has occurred in several mammalian species, and it likely is only a matter of time before someone announces the appearance of the first human clone. It is our personal belief that somewhere on this planet, a surrogate mother already is carrying the first cloned embryo—or will be shortly. In fact, Italian *in vitro* expert Severino Antinori announced on Friday, April 5, 2002, that a woman taking part in his controversial human cloning project already was eight weeks pregnant with a cloned embryo (see Daniel, 2002). Nineteen days later, on Wednesday, April 24, 2002, Dr. Antinori claimed that as of that date, three cloned pregnancies were in progress (see "Italian Cloning Scientist...," 2002). Once we cross this threshold, human reproduction no longer will take place as God ordained, but will occur instead solely at the discretion of man (or woman!). [NOTE: In July 2002, researcher Orly Lacham-Kaplan at Monash University in Melbourne, Australia, announced that she had discovered a method by which to fertilize eggs using genetic material harvested from somatic (body) cells–without the use of sperm (see "Eggs Fertilised without Sperm," 2002). The implications of such a procedure are obvious. As one news report observed, this process "could help lesbian couples to have baby girls that are genetically their own" (Highfield, 2002). This is what we meant when we commented that future human reproduction no longer will take place as God ordained, but instead will occur instead solely at the discretion of man (**or woman!**).]

In the September 2003 issue of *Fertility and Sterility*, James Grifo and his colleagues at New York University School of Medicine, along with researchers at Sun Yat Sen University Medi-

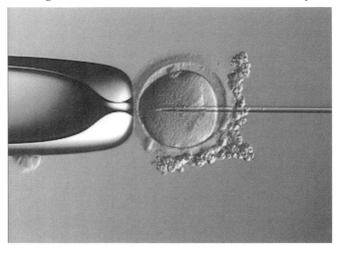

Figure 4 — Insertion into oocyte, during cloning process, of full complement of genetic material from somatic cell

cal Science in China, created the first human pregnancy using techniques related to cloning. The procedure was carried out in China, in an effort to avoid laws and regulations regarding human experimentation. As Helen Pearson noted in an article that appeared on *Nature* magazine's Web site:

> The team fertilized eggs from two women in test tubes. They then sucked out the nucleus of one egg and injected it into the other, which they had stripped of its own nucleus. The idea is that the second egg will better direct the growth of an embryo (2003a).

After creating seven "reconstructed" zygotes, the team implanted five of those into a 30-year-old woman who already had undergone two failed attempts at *in vitro* fertilization. Scientists reported a successful triplet pregnancy, and even were able to detect fetal heartbeats. At 33 days, a "fetal reduction to a twin pregnancy was performed" (see Zhang, et al., 2003). One of the two remaining babies was lost after 24 weeks, due to "premature rupture of membranes," and was pronounced dead as a result of "respiratory distress" (Zhang, et al.). The final remaining infant died at 29 weeks after suffering from a cord prolapse.

In light of this evidence, and the unfortunate deaths of the children that resulted from the experiment, it is as unbelievable as it is terrifying that Grifo and his colleagues would dare to conclude: "Viable human pregnancies with normal karyotype [the chromosomal characteristics of an individual—BH/BT] can be achieved through nuclear transfer." How tragic that we already have lost three innocent lives because scientists are resolved to further "improve" this technique. How many more humans will have to die before we realize human cloning is morally and ethically reprehensible?

Cloning bypasses the normal fertilization process between an egg and a sperm cell. Cloning allows scientists to take a mature body cell, subject it to harsh treatment so that it reverts to an "embryonic" mode, and then transfer its genetic material into an egg cell whose nucleus has been removed (leaving the egg empty, but healthy). Upon realizing that it no longer is in a hostile environment, the body cell "wakes up" and begins to develop–having forgotten where it came from and what it was on its way to becoming. As it begins to grow once more, it creates a whole new organism. This new organism then will be an exact **genetic** duplicate of the original body cell from which it was taken. But is this a safe method of reproduction? Ask yourself what happens to all of the embryos that are used to try to get the procedure "up and running," so-to-speak. How many failed human clones will we have to produce before we realize how morally bankrupt such a procedure really is? [For a brief look at humanity's future from an evolutionist's point of view, see Peter Ward's 2001 book, *Future Evolution*, pp. 139-153.]

Human reproduction was designed and created by God. During the activities of the Creation week (described in Genesis 1), it was only at the creation of man that a "divine conference" of the members of the Godhead occurred. Additionally, the Bible specifically denotes a **separate creation of males and females**. The sexes were not created simultaneously as in the case of the members of the animal kingdom. Genesis 1:26-27 records: "And God said, 'Let us make man in our image, after our likeness: and let them have dominion over the fish of the sea, and over the birds of the heavens, and over the cattle, and over all the earth, and over every creeping thing that creepeth upon the earth.' And God created man in his own image, in the image of God created he him; **male and female created he them**" (emp. added). He commanded Adam and Eve to "be fruitful, and multiply, and replenish the earth, and subdue it; and have dominion over the fish of the sea, and over the birds of the heavens, and over every living thing that moveth upon the earth" (Genesis 1:28). This command came from the God Who spoke life into man, and Who designed humans and their means of reproduction completely separate from the animals.

Sexual reproduction is not merely the product of millions of years of evolution. **As these numerous examples of differences adequately demonstrate, the highly complex and intricate manner in which the human body reproduces is not a matter of mere chance or a "lucky role of the dice." Rather, it is the product of an intelligent Designer.**

5

THE PROBLEM OF LANGUAGE

In 1994, an article appeared in *Time* magazine titled "How Man Began." Within that article was the following bold assertion: "No single, essential difference separates human beings from other animals" (Lemonick, 143[11]:81). Yet, in what is obviously a contradiction to such a statement, evolutionists admit that communication via speech is uniquely human—so much so that it often is used as the singular most important dividing line between humans and animals. In a book titled *Eve Spoke*, evolutionist Philip Lieberman admitted: "Speech is so essential to our concept of intelligence that its possession is virtually equated with being human. Animals who talk **are** human, because what sets us apart from other animals is the 'gift' of speech" (1998, p. 5, emp. in orig.). In *The Cambridge Encyclopedia of Human Evolution*, editors Jones, Martin, and Pilbeam conceded that "[t]here are no non-human languages," and then went on to observe that "language is an adaptation unique to humans, and yet the nature of its uniqueness and its biological basis are notoriously difficult to define" (1992, p. 128). Terrance Deacon noted:

> In this context, then, consider the case of human language. It is one of the most distinctive behavioral adaptations on the planet. Languages evolved in only one species, in only one way, without precedent, except in the most general sense. And the differences between languages and all other natural modes of communicating are vast (1997, p. 25).

What events transpired that have allowed humans to speak, while animals remained silent? If we are to believe the evolutionary teaching that currently is taking place in colleges and universities around the world, speech evolved as a natural process through time. Yet no one is quite sure how, and there are no known animals that are in a transition phase from non-speaking to speaking. In fact, in the *Atlas of Languages*, this remarkable admission can be found: "No languageless community has ever been found" (Matthews, et al., 1996, p. 7). This represents no small problem for evolutionists. In fact, the origin of speech and language (along with the development of sex and reproduction) remains one of the most significant hurdles in evolutionary theory, even in the twenty-first century. In fact, some evolutionists simply have stopped discussing the matter. Jean Aitchison noted: "In 1866, a ban on the topic was incorporated into the founding statues of the Linguistic Society of Paris, perhaps the foremost academic linguistic institution of the time: 'The Society does not accept papers on either the origin of language or the invention of a universal language'" (2000, p. 5). That is an amazing (albeit inadvertent) admission of defeat, especially coming from a group of such eminent scientists, researchers, and scholars.

The truth of the matter is, however, that the origin of human languages **can** be discerned—**but not via the theory of evolution**. We invite your close attention to the information that follows, which demonstrates conclusively that humans were created by God with the special unique ability to employ speech for communication.

EVOLUTIONARY THEORIES ON THE ORIGIN OF SPEECH

Many animals are capable of using sounds to communicate. However, there is a colossal difference between the grunt of a pig or the hoot of an owl, and a human standing before an audience reciting Robert Frost's "The Road Not Taken." This enormous chasm between humans and animals has led to a multiplicity of theories on exactly how man came upon this unequaled capability. But there is one common theme that stands out amidst all the theories: "The world's languages evolved spontaneously. They were not designed" (Deacon, p. 110).

Design indicates that there was a Designer; thus, evolutionists have conjured up theories that consider language nothing more than a fortuitous chain of events. Most of these theories involve humans growing bigger brains, which then made it physiologically possible for people to develop speech and language. For instance, in the foreword of her book, *The Seeds of Speech,* Jean Aitchison hypothesized:

> Physically, a deprived physical environment led to more meat-eating and, as a result, a bigger brain. The enlarged brain led to the premature birth of humans, and in consequence a protracted childhood, during which mothers cooed and crooned to their offspring. An upright stance altered the shape of the mouth and vocal tract, allowing a range of coherent sounds to be uttered (2000, p. x).

Thus, according to Aitchison, we can thank "a deprived physical environment" for our current ability to talk and communicate. Another evolutionist, John McCrone, put it this way:

> It all started with an ape that learned to speak. Man's hominid ancestors were doing well enough, even though the world had slipped into the cold grip of the ice ages. They had solved a few key problems that had held back the other branches of the ape family, such as how to find enough food to feed their rather oversized brains. Then man's ancestors happened on the trick of language. Suddenly, a whole new mental landscape opened up. Man became self-aware and self-possessed (1991, p. 9).

Question: How (and why) did that first ape learn to speak? It is easy to suggest that "it all started with an ape that learned to speak." But it is much more difficult to describe **how** this took place, especially in light of our failure to teach apes to speak today. In his book, *From Hand to Mouth: The Origins of Language,* Michael Corballis stated:

> My own view is that language developed much more gradually, starting with the gestures of apes, then gathering momentum as the bipedal hominins evolved.

The appearance of the larger-brained genus *Homo* some 2 million years ago may have signaled the emergence and later development of syntax, with vocalizations providing a mounting refrain. What may have distinguished *Homo sapiens* was the final switch from a mixture of gestural and vocal communication to an autonomous vocal language, embellished by gesture but not dependent on it (2002, p. 183).

The truth, however, is that evolutionists can only speculate as to the origin of language. Evolutionist Carl Zimmer summed it up well when he wrote:

No one knows the exact chronology of this evolution, because language leaves precious few traces on the human skeleton. The voice box is a flimsy piece of cartilage that rots away. It is suspended from a slender C-shaped bone called a hyoid, but the ravages of time usually destroy the hyoid too (2001, p. 291).

Thus, theories are plentiful—while the evidence to support those theories remains mysteriously unavailable. Add to this the fact that humans acquire the ability to communicate (and even learn some of the basic rules of syntax) by the age of two, and you begin to see why Aitchison admitted: "Of course, holes still remain in our knowledge: in particular, at what stage did language leap from being something new which humans discovered to being something which every newborn human is scheduled to acquire? This is still a puzzle" (p. ix). Yes, it is "a puzzle."

ADAM–THE FIRST HUMAN TO TALK AND COMMUNICATE

In a chapter titled "What, When, and Where did Eve Speak to Adam and He to Her?," Philip Lieberman stated:

In the five-million-year-long lineage that connects us to the common ancestors of apes and human beings, there have been many Adams and many Eves. In the beginning was the word, but the vocal communications of our most distant hominid ancestors five million years or so ago probably didn't really differ from those of the ape-hominid ancestor (1998, p. 133).

Using biblical terminology, Lieberman had written a year earlier: "For with speech came a capacity for thought that had never existed before, and that has transformed the world. In the beginning was the word" (1997, p. 27).

When God created the first human beings—Adam and Eve—He created them in His own image (Genesis 1:26-27). This likeness unquestionably included the ability to engage in intelligible speech via human language. In fact, God spoke to them from the very beginning of their existence as humans (Genesis 1:28-30). Hence, they possessed the ability to understand verbal communication—**and to speak themselves!**

God gave very specific instructions to the man **before** the woman was even created (Genesis 2:15-17). Adam gave names to the animals **before** the creation of Eve (Genesis 2:19-20). Since both the man and the woman were created on the sixth day, the creation of the man preceded the creation of the woman by only hours. So, **Adam had the ability to speak on the very day he was brought into existence!**

That same day, God put Adam to sleep and performed history's first human surgery. He fashioned the female of the species from a portion of the male's body. God then presented the woman to the man (no doubt in what we would refer to as the first marriage ceremony). Observe Adam's recorded response: "And Adam said, 'This is now bone of my bones and flesh of my flesh; she shall be called Woman, because she was taken out of man'" (Genesis 2:23). Here is Adam—less than twenty-four hours old—articulating intelligible speech with a well-developed vocabulary and advanced powers of expression. Note, too, that Eve engaged in intelligent conversation with Satan (Genesis 3:1-5). An unbiased observer is forced to conclude that Adam and Eve were **created by God** with oral communication capability. Little wonder, then, that God told Moses: "Who had made man's mouth?... Have not I, the Lord? Now therefore, go, and I will be with your mouth and teach you what you shall say" (Exodus 4:11-12).

This circumstance should not surprise us, since the rest of the created order also was brought into existence fully formed and operational. Adam's body was that of a man—not a child. His body possessed reproductive capability (Genesis 1:28). His mind was mentally and psychologically functional on the level of an adult. Likewise, trees and plants were completely operational in their photosynthetic, reproductive, and fruit-bearing capability (Genesis 1:11-12). Animals, too, were created fully functional (Genesis 1:20-25). And, the Sun, Moon, planets, and stars were created instantaneously to provide the services they were intended to provide (Genesis 1:14-18). Once again, the biblical explanation of the beginning of the human race and linguistic functionality is logical, reasonable, and scientifically feasible. The evolutionary model is not.

TOWER OF BABEL–AND THE UNIVERSAL LANGUAGE

Nobody knows exactly how many languages there are in the world, partly because of the difficulty of distinguishing between a language and a sub-language (or dialects within it). One authoritative source that has collected data from all over the world, *The Ethnologue*, lists the total number of languages as 6,809.

The Bible's explanation of the origins of multiple human languages is given in the Tower of Babel incident (Genesis 11: 1-9). Scripture simply and confidently asserts: "Now the whole earth had one language and one speech" (11:1). When Noah and his family stepped off of the ark, they spoke a single language that was passed on to their offspring. As the population increased, it apparently remained localized in a single geographical region. Consequently, little or no linguistic variation ensued. But when a generation defiantly rejected God's instructions to scatter over the planet, God miraculously intervened and generated the major language groupings of the human race. This action forced the population to proceed with God's original intention by clustering according to shared languages.

This depiction of the origin of human languages coincides well with the present status of the world's languages. The extant linguistic evidence does not support the model postulated by evolutionists for the origin of languages. Many evolutionary linguists believe that all human languages descended from a single, primitive language, which itself evolved from grunts and noises of the lower animals. The single most influential "hopeful monster" theory of the evolution of human language was proposed by Noam Chomsky, the famed MIT linguist, and has since been echoed by numerous anthropologists, philosophers, linguists, and psychologists.

Chomsky argued that the ability of children to acquire the grammar necessary for a language can be explained only if we assume that all grammars are variations of a single, generic "universal grammar," and that all human brains come "with a built-in language organ that contains this language blueprint" (Deacon, 1997, p. 35). However, the existing state of human language suggests that the variety of dialects and sub-languages has developed from a relatively few (perhaps less than twenty) languages. These so-called "proto-languages," from which all others supposedly developed, were distinct among themselves—with no previous ancestral language. Creationist Carl Wieland thus observed: "The evidence is wonderfully consistent with the notion that a small number of languages, separately created at Babel, has diversified into the huge variety of languages we have today" (1999, p. 22).

THE BRAIN'S LANGUAGE CENTERS–CREATED BY GOD

In contemplating how language arose, evolutionists frequently link the evolution of the brain to the appearance of languages. But consider that over 5,000 languages exist, and you begin to understand that the development of language cannot be viewed as a simple, clear-cut addition to human physiology that was made possible by an enlarged brain unique to *Homo sapiens*. Terrance Deacon commented on the intricacy of evolving a language when he stated: "For a language feature to have such an impact on brain evolution that all members of the species come to share it, it must remain invariable across **even the most drastic language change possible**" (p. 329, emp. in orig.).

The complexity underlying speech began to reveal itself in patients who were suffering various communication problems. Researchers began noticing analogous responses among patients with similar injuries. The ancient Greeks noticed that brain damage could cause the loss of the ability to speak (known as aphasia). Centuries later, in 1836, Marc Dax described a group of patients that could not speak normally. Dax reported that all of these patients experienced damage to the left hemisphere of their brain. In 1861, Paul Broca described a patient who could speak only a single word (the word "tan"). When this patient died, Broca examined his brain and noted damage to the left frontal cortex, which has since become known anatomically as "Broca's area." While patients with damage to Broca's area can understand language, they generally cannot produce speech because words are not formed properly and thus their speech is slurred and slow.

In 1876, Carl Wernicke found that language problems also could result from damage to another area of the brain. This area, later termed "Wernicke's area," is located in the posterior part of the temporal lobe. **Damage to Wernicke's area results in a loss of the ability to understand language**. Thus, patients can continue to speak, but the words are put together in such a way that they make no sense. Interestingly, in most people (around 97%), both Broca's area and Wernicke's area are found only in the left hemisphere, which explains the language deficits observed in patients with brain damage to the left side of the brain. Evolutionists freely acknowledge that

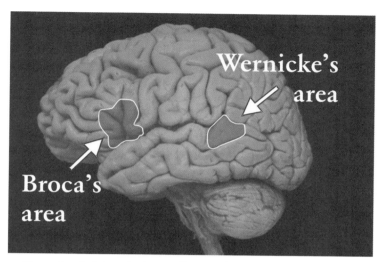

Figure 1 — Left hemisphere of human brain with language centers—Broca's area and Wernicke's area—highlighted. LifeART image copyright © (2003) Lippincott, Williams & Wilkins. All rights reserved. Used by permission.

> [t]he relationship between brain size and language is unclear. Possibly, increased social interaction combined with tactical deception gave the brain an initial impetus. Better nourishment due to meat-eating may also have played a part. Then brain size and language possibly increased together (Aitchison, 2000, p. 85).

But the brain is not simply larger. The connections are vastly different as well. As Deacon went on to admit: "Looking more closely, we will discover that a radical re-engineering of the whole brain has taken place, and on a scale that is unprecedented" (p. 45). In order to speak a word that has been read, information is obtained from the eyes and travels to the visual cortex. From the primary visual cortex, information is transmitted to the posterior speech area (which includes Wernicke's area). From there, information travels to Broca's area, and then to the primary motor cortex to provide the necessary muscle contractions to produce the sound. To speak a word that has been heard, we must invoke the primary auditory cortex, not the visual cortex. Deacon commented on this complex neuronal network—not found in animals—when he wrote:

There is, without doubt, something special about human brains that enables us to do with ease what no other species can do even minimally without intense effort and remarkably insightful training. We not only have the ability to create and easily learn simple symbol systems such as the chimps Sherman and Austin struggled to learn, but in learning languages we acquire an immensely complex rule system and a rich vocabulary at a time in our lives when it is otherwise very difficult to learn even elementary arithmetic. Many a treatise on grammatical theory has failed to provide an adequate accounting of the implicit knowledge that even a four-year-old appears to possess about her newly acquired language (p. 103).

ANATOMY OF SPEECH

The mechanics involved in speaking have anatomical requirements that are found primarily in humans. There is no animal living presently, nor has one been observed in the fossil record, that possesses anything close to the "voice box" (as we commonly call it) that is present in humans. As information scientist Werner Gitt observed in his intriguing book, *The Wonder of Man*:

> Only man has the gift of speech, a characteristic otherwise only possessed by God. This separates us clearly from the animal kingdom…. In addition to the necessary "software" for speech, we have also been provided with the required "hardware" (1999, p. 101).

Furthermore, the lack of any "transitional" animal form (with the requisite speech hardware) in the fossil record poses a significant continuity problem for evolutionists. As Deacon noted:

> This lack of precedent makes language a problem for biologists. Evolutionary explanations are about biological continuity, so a lack of continuity limits the use of the comparative method in several important ways. We can't ask, "What ecological variable correlates with increasing language use in a sample spe-

cies?" Nor can we investigate the "neurological correlates of increased language complexity." There is no range of species to include in our analysis (p. 34).

To simplify the anatomy required for speech by using an analogy, think of a small tube resting inside a larger tube. The inner tube consists of the trachea going down to the lungs, and the larynx (which houses the voice box). At the larynx, the inner tube opens out to the larger tube, which is known as the pharynx. It not only carries sound **up** to the mouth, but also carries food and water from the mouth **down** to the stomach. A simplistic description of how humans utter sounds in speech can be characterized by the control of air generated by the lungs, flowing through the vocal tract, vibrating over the vocal cord, being filtered by facial muscle activity, and then being released out of the mouth and nose. Just as sound can be generated by forcing air across the narrow mouth of a bottle, air is streamed across the vocal cords, which can be tightened or relaxed to produce a variety of different resonances. The physiological components necessary can be divided into: (1) the supralaryngeal vocal tract; (2) the larynx; and (3) the subglottal system.

In 1848, Johannes Muller demonstrated that human speech involved modulation of acoustic energy by the airway above the larynx (called the supralaryngeal tract). The sound en-

Anatomy Used During Speech

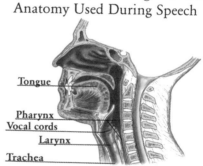

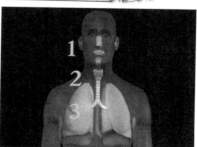

Figure 2 — Physiological components involved in speech. LifeART image copyright © (2003) Lippincott, Williams & Wilkins. All rights reserved. Used by permission.

ergy for speech is generated in the larynx at the vocal folds. The subglottal system, which consists of the lungs, trachea, and their associated muscles, provides the necessary power for speech production. The lungs produce the initial air pressure that is essential for the speech signal; the pharyngeal cavity, oral cavity, and nasal cavity shape the final output sound that is perceived as speech.

BIRDS OF A FEATHER—OR NAKED APE?

Imagine the conundrum in which evolutionists find themselves when it comes to speech and language. The animal that comes closest to producing anything that even vaguely resembles human speech is not another primate, but rather a bird. Deacon noted:

> In fact, most birds easily outshine any mammal in vocal skills, and though dogs, cats, horses, and monkeys are remarkably capable learners in many domains, vocalization is not one of them. Our remarkable vocal abilities are not part of a trend, but an exception (pp. 30-31).

For instance, a famous African gray parrot in England named Toto is able to pronounce words so clearly that he sounds rather human. Like humans, birds can produce fluent, complex sounds. We both share a double-barreled, double-layered system involving tunes and dialects, which is controlled by the left side of our brains. And just like young children, juvenile birds experience a period termed "sub-song" where they twitter in what resembles the babbling of a young child learning to speak. Yet Toto does not have "language" as humans understand it. Humans use language for many more purposes than birds use song. Consider also that it is mostly male birds that sing. Females remain songless unless they are injected with the male hormone testosterone (see Nottebohm, 1980). Consider also that humans often communicate intimately between two or three people, while bird communication is a fairly long-distance affair.

Oddly, some researchers have even gone so far as to suggest that both animate and inanimate objects can communicate. According to a group that refers to itself as the Global Psychic Team, "animals, trees, plants, rocks—all of nature —telepathically communicate with us, sending images, feelings, even words. The key is in learning how to listen and respond" (see "Animals Talk," 2002). But what evidence exists to demonstrate that animals (much less plants and rocks!) have the unique ability to communicate that is possessed by humans? While evolutionary language scientists assert differently, the truth is that animals do not possess the ability to talk and communicate like humans.

One of the big "success" stories in looking at the human-like qualities of non-human primates is a male bonobo chimp known as Kanzi (see Savage-Rumbaugh and Lewin, 1994; Skoyles and Sagan, 2002, pp. 217-220). Kanzi was born October 28, 1990, and began his journey to learn to "speak" as a result of the training given to his mother, Matata, via a "talking" keyboard. Matata never did master the keyboard, but Kanzi did. Through many years of intense training and close social contact with humans, this remarkable animal attained the language abilities of an average two-year-old human. By age ten, he had a "spoken" vocabulary (via the keyboard) of some two hundred words. In fact, Kanzi was able to go beyond the mere parroting or "aping" of humans; he actually could communicate his wants and needs, express feelings, and use tools. When tested against a two-year-old girl by the name of Alia (where both the girl and the chimp were given verbal instructions to carry out certain tasks), Kanzi performed better than Alia. And, as he grew into adulthood, Kanzi began to prefer the company of humans to that of other chimps. Inasmuch as Kanzi can accomplish these things, does this prove that chimps are merely hairy, child-like versions of humans?

Hardly. To use the words of the famous American news commentator, Paul Harvey, someone needs to tell "the rest of the story." For example, in their 2002 volume, *Up from Dragons,* John Skoyles and Dorion Sagan discussed Kanzi at great length. Among other things, they wrote:

Kanzi did this when he was 5, and Alia was only 2. But it was not really a fair contest. Alia was learning not only to understand spoken speech, but also to speak, something that would provide feedback on her comprehension. Since **Kanzi could not make speech sounds**, he was working under a handicap when trying to understand spoken English. It is remarkable that he could understand single words, let alone the short sentences above. Interestingly, **while Kanzi will never, for anatomical reasons, be able to speak,** he does have a far wider range of vocal sounds than other chimps....

Kanzi shows that while chimps may have the potential to learn language, they require a "gifted" environment to do so. Kanzi was surrounded by intelligent apes with PhDs [i.e., humans—BH/BT] who spoke to him and gave him a stream of rich interactions. They gave Kanzi's brain a world in which it could play at developing its ability to communicate.... Therefore, as much as in his brain, **Kanzi's skill lies in the environment that helped shape it** (2002, pp. 215,216, emp. added).

Kanzi does not have the anatomical equipment required for speech. Aside from the mimicking ability of parrots, no animal does. As Skoyles and Sagan noted: "Chimps lack the vocal abilities needed for making speech sounds—speech requires a skilled coordination between breathing and making movements with the larynx that chimps lack" (p. 214). Humans, however, **do** possess the anatomical equipment required for speech.

But there is more. Regardless of the amount of instruction such animals receive, there appear to be built-in limits on their progress. On February 15, 1994, the public television program NOVA aired a show titled "Can Chimps Talk?" (for a full transcript of the show go to www.primate.wisc.edu/pin/nova.html). The show began with a "conversation" with Kanzi, who was required to use a talking keyboard to respond to queries from his human counterpart. As the television program demonstrated quite effectively, he often responded incorrectly when asked a question. For instance, one of the humans asked, "Is there any other food you'd like me to bring in the backpack?" Kanzi's talking keyboard response was: "ball."

The program then focused on Washoe, a chimpanzee that, in the 1970s, was taught a portion of American Sign Language by Allen and Beatrice Gardner at the University of Nevada. By the time Washoe was five, the trainers reported that she could use 133 signs. Headlines were quick to report that a non-human primate was using human language. This spurred other scientists, such as Herb Terrace, to begin experimenting with animal language. Terrace set out to replicate some of the Gardners' study by using his own ape, Nim Chimsky (sarcastically named after Noam Chomsky, who believes language is confined solely to humans). The main goal of the project was to determine if a chimpanzee could create a sentence. In the documentary, Terrace stated: "I have concluded that, unfortunately, the answer to that question is no." Nim's sign usage could best be interpreted as a series of "conditioned discriminations" similar to behaviors seen in many less-intelligent animals. This work suggested that Nim, like circus animals, was using words only to obtain food rewards. Terrace realized that while Nim seemed to be using a combination of signs, he actually was imitating the trainer. This caused Terrace to look at some of Gardners' films. He decided that Washoe, too, was being led by his teacher and was merely imitating.

As Skoyles and Sagan candidly admitted, Kanzi's skill was "in the environment that helped shape it." That is exactly what Terrace discovered. Such an assessment always will be true of "talking animals." But it is not always true of humans. Consider the following case in point.

As we mentioned earlier, the eminent linguist Noam Chomsky has championed the idea that humans are born with a built-in "universal grammar"—a series of biological switches for complex language that is set in place in the early years of childhood. This, he believes, is why children can grasp elaborate language rules even at an early age—**even without adults to teach them**. Chomsky noted: "The rate of vocabulary acquisition is so high at certain stages in life, and the precision and delicacy of the concepts acquired so remarkable, that it seems necessary to conclude that in some manner the conceptual system with which lexical items are connected is already in place" (1980, p. 139). John W. Oller and John L. Omdahl went on to comment:

> In other words, the conceptual system is not really constructed in the child's mind as if out of nothing, but must be, in an important sense, known before the fact. The whole system must be in place before it can be employed to interpret experience (1997, p. 255, emp. in orig.).

Powerful support for Chomsky's theory emerged from a decade-long study of 500 deaf children in Managua, Nicaragua, which was reported in the December 1995 issue of *Scientific American* (Horgan, 1995, 273[6]:18-19). These children started attending special schools in 1979, but none was taught (or used) a formal sign language. Within a few years, and under no direction from teachers or other adults, they began to develop a basic "pidgin" sign language. This quickly was modified by younger children entering school, with the current version taking on a complex and consistent grammar. If Chomsky is correct, where, then, did humans get their innate ability for language? Chomsky himself will not even hazard a guess. In his opinion, "very few people are concerned with the origin of language because most consider it a hopeless question" (as quoted in Ross, 1991, 264[4]:146). The development of language, he admits, is a "mystery." The fundamental failing of naturalistic theories is that they are inadequate to explain the origins of something so complex and information-rich as human language, which itself is a gift of God and is part of man's having been created "in His image" (see Thompson, 2002, pp. 85-134).

The fact is, no animal is capable of speaking in the manner in which people can speak. Speech is a peculiarly **human** trait. In an article titled "Chimp-Speak" that dealt with this very point, Trevor Major wrote:

First, chimps do not possess the anatomical ability to speak. Second, the sign language they learn is not natural, even for humans. Chimps have to be trained to communicate with this language; it is not something they do in the wild. And unlike humans, trained chimps do not seem to pass this skill on to their young. Third, chimps never know more than a few hundred words—considerably less than most young children.... [E]volutionists have no way to bridge the gap from innate ability to language relying on natural selection or any other purely natural cause. Why? Because language is complex and carries information—the trademarks of intelligent design (1994, 14[3]:1).

Another MIT scientist, Steven Pinker (director of the university's Center of Cognitive Neuroscience), stated in *The Language Instinct: The New Science of Language and Mind*:

As you are reading these words, you are taking part in one of the wonders of the natural world. For you and I belong to a species with a remarkable ability: we can shape events in each other's brains with remarkable precision. I am not referring to telepathy or mind control or the other obsessions of fringe science; even in the depictions of believers, these are blunt instruments compared to an ability that is uncontroversially present in every one of us. **That ability is language**. Simply by making noises with our mouths, we can reliably cause precise new combinations of ideas to arise in each other's minds. The ability comes so naturally that we are apt to forget what a miracle it is....

Language is obviously as different from other animals' communication systems as the elephant's trunk is different from other animals' nostrils.... As we have seen, human language is based on a very different design. The discrete combinatorial system called "grammar" makes human language infinite (there is no limit to the number of complex words or sentences in a language), digital (this infinity is achieved by rearranging discrete elements in particular orders and combinations, not by varying some signal along a continuum like the mercury in a thermometer), and compositional (each of the infinite combinations has a different meaning predictable from the meanings of its parts and the rule and principles arranging them). Even the seat of human language in the brain is special... (1994, pp. 1,365, parenthetical comments in orig., emp. added).

The Bible mentions only two (supernaturally caused) exceptions to this rule: the serpent in the Garden of Eden and Balaam's donkey. However, unlike man, both of these animals were controlled externally; Satan controlled the serpent, and God controlled the donkey. It is evident that only man was given the gift of speech. It is an intrinsic part of his nature that associates him with God and separates him from the rest of creation.

Without detracting anything from primates like Kanzi and Washoe, fundamental differences between animals and humans nevertheless remain. Unlike human children, animals: (1) do not have a special region in the brain devoted to language; (2) have a much smaller brain overall; and (3) lack the anatomy to speak the words they may think. In summary, humans have an innate, built-in, hard-wired ability to acquire and communicate complex languages from the moment of their birth.

Admittedly, animals **do** possess a measure of understanding. They can learn to respond to commands and signs, and in some cases even can be trained to use minimal portions of human sign language. But, as biologist John N. Moore has pointed out:

> Although the chimpanzee Washoe has been taught the American Sign Language, such an accomplishment is **primarily** an increase in an ability of the anthropoid to respond to direct presentation of **signs**. And, further, the learned capability of the chimpanzee Lana to utilize push buttons connected with a computer to "converse" with a human trainer depends fundamentally upon increased conditional reflex response to **signs** (1983, p. 341, emp. in orig.).

Even though apes, dogs, and birds can be "trained" to do certain things, they cannot reason and communicate ideas with others so as to have true mental communion. The intelligence of animals is unlike that of humankind. As Moore went on to discuss,

> [t]he purest and most complex manifestation of man's symbolic nature is his capacity for conceptual thought, that is, for thought involving sustained and high order abstraction and generalization. Conceptual thought enables man to make himself independent of stimulus boundness that characterizes animal thinking. Animals, especially primates, give undeniable evidence of something **analogous** to human thought—analogous yet medically different in that their thought is bound to the immediate stimulus situation and to the felt impulse of the organism. Animal thinking, too, is riveted to the realm of survival (broadly taken) and therefore encompasses a variety of needs pertinent to the species as well as to the individual. These differences account for the distinction between **conceptual** thought, which is the exclusive prerogative of man, and **perceptual** thought, a cognitive function based directly upon sense perception, which man shares with other animals (p. 344, emp. in orig.).

Thus, the issue is not "can animals think?," but rather "can they think the way humans do?" The answer, obviously, is a resounding "No!" In summarizing his thoughts on this subject, Trevor Major offered the following conclusion concerning the intelligence of chimpanzees.

> Are chimps intelligent? The answer is yes. Do chimps possess the **same kind** of intelligence as humans? The answer would have to be no. Humans are more intelligent, **and** they possess additional forms of intelligence. What we must remember, also, is that the greatest capabilities of the apes belong to a handful of superstars like Kanzi and Sheba. Even these animals lack the empathy, foresight, and language capabilities of all but the youngest or most intellectually challenged of our own species (1995, 15:88, emp. in orig.).

Moore commented further:

> Animals can think in several ways...though only on the perceptual, not on the conceptual level. The key difference here is one between conceptual and perceptual thinking. The latter, which is typical of animal thinking, requires the actual or nearly immediate presence of the pertinent objects. Man's thinking, on the other hand, is independent of the presence of pertinent objects. It is, in fact, independent of objects altogether, as is the case with logical or mathematical exercises. Secondly, the difference between human and animal thinking resides in the fact that, whether or not the object of the mental operation is present, animals cannot make judgments or engage in reasoning. For example, animals are unable to conclude that such and such **is** or **is not** the case in a given situation or that **if** such and such is the case, **then** so and so is not (p. 344, ellipses and emp. in orig.).

Although animal trainers and investigators since the seventeenth century have tried to teach chimpanzees to talk, no chimpanzee has ever managed it. A chimpanzee's sound-producing anatomy is simply too different from that of humans. Chimpanzees might be able to produce a muffled approximation of human speech—if their brains could plan and execute the necessary articulate maneuvers. But to do this, they would have to have our brains, **which they obviously do not** (Lieberman, 1997, p. 27).

COMPLEXITY OF LANGUAGE— UNIQUELY HUMAN

No known language in all of human history can be considered "primitive" in any sense of the word. In her book, *What is Linguistics?*, Suzette Elgin remarked: "The most ancient languages for which we have written texts—Sanskrit for example—are often far more intricate and complicated in their grammatical forms than many other contemporary languages" (1973, p. 44). Lewis Thomas, a distinguished physician, scientist, and longtime director and chancellor of the Sloan Kettering Cancer Center in Manhattan, acknowledged: "...[L]anguage is so incomprehensible a problem that the language we use for discussing the matter is itself becoming incomprehensible" (1980, p. 59). It appears that, from the beginning, human communication was designed with a great amount of complexity and forethought, and has allowed us not only to communicate with one another, but also with our Creator.

In a paper titled "Evolution of Universal Grammar" that appeared in the January 2001 issue of *Science*, M.A. Nowak and his colleagues attempted to discount the gulf that separates humans and animals (Nowak, et al., 2001). This paper, which was a continuation of a 1999 paper titled "The Evolution of Language" (Nowak and Krakauer, 1999), used mathematical calculations in an effort to predict the evolution of grammar and the rules surrounding it. While Nowak and his team inferred that the evolution of universal grammar can occur via natural selection, they freely admitted that **"the question concerning why only humans evolved language is hard to answer"** (96:8031, emp. added). Hard to answer? The mathematical models presented in these papers do not tell us anything about the origination of the multitude of languages used in the world today. If man truly did evolve from an ape-like ancestor, how did the phonologic [the branch of linguistics that deals with the sounds of speech and their production] component of our languages become so diverse and variegated? Nowak's paper also did not clarify the origination of written languages, or describe how the language process was initiated in the first humans, considering we know today that parents teach languages to their offspring.

Nowak and his collaborators believe that the "first step" in the evolution of language was "signal-object associations." They speculate that common objects, frequently utilized, were given a representative signal or sign (in a manner similar to modern sign language). These researchers also believe that early in evolution, these signals were "likely to have been noisy" and therefore "mistaken for each other." Nowak suggests that these errors necessitated the formation of words, and describes this step in the evolution of language as comparable to going "from an analogue to a digital system." However, there is no evidence that demonstrates how these "prehistoric" people made the quantum leap from signals to words. The last step Nowak describes is the evolution of basic grammatical rules in an effort to convey even more information than just simple words. While these speculations make a nice, neat, progressive path toward human language, they do little to explain adequately the anatomical differences found in animals and humans. The human supralaryngeal airway differs from that of any other adult mammal, and is quite essential for speech. While chimpanzees have been taught to communicate via sign language, they cannot speak, and do not appear to use any complex syntax in communication.

Nowak and his colleagues began with the assumption that language "evolved as a means of communicating information between individuals" (96:8030), and then went on to speculate that natural selection favors the emergence of a universal, rule-based language system. But if natural selection "favors" a complex language, how do we account for the nonvocal communication observed in animals, and why hasn't this communication "emerged" into a formal language in those animals? In an effort to explain this embarrassing lack of understanding, Nowak, et al., offered several speculations as to why animals have not evolved a better form of communication. In their explanation, they listed:

- Signal-object associations form only when information transfer is beneficial to both speaker and listener.
- In the presence of errors, only a very limited communication system describing a small number of objects can evolve by natural selection.
- Although grammar can be an advantage for small systems, it may be necessary only if the language refers to many events.
- Thus, animals may not possess the need to describe "many" events.

But such speculations leave gaping holes in regard to potential explanations as to why animals cannot use speech. As Deacon noted:

> How could anyone doubt that language complexity is the problem? Languages are indeed complicated things. They are probably orders of magnitude more complicated than the next-most-complicated communication system outside of the human sphere. And they are indeed almost impossibly difficult for other species to acquire (1997, p. 40).

Also, consider that when language first appears on the scene, it already is fully developed and very complex. The late Harvard paleontologist George Gaylord Simpson described it this way:

> Even the peoples with least complex cultures have highly sophisticated languages, with complex grammar and large vocabularies, capable of naming and discussing anything that occurs in the sphere occupied by their speakers. The oldest language that can be reconstructed is already modern, sophisticated, complete from an evolutionary point of view (1966, p. 477).

Chomsky summed it up well when he stated:

> Human language appears to be a unique phenomenon, without significant analogue in the animal world.... There is no reason to suppose that the "gaps" are bridgeable. There is no more of a basis for assuming an evolutionary development from breathing to walking (1972, pp. 67-68).

CONCLUSION

The fact of the matter is, language is quintessentially a human trait. All attempts to shed light on the evolution of human language have failed—due to the lack of knowledge regarding the origin of **any** language, and due to the lack of an animal that possesses any "transitional" form of communication. This leaves evolutionists with a huge gulf to bridge between humans with their innate communication abilities, and the grunts, barks, and chatterings of animals. Deacon lamented:

So this is the real mystery. Even under these loosened criteria, there are no simple languages used among other species, though there are many other equally or more complicated modes of communication. Why not? And the problem is even more counterintuitive when we consider the almost insurmountable difficulties of teaching language to other species. This is surprising, because there are many clever species. Though researchers report that languagelike communication has been taught to nonhuman species, even the best results are not above legitimate challenges, and the fact that it is difficult to prove whether or not some of these efforts have succeeded attests to the rather limited scope of the resulting behaviors, as well as to deep disagreements about what exactly constitutes language-like behavior (1997, p. 41).

Evolutionist R.L. Holloway, in an article on "Paleoneurological Evidence for Language Origins" written for the New York Academy of Sciences, recognized this gaping chasm between humans and animals, and admitted: "The very fact... that human animals are ready to engage in a great 'garrulity' over the merits and demerits of essentially unprovable hypotheses, is an exciting testimony to the gap between humans and other animals" (1976, 280:330). Toward the end of his book, as Deacon was summarizing the conundrum, he noted:

Evolution has widened the cognitive gap between the human species and all others into a yawning chasm. Taken together, the near-universal failure of nonhumans and the near-universal success of humans in acquiring symbolic abilities suggests that this shift corresponds to a major reassignment of cognitive resources to help overcome natural barriers to symbol learning. Other species' failures at symbol learning do not result from the lack of some essential structure present only in human brains. As we have seen, chimpanzees can, under special circumstances, be brought to understand symbolic communication, though at best on a comparatively modest scale (p. 412).

Should you be suspicious when someone says that language evolved? In his paper titled "A Physicist Looks at Evolution," British physicist H.S. Lipson put it well when he wrote:

> I have always been slightly suspicious of the theory of evolution because of its ability to account for any property of living things (the long neck of the giraffe, for example). I have therefore tried to see whether biological discoveries over the last thirty years or so fit in with Darwin's theory. I do not think that they do. To my mind, the theory does not stand up at all (1980, 31:138).

Indeed, the Bible still offers the only plausible explanation for the origin of human language: "Then God said, 'Let Us make man in Our image, according to Our likeness;' ...So God created man in His own image; in the image of God He created him; male and female He created them" (Genesis 1:26-27; cf. Genesis 11:1-9). Humans are capable of communicating in human language because God created them to do so!

6

THE PROBLEM OF THE BRAIN

INTRODUCTION [by Brad Harrub]

On July 17, 1990, U.S. President George H.W. Bush declared that the years between 1990 and 2000 were to be designated as the "Decade of the Brain," and announced that this declaration was intended "to enhance public awareness of the benefits to be derived from brain research" through "appropriate programs, ceremonies, and activities." Millions of grant dollars were shifted toward neurobiological studies to encourage neuroscientists to try to answer some basic questions in this area. It was during this "decade of the brain" that I found myself completing my graduate degree in the neurobiology department at the University of Tennessee Medical School. Those years of in-depth study taught me a great deal about the anatomy and physiology of the brain, and about how it works within the body as a whole. But they also taught me that, as scientists, we are far from unlocking all the secrets that this incredible structure holds. In fact, scientists are not agreed as to how we can unlock the remaining secrets. We now possess the ability to record the activity from a single neuron located deep within the brain, but we can only speculate about the role that particular activity plays in such things as memories or emotions. The more we learn about this complex group of cells, the more we realize we do not know much about the "big picture."

I vividly recall an occasion in which those of us in one of my graduate classes were being asked to explain the molecular events that transpire when a neuron fires. The professor phrased the question something like this: "Suppose for a minute that you want to remember a phone number, what events would take place at the cellular level within the basal ganglia during that thought process?" After a lengthy discussion about calcium and sodium channels, a student in the back of the class spoke up and said, "Yeah, but exactly where would that phone number be stored, and how does the brain remember things?" The professor's answer: We don't know. Robert Ornstein and Richard Thompson summed it up well when they stated: "After thousands of scientists have studied it for centuries, the only word to describe it remains **amazing**" (1984, p. 21, emp. in orig.).

Consider this simple test. Read the following sentence: *Mom had hot apple cider ready for us on that cold snowy day.* In the seconds that were required for you to complete the sentence, your brain already had carried out a multitude of tasks. Initially, your eyes focused on the piece of paper on which the sentence was written, and then transmitted the visual stimuli chemically via your optic nerve to your brain. The brain received that chemical signal, and immediately recognized the symbols on the page as English letters. It then compiled those letters into an entire sentence (using rules that you learned long ago in elementary school), which it analyzed and comprehended. In addition, your brain also may have painted a mental image of this snowy day and your mother. You may even have found yourself suddenly craving a mug of hot apple cider. Also during that short span, your ears reported any unusual sounds, and your nose constantly was sampling the air for new odors. All the while, your brain was keeping your body at homeostasis—that is, it signaled your heart to beat and your lungs to respire, it measured hormone levels in your blood stream (and made adjustments as needed), and relayed any pain or sensation that you might be feeling during those few short seconds. And all of this is merely the proverbial "tip of the iceberg." The brain, and the nerves associated with it, carry out countless physiological functions, most of which we understand at only a very basic level. Again, truth be told, we have yet to understand exactly how this unique organ can perform all of these functions—simultaneously and with such marvelous precision.

And therein lies the enigma surrounding the brain. How can we take three pounds of matter, and in that small space cram all of our education, memories, communication skills, emotions, likes, and dislikes—yet, all the while it is those same three pounds of matter that keep our heart beating, cause our lungs to respire, and give us a detailed internal map of the position of our arms or legs? How is it that a certain smell instantaneously can carry us back to a period in our childhood, offering us crystal clear images of that particular time in our life? Exactly how is it that we can distinguish between a banana and an orange, just by using our nose? What chemical reactions occur to tell us which one is an orange? **Where** is that memory stored, and how long will that memory **remain** stored? What part of our brain controls our emotions? Where do we hold feelings such as love and hate? How is it that the sound of one voice can bring tears of joy, while sounds from another can cause our blood pressure to begin to climb? In fact, why is it that humans love at all?

As vexing as these questions are, they are even more troubling for individuals who espouse that the brain arrived here by Darwinian mechanisms. Evolutionists would like us to believe that the brain is nothing more than an advanced computer—it receives input (via the senses), and after the input makes its way through various neuronal circuits, output is the end result. Input equals output. Ornstein and Thompson speculated: "What exists as only a few extra cells in the head of the earthworm, handling information about taste and light, has evolved in us humans into the incredibly complex and sophisticated structure of the human brain" (1984, p. 22). These sentiments no doubt are shared by thousands of individuals who stand in utter awe of the brain, yet who chalk up its existence to pure happenstance. Is the brain merely the product of evolution, or were humans created differently than animals?

HISTORY OF THE BRAIN

The earliest known reference to the brain anywhere in human records was written on papyrus in the seventeenth century B.C. (see Breasted, 1930). According to James Breasted, the individual who translated and published the contents of that document, the word "brain" occurs only eight times in Egyptian history, six of them on the pages of the Smith Papyrus describing the symptoms, diagnosis, and prognosis of two patients suffering from compound fractures of the skull. The organ that we commonly refer to as the brain has not always held a revered status in the eyes of men. In fact, the brain was given little importance by ancient Egyptians who believed that it cooled the body and did little else. As these skilled preservers of the dead prepared bodies for mummification, they excised the brain through the nose with a wire loop and discarded it. Often, the brain simply was pitched into the sand (primary attention was given to the heart, which they considered the most important organ of the body). The classical Greeks, to whom we owe so many ideas, also were divided over whether the heart or the brain served as the seat of one's intellect. The famed Hippocratic writers rightly believed the brain to be the dominant location for things like intelligence and passion. Plato also taught that the brain was the supreme organ of the body, assigning to it such things as passions of the heart, emotions, and even appetites of the belly. Aristotle, a student of Plato, contended on the other hand that the heart was the center of thought and sensation, believing that the brain worked

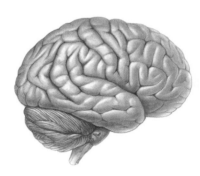

Figure 1 — The human brain. LifeART image copyright © (2003) Lippincott, Williams & Wilkins. All rights reserved. Used by permission.

as a refrigerator to cool the heart (which is ironic, now that we know the brain generates the most heat!). And so, the debate continued for centuries.

At the time the Old Testament was translated into Greek (finished sometime during the second century B.C.), the majority of people adhered to Aristotle's viewpoint, and believed that the heart was the center of understanding. The Scriptures are replete with references to man's intellect and emotions as residing in "the heart"–what we now refer to as "the mind." The King James Version lists 830 occurrences of the word heart in over 762 verses. Just a short period after Christ walked this Earth, a philosopher by the name of Galen (A.D. 130-200) realized Aristotle's mistake, and noted that the "power of sensations and of movement flows from the brain" and that "what is rational in the soul has its existence there" (as quoted in Fincher, 1984, p. 13). He went on to question: "Why is the brain capable of cooling the heart, and why is the heart not rather capable of heating the brain which is placed above it, since all heat tends to rise? And why does the brain send to the heart only an imperceptible nerve impulse, while all the sensory organs draw a large part of their substance from the brain?" Unfortunately, however, early human anatomy was based on a combination of animal dissections and fertile imagination, which only perpetuated the confusion, allowing Shakespeare (1546-1616) to have Portia frame the question, "Tell me, where is fancy bred, Or in the heart or in the head?"

Great discoveries about human physiology and the structure of the human brain were made during the Renaissance Period. Leonardo da Vinci discovered that he could pour wax into the ventricles (open spaces) of an ox brain, and then strip away the flesh after it had cooled. The hardened wax model that resulted, represented the true shape of the cavities that had remained clandestine within the brain for millennia. In the nineteenth century, the debate over the brain/mind erupted into a furor, led by these famous words:

"What is mind?" ––"No matter."

"What is matter?" ––"Never mind."

Eventually, anatomy revealed the truth, and cardiocentric believers found themselves jarred by the fact that during embryonic formation, nerves developed directly from the brain, while blood vessels developed independently from the heart. Further human dissections firmly established that the heart was more or less a pump, while the brain held all of the intricate secrets of consciousness and the senses, including emotions such as love. However, some theories die hard. For instance, we challenge you to find a Valentine's card with a picture of a **brain** with an arrow going through it. While we know that the heart is not the center of our emotions, many people still make references such as "you always will hold a special place in my heart."

Thus, after years of deliberating and conjecture, the cerebral cortex began to be viewed as more than a mere radiator for the heart. Paradoxically, before men even speculated on its higher functions, part of the answers already had been recorded: "…It is to be conceived that the motor force, or the nerves themselves, take their origin from the brain, where fantasy is located" (see Fincher, p. 16). French mathematician René Descartes, who was born in France in 1596, made this fitting declaration. During his lifetime, a series of biological discoveries rocked the scientific world, and stimulated Descartes to probe the brain. He was devoutly religious, and his philosophy was a bold attempt to reconcile scientific methods while remaining true to his faith in God. Descartes was the one who penned the famous words, "*cogito ergo sum*" ("I think, therefore I am"). Accordingly, Descartes defined thinking as the whole range of conscious mental processes–in-

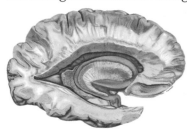

Figure 2 — Cerebral hemisphere dissection demonstrating the cortex. LifeART image copyright © (2003) Lippincott, Williams & Wilkins. All rights reserved. Used by permission.

tellectual thoughts, feeling, will, and sensations. He was of the firm opinion that the mind always was at work, even during periods of sleep. Based on his work, Descartes made a complete and total division between mind and body—one far more drastic than Plato's.

Descartes' work was very important because it established "a modern philosophical basis for the belief that a human being lives a dual existence involving a spiritual soul and a body" (Elbert, 2000, p. 217). However, he believed that the body and soul interacted at a particular place, and he unfortunately felt obligated to try to determine that place. Due to the insufficient knowledge of Descartes' day, he concluded that the interaction took place in the pea-sized pineal gland—a structure that we now know is an endocrine gland that manufactures and secretes melatonin in accordance with our circadian rhythms.

THE EVOLUTION OF THE BRAIN

If you were to walk into a neuroanatomy class at a major medical school, you very likely would find more than fifty white porcelain buckets—each filled with preservative fluids, and containing a brain that had been collected from a donor cadaver. The first thing you would notice as you examined the physical mass of the brain probably would be the various convolutions and wrinkles (known as sulci) that cover the entire surface. Had the brain not been soaking for weeks in a fixative such as formaldehyde, you would be able to see that the brain itself is extremely soft, with almost a custard-like consistency. Upon cutting the brain in half, you would observe what appear to be striations in various areas, and you would find various hollow ventricles that normally are bathed in cerebrospinal fluid. Hidden within this gray and white tissue is the most intricately wired communication network in the world.

Those three pounds of "matter" represent literally billions of interconnected nerve cells and millions of protective glial cells—which, according to evolutionists, arose by the effects of time, natural law, and chance from nonliving matter. The brain has been estimated to contain 100 billion (10^{11}) neurons (Kandel, 1991, p. 18), each a living unit within itself. While most neurons share similar properties, they can be classified into "perhaps as many as 10,000 different types" (p. 18). Over 100 thousand billion electrical connections are estimated to be present throughout the human brain, which has been said to be more than "all the electrical connections in all the electrical appliances in the world." In describing this awesome organ, R.L. Wysong wrote:

> The human brain weighs about three pounds, contains ten billion neurons with approximately 25,000 synapses (connections) per neuron. Each neuron is made up of 10,000,000,000 macromolecules. The human mind can store almost limitless amounts of information (a potential millions of times greater than the 10^{15} bits of information gathered in a lifetime), compare facts, weigh information against memory, judgment and conscience and formulate a decision in a fraction of a second (1976, p. 340, parenthetical item in orig.).

Arguably, the brain is the most unique organ in the entire body—not merely because of its physical make-up, but because of **what** it does and **how** it does it. As evolutionist George Bartelmez put it many years ago: "Only a single fundamental organ has undergone great specialization in the genus *Homo*. This is the brain" (1926, p. 454). Today, from an evolutionary perspective, that assessment still is viewed as correct. As Johanson and Edgar noted seventy years later: "This change in both size and shape represents one of the most remarkable morphological shifts that has been observed in the evolutionary history of any mammal, for it entailed both an enhanced cranial capacity and a radical reorganization of brain proportions" (1996, p. 83).

We believe that the brain deserves a great deal more respect than evolutionists are willing to afford it. The late evolutionist Isaac Asimov characterized the human brain as "the most complex and orderly arrangement of matter in the universe" (1970, p. 10). When Paul Davies, professor of mathematics and physics at the Universe of Adelaide, referred to it as "the most developed and complex system known to science" (1992, 14[5]:4), he did not overstate the case. Sherwin Nuland, in *The Wisdom of the Body*, wrote in regard to the human brain:

> Though the three pounds represent a mere 2 percent of the body weight of a 150-pound person, the quartful of brain is so metabolically active that it uses 20 percent of the oxygen we take in through our lungs. To supply this much oxygen requires a very high flow of blood. Fully 15 percent of the blood propelled into the aorta with each contraction of the left ventricle is transported directly to the brain. Not only does the brain demand a large proportion of the body's oxygen and blood but it also begins its life requiring an equivalent share, or even more, of its genes. Of the total of about 50,000 to 100,000 genes in *Homo sapiens*, some 30,000 code for one or another aspect of the brain. Clearly, a huge amount of genetic information is required to operate the human brain…. From all of this emerges the brain's overarching responsibility—it is the chief means by which the body's activities are coordinated and governed (1997, pp. 328,346).

James Trefil addressed the brain's complexity when he wrote:

> The brain is a physical system. **It contains about 100 billion interconnected neurons—about as many neurons as there are stars in the Milky Way galaxy**…. In the end, by mechanisms we still haven't worked out (but we will do so!), these signals are converted, by neurons in different parts of the brain, into the final signals that produce images or smells or sounds (1996, pp. 217-218, parenthetical item in orig., emp. added).

Notice Trefil's admission that the brain works "by mechanisms we still haven't worked out." Ian Tattersall, in his book, *Becoming Human*, wrote in a similar fashion in describing the brain's marvelous sophistication—while admitting that "there's a huge amount that we don't know."

[T]he brain is an extremely power-hungry mechanism that, because of its size, monopolizes some 20 percent of our entire energy intake.... But the matter doesn't rest there, for sheer brain size is far from the full story. **The organization—the structure—of our brains is also unique, and it is this that appears to hold the ultimate key to our remarkable cognitive powers**. There's a huge amount, of course, that we don't know about how the brain works and especially about how a mass of chemical and electrical signals can give rise to such complex effects as cognition and consciousness (1998, pp. 69,70, emp. added).

The point in Dr. Tattersall's last sentence is well taken. There is a **"huge amount that we don't know"**—including (among other things) how "a mass of chemical and electrical signals can give rise to such complex effects as cognition and consciousness." [Pardon us if we are a bit skeptical of Trefil's exuberant suggestion, "but we will do so!" On this topic, we agree wholeheartedly with Robert Jastrow of NASA, who admitted: "Is it possible that man, with his remarkable powers of intellect and spirit, has been formed from the dust of the earth by chance alone? It is hard to accept the evolution of the human eye as a product of chance; it is even harder to accept the evolution of human intelligence as the product of random disruptions in the brain cells of our ancestors.... Among the organs of the human body, none is more difficult than the brain to explain by evolution. The powers that reside in the brain make man a different animal from all other animals" (1981, pp. 98-99,104).] Tattersall suggested: "Little as we understand the highly complex workings of our brains in producing consciousness, it is clear that there is a 'whole brain' effect in the production of our prized awareness" (2002, p. 73). But, the "whole brain" idea doesn't get us very far, as Daniel Dennett admitted in *Consciousness Explained*.

[T]he trouble with brains, it seems, is that when you look in them, you discover that **there's nobody home**. No part of the brain is the thinker that does

the thinking or the feeler that does the feeling, and
the whole brain appears to be no better a candidate
for that very special role (1991, p. 29, emp. in orig.).

Yet in spite of the fact that when we look at the brain, "there's
nobody home," and in spite of the fact that "neuroscience is
said to be awash with data about what the brain does, but virtually devoid of theories about how it works" (Lewin, 1992, p.
163), there are some things we **do** know.

> The brain, although being **the most complex structure existing on Earth—and perhaps in the Universe**—is a well-defined object: it is a material entity
> located inside the skull, which may be visualized,
> touched and handled. It is composed of chemical substances, enzymes and hormones which may be measured and analyzed. Its architecture is characterized
> by neuronal cells, pathways and synapses. Its functioning depends on neurons, which consume oxygen, exchanging chemical substance through their membranes,
> and maintaining states of electrical polarization interrupted by brief periods of depolarization (Cardoso,
> 1997/1998, emp. in orig.).

> The brain is a helmet-shaped mass of gray and white
> tissue about the size of a grapefruit, one to two quarts
> in volume, and on average weighing three pounds
> (Einstein's brain, for example, was 2.75 pounds). Its
> surface is wrinkled like that of a cleaning sponge, and
> its consistency is custardlike, firm enough to keep from
> puddling on the floor the brain case, soft enough to
> be scooped out with a spoon…. **The human genome
> database accumulated to 1995 reveals that the
> brain's structure is prescribed by at least 3,195
> distinctive genes, 50 percent more than for any
> other organ or tissue**… (Wilson, 1998, p. 97, parenthetical item in orig., emp. added).

> Some overall descriptions of the properties of the human brain are instructive. For instance, **10 billion neurons are packed into the brain, each of which, on
> average, has a thousand links with other neurons,
> resulting in more than sixty thousand miles of writ-**

ing. Connectivity on that scale is beyond comprehension, but undoubtedly it is fundamental to the brain's ability to generate cognition. Although individual events in an electronic compute happen a million times faster than in the brain, **its massive connectivity and simultaneous mode of activity allows biology to outstrip technology for speed**. For instance, the faster computer clocks up a billion or so operations a second, which pales to insignificance beside the 100 billion operations that occur in the brain of a fly at rest.... To say that the brain is a computer is a truism, because, unquestionably, what goes on in there is computation. But so far, no man-made computer matches the human brain, either in capacity or design.... Can a computer think? And, ultimately, can a computer generate a level of consciousness... (Lewin, 1992, pp. 160,163, emp. added).

The human brain's increase in neurons is due to its greater size, not to greater density, since humans have only about 1.25 as many neurons per cubic centimeter as chimpanzees do. There are approximately 146,000 neurons per square millimeter of cortical surface. The human brain has an area of about 2,200 square centimeters and about 30 billion neurons (more than assumed until quite recently). The chimpanzee and the gorilla have brains of about 500 square centimeters, and with about 6 billion neurons (Ornstein, 1991, p. 63, parenthetical item in orig.).

Can anyone—after reading descriptions (and admissions!) such as these—really believe that the human brain is "only another organ" as Michael Lemonick claimed in *Time* magazine (2003a, 161[3]:66)? Not without denying the obvious! In the January 16, 1997 issue of *Nature*, Sir Francis Crick's close collaborator, Christof Koch, wrote: "The latest work on information processing and storage at **the single cell (neuron) level reveals previously unimagined complexity and dynamism**" (385:207, parenthetical item in orig., emp. added). His concluding remarks were: "As always, we are left with a feeling of awe for the amazing complexity found in Nature" (385:210). Amazing complexity? What an understatement!

A case in point is British evolutionist Richard Dawkins. In the preface to his book, *The Blind Watchmaker*, he discussed the brain's incredible complexity and "apparent design," and the problem posed by both.

> The computer on which I am writing these words has an information storage capacity of about 64 kilobytes (one byte is used to hold each character of text). The computer was consciously designed and deliberately manufactured. The brain with which you are understanding my words is an array of some ten million kiloneurones. Many of these billions of nerve cells have each more than a thousand "electric wires" connecting them to other neurons. Moreover, at the molecular genetic level, every single one of more than a trillion cells in the body contains about a thousand times as much precisely coded digital information as my entire computer. **The complexity of living organisms is matched by the elegant efficiency of their apparent design. If anyone doesn't agree that this amount of complex design cries out for an explanation, I give up** (1986, p. ix, emp. added).

But, after having described the brain's immense complexity and "apparent" design, and after being just about ready to "give up," he reconsidered, and wrote:

> No, on second thought I don't give up, because one of my aims in the book is to convey something of the sheer wonder of biological complexity to those whose eyes have not been opened to it. But having built up the mystery, my other main aim is to remove it again by explaining the solution (p. ix).

He then spent the remainder of the book informing the reader (using, of all things, well-designed computer programs!) that the design in nature is merely "apparent," not "real."

But, the question lingers: How did natural selection produce the human brain? Basically, there are two views within the evolutionary camp. Some, like MIT's Steven Pinker, believe that the brain can be broken down into individual components, each of which evolved for specific purposes (see Morris, 2001, p. 208). To quote Pinker:

> The mind, I claim, is not a single organ but a system of organs, which we can think of as psychological faculties or mental modules…. The word "module" brings to mind detachable, snap-in components, and that is misleading. Mental modules are not likely to be visible to the naked eye as circumscribed territories on the surface of the brain, like the flank steak and the rump roast on a supermarket cow display. A mental module probably looks more like roadkill, sprawling messily over the bulges and crevasses of the brain (1997a, pp. 27,30).

Others, having been heavily influenced by a theory set forth by the late paleontologist, Stephen Jay Gould, and his close friend, population geneticist Richard Lewontin, take a different approach. These two Harvard professors advocated the view that the brain evolved for its own set of reasons, and that certain human traits then followed that had nothing whatsoever to do with natural selection. According to Gould:

> …[T]he brain got big by natural selection for a small set of reasons having to do with what is good about brains on the African savannas. But by virtue of that computational power, **the brain can do thousands of things that have nothing to do with why natural selection made it big in the first place**…. Natural selection didn't build our brains to write or to read, that's for sure, because we didn't do those things for so long (1995, emp. added).

Since written language is allegedly a relatively recent evolutionary invention, then it could not be an ability that evolved during ancestral times as hominids roamed the savannas of Africa. Gould's point, then, is that the ability to read and write must be a by-product of the way the brain itself is constructed. Indeed, says Gould, it would be easy to construct quite a large list of human intellectual abilities that could not have been shaped by natural selection. Such a list might include such things as the ability to learn higher mathematics, to understand complicated games like chess, to play a violin, and perhaps even to form linguistic constructions.

In addition to reading and writing, Dr. Gould cited consciousness as a "quirky accident" that was simply a fortuitous, unexpected by-product of the brain having evolved and gotten bigger. A brief history lesson is in order.

In 1978, the Royal Society of London sponsored a symposium on the subject of "adaptation." Dr. Lewontin had been invited to attend, but he does not care much for airplanes. He asked his friend Dr. Gould to co-author the paper with him, and then to present it at the British Symposium. The paper was titled "The Spandrels of San Marco and the Panglossian Paradigm: A Critique of the Adaptationist Programme" (see Gould and Lewontin, 1979), and became famous practically overnight. [NOTE: When Gould and Lewontin referred to the "Panglossian paradigm" in the title of their paper, they were alluding to the ideas espoused by Dr. Pangloss in Voltaire's famous novel, *Candide*. In his novel, Voltaire satirized the beliefs of the eminent German philosopher Gottfried Wilhelm von Leibniz, who maintained that this was "the best of all possible worlds." According to Dr. Pangloss, in this best of all worlds, everything existed for a purpose. For example, in explaining to Candide why he had contracted syphilis, Dr. Pangloss said: "It is indispensable in this best of all possible worlds. For if Columbus, when visiting the West Indies, had not caught this disease, which poisons the source of generation, which frequently even hinders generation, and is clearly opposed to the great end of Nature, we should have neither chocolate nor cochineal" (see Morris, 2001, p. 85).]

The Gould/Lewontin paper (which was published a year later in 1979) began with a description of the central dome of St. Mark's Church (*San Marco* in Italian), located in Venice see Figure 3). The dome is supported by two distinct arches that meet at right angles. The arches divided the dome into four tapering, triangular spaces. As Gould and Lewontin noted, these spaces are an unavoidable by-product of mounting a dome on two rounded arches; the arches could not divide the inner surface of the dome in any other way.

These spaces are known as spandrels. [The term spandrel actually was misapplied by Gould and Lewontin. As it turns out, the correct term is "pendentive," as several authors have pointed out; see Houston, 1990, pp. 498-509; Dennett, 1995, pp. 271-275; Ruse, 2001b, p. 236.] In the spandrels, artisans painted mosaics of the four biblical evangelists (Matthew, Mark, Luke, and John) and mosaic images representing the Tigris, Euphrates, Nile, and Indus rivers. Gould and Lewontin remarked that the spandrels were not created by the architect for any specific purpose. Rather, they were "non-adaptive side effects"; the spandrels **had** to be there. They were not created for the **purpose** of housing mosaics; they were decorated because there were **empty spaces** to be filled.

According to Gould and Lewontin, a similar phenomenon occurs during the course of evolution. Organisms, they suggested, possess numerous traits that were not molded by natural selection. Such traits exist because they are, in effect, by-products of something else (see Schwartz, 1999). This does not mean that these traits are not useful. Once a spandrel exists, natural selection supposedly was able to modify it in some way to make it useful, just as the architects of San Marco found that the triangular spaces (spandrels) could be used for decorative mosaics. The spandrels often turned out to be useful when adapted for **some** purpose, but, as Gould and Lewontin noted, the spandrels originally evolved for secondary purposes. They therefore could not be attributed directly to natural selection.

Figure 3 — The spandrels of San Marco. Image courtesy of Alan Humm.

Three years later, Gould and Yale University paleontologist Elisabeth Vrba invented the term "exaptation" to define and illuminate the role played by spandrels. What, exactly, is an exaptation? Gould explained: "…[W]hat shall we call structures that contribute to fitness but evolved for other reasons and were later co-opted for their current role? They have no name at present, and [Elisabeth] Vrba and I suggest that they be called 'exaptations'" (1984a, p. 66; for Vrba reference, see Gould and Vrba, 1982). Thus, exaptations are spandrels that organisms have adapted for some useful purpose. In a 1997 article he authored for the *New York Review of Books* ("Evolution: The Pleasures of Pluralism"), Gould wrote: "Natural selection made the human brain big, but most of our mental properties and potentials may be spandrels—that is, nonadaptive side consequences of building a device with such structural complexity" (1997a, 44[11]:52).

From an evolutionary viewpoint, the "extraordinary increase in the human brain size was **the fastest evolutionary transformation known**" (Ornstein, 1991, p. 35, emp. added). On some levels, it might make sense that the larger the brain, the more intelligent the animal. However, we now know that brain size does not determine intelligence. The tiny mouse lemur (*Microebus murinus*) has a brain that represents three percent of its overall body weight, whereas the human brain accounts for only two percent, and yet this tiny mouse cannot talk or make complex tools. Simply put, brain size does not determine intelligence. Tattersall put it this way:

> **We know remarkably little about the actual sequence of events in human brain enlargement over time. Even less do we understand the effects of these events….** Intuitively, from a human vantage point, it's hard to avoid the conclusion that, somehow, brain expansion is intrinsically a good thing —though perhaps the contemplation of the extreme rarity of this phenomenon in nature should make us think again…. **[A]s it turns out, the concept of a gradual increase in brain size over the eons is**

> actually rather problematic. For a start, this idea
> strongly implies that every ounce of extra brain
> matter is equivalent in intelligence production
> to every other brain ounce—which is clearly not
> the case (2002, pp. 67,68, emp. added).

No evidence exists that demonstrates a relationship between brain size and intelligence within any given species. The human brain, for example, is known to have a range in volume from less than 1,000 to more than 2,000 cubic centimeters. In fact, some of the most intelligent people in history had small brains.

Yet, evolutionists often classify hominid fossils largely according to brain size (see the chart in Pinker, 1997a, pp. 198-199). They assume that the human brain started out in primates as a relatively small organ, and then evolved through time to the size we now see it. Peter Wilson commented on this in his book, *Man the Promising Primate:*

> We distinguish hominid fossils from other primate
> remains partly by the relative size of the braincase.
> As we move from *Australopithecus africanus* to *Homo
> habilis, Homo erectus,* and finally *Homo sapiens,* we have
> a creature whose probable brain size increases from
> 400 cubic centimeters to 1,500 cubic centimeters. That
> brain is housed in a cranium that becomes more and
> more vaulted, loses its ridges and crests, and shows
> more and more evidence of a forehead and backhead
> (1980, p. 45).

Gould, however, concluded one of the chapters in his book, *Ever Since Darwin,* by asking:

> But **why** did such a large brain evolve in a group of
> small, primitive, tree-dwelling mammals, more sim-
> ilar to rats and shrews than to mammals convention-
> ally judged as more advanced? And with this pro-
> vocative query I end, for **we simply do not know the
> answer to one of the most important questions we
> can ask** (1977a, p. 191, emp. added).

Growing a bigger brain is not quite as straightforward as it first might appear. It is not simply a matter of "putting on weight" like one does with his or her body. Every neuron that is "added" must be of the right kind (excitatory or inhibitory), must possess the right neurotransmitters, and must be "interconnected" with literally thousands of other neurons. Harvard's Ernst Mayr correctly remarked: "The unique character of our brain seems to lie in the existence of many (perhaps as many as forty) different types of neurons, some perhaps specifically human" (2001, p. 252, parenthetical item in orig.).

Also, a rich supply of oxygenated blood must be present, which would entail allowing additional blood vessels to reach these new neurons. Additionally, our brains require a tremendous amount of energy. As an example, a newborn's brain consumes 60% of the energy that the baby produces (Gibbons, 1998b, 280:1345), while adults devote only 20% of their cardiac output to this organ (which accounts for only two percent of our body weight–Van De Graaf and Fox, 1989, p. 438). So the question then becomes, if humans (and their brains) evolved, why would nature "select" for a larger brain that is more energy consuming? Michael Ruse recognized the huge hurdle to be overcome in "evolving" brains when he stated: "When we developed brains, they are so expensive to produce that one needs really big ones or their benefits do not outweigh their costs" (2001a, p. 70). Furthermore, the question must be asked: Where does the energy come from in the first place? It would make sense that supporting a "bigger" brain would require a higher energy consumption, yet a human's basal metabolic rate is no higher than that of a large sheep, which has a brain one-fifth as large. As Gibbons noted: "Humans are apparently getting enough energy to feed their brains without increasing their overall energy intake, so it must be coming from some other source" (1998b, 280:1345). But exactly what that source is, remains to be determined.

Researchers have long known that an animal's body size plays a critical role in brain size (see Gibbons, 280:1345). Whales and elephants compensate for their large brains by an increased size in other organs that can provide energy (e.g., larger heart and lungs provide more oxygen). But humans do not follow this rule. In the context of simian primates, for example, the human brain is approximately "three times larger than the value predicted for an 'average' monkey or ape with our body size" (Jones, et al., 1992, p. 116). If evolutionists are correct, then the human brain has tripled in size since "Lucy" walked the Earth, yet our bodies have yet to even double. According to primatologist Robert D. Martin, humans "have the largest brain size relative to body size among placental mammals" (as quoted in Gibbons, 280:1345). Yet, as Mayr has admitted:

> **What is perhaps most astonishing is the fact that the human brain seems not to have changed one single bit since the first appearance of _Homo sapiens_, some 150,000 years ago**. The cultural rise of the human species from primitive hunter-gatherer to agriculture and city civilizations took place without an appreciable increase in brain size. It seems that in an enlarged, more complex society, a bigger brain is no longer rewarded with a reproductive advantage (2001, p. 252, emp. added).

One question that evolutionists admittedly have difficulty answering is why "other animals" have not similarly "evolved" larger brains. If humans were able to somehow surmount all of the physiological and energy-related obstacles standing in the way of growing larger brains, why have reptiles, birds, or fish not followed suit? Exactly how is our brain different from those of animals? Was it forced to grow larger and "rewire" as we climbed out of trees and changed our diets? Hardly! Evolutionists admit that "our brain is unusually large" and that "its internal wiring shows only subtle differences from other mammals" (Jones, et al., p. 107). But if the wiring is essentially the same, and if we know of animals that have larger brains, then what accounts for the vast differences we see between human intelligence and animal intelligence?

Equally important, of course (at least from the human vantage point) is the question: What caused the tremendous increase in **human** brain size? Scientists admit that no one knows. Johanson and Edgar wrote: "**We cannot answer exactly why we evolved our large brains**" (1996, p. 80, emp. added). Ornstein admitted:

> **We look at whether the human mind is, in part, an accident. Its evolution turns around a central question: Why is our brain so big?** Why have a brain capable of not only chess when there was no game, but of building guided missiles when there was no metal or chemistry or writing? For the brain (which is the most "costly" neural material in the body) ballooned up radically 2 million years ago, and the "usual suspects" for this expansion don't seem to have primary responsibility. It was not language, it was not tools, it was not bipedalism alone. **The brain seems to have increased in size before all the organized societies, cooperation, and language would have had any call for such a development.**

> **This is the central mystery of the mind**: It is difficult to see why we are so advanced relative to our nearest ancestors. We aren't just a slightly better chimp, and it's difficult, on reflection, to figure out why. This gigantic cortex has given us our adaptability as well as the extra capacity to adapt to the heights of the Himalayas, the Sahara Desert, the wilds of Borneo, even to central London....

> Life challenges alone were probably not enough to inspire the astonishing rapidity of brain growth. **There must have been another reason**.... This development occurred well before organized society or language and long before technology. It is an amazing spurt in growth in the most complicated structure in all biology (1991, pp. 8,37, parenthetical item in orig., emp. added).

But was it the brain's size alone that allowed these "nonadaptive side consequences"? Apparently not, as Johanson and Edgar went on to note.

> In absolute size, the human brain breaks no records. Elephant brains exceed ours by a factor of four, and some whale brains are even bigger.... Monkeys, apes, and humans possess the biggest brains relative to body weight of any terrestrial mammal. So, part of the answer is that the human brain is just a highly elaborated ape brain. Yet this is still something different, something unique, about the size of the human brain. Our brain is three times larger than the predicted size for a hypothetical non-human primate of average body size.... **But size isn't everything.** Our brain also differs significantly from those of apes in the proportion of various parts.... The human brain is a sponge that soaks up sensations and observations, and it is a masterful organ for storing, retrieving, and processing a wide range of detailed and complicated information.... So, **size alone does not explain our unusual mental abilities.** What counts is what's inside the package and how it is all arranged... (p. 80, emp. added).

Earlier, we quoted Ian Tattersall, who ended his assessment of the brain with these comments: "There's a huge amount, of course, that we don't know about how the brain works and especially about how a mass of chemical and electrical signals can give rise to such complex effects as cognition and consciousness" (1998, p. 70). We also quoted Richard Morris, who lamented:

> Scientific knowledge of the brain is woefully incomplete. **Scientists do not know how the brain acquires and stores information, how it produces feelings of pleasure and pain, or how it creates consciousness. The functioning of the human brain is a profound mystery** (2001, p. 200, emp. added).

We could not have said it better ourselves. Evolutionists do not know how the brain evolved. Nor do they have much understanding about how the brain acquires and stores information, in spite of decades of intensive research. Ernst Mayr of Harvard admitted: "The synapses, for instance, apparently play an important role in memory retention, but how they do so is almost entirely unknown" (2001, p. 252). Similarly, evolutionists do not know how the brain creates consciousness (a subject we will examine in the next chapter). Yet the leading candidate to serve as a potential evolutionary explanation for the mind (and then, ultimately, consciousness) is, perhaps somewhat conspicuously, the brain. Some (like Pinker and his colleagues) believe that the brain evolved its specific regions with a purpose (if you will pardon the pun) "in mind." Others, like Gould and his followers, believe that, to quote Ornstein, "structures that evolved for one purpose later changed their function" and gave rise to consciousness (1991, p. 33). Not much agreement here, to be sure.

But there is one place where a consensus **does** exist. Monroe Strickberger, in his textbook, *Evolution*, put it like this: "[A]lthough we do not yet know the precise relationship between the matter of the brain (neurons, synapses, and so on) and the thoughts and feelings it produces, **that such a relationship exists is no mystery**" (2000, p. 56, parenthetical item in orig., emp. added). **That** a relationship between brain, mind, and consciousness exists may be "no mystery." But **why** and **how** that relationship exists, certainly **is**!

Perhaps it is because of the mystery that surrounds the various functions and attributes of the brain that, as our knowledge of the brain has multiplied in what sometimes seems to be almost a geometric progression, it has becoming increasingly popular to "downplay" the extreme complexity of the brain itself—no doubt in the hope that the general populace will begin to think like this: "Well, if the once-impenetrable fortress of humanity that is the human brain has now been breached and explained by science, we have answered the most basic issue: evolution's major problem is solved!" Attempts to minimize the brain's amazing abilities have become rather commonplace. Consider just one example.

In an article on mind/body problems titled "The Power of Mood" that he authored for the January 20, 2003 issue of *Time* magazine, Michael D. Lemonick commented:

> **The brain, after all, is only another organ**, and it operates on the same biochemical principles as the thyroid or the spleen. What we experience as feelings, good or bad, are at the cellular level no more than a complex interaction of chemicals and electrical activity (2003a, 161[3]:66, emp. added).

In the introductory article ("Your Mind, Your Body") he wrote to accompany the feature articles in that same issue of *Time*, he suggested:

> **Mind and body, psychologists and neurologists now agree, aren't that different.** The brain is just another organ, albeit more intricate than the rest.... Scientists are also learning something else. Not only is the mind like the rest of the body, but the well-being of one is intimately intertwined with that of the other. **This makes sense because they share the same systems**—nervous, circulatory, endocrine and immune (2003b, 161[3]:63, emp. added).

In *The God Experiment,* Russell Stannard wrote:

> It is a widely held assumption that nothing goes on in the brain that is markedly different from what happens in inanimate matter. Although the processes occurring in the brain are undoubtedly more intricate because of the extreme complexity of the physical structure, **they are nevertheless all to be held accountable for—in principle—through the operation of the well-established laws of nature** (2000, p. 45, emp. added).

Tufts University philosopher Daniel Dennett, in an interview on this very subject, said matter-of-factly: "The mind is somehow nothing but a physical phenomenon. **In short, the mind is the brain**..." (as quoted in Lewin, 1992, p. 157, emp. added). Nuland took the same approach.

The mind is a man-made concept, a way to categorize and contemplate the manifestations of certain physical and chemical actions that occur chiefly in the brain. It is a product of anatomic development and physiologic functioning. What we call the mind is an activity, made up of a totality of the innumerable constituent activities of which it is composed, brought to awareness by the brain. The brain is the chief organ of the mind, but not its only one. In a sense, every cell and molecule in the body is a part of the mind, and every organ contributes to it. **The living body and its mind are one—the mind is a property of the body** (1997, p. 349, emp. added).

In *The Astonishing Hypothesis*, Francis Crick even went so far as to suggest that it soon may be possible to identify specific neurons in the brain that cause consciousness. He asserted that, eventually, all mind processes, including consciousness, will be explicable as nothing more than the firing of neurons—i.e., in terms of interactions between atoms and molecules (1994, pp. 3,259). Steven Pinker is on record as stating: **"Nothing in the mind exists except as neural activity"** (1997b, emp. added). B.A. Farrel announced bluntly: "A human being is a modulator of pulse frequencies, and nothing more" (as quoted in Allan, 1989, p. 63). Or, as Jerome Elbert put it: "I **do** maintain that 'mental events can be reduced to brain events'" (2000, p. 265, emp. in org.). He then predicted:

> Science will probably succeed in describing how our consciousness arises from natural processes. It will probably explain how thinking, reasoning, emotions, motivations, and intuition function as a result of the activity of the brain, and as a result of the brain interacting with the rest of the body and the outside world (p. 268).

Think with us for a moment, however, about the implications of what you have just read. Beliefs have consequences! If: (a) "what we experience as feelings, good or bad, are at the cellular level no more than a complex interaction of chemicals and electrical activity"; (b) "mind and body...aren't that different"; (c) "the mind is a property of the body" and "mind is a man-made concept"; (d) "nothing in the mind exists except as neural activity," **what does all of this mean**?

Let Steven Pinker explain. He believes (as noted above) that "nothing in the mind exists except as neural activity." Would it surprise you to learn, then, that in a *New York Times* article, Pinker suggested that women who murder their newborn babies may not be either mad or evil, but simply unconsciously obeying "primeval instincts to sacrifice their children for the good of the tribe"? (see Blanchard, 2000, p. 382). In his fascinating book, *Does God Believe in Atheists?*, John Blanchard addressed Dr. Pinker's suggestion: "This is the logical outworking of materialism, **but if reducing the brain's activity to electrical impulses can sanction murder, what can it condemn?**" (p. 382, emp. in orig.).

What indeed? Atheistic philosopher Michael Ruse admitted that if evolution is accepted as true, then **"morality is no more...than an adaptation**, and as such has the same status as such things as teeth and eyes and noses" (1995, p. 241, emp. added). But if, as Ruse went on to say, "morality is a creation of the genes" (p. 290), then by what criterion, or group of criteria, do humans make moral decisions? Reichenbach and Anderson commented on this very issue when they wrote:

> Reductionism, however, threatens the very concept of the person. Where persons' actions and beliefs are ultimately explainable in terms of unpredictable neural firings and chemical transfers, those acts and beliefs are no longer the purposeful product of human choice.... **This means that reductionism is particularly disastrous for morality, not to mention our concept of personhood itself** (1995, p. 279, emp. added).

And what place is there for the famed human possession, "free will"? Are we merely products of our environment? Does input truly equal output? Nancey Murphy recognized the quandary of losing our free will and reducing the brain to little more than matter.

> First, if mental effects can be reduced to brain events, and the brain events are governed by the laws of neurology (and ultimately by the laws of physics), then in what sense can we say that humans have free will? Are not their intendings and willings simply a product of blind physical forces, and thus are not their willed actions merely the product of the blind forces? (1998, p. 131).

She went on to comment:

> Second, if mental events are simply the products of neurological causes, then what sense can we make of reasons? That is, we give reasons for judgments in all areas of our intellectual lives—moral, aesthetic, scientific, mathematical. It seems utter nonsense to say that these judgments are merely the result of the blind forces of nature (p. 131).

Have we no option but to do whatever our genes have programmed us to do? In other words, how can the materialist escape from the stranglehold of determinism—the idea which suggests, as its name implies, that everything we do is "determined," and that we have, in essence, no free will. This farcical idea is exactly what Cornell professor William Provine has advocated. In 1998, during "Darwin Day" at the University of Tennessee at Knoxville, he delivered the keynote lecture titled "Evolution: Free Will and Punishment and Meaning in Life." During that lecture, he displayed a slide that stated: "Finally, free will is nonexistent." It went on to note: "Free will is the worst of all cultural inventions. Belief in free will fuels our revenge-minded culture" (Provine, 1998).

In the now-famous text of his Compton Lectures, *Objective Knowledge: An Evolutionary Approach*, British philosopher Sir Karl Popper made the point that even if determinism **were** true, it could not be argued, since any argument is itself presumably predetermined by purely physical conditions—as would be any opposing arguments. As Popper put it:

> According to determinism, any such theories—such as, say, determinism—are held because of a certain physical structure of the holder (perhaps of his brain).

> Accordingly, we are deceiving ourselves (and are physically so determined as to deceive ourselves) whenever we believe that there are such things as arguments or reasons which make us accept determinism. Or in other words, physical determinism is a theory which, if it is true, is not arguable, since it must explain all our reactions, including what appear to us as beliefs based on arguments, as due to **purely physical conditions**. Purely physical conditions, including our physical environment, make us say or accept whatever we say or accept… (1972, p. 223, emp. added).

In their book, *The Wonder of Being Human: Our Brain and Our Mind*, Sir John Eccles and his co-author Daniel Robinson commented on the correctness of Popper's assessment—and the absurd nature—of determinism when they observed: "This is an effective *reductio ad absurdum*" (reduction to the absurd —BH/BT]. They then went on to state: "This stricture applies to all of the materialist theories" (1984, p. 38; cf. also Eccles, 1992, p. 21). Yes, it **is** absurd. And yes, it **does** apply to "all of the materialist theories."

A good illustration of this is the life, teachings, and actions of the French novelist commonly known as the Marquis de Sade (1740-1814), who gave his name to sadism, in which a person derives sexual satisfaction from inflicting pain and humiliation on others. De Sade argued that, since everything is chemically determined, whatever is, is right. The distinguished microbiologist, Lynn Margulis, and her co-author/son Dorion Sagan, discussed this very point in their book, *What is Life?*

> The high-born Frenchman Donatien Alphonse Francois de Sade (1740-1814) keenly felt the vanishing basis for morality. **If Nature was a self-perpetuating machine and no longer a purveyor of divine authority, then it did not matter what he, as the infamous marquis de Sade, did or wrote** (1995, p. 40, emp. added).

Or, as Ravi Zacharias put it: "Thinking atoms discussing morality is absurd" (1990, p. 138).

In his book, *In the Blood: God, Genes and Destiny*, Steve Jones suggested that criminal behavior was determined largely by genetic make-up (1996, pp. 207-220). In discussing Jones' book, one writer, Janet Daley, insisted that if genetics is found to be ultimately responsible for "bad" traits, then it also must account for "good" ones. As she observed: "If we can never be truly guilty, then we can never be truly virtuous either." Daley went on to say:

> Human beings are only capable of being moral insofar as they are free to choose how they behave. If they have no power to make real choices–if their freedom to decide how to act is severely limited by forces outside their control–then it is nonsense to make any ethical judgements about them. It would be wrong, as well, to base a judicial system on the assumption that people are free to choose how they will act. The idea of putting anyone on trial for anything at all becomes absurd (1996).

In fact, attempting to locate a "basis for morality" in the blind outworkings of nature is futile. As Ruse put it: "There is no justification for morality in the ultimate sense" (as quoted in O'Hear, 1997, p. 140). In Dave Hunt's words, "There are no morals in nature. Try to find a compassionate crow or an honest eagle–or a sympathetic hurricane" (1996, p. 41). Are those who advocate the idea that "nothing in the mind exists except as neural activity," willing to accept the consequences of their belief?

GROWING NEURONS

Every human begins life as a single fertilized cell. When the male and female gametes join to form the zygote that will grow into the fetus, it is at that very moment that the formation of a new body begins. It is the result of a **viable** male gamete joined sexually with a **viable** female gamete, which has formed a zygote that will move through a variety of important stages.

The first step in the process—which eventually will result in the highly differentiated tissues and organs that compose the body of the neonatal child—is the initial mitotic cleavage of that primal cell, the zygote. At this point, the genetic material doubles, matching copies of the chromosomes move to opposite poles, and the cell cleaves into two daughter cells. Shortly afterwards, each of these cells divides again, forming the embryo. [In humans and animals, the term "embryo" applies to any stage after cleavage but before birth (see Rudin, 1997, p. 125).]

As the cells of the embryo continue to divide, they form a cluster of cells. These divisions are accompanied by additional changes that produce a hollow, fluid-filled cavity inside the ball, which now is a one-layer-thick grouping of cells known as a blastula. Early on the second day after fertilization, the embryo undergoes a process known as gastrulation, in which the single-layer blastula turns into a three-layered gastrula consisting of ectoderm, mesoderm, and endoderm, surrounding a cavity known as the archenteron. Each of these layers will give rise to very specific structures. For example, the ectoderm will form the outermost layer of the skin and other structures, including the sense organs, parts of the skeleton, and the nervous system. The mesoderm will form tissues associated with support, movement, transport, reproduction, and excretion (i.e., muscle, bone, cartilage, blood, heart, blood vessels, gonads, and kidneys). The endoderm will produce structures associated with breathing and digestion (including the lungs, liver, pancreas, and other digestive glands) [see Wallace, 1975, p. 187].

Within 72 hours after fertilization, the embryo will have divided a total of four times, and will consist of sixteen cells. Each cell will divide before it reaches the size of the cell that produced it; hence, the cells will become progressively smaller with each division. About twenty-two days after fertilization, the brain begins its embryonic development with the formation of the neural tube. About twenty-two days after fertilization, this hollow region begins to develop (Moore and Persaud, 1993, p. 385). The cells located within this hollow tube eventually will multiply, migrate, and become the brain and spinal cord. Once the brain is fully developed, three distinct regions can be identified: forebrain, midbrain, and hindbrain. Structures such as the cerebrum, thalamus, and hypothalamus are located within the forebrain. The midbrain is made up of the superior and inferior colliculi and the cerebral peduncles. The hindbrain is composed primarily of the cerebellum, pons, and medulla oblongata. Literally millions of neurons are housed in each of these structures, from which radiate communicating axons to other regions to allow the entire brain the unique ability to communicate with itself (thanks to a small structure known as the corpus callosum, the left and right hemispheres of the brain possess the ability to communicate with one another).

While regions and structures within the brain have been dissected exhaustively and mapped out considerably, what can those neurological pathways tell us about **function**? Can we look at the exterior surface of the brain and determine the intellectual capabilities of an individual? Evolutionists must think so; look at the "dumb," hairy, club-carrying creatures that they portray as our ancestors. These evolutionists would like to be able to look at a fossilized skull, or even an endocranial cast, and determine what "prehuman" brains were capable of doing in the distant past. However, as Terrence Deacon admitted: "Surface morphology and underlying brain functions are not directly correlated in most cases." He went on to say, therefore, that "we must be careful when drawing functional interpretations from endocasts" (1999, p. 116).

Many materialists are adamant that the human brain has evolved through a layering process—with each "higher species" adding a new layer. Thus, as Ian Tattersall remarked in his book, *The Monkey in the Mirror*, "as far as is known, not much if anything has been 'lost' in the course of human brain evolution. Our skulls still house the descendants of structures that eons ago governed the behavior of ancient fish, of primitive mammals, and of early primates" (2002, p. 72).

According to this "triune" brain theory, the brain evolved in three stages: the reptilian brain, followed by the paleocortex, and then the neocortex. Thus, the innermost portion of our brain is said to be the reptilian brain—since evolutionists believe it to be the oldest and most primitive portion. It therefore would include structures such as the pons and medulla, and would handle many of the autonomic tasks needed for survival (e.g., breathing). According to evolutionists, this portion of our brain has remained basically unchanged by evolution, and we therefore share it with all animals that possess a backbone. The next layer is said to be the mammalian brain or the paleocortex, which is alleged to have arisen when mammals evolved from reptiles. It would include structures such as the amygdala and hypothalamus. Then, on top of this, evolutionists claim we have added another layer—the neocortex or human brain, which allows humans to handle logic. This new layer is said to "envelop" the other layers in gray matter, and amounts to 85% of the human brain mass. In his biography of Carl Sagan, William Poundstone observed that even Sagan propagated this myth. He noted: "His extended discussion of the triune brain implicitly endorses it as (at least) an interesting idea. That was what some neurologists found objectionable. 'It's dismaying for people like us,' complained Boyd Campbell of Walter Reed Army Medical Center, 'to see Sagan come and swallow all that stuff, write *The Dragons of Eden*, and get a Pulitzer Prize for it' " (1999, p. 254, parenthetical item in orig.). Dismaying, to be sure. As James Trefil pointed out, this way of thinking is "completely wrong":

> Unfortunately, this understanding of the brain has led to a rather oversimplified notion of brain function in some parts of the popular press—in which the brain is seen as a set of successive overlays. At the bottom (the brain stem and diencephalons) is a kind of primitive, reptilian brain shared with all animals, with progressive overlying refinements added until we get to the cerebral cortex, which reflects the highest brain functions. In its extreme form, this view presents the

idea of the brain as a kind of sedimentary structure, like the stratifications of the Grand Canyon. Each new layer adds a new function, while underlying layers stay more or less the same. This is another of those concepts that the French call a *fausse idée claire*. **It's simple, elegant, clear, and completely wrong** (1997, p. 75, parenthetical item in orig., emp. added).

And yet the textbooks still show a progression through fish, amphibians, reptiles, and mammals. This theory of how the brain evolved in layers has suffered the same fate as that of a soufflé when the oven door is slammed—it has fallen flat.

THE BRAIN VERSUS A COMPUTER

Walk into any office, hospital, or even grocery store, and you will find yourself in the presence of computers. Computers have become an integral part of our everyday lives—they even played a role in getting this book to you. But most intelligent individuals will agree that computers did not arrive on this planet by time, natural law, and chance. Computers are designed and manufactured, and they constantly are being improved to increase their speed and capabilities. But the computer fails miserably in comparison to the human brain. When is the last time a computer grabbed a pencil to compose a sonnet, a short story, or a poem? How many computers are capable of taking a piece of wood, fashioning it in the shape of a violin, and then sitting down to play Barber's *Adagio for Strings*. And yet evolutionists insist that the human brain—an object far more complex, and with far more capabilities than a computer—"evolved" in order to provide us with memories, emotions, the ability to reason, and the ability to talk. Other individuals like to "simplify" the human brain down to the level of modern-day computers. They rationalize that, like computers, the human brain can rapidly process, store, and recall bits of information. Also, some scientific investigators compare neuronal connections to the wiring found within computers. However, the inner workings of a computer always can be reduced to one thing—electronics. The basic function of computers always involves the movement of an electrical charge in a semiconductor. The brain, on the other hand, operates purely on electrochemical reactions. The transmission of nerve signals involves chemicals known as neurotransmitters. Once a neuron is caused to fire, it moves these neurotransmitters into the tiny space between itself and the neighboring neurons (at the synapse), in order to stimulate them.

Additionally we know that the human brain can reason and think—i.e., we possess self-awareness. Computers have the ability to carry out multiple tasks, and they can even carry out complex processes—but not without the programming and instruction they receive from humans. Additionally, computers do not possess the ability to reason. When asked to translate into Russian the sentence—"the spirit is willing but the flesh is weak" —one computer came up with words that meant "the vodka is fine, but the meat is tasteless" (Allan, 1989, p. 68)—which is a far cry from the original meaning. Nor are computers self-aware. In comparing a modern-day computer to the awesome power of the human brain, astrophysicist Robert Jastrow admitted: "The machine would be a prodigious artificial intelligence, but it would be only a clumsy imitation of the human brain" (1981, p. 143).

It has been estimated that if we learned something new every second of our lives, it would take three million years to exhaust the capacity of the human brain (Weiss, 1990, p. 103). Plainly put, the brain is not just an advanced computer. All those convolutions and neuronal networks are the result of an intelligent Creator. If we are able to rationalize that a computer found in the middle of the Sahara Desert did not just "happen" by random chance, then why are so many willing to believe that a far more complex human brain occurred in such a fashion?

TWELVE CRANIAL NERVES

We all have experienced the unpleasantness of sitting in front of a doctor with our tongue outstretched, saying "Ah," while the physician gags us with a wooden tongue depressor.

Interestingly, this dreadful routine, which is performed on a daily basis in clinics and doctors' offices around the world, has an important purpose. By having you open your mouth, protrude your tongue, vocalize the word "Ah," and confirm an intact gag reflex, doctors are able to not only look at the back of your throat, but also to assess many of your cranial nerves. Every human is born with twelve pairs of these special nerves, each performing a different function, and each going to a different location within the body.

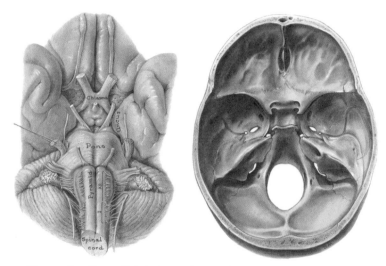

Figure 4 — Superficial view of cranial nerves and the interior base of the skull demonstrating the various foramina. LifeART image copyright © (2003) Lippincott, Williams & Wilkins. All rights reserved. Used by permission.

Unlike nerves that originate from your spinal cord, cranial nerves drop directly out of the brain and then proceed to their target organs. Recall, however, that your brain is completely encased in bone—your skull. So, exactly how do these twelve cranial nerves get to where they need to go? Quite simply, they travel through well-placed foramina or "holes." Each pair of nerves has a specific "hole" through which it descends in order to reach a target such as the eye (optic nerve) or the heart (vagus nerve). If you were to take a skull and pour water where the brain normally would be sitting, you soon would notice water coming out of several different holes. These holes allow the cranial nerves to travel from the brain to their target organs. But ask yourself this question: How did the holes get there? Did they evolve, too? Did these cranial nerves simply "evolve" out of the brain and then wait around until holes evolved in the skull? And let's not make a small issue out of these tiny holes: the brain is constantly bathed in cerebro-spinal fluid—a fluid that you do not want "leaking" out of the cranium. The formation of the holes and the dural layers that prevent this "leakage" definitely point to an intelligent Designer.

CONCLUSION

Neuroscientists already have gone, to use the Star Trek mantra, "where no one has gone before." Scientists now possess the ability to record the neurological activity from a single neuron. Using ultra-fine microelectrodes, we can proceed down through the cortex of the brain and patch-clamp neurons in order to determine exactly what ionic changes are occurring across the neuronal membranes. We have the ability to use tracer dyes to detect where a nerve sends a specific signal. Entire maps have been made that demonstrate the neurological pathways of specific types of neurons. We have tremendous hope that new areas of research, such as neuronal stem cells and nerve growth factors, will relieve or cure some of the neurological diseases that exist today. But science is far from understanding and comprehending the complexity of the brain. In fact, the brain remains a puzzle with far more pieces missing than have been properly set in place to complete the puzzle.

Upon hearing of the death of a child, a mother will begin to weep uncontrollably. What actually caused the tears to flow down her face? Where does she hold those treasured memories of her offspring? Some scientists would have us believe that those tears are merely a product of organic evolution, and that through time, humans "naturally selected" for them. But why? Man can reason, laugh, cry, and even worship. Why would we selectively want to cry at the loss of a loved one? Or why would our fleshly "brain" go to great lengths to worship and praise something it has never seen—unless we are more than mere matter? Evolutionist Steven Pinker wrestled with this point in his book, *How the Mind Works.*

> How does religion fit into a mind that one might have thought was designed to reject the palpably not true? The common answer—that people take comfort in the thought of a benevolent Sheperd, a universal plan, or an afterlife—is unsatisfying, because it only raises the question of why a mind would evolve to find comfort in beliefs it can plainly see are false. A freezing person finds no comfort in believing he is warm; a person face-to-face with a lion is not put at ease by the conviction that it is a rabbit (1997a, pp. 554-555).

The precision and complexity of our brain, and the manner in which it is able to interact with our mind, clearly point to an intelligent Designer. Writing in the *Bulletin of Atomic Scientists,* psychologist Roger Sperry of the California Institute of Technology observed:

> Before science, man used to think himself a free agent possessing free will. Science gives us, instead, causal determinism wherein every act is seen to follow inevitably from preceding patterns of brain excitation. Where we used to see purpose and meaning in human behavior, science now shows us a complex bio-physical machine composed entirely of material elements, all of which obey inexorably the universal laws of physics and chemistry.... I find that my own conceptual working model of the brain leads to inferences that are in direct disagreement with many of the foregoing; especially I must take issue with that whole general materialistic-reductionist conception of human nature and mind that seems to emerge from the currently prevail-

ing objective analytic approach in the brain-behaviour sciences. When we are led to favour the implications of modern materialism in opposition to older, more idealistic values in these and related matters, **I suspect that science may have sold society and itself a somewhat questionable bill of goods** (1966, pp. 2-3, emp. added)

We suspect so, too.

7

THE EVOLUTION OF CONSCIOUSNESS [PART I]

"Once consciousness was established, there was no going back" (Richard Leakey, 1994, p. 149).

"We have reached the stage where ignoring the problem will not cause it to go away" (Eccles and Robinson, 1984, p. 17).

In a book review that Joel Peck authored about the *Encyclopedia of Evolution* for the February 27, 2003 issue of *Nature*, he commented: "Given the relatively small number of working evolutionary biologists, the field receives a surprisingly large amount of media attention" (421:895). Yes, it does. However, while it might be said that sifting through the jumble of scientific and philosophical literature on organic evolution makes for a somewhat interesting journey, truth be told, it is not always an educational one. At practically every turn, the things that evolutionists admittedly recognize as **unknown** far outweigh those that they claim are **known**. Questions vastly outnumber answers. Problems greatly exceed solutions. Theories increasingly eclipse facts. Doubts routinely overshadow certainties. Nothing is what it seems.

Think this is an exaggeration? Think again. In the specific areas of evolutionary thought that are incontrovertibly the most important for the theory's hegemony and success, one finds everywhere "challenges," "problems," "enigmas," "mysteries," "puzzles," "disappointments," and yes, at times, even a strong dose of obfuscation. We would like to illustrate this claim by presenting a few brief examples.

THE ORIGIN OF LIFE

Take, for example, the very origin of life itself. As long ago as 1957, evolutionary anthropologist Loren Eiseley summed up the matter in his classic text, *The Immense Journey*, when he wrote:

> With the failure of these many efforts, science was left in the somewhat embarrassing position of having to postulate theories of living origins which it could not demonstrate. **After having chided the theologian for his reliance on myth and miracle, science found itself in the unenviable position of having to create a mythology of its own: namely, the *assumption* that what, after long effort, could not be proved to take place today, had, in truth, taken place in the primeval past** (pp. 201-202, emp. and italics added).

From that day to this, the situation has not changed one iota. Follow the time line. In 1961, Harry Fuller and Oswald Tippo admitted in their text, *College Botany*:

> The evidence of those who would explain life's origin on the basis of the accidental combination of suitable chemical elements is no more tangible than that of those people who place their faith in Divine Creation as the explanation of the development of life. Obviously the latter have just as much justification for their belief as do the former (p. 25).

Six years later, in speaking of the concept of spontaneous generation, evolutionists D.E. Green and R.F. Goldberger wrote in their text, *Molecular Insights into the Living Process:*

> There is one step [in evolution—BH/BT] that far outweighs the others in enormity: the step from macromolecules to cells. All the other steps can be accounted

for on theoretical grounds—if not correctly, at least elegantly. However, **the macromolecule to cell transition is a jump of fantastic dimensions, which lies beyond the range of testable hypothesis**. In this area, all is conjecture. The available facts do not provide a basis for postulation that cells arose on this planet. This is not to say that some paraphysical forces were not at work. **We simply wish to point out that there is no scientific evidence** (1967, pp. 406-407, emp. added).

Almost a decade-and-a-half after that, Nobel laureate Sir Francis Crick wrote:

An honest man, armed with all the knowledge available to us now, could only state that in some sense, **the origin of life appears at the moment to be almost a miracle**, so many are the conditions which would have had to have been satisfied to get it going (1981, p. 88, emp. added).

After another four years had passed, evolutionist Andrew Scott authored an article in *New Scientist* on the origin of life titled "Update on Genesis," in which he observed:

Take some matter, heat while stirring, and wait. That is the modern version of Genesis. The "fundamental" forces of gravity, electromagnetism and the strong and weak nuclear forces are presumed to have done the rest.... But how much of this neat tale is firmly established, and how much remains hopeful speculation? In truth, the mechanism of almost every major step, from chemical precursors up to the first recognizable cells, is the subject of either controversy or complete bewilderment.

We are grappling with a classic "chicken and egg" dilemma. Nucleic acids are required to make proteins, whereas proteins are needed to make nucleic acids and also to allow them to direct the process of protein manufacture itself.

The emergence of the gene-protein link, an absolutely vital stage on the way up from lifeless atoms to ourselves, is still shrouded in almost complete mystery....

We still know very little about how our genesis came about, and to provide a more satisfactory account than we have at present remains one of science's great challenges (1985, 106:30-33, emp. added).

John Horgan concluded that if he were in the creationist camp today, he would focus on the subject of the origin of life because, he has suggested, this

...is by far the weakest strut of the chassis of modern biology. The origin of life is a science writer's dream. It abounds with exotic scientists and exotic theories, which are never entirely abandoned or accepted, but merely go in and out of fashion (1996, p. 138).

In an article titled "The Origin of Life: More Questions Than Answers," well-known origin-of-life researcher Klaus Dose pointed out:

More than 30 years of experimentation on the origin of life in the fields of chemical and molecular evolution have led to a better perception of the immensity of the problem of the origin of life on Earth rather than to its solution. **At present all discussions on principal theories and experiments in the field either end in stalemate or in a confession of ignorance** (1988, 13[4]:348, emp. added).

Or, as renowned physicist Paul Davies and his coworker, Phillip Addams, noted:

Some scientists say, just throw energy at it and it will happen spontaneously. That is a little bit like saying: put a stick of dynamite under the pile of bricks, and bang, you've got a house! Of course you won't have a house, you'll just have a mess. **The difficulty in trying to explain the origin of life is in accounting for how the elaborate organizational structure of these complex molecules came into existence spontaneously from a random input of energy. How did these very specific complex molecules assemble themselves?** (1998, pp. 47-48, emp. added).

THE ORIGIN OF THE GENETIC CODE

Or, consider the origin of the genetic code. Evolutionist Douglas Hofstadter remarked:

> A natural and fundamental question to ask on learning of these incredibly interlocking pieces of software and hardware is: "How did they ever get started in the first place?" It is truly a baffling thing. One has to imagine some sort of bootstrap process occurring, somewhat like that which is used in the development of new computer language–but a bootstrap from simple molecules to entire cells is almost beyond one's power to imagine. There are various theories on the origin of life. They all run aground on this most central of all central questions: "How did the Genetic Code, along with the mechanisms for its translation (ribosomes and RNA molecules) originate?" **For the moment, we will have to content ourselves with a sense of wonder and awe, rather than with an answer** (1980, p. 548, emp. added).

Leslie Orgel, one of the "heavyweights" in origin-of-life studies, similarly admitted:

> We do not yet understand even the general features of the origin of the genetic code.... **The origin of the genetic code is the most baffling aspect of the problem of the origins of life**, and a major conceptual or experimental breakthrough may be needed before we can make any substantial progress (1982, p. 151, emp. added).

Writing in *Nature* on "The Genesis Code by Numbers," evolutionist John Maddox commented:

> It was already clear that the genetic code is not merely an abstraction but the embodiment of life's mechanisms; the consecutive triplets of nucleotides in DNA (called codons) are inherited but they also guide the construction of proteins. So **it is disappointing that the origin of the genetic code is still as obscure as the origin of life itself** (1994, 367:111, emp. added).

THE ORIGIN OF SEX

Consider, too, the origin of sex. In his book, *The Master-piece of Nature: The Evolution of Genetics and Sexuality*, Graham Bell described the dilemma in the following manner:

> **Sex is the queen of problems in evolutionary biology**. Perhaps no other natural phenomenon has aroused so much interest; certainly none has sowed as much confusion. The insights of Darwin and Mendel, which have illuminated so many mysteries, have so far failed to shed more than a dim and wavering light on the central mystery of sexuality, emphasizing its obscurity by its very isolation (1982, p. 19, emp. added).

Much of nature reproduces sexually, yet evolutionists do not have the first clue as to how sex evolved. Sir John Maddox (quoted above), who served for over twenty-five years as the distinguished editor of *Nature*, the prestigious journal published by the British Association for the Advancement of Science (and who was knighted by Queen Elizabeth II in 1994 in recognition of his "multiple contributions to science"), authored an amazing book titled *What Remains to be Discovered*, in which he addressed the origin of sex, and stated forthrightly: "The overriding question is when (and then how) sexual reproduction itself evolved. **Despite decades of speculation, we do not know**" (1998, p. 252, parenthetical item in orig., emp. added).

THE ORIGIN OF LANGUAGE AND SPEECH

Then, think about the origin of language and speech, which remains one of the most significant hurdles in evolutionary theory, even in the twenty-first century. In fact, some evolutionists simply have stopped discussing the matter completely. Earlier in this book, we quoted from *The Seeds of Speech: Language Origin and Evolution* by Jean Aitchison, who wrote:

In 1866, a ban on the topic was incorporated into the founding statues of the Linguistic Society of Paris, perhaps the foremost academic linguistic institution of the time: "The Society does not accept papers on either the origin of language or the invention of a universal language" (2000, p. 5).

Our observation was (and is) that this is an amazing (albeit perhaps inadvertent) admission of defeat, especially coming from a group of such eminent scientists, researchers, and scholars. In regard to the origin of language, Aitchison commented:

> Of course, holes still remain in our knowledge: in particular, at what stage did language leap from being something new which humans discovered to being something which every newborn human is scheduled to acquire? **This is still a puzzle** (p. ix, emp. added).

Again, we concur; it is "a puzzle."

THE ORIGIN OF CONSCIOUSNESS– "THE GREATEST OF MIRACLES"

Earlier, we quoted evolutionist Graham Bell, who opined in regard to the origin of sex that "perhaps no other natural phenomenon has aroused so much interest; certainly none has sowed as much confusion." We beg to differ. In our estimation, there can be little doubt that there is one challenge/problem/enigma/mystery/puzzle that outranks all others in regard to the difficulty it presents for evolutionary theory– **the evolution of consciousness**. And if the scientific literature can be taken as any type of accurate gauge, the evolutionists themselves agree with us. If sex is the "queen" of problems in evolutionary biology, then the evolution of consciousness must surely rank as the "king" of such problems.

The Importance of Human Consciousness

When speaking of consciousness (also referred to in the literature as "self-awareness"), evolutionists freely admit that, from their vantage point at least, "consciousness is one's most precious possession" (Elbert, 2000, p. 231). David MacKay of the University of Keele in England wrote: "[Consciousness is] for us, the most important aspect of all" (1965, p. 498). As famed paleoanthropologist Richard Leakey put it: "The sense of self-awareness we each experience is so brilliant it illuminates everything we think and do…" (1994, p. 139). In their book, *Evolution,* the late geneticist Theodosius Dobzhansky (of the Rockefeller University) and his co-authors wrote: "In point of fact, **self-awareness is the most immediate and incontrovertible of all realities**. Without doubt, the human mind sets our species apart from nonhuman animals" (Dobzhansky, et al., 1977, p. 453, emp. added). Ervin Laszlo, in his volume, *Evolution: The Grand Synthesis*, commented:

> **The phenomenon of mind is perhaps the most remarkable of all the phenomena of the lived and experienced world**. Its explanation belongs to a grand tradition of philosophy—to the perennial "great questions" that each generation of thinkers answers anew…or despairs of answering at all (1987, p. 116, ellipsis in orig., emp. added).

The late Robert Wesson, a Hoover Institution Senior Research Fellow, observed in his book, *Beyond Natural Selection*:

> Life has a dual nature: its material basis and the essence of functionality and responsiveness that distinguishes living things and flourishes at higher levels of evolution. **The material and the mental are both real**, just as are causation and will. The mind derives richness from these two sides, like feeling and bodily function, love and sex, the spiritual and the carnal, the joy of creation and the satisfaction of bodily wants (1997, p. 278, emp. added).

Or, as philosopher Michael Ruse remarked: "**The important thing from our perspective is that consciousness is a real thing**. We are sentient beings" (2001b, p. 200, emp. added). Sir Cyril Hinshelwood, professor of chemistry at the Imperial College in London, commented: "I almost hesitate to say this in a scientific gathering; but one does just wonder

what would be the point or purpose of anything at all if there were not consciousness anywhere" (1965, p. 500, emp. added).

And creationists certainly agree. In his work, *Understanding the Present: Science and the Soul of Modern Man,* theist Bryan Appleyard observed:

> A moment's thought would convince a child that the most striking thing about us is that we are utterly unlike anything else in nature. Light, gravity, even the whole biological realm are related to us only in the most superficial way: we reflect light, if dropped we fall, and we have a body system roughly comparable to a large number of animals. **All of which is trivial compared with the one attribute we have that is denied to the rest of nature—consciousness** (1992, pp. 193-194, emp. added).

Yes, consciousness is a "real thing." But why is it an "important thing"? The late evolutionist and Harvard professor, Stephen Jay Gould, concluded:

> Consciousness, vouchsafed only to our species in the history of life on earth, is the most god-awfully potent evolutionary invention ever developed. Although accidental and unpredictable, it has given *Homo sapiens* unprecedented power both over the history of our own species and the life of the entire contemporary biosphere (1997b, p. ix).

With consciousness has come the ability to control—well—almost everything! But with that "unprecedented power" has come unprecedented responsibility because, as even evolutionists are wont to admit, actions have consequences. Well-known evolutionist Donald Griffin, in the 2001 revised edition of his classic text, *Animal Minds: Beyond Cognition to Consciousness,* admitted as much when he wrote:

> It is self-evident that we are aware of at least some of what goes on around us and that we think about our situation and about the probable results of various actions that we might take. **This sort of conscious sub-**

jective mental experience is significant and useful because it often helps us select appropriate behavior (p. ix, emp. added).

"Selecting appropriate behavior" (or, as the case may be, **not** selecting appropriate behavior) becomes a key point in this discussion. As evolutionists John Eccles and Daniel Robinson correctly observed in *The Wonder of Being Human: Our Brain and Our Mind:* "Whether one takes human beings to be 'children of God,' 'tools of production,' 'matter in motion,' or 'a species of primate' has consequences" (1984, p. 1). Yes, as we will show, it certainly does.

The "Mystery" of Human Consciousness

Consciousness is undeniably real. And it does have consequences—something that practically every rational human freely admits. But admitting all of that is the easy part. The difficulty arises in explaining **why**—why consciousness exists; why it is real; why it works the way it does; and why it "has consequences." When it comes to explaining the origin of consciousness, evolutionists admit (to use their own words): "Clearly, we are in deep trouble" (Eccles and Robinson, 1984, p. 17). Just how "deep" that "trouble" really is, appears to be one of the most widely known, yet best-kept secrets in science. In a chapter ("The Human Brain and the Human Person") that he authored for the book, *Mind and Brain: The Many-Faceted Problems*, Sir John Eccles wrote: "The emergence and development of self-consciousness...is an utterly mysterious process.... The coming-to-be of self-consciousness is a mystery that concerns each person with its conscious and unique selfhood" (1982, pp. 85,97). Or, as British physicist John Polkinghorne was wont to admit: "The human psyche has revealed its shadowy and elusive depths" (1986, p. 5).

Consider the following admissions from those within the evolutionary community, and as you do, notice the descriptive terms ("problem," "mystery," "puzzle," "riddle," "challenge," "muddle," etc.) that generally are employed in any discussion of consciousness. [AUTHORS' NOTE: While we might just as easily have quoted from only one or two sources, we wanted to provide extensive documentation of just how serious this concern actually is. To do so, we have quoted from a wide variety of sources among those within the evolutionary establishment. We do not believe that any fair-minded reader could possibly consider the concessions below and fail to realize that evolutionary theory has absolutely no adequate explanation for the origin of human consciousness—"our most precious possession."]

Consciousness in General

Consciousness is the highest manifestation of life, but as to its origin, destiny, and the nature of its connection with the physical body and brain— these are as yet unsolved metaphysical questions, the answer to which can only be found by continued research in the direction of higher physical and psychical science (Carrington, 1923, p. 54, emp. added).

Nobody has the slightest idea how anything material could be conscious. Nobody even knows what it would be like to have the slightest idea about how anything material could be conscious (Fodor, 1992, p. 5, emp. added).

There is nothing strange about consciousness except that we don't understand it.... You can't explain consciousness on the cheap.... **I admit that I am not able to explain consciousness** (Scott, 1995, pp. 132,141,163, emp. added).

We still have no clue how mind and matter are related, or what process led to the emergence of mind from matter in the first place (Davies, 1995, emp. added).

It seems to me that there is a fundamental problem with the idea that mentality arises out of physicality— that is something which philosophers worry about for very good reasons. The things we talk about in physics are matter, physical things, massive objects, particles, space, time, energy and so on. How could our feelings, our perception of redness, or of happiness have anything to do with physics? **I regard that as a mystery** (Penrose, 1997, p. 94, emp. added).

We need to close the gap between the physical and subjective realms of this topic before we can hope to reach an understanding of consciousness. **Until then it remains**, according to *Scientific American,* "**biology's most profound riddle**" (Johanson and Edgar, 1996, p. 107, emp. added).

The problem of consciousness tends to embarrass biologists. Taking it to be an aspect of living things, they feel they should know about it and be able to tell physicists about it, whereas they have nothing relevant to say (Wald, 1994, p. 129, emp. added).

The "problem of consciousness" has been identified as an outstanding intellectual challenge across disciplines ranging from basic neuroscience through psychology to philosophy, although **opinions vary widely on the chances of achieving a solution** (Zeman, 2001, 124:1264, emp. added).

Human consciousness is just about the last surviving mystery.... **With consciousness, however, we are still in a terrible muddle**. Consciousness stands alone today as a topic that often leaves even the most sophisticated thinkers tongue-tied and confused. And, as with all the earlier mysteries, there are many who insist—and hope—that there will never be a demystification of consciousness. Science does not answer all good questions. Neither does philosophy (Dennett, 1991, pp. 21,22, emp. added).

Why do we have "sentience," as we might call it? Why do we have the capacity of self-awareness?... Why is it that what is essentially no more than a bunch of atoms should have thinking ability?... **I'm afraid that at this point, we start to run out of answers**. The Darwinian qua Darwinian is reduced to silence. This is not to deny the existence of consciousness. Anything but!... **The point is that as a Darwinian, that is to say as a scientist and an evolutionist, there seems to be no answer**. At least, no answer at the moment (Ruse, 2001b, pp. 197,198,199, emp. added).

The evolution of the capacity to simulate seems to have culminated in subjective consciousness. **Why this should have happened is, to me, the most profound mystery facing modern biology**... (Dawkins, 1976, p. 59, emp. added).

Clearly we are in deep trouble.... It will be realized that the modern Darwinian theory of evolution is defective in that it does not even recognize the extraordinary problem presented by living organisms' acquiring mental experiences of a nonmaterial kind that are in another word from the world of matter-energy, which heretofore was globally comprehensive. ...We believe that **the emergence of consciousness is a skeleton in the closet of orthodox evolutionism**.... It remains just as enigmatic as it is to an orthodox evolutionist as long as it is regarded as an exclusively natural process in an exclusively materialist world (Eccles and Robinson, 1984, pp. 17,18).

Consciousness and the Brain

[W]e infer a close, highly intimate relation between brain and consciousness. But there is a seemingly unbridgeable conceptual gap between the brain as a *physical* object and *mental* consciousness. **This is the most baffling problem** (Gregory, 1977, pp. 275-276, italics in orig., emp. added).

We can turn now to what is probably **the "most unanswered" problem in brain evolution...conscious awareness** (Sperry, 1977, p. 424, emp. added).

What the connection, or the relationship, is between what goes on mentally in the mind and what goes on physically in the brain, nobody knows. Perhaps we shall never know. **The so-called mind/brain problem has proved so elusive, many have come to regard it as a mystery of ultimate significance**.... Unlike less complicated physical structures, **the brain is accompanied by consciousness. As we said earlier, we do not know why this should be**. For the time being at least, we must simply accept it as a brute fact (Stannard, 2000, pp. 41-42,44, emp. added)

One immediate question, which seems not to have been answered, is: Why, of all physical objects, are only brain states conscious? Or is it supposed that consciousness is widespread among objects? If so we have no knowledge of this. But if not, what makes brains *uniquely* conscious objects? (Gregory, 1977, p. 280, italics in orig., emp. added).

Just what sort of neural activity leads to consciousness remains a **challenging mystery...**" (Griffin, 2001, p. 5, emp. added).

Scientific knowledge of the brain is woefully incomplete. **Scientists do not know how the brain acquires and stores information, how it produces feelings of pleasure and pain, or how it creates consciousness. The functioning of the human brain is a profound mystery**, one that scientists have only begun to understand (Morris, 2001, p. 200, emp. added).

Exactly what it is about our brains that leads to our extraordinary consciousness remains obscure... (Tattersall, 1998, p. 69, emp. added).

The key philosophical question posed by consciousness concerns its relationship to the neural processes which correlate with it. How do the events which register in our experience relate to those occurring in our brains? **This "problem of consciousness" is the modern formulation of the ancient "mind-body problem"** (Zeman, 2001, 124:1282, emp. added).

Consciousness and the Mind

It is amazing to verify that even after several centuries of philosophical ponderings, hard dedication to brain research, and remarkable advances in the field of neuroscience, the **concept of mind still remains obscure, controversial and impossible to define within the limits of our language** (Cardoso, 1997/1998, emp. added).

Of all the problems which arise in connection with the notion of "mind" the most difficult is the fact of consciousness itself. Consciousness is often defined as awareness—awareness of self and of the environment—but this does no more than substitute one word for another, since we are equally unable to explain the subjective aspects of awareness. But even if we have to take the fact of awareness as a given, just as we take light or gravity as givens, we can still usefully ask certain questions, such as: where in the brain is awareness, or consciousness, located? Is it a function of the whole brain or only of part? Is it a property of neurones [the British spelling of neurons —BH/BT] or nerve cells? Is there more than one kind or level of consciousness? What does it mean to be unconscious and what mechanisms determine whether we are conscious or not? (Taylor, 1979, pp. 73-74, emp. added).

The intangible mind...defies explanation in terms of evolutionary theory (Wesson, 1997, p. 276, emp. added).

...[S]cientists remain unsure about the precise basis of mind (Wilson, 1998, p. 99, emp. added).

Unfortunately, what we call the mind is notoriously refractory to scientific study... (Dobzhansky, et al., 1977, p. 453, emp. added).

What kind of thing is a mind? What is the relation between our minds and our bodies and, more specifically, what is the relation between what goes on in our minds and what goes on in our brains? How did brains and minds originate? Can our brains be regarded as nothing more than exceedingly complicated machines? Can minds exist without brains? Can machines have minds? Do animals have minds? **None of these questions is new, and some of them are extremely old. None of them can be answered in a way that is wholly satisfactory** (Glynn, 1999, p. 4, emp. added).

The emergence of full consciousness...is indeed one of the greatest of miracles (Popper and Eccles, 1977, p. 129, emp. added).

CONSCIOUSNESS DEFINED

The past three decades have witnessed a serious and noticeable increase in interest in the subject of consciousness, accompanied by a surge of publications, new scientific and/ or philosophical journals, and scientific meetings (see, for example: Eccles, 1966, 1967, 1970; 1973; 1979; 1982; 1984; 1989; Dennett, 1991; McGinn, 1991; Ornstein, 1991; Eccles, 1992; Edelman, 1992; Flanagan, 1992; Fodor, 1992; Milner and Rugg, 1992; Searle, 1992; Beloff, 1994; Crick, 1994; Eccles, 1994; Penrose, 1994; Pinker, 1994; Sperry, 1994; Metzinger, 1995; Scott, 1995; Chalmers, 1996; Dennett, 1996; Libet, 1996; Velmans, 1996; Koch, 1997; Penrose, 1997; Pinker, 1997a; Weiskrantz, 1997; Cotterill, 1998; Hurley, 1998; Jasper, et al., 1998; Rose, 1998; Glynn, 1999; Velmans, 2000; Wright, 2000; Donald, 2001; Griffin, 2001; Greenfield, 2002; Tolson, 2002; Lemonick, 2003a, 2003b; Pinker, 2003).

One would think that since **so much** has been written on the subject of consciousness, surely, the definition of this oft'-discussed topic would be a straightforward, simple matter. Think again! [One dictionary on psychology had the following entry under "consciousness": "Consciousness is a fascinating but elusive phenomenon; it is impossible to specify what it is, what it does or why it evolved. Nothing worth reading has been written about it" (Sutherland, 1989).] Scientists and philosophers cannot even agree on the definition of the term, much less on the origin of that which they are attempting to define.

Our English word "consciousness" has its roots in the Latin *conscio*, formed by the coalescence of *cum* (meaning "with") and *scio* (meaning "know"). In its original Latin sense, to be conscious of something was to share knowledge of it, with someone else, or with oneself. As C.S. Lewis noted in his book, *Studies in Words:*

> A "weakened" sense of *conscientia* coexisted in Latin with the stronger sense, which implies shared knowledge: in this weak sense *conscientia* was, simply, knowl-

edge. All three senses (knowledge shared with another, knowledge shared with oneself and, simply, knowledge) entered the English language with "conscience," the first equivalent of *conscientia.* The words "conscious" and "consciousness" first appear early in the 17th century, rapidly followed by "self-conscious" and "self-consciousness" (1960).

Consciousness, however, has become a rather ambiguous term in its everyday usage. It can refer to: (1) a waking state; (2) experience; and (3) the possession of any mental state. It may be helpful to the reader to provide an example of each of these three main usages: (1) the injured worker lapsed into unconsciousness; (2) the criminal became conscious of a terrible sense of dread at the thought of being apprehended; and (3) I am conscious of the fact that sometimes I get on your nerves. Anthony O'Hear suggested:

> In being conscious of myself as myself, I see myself as separate from what is not myself. In being conscious, a being reacts to the world with feeling, with pleasure and pain, and responds on the basis of felt needs.... Consciousness involves reacting to stimuli and feeling stimuli (1997, pp. 22,38).

The phrase "self-consciousness," at times, can be equally ambiguous, as it may include: (1) proneness to embarrassment in social settings; (2) the ability to detect our own sensations and recall our recent actions; (3) self-recognition; (4) the awareness of awareness; and (5) self-knowledge in the broadest sense (see Zeman, 2001, 124:1264). O'Hear went on to suggest:

> Self-consciousness, though, is something over and above the sensitivity and feeling implied by consciousness. As self-conscious I do not simply have pleasures, pains, experiences, and needs, and react to them: I am also aware that I have them, that there is an "I" which is a subject of these experiences and which is a possessor of needs, experiences, beliefs, and dispositions....

A self-conscious person, then, does not simply have beliefs or dispositions, does not simply engage in practices of various sorts, does not just respond to or suffer the world. He or she is aware that he or she has beliefs, practices, dispositions, and the rest. It is this awareness of myself as a subject of experience, as a holder of beliefs, and an engager in practices, which constitutes my self-consciousness. A conscious animal might be a knower, and we might extend the epithet "knower" to machines if they receive information from the world and modify their responses accordingly. **But only a self-conscious being knows that he is a knower** (pp. 23-24, emp. added).

Neurobiologist Antonio Damasio believes that consciousness comes in two forms. First is **"core consciousness,"** which is limited to the here and now, and is what we share with other higher primates. The second, which is the ingredient humans possess that makes us unique, he has labeled as **"extended consciousness."** This type of consciousness adds awareness of past and future to the mix (see Tattersall, 2002, p. 73). Nobel laureate Gerald Edelman, director of neurosciences and chairman of the department of neurobiology at the Scripps Research Institute (1992, pp. 117-123), believes that we should distinguish between what he calls "primary consciousness" (equivalent to Damasio's "core consciousness") and "higher-order consciousness" (equivalent to Damasio's "extended consciousness"). [Stanford University biologist Paul Ehrlich prefers the terms "consciousness" and "intense consciousness" (2000, pp. 110-112).] What is involved in the transition from primary to higher consciousness is that the subject of the consciousness does not merely "have" experiences, but is able, over and above that, to refine, alter, and report its experiences. Primary consciousness lacks any notion of an experience or self. In other words, a "non-self-conscious" creature is aware of and/or able to react to stimuli. But higher-order consciousness represents an awareness of the plans and concepts by which one makes one's way in the world.

Ian Tattersall commented: "…[I]f consciousness were something more susceptible to scientific analysis than it is, we would certainly know a lot more about it by now than we do—which is very little indeed" (2002, p. 59). Donald Johanson and Blake Edgar, in their book, *From Lucy to Language*, admitted that "consciousness, being inherently singular and subjective, is a tricky prospect for objective scientific analysis…" (1996, p. 107). True enough. But, as it turns out, defining it is no less of a "tricky prospect." Nobel laureate Sir Francis Crick was not even willing to give it a try. In his book, *The Astonishing Hypothesis: The Scientific Search for the Soul,* he lamented:

> Everyone has a rough idea of what is meant by consciousness. It is better to avoid a **precise** definition of consciousness because of the dangers of premature definitions. Until the problem is understood much better, any attempt at a formal definition is likely to be either misleading or overly restrictive or both. If this seems like cheating, try defining for me the word **gene**. So much is now known about genes that any simple definition is likely to be inadequate. How much more difficult, then, to define a biological term when rather little is known about it (1994, p. 20, emp. in orig.).

Richard Leakey, on the other hand, was at least willing to inquire: "What **is** consciousness? More specifically, what is it **for**? What is its **function**? Such questions may seem odd, given that each of us experiences life through the medium of consciousness, or self-awareness" (1994, p. 139, emp. in orig.). Yes, such questions **do** seem a bit odd, considering all the "press" given to the subject of consciousness over the past many years. But, as Adam Zeman wrote in the extensive review of consciousness he prepared for the July 2001 issue of the scientific journal, *Brain*: "Whether scientific observation and theory will yield a complete account of consciousness remains a live issue" (124:1264). A "live issue" indeed! Just getting scientists and philosophers to agree on a standard, coherent definition seems to be an almost impossible task. In his 1997 volume,

The Large, the Small and the Human Brain, British mathematical physicist Roger Penrose asked: "**What is consciousness?
Well, I don't know how to define it. I think this is not the
moment to attempt to define consciousness, since we do
not know what it is**..." (p. 98, emp. added; Penrose's central
thesis is basically that "there should be something outside of
known physics," p. 102).

But the fact that "we do not know what it is" has not prevented people from offering a variety of definitions for "our
most precious possession," consciousness. Johanson and Edgar went on to say:

> But what about the apparently extrasomatic structure
> of the mind, or consciousness? Where does the brain
> end and the mind begin, or are they one and the same?
> Is it consciousness—more than bipedalism, language,
> or evolved culture—that really sets humans apart? First,
> **what is consciousness? No single definition may
> suffice for such an elusive concept**, but we can de-
> scribe consciousness as self-awareness and self-re-
> flection, the ability to feel pain or pleasure, the sen-
> sation of being alive and of being us, the sum of what-
> ever passes through the mind (p. 107, emp. added).

Their suggestion that "no single definition may suffice for
such an elusive concept" has been echoed by others who have
broached the puzzle of consciousness. In his 2001 book, *A
Mind So Rare,* Canadian psychologist Merlin Donald noted:

> [W]e must mind our definition of consciousness. It is
> not really a unitary phenomenon, and allows more
> than one definition. In fact, it encompasses at least
> three classes of definition. The first is the definition
> of consciousness as a **state**.... A second class of func-
> tional definition takes an **architectural** approach,
> whereby consciousness is defined as a place in the
> mind.... This does not imply that there is a single neu-
> ral locus, a "consciousness module" somewhere in
> the brain. We have already dismissed that as a possi-
> bility.... This definition acknowledges the very wide
> reach of awareness and the fact that it can bring cog-

nition, emotion, and action under a unified command. ...It gives an organism more focused intellectual power....

The third definition of consciousness takes a frankly human-centered view of cognition and has more to do with enlightenment, or illumination, than with mere attention. This is the **representational** approach.... This rigorous standard of awareness invariably excludes animals from true consciousness, primarily because we have language and they don't. This is a bit circular, however. If awareness is defined in advance as a direct product of language, it is hardly surprising that it should be special to humans. Moreover, it is not obvious that language is a good criterion for awareness. The use of language is driven by many agendas, very few of which originate in language. Language is an add-on, a Johnny-come-lately in the evolutionary sequence, and it gets most of its material and its content from much older parts of our mental universe.... In itself, language cannot bestow self-awareness.... The mere possession of symbols will not alter basic ability. The capacity to take a perspective on one's own mental states cannot be changed simply by one's possessing a lexicon or vocabulary (pp. 118,119,120, emp. in orig.).

For University of Washington neurobiologist William Calvin, consciousness consists of "contemplating the past and forecasting the future, planning what to do tomorrow, feeling dismay when seeing a tragedy unfold, and narrating our life story." For Cambridge University psychologist Nicholas Humphrey, an essential part of consciousness is "raw sensation." According to Steven Harnad, editor of the respected journal, *Behavioral and Brain Sciences*, "consciousness is just the capacity to have experiences" (for documentation of statements by Calvin, Humphrey, and Harnad, see Lewin, 1992, pp. 153-154). And, even though Roger Penrose started out by admitting, "I don't know how to define it; I think this is not the moment to attempt to define consciousness, since we do not know what it is," that did not keep him from offering up his own set of definitions for consciousness.

It seems to me that there are at least two different aspects to consciousness. On the one hand, there are **passive** manifestations of consciousness, which involve **awareness**. I use this category to include things like perceptions of colour, of harmonies, the use of memory, and so on. On the other hand, there are its **active** manifestations, which involve concepts like free will and the carrying out of actions under our free will. The use of such terms reflects different aspects of our consciousness (1997, pp. 98-99, emp. in orig.).

Notice how frequently "consciousness" seems to be tied to "awareness" (or "self-consciousness" with "self-awareness")? There's a reason for that: the two commonly are used interchangeably in the scientific and philosophical literature. Eccles noted: "One can also use the term self-awareness instead of self-consciousness, but I prefer self-consciousness because it relates directly to the self-conscious mind" (1992, p. 3). The late evolutionist of Harvard, Kirtley F. Mather, offered his personal opinion when he said: "[A]wareness is a term that I prefer to consciousness" (1986, p. 126). In his book, *The Evolution of Consciousness*, Stanford University biologist Robert Ornstein suggested: **"Being conscious is being aware of being aware**. It is one step removed from the raw experience of seeing, smelling, acting, moving, and reacting" (1991, pp. 225-226, emp. added). New Zealand anthropologist Peter J. Wilson, in his volume, *Man: The Promising Primate*, addressed the concept of "self" consciousness.

[S]elf-consciousness means that an individual perceives difference **in himself**, regarding himself as a complex and heterogeneous entity made up of separate but interrelated parts…. The main division of the human person separates what he sees of himself, the surface of his body, from what he cannot see but supposes of himself—what is inside. The "inside" is most frequently the subject, that which perceives yet can also consider itself as an object, something to be perceived or conceived. What is within is frequently acknowledged to be the owner of the body yet is also thought of as being possessed. We can speak of "my mind" or "my spirit" as easily as "my body." This self-consciousness or individuality is the basis of bonding and of permanent in relationships (1980, p. 85, emp. in orig.).

Paul Ehrlich, in his 2000 text, *Human Natures: Genes, Cultures, and the Human Prospect*, also addressed the intriguing concept of "self" consciousness.

> We have a continuous sense of "self"—of a little individual sitting between our ears—and, perhaps equally important, a sense of the threat of death, of the potential for that individual—our self—to cease to exist. I call all of this sort of awareness **"intense consciousness"; it is central to human natures and is perhaps the least understood aspect of those natures** (p. 110, emp. added).

He went on to note, however:

> Consciousness may well be limited to higher vertebrates, perhaps restricted to *Homo sapiens*.... Intense consciousness, as I've defined it, appears unique to *Homo sapiens* among modern organisms.... Consciousness itself, a broader concept than that implied by the term **intense consciousness** as I am using it, has many meanings. I prefer to define consciousness simply as the capacity of some animals, including human beings, to have, when awake, mental representations of real-time events that are happening to them or are being perceived by them (pp. 112,111, emp. in orig.).

And, last but not least, of course, let it be noted that even though certain scientists and philosophers do not know what consciousness **is**, they do know what it **is not**. As evolutionary humanist Jerome W. Elbert put it in his 2000 book, *Are Souls Real?*:

> We can define consciousness as **what it is like to be a person who is awake or dreaming and has a normally functioning brain**.... By our definition, consciousness is interrupted by dreamless sleep, and it returns when we awaken or have a dream. By almost

anyone's definition, consciousness leaves when a person is under general anesthetic during surgery. The fact that consciousness can be halted and restarted is evidence that it is due to the operation of a **process**, rather than the presence of a **spiritual entity**. This is consistent with the view that consciousness arises from a dynamic process within the brain, rather than from the presumable continuous indwelling of a soul (p. 223, emp. in orig.).

Or, to quote Roger Penrose: "I am suggesting that **there are not mental objects floating around out there which are not based in physicality**" (1997, p. 97, emp. added). So much, then, for the idea that self-consciousness or self-awareness has any "spiritual" origin or significance. [We will have more to say on this point later.]

Before we leave this section on the definition of consciousness, perhaps we should say something about the prickly subject of "qualia," which is a term that certain philosophers have coined to refer to what they believe are "subjective dimensions of experience" that are real "only in the eye of the beholder." In his article reviewing the subject of consciousness, Zeman discussed not only the definition of the term, but also the contentious nature of the claim that qualia actually exist.

Consciousness in its first sense is the behavioural expression of our normal waking state. But when we are conscious in this first sense we are always conscious **of** something. In its second sense consciousness is the content of experience from moment to moment: what it feels like to be a certain person, now, in a sense in which we suppose there is nothing it feels like to be a stone or lost in dreamless sleep. This second sense of consciousness is more inward than the first. It highlights the qualitative, subjective dimension of experience. Philosophers sometimes use the technical (and controversial) term "qualia" to refer to the subjective texture of experience which is the essence of this second sense of consciousness (2001, 124:1265, parenthetical item and emp. in orig.).

These so-called "subjective dimensions" parade through the literature under quite a variety of names, as Daniel Dennett explained:

> Philosophers have adopted various names for the things in the beholder (or properties of the beholder) that have been supposed to provide a safe home for the colors and the rest of the properties that have been banished from the "external" world by the triumphs of physics: **raw feels, sensa, phenomenal qualities, intrinsic properties of conscious experiences, the qualitative content of mental states** and, of course, **qualia**, the term I will use (1998, p. 141, parenthetical item and emp. in orig.).

Certain philosophers (e.g., Owen Flanagan, 1992, and David Chalmers, 1995) steadfastly insist that, to quote Flanagan, "qualia are for real" (p. 61). Others, like Dennett, argue just as strongly that they are not. As Dennett went on to say: "There are subtle differences in how these terms have been defined, but I'm going to ride roughshod over them. I deny that there are **any** such properties" (p. 141, emp. in orig.). Dennett does, in fact, deny that qualia exist. In his 1998 book, *Brainchildren*, he wrote in a chapter titled "Instead of Qualia": "[T]here are no qualia...so I have recommended abandoning the word, but I seem to have lost that battle" (p. 141).

As we write this, the battle is raging over whether qualia are real or not. At this point in time, all we can say is "stay tuned," while the philosophers try to reach a consensus regarding whether we actually **see** a green leaf on the tree, or whether we just "think" we see a green leaf (or a tree!).

WHY–AND HOW–DID CONSCIOUSNESS ARISE?

When Sir Karl Popper and Sir John Eccles stated in their classic text, *The Self and Its Brain*, that "**the emergence of full consciousness...is indeed one of the greatest of miracles**," they did not overstate the case (Popper and Eccles, 1977,

p. 129, emp. added). Be sure to notice their use of the word "emergence." The "miracle" of the "emergence" of consciousness has to do with two things: (1) the **fact** of its existence; and (2) the **reason** for its existence. In other words, **why** did consciousness arise, and **how** did it do so?

Why Did Consciousness Arise?

At the outset, let us state what is common knowledge (and readily admitted) within the scientific community: evolutionary theory cannot begin to explain **why** consciousness arose. In our estimation, one of the most fascinating books published within the last thirty years was a volume with the seemingly unprofessional title, *The Encyclopaedia of Ignorance* (see Duncan and Weston-Smith, 1977). But, although the title may appear somewhat whimsical, the content of the volume is anything but. In chapter after chapter, distinguished, award-winning scientists (such as Nobel laureate Sir Francis Crick and two-time Nobel laureate Linus Pauling) enunciated and explained some of the most important things in the world–**things of which science is completely ignorant**. Interestingly, one of the chapters in the book, written by Richard Gregory (professor of neuropsychology and director of the brain and perception laboratory at the University of Bristol in England), was "Consciousness." In his discussion, Dr. Gregory asked:

> Why, then, do we **need** consciousness? What does consciousness have that the neural signals (and physical brain activity) do not have? Here there is something of a paradox, for if the awareness of consciousness does not have any effect–if consciousness is not a causal agent–then it seems useless, and so should not have developed by evolutionary pressure. If, on the other hand, it is useful it must be a causal agent: but then physiological description in terms of neural activity cannot be complete. Worse, we are on this alternative stuck with mentalistic explanations, which seem outside science. To develop science in this direction we would have to reverse the direction of physical explanations which have so far proved so suc-

cessful. It might be argued that the "inner" world of consciousness is essentially different from the physical world: but then it seems strange that the physical signals of the nervous system are so important (1977, p. 277, parenthetical item and emp. in orig.).

In this brief assessment, Gregory has isolated several key points. First, what does consciousness have that the brain, by itself, does not? Second, if consciousness does not have some "real function," then, obviously, nature would have "selected against" it–and it never would have appeared in the first place. Third, if it does actually have some function, in light of our current knowledge about how the neural network of the brain operates, **what is that function**? And if there is beneficial function, why haven't the brains of animals selected for it? To echo Gregory's question, "Why do we **need** consciousness?"

Why indeed? Philosopher Michael Ruse noted some of the major hurdles involved in "nature" being able to "select" for consciousness when he asked:

> What of the ultimate question, namely that of consciousness? Darwinians take consciousness very seriously. Consciousness seems so large a part of what it is to be a human that it would be very improbable that natural selection had no role in its production and maintenance. Even if one agrees that consciousness is in some sense connected to or emergent from the brain–and how could one deny this?–**consciousness must have some biological standing in its own right**.... But what is consciousness, and what function does it serve? Why should not an unconscious machine do everything that we can do? (2001a, p. 72, emp. added).

Some materialists, of course, have suggested that a machine **can** do "everything we can do." The eminent British physiologist Lord E.D. Adrian, in the chapter he authored on "Consciousness" for the book, *Brain and Conscious Experience*, concluded: "As far as our public behavior is concerned, **there is** nothing that could not be copied by machinery, nothing therefore that could not be brought within the framework of physical science" (1965, p. 240, emp. added). [Lord Adrian's remarks were made at a scientific symposium held at the Vatican during the week of September 28-October 4, 1964. Following his speech, the seminar participants engaged in a roundtable discussion that centered on Adrian's lecture. One of those in attendance was Wilder Penfield, the world-renowned Canadian neurosurgeon, who dryly responded to Lord Adrian: "I had in mind to ask whether the robot could, in any conceivable way, see a joke. I think not. Sense of humor would, I suspect, be the last thing that a machine would have" (as quoted in Eccles, 1966, p. 248). Brilliant stroke!]

Evolutionary theory has no adequate answer to the question of how consciousness arose, as evolutionists Eccles and Robinson admitted.

> **[A]ll materialist theories of the mind are in conflict with biological evolution**.... Evolutionary theory holds that only those structures and processes that significantly aid in survival are developed in natural selection. **If consciousness is causally impotent, its development cannot be accounted for by evolutionary theory** (1984, p. 37, emp. added).

Dr. Eccles addressed this critically important point once again in his 1992 book, *The Human Psyche.*

> In accord with evolutionary theory only those structures and processes that significantly aid in survival are developed in natural selection. If consciousness is causally impotent, its development cannot be accounted for by evolutionary theory. According to biological evolution, mental states and consciousness could have evolved and developed **only if they were causally effective** in bringing about changes in neural happenings in the brain with the consequent changes in behaviour (p. 20, emp. in orig.).

Or, as Gregory had asked several years earlier:

If the brain was developed by Natural Selection, we might well suppose that consciousness has survival value. But for this it must, surely, have causal effects. **But what effects could awareness, or consciousness, have?** (1977, p. 276, emp. added).

In his 2000 book, *Nonzero: The Logic of Human Destiny*, Robert Wright (former senior editor of *The Sciences*) addressed this same point when he wrote:

> [B]rains have consciousness. They don't just process information; they have the subjective **experience** of processing information. They feel pleasure and pain, have epiphanies of insight, and so on…. [A]ccording to this mainstream scientific view, consciousness—subjective experience, sentience—has zero behavioral manifestations; it doesn't **do** anything…. In technical terms: consciousness, subjective experience, is "epiphenomenal"—it is always an effect, never a cause. …[I]f consciousness doesn't **do** anything, then its existence becomes quite the unfathomable mystery. If subjective experience is superfluous to the day-to-day business of living and eating and getting our genes into the next generation, then why would it have ever arisen in the course of natural selection? Why would life acquire a major property that has no function? (pp. 305, 306, 307, emp. in orig.).

Evolutionists may not be able to explain what causal effect(s) consciousness might possibly have that would endow it with a "survival value" significant enough for "nature" to "select," but one thing is certain: most of them are not willing to go so far as to suggest that consciousness does not exist, or that it is unimportant to humanity. As Ruse put it:

> Of course, this does not address the ultimate question, namely, that of consciousness. As you might expect, there are divided opinions on this matter. There are those who, even today, want to deny that consciousness has any great biological significance. Others, relatedly, feel that consciousness is something very recently acquired, and so it cannot have been a major factor in

human evolution. The average evolutionist, however, particularly the average Darwinian, feels extremely uncomfortable with such a dismissive attitude. **Consciousness seems a very important aspect of human nature**. Whatever it may be, consciousness is so much a part of what it is to be human that Darwinians are loath to say that natural selection had no or little role in its production and maintenance (2001b, pp. 197, emp. added).

While the "average Darwinian" may indeed be "extremely uncomfortable" with the suggestion that natural selection had "little or no role in the production and maintenance of consciousness," the truth of the matter is that no Darwinian can explain **why**, or **how**, natural selection could have played any part whatsoever in such a process. Yet, as Richard Heinberg observed in his book, *Cloning the Buddha: The Moral Impact of Biotechnology*: "Since no better material explanation is apparently available, it is assumed that whatever explanation is at hand—however obvious its shortcomings—**must be** true. Natural selection thus becomes an inscrutable, godlike agency capable of producing miracles" (1999, p. 71, emp. in orig.).

From an evolutionary viewpoint, consciousness doesn't **do** anything. It doesn't "help" the neural circuits in the brain. It apparently doesn't have any "great biological significance," and it doesn't seem to bestow any innate "survival benefit" on its possessor. We ask, then, **what is left**? Or, to repeat Gregory's question: "Why do we **need** consciousness?"

Why Do We Need Consciousness?

Why **do** we need consciousness? From an evolutionary viewpoint, maybe we don't. W.H. Thorpe, in his chapter, "Ethology and Consciousness," for the book, *Brain and Conscious Experience*, asked regarding consciousness: "Is there a good selective reason for it or is there just no reason at all why the animal should not have got on quite as well without having developed this apparently strange and new faculty" (1965, p.

497). Perhaps, amidst all the other "happenstances" resulting from billions of years of evolution, consciousness is, to put it bluntly, a "quirky accident." Ironically (or maybe not), those are the exact words the late evolutionist of Harvard, Stephen Jay Gould, used to describe the origin of consciousness when he said: "The not-so-hidden agenda in all this is a concern with human consciousness. You can't blame us for being fascinated with consciousness; it's an enormous punctuation in the history of life. **I view it as a quirky accident**" (as quoted in Lewin, 1992, pp. 145-146, emp. added). Or, as Sir Fred Hoyle observed of Gould's reference to consciousness being "an enormous punctuation in the history of life": "Professor Gould accepts human consciousness as an exception to his general thesis; it is a phenomenon sudden in its appearance and exceptional in its nature" (Hoyle and Wickramasinghe, 1993, p. 177). Theodosius Dobzhansky suggested:

> Self-awareness is, then, one of the fundamental, and possibly the most fundamental, characteristic of the human species. **This characteristic is an evolutionary novelty**; the biological species from which mankind has descended had only rudiments of self-awareness, or perhaps lacked it altogether (1967, p. 68, emp. added).

An "exceptional evolutionary novelty"? In fact, it is **so** exceptional that some evolutionists have given up altogether trying to figure out why consciousness exists at all. One such prominent figure in the field is British philosopher Colin McGinn. In speaking about McGinn's views on our inability to explain the origin of consciousness, James Trefil wrote in his book, *Are We Unique?*:

> Others have suggested more esoteric arguments about the fundamental unknowability of consciousness. For example, philosopher Colin McGinn of Rutgers University has suggested, on the basis of an argument from evolutionary theory, that the human mind is simply not equipped to deal with this particular problem. His basic argument is that **nothing in evolution has**

ever required the human mind to be able to deal with the operation of the human brain. Consequently, the argument goes, although we may be able to pose the problem of consciousness, our brains have not developed to the point where we can hope to solve it (1997, p. 186, emp. added).

In his 2000 volume, *Human Natures: Genes, Cultures, and the Human Prospect,* Paul Ehrlich discussed the situation as well when he wrote that McGinn doubts

> ...that we will ever understand how a pattern of electrochemical impulses in our nervous systems is translated into the rich experience of, say, watching an opera or flying an airplane. He believes that **our minds did not evolve in such a way as to enable us to answer that question, which may be fated to remain unanswered for a very long time, if not forever** (p. 112, emp. added).

To quote McGinn himself:

> What I argue is that an understanding of consciousness is beyond the reach of the human mind, that cognitively we are not equipped to understand it in the way we understand other phenomena we experience in the physical world. You can analyze brain structure and function in the way we analyze other phenomena, but the information you get tells you about nerve cells and circuits. Alternatively, you can think about consciousness as subjective experience. And what you find is that the two sides of inquiry never meet and, I think, never will. There's nothing mysterious about the physics and chemistry underlying consciousness. Our problem is that the phenomenon that arises from that chemistry and physics—consciousness—isn't available to the kind of analytical thinking of which humans are capable (as quoted in Lewin, 1992, p. 168)

Some evolutionists, however, are not quite ready to throw in the towel just yet. Rather than admit defeat, they have opted to defend the view that the "why" of consciousness has something to do with the brain—although they are not quite sure **what** or **how**. Stephen Jay Gould believed that the brain evolved, got bigger, and somehow produced consciousness as an "exaptation." What, exactly, is an exaptation? Allow us to remind you of Gould's definition:

> …[W]hat shall we call structures that contribute to fitness but evolved for other reasons and were later co-opted for their current role? They have no name at present, and [Elisabeth] Vrba and I suggest that they be called "exaptations" (1984a, p. 66; for the Vrba reference, see Gould and Vrba, 1982).

In other words, a big brain did not "evolve" in order to produce consciousness. Instead, for one reason or another (that no one seems quite able to explain), consciousness "just happened" as a fortuitous, unexpected by-product. Gould discussed human consciousness as one of the brain's "exaptive possibilities" when he wrote:

> I do not doubt that the brain became large for an adaptive reason (probably a set of complex reasons) and that natural selection brought it to a size that made consciousness possible. But, surely, most of what our brain does today, most of what makes us so distinctively human (and flexible), arises as a consequence of the non-adaptive sequelae, not of the primary adaptation itself—for the sequelae must be so vastly greater in number and possibility. The brain is a complex computer constructed by natural selection to perform a tiny subset of its potential operations. An arm built for one thing can do others (I am now typing with fingers built for other purposes). But a brain built for some functions can do orders of magnitude more simply by virtue of its basic construction as a flexible computer. **Never in biological history has evolution built a structure with such an enormous and ramifying set of exaptive possibilities**. The basis of human flexibility lies in the unselected capacities of our large brain (1984a, pp. 67-68, parenthetical items in orig., emp. added).

We covered the Gould/Vrba idea of "exaptations" in chapter six, and so we will not repeat that material here. For now, however, one thing is certain: consciousness does appear to be connected to the brain. Yet that causes as many problems as it presents solutions, as Gregory observed:

> We believe that consciousness is tied to living organisms: especially human beings, and more particularly to specific regions of the human brain.... This in turn generates the question: "What is the relation between consciousness and the matter or functions of the brain?" ...One trouble about consciousness is that it cannot be (or has not yet been) isolated from brains, to study it in different contexts. So the classical methods of scientific inquiry are not fully available for investigating the brain/mind relation (1977, pp. 274, 276, parenthetical item in orig.).

Paleoanthropologist Richard Leakey chimed in to agree:

> The most obvious change in the hominid brain in its evolutionary trajectory was, as noted, a tripling of size. Size was not the only change, however; the overall organization changed, too. The brains of apes and humans are constructed on the same basic pattern: both are divided into left and right hemispheres, each of which has four distinct lobes: frontal, parietal, temporal, and occipital. In apes, the occipital lobes (at the back of the brain) are larger than the frontal lobes; in humans, the pattern is reversed, with large frontals and small occipital lobes. **This difference in organization presumably underlies in some way the generation of the human mind** as opposed to the ape mind. If we knew when the change in configuration occurred in human prehistory, we would have a clue about the emergence of human mind.

Alas, Leakey lamented:

> **Much of this, of course, is speculation. How can we know what happened to our ancestors' level of consciousness** during the past 2.5 million years? How can we pinpoint when it became as we experience it today? **The harsh reality anthropologists**

face is that these questions may be unanswerable. If I have difficulty proving that another human possesses the same level of consciousness I do, and if most biologists balk at trying to determine the degree of consciousness in nonhuman animals, how is one to discern the signs of reflective consciousness in creatures long dead? (1994, pp. 145,154-155, parenthetical item in orig., emp. added).

To be sure, brains are terribly important from an evolutionary perspective. Brain scientist Roger Sperry remarked:

> It is clear that the human brain has come a long way in evolution.... Maybe the total falls a bit short of universal causal contact; maybe it is not even quite up to the kind of things that evolution has going for itself over on Galaxy Nine; and maybe, in spite of all, any decision that comes out is still predetermined. Nevertheless, it still represents a very long jump in the direction of freedom from the primeval slime mold, the Jurassic sand dollar, or even the latest model orangutan (1977, p. 433).

One widely held view regarding the "very long jump" from the three pounds of matter inside a human skull being "just" a brain, to the type of complex brain that permits and/or produces consciousness, appears to be that once the brain reached a certain size, consciousness merely "came along for the ride." Or, as Ruse theorized:

> Whatever position is taken on evolution, no one is denying that consciousness is in some sense connected to or emergent from the brain. The question—at least the question that concerns Darwinians—is whether, over and above the brain, consciousness has some biological standing in its own right. General opinion (my opinion!) is that somehow, as brains got bigger and better during animal evolution, consciousness started to emerge in a primitive sort of way. Brains developed for calculating purposes and **consciousness emerged and, as it were, got dragged along**. Most Darwinians think that at some point, consciousness came into its own right (2001b, pp. 197-198, parenthetical item in orig., emp. added).

There are, however, a number of "alternative explanations" for why the brain ultimately developed consciousness. Gregory listed just a few when he wrote: "It has been suggested that: (1) mind and brain are not connected (epiphenomenalism); or (2) that the brain generates consciousness; or (3) that consciousness drives the brain; or (4) that they both work in parallel (like a pair of identical clocks) without causal connection" (1977, p. 279, parenthetical items in orig.). Then again, not everyone is ecstatic about the concept of increased brain size being responsible for something as important and quixotic as consciousness. Roger Lewin, in *Complexity: Life at the Edge of Chaos,* observed:

> I found many biologists distinctly uncomfortable with talking about increase in brain size as a measure of complexity. "I'm hostile to all sorts of mystical urges toward great complexity," said Richard Dawkins when I asked him whether an increase in computational complexity might be considered an inevitable part of the evolutionary process. "You'd like to think that being able to solve problems contributes to Darwinian fitness, wouldn't you?," said John Maynard Smith. "But it's hard to relate increased brain size to fitness. After all, bacteria are fit" (1992, p. 146).

Steven Pinker, the eminent psychologist from MIT, is no happier with the idea that "a big brain explains it all." In his book, *The Language Instinct,* he lamented:

> At the level of the whole brain, that there has been selection for bigger brains is, to be sure, common among writings about human evolution (especially from paleoanthropologists). Given that premise, one might naturally think that all kinds of computational abilities might come as a by-product. But if you think about it for a minute, you should quickly see that the premise has it backwards. Why would evolution ever have selected for sheer bigness of brain, that bulbous, metabolically greedy organ? **A large-brained creature is sentenced to a life that combines all the disadvantages of balancing a watermelon on a broom-**

stick, running in place in a down jacket, and for women, passing a large kidney stone every few years. Any selection on brain size itself would surely have favored the pinhead. Selection for more powerful computational abilities (language, perception, reasoning, and so on) must have given us a big brain as a by-product, not the other way around! (1994, pp. 374-375, parenthetical items in orig., emp. added).

Furthermore, "brain size," as it turns out, doesn't live up to its vaunted reputation. Brain size and intellect among living people have been thoroughly explored by, among others, such scientists as evolutionist W. LeGros Clark, who reported that skulls from humans of normal intelligence vary in cranial capacity anywhere from 900cc to 2,300 cc. In fact, Dr. Clark discussed one completely normal human being whose brain size was a mere 720 cc (see Clark, 1958; pp. 357-360, Howe, 1971, p. 213).

If natural selection didn't "choose" consciousness (because it has no "causal effects"), if consciousness has no known function (from an evolutionary point of view), and if "evolving a big brain" isn't an adequate explanation for consciousness—then, to repeat our original question, **why** did consciousness arise in the first place? What does it **do**?

Some evolutionists have suggested that consciousness arose "so that people could process language." But, as Wright pointed out:

> People who claim to have a scientific answer usually turn out to have misunderstood the question. For example, some people say that consciousness arose so that people could process language. And it's true, of course, that we're conscious of language. As we speak, we have the subjective experience of turning our thoughts into words. It even feels as if our inner, conscious self is **causing** the words to be formed. But, whatever it may feel like, the (often unspoken) premise of modern behavioral science is that when you are in conversation with someone, all the causing hap-

pens at a physical level. That someone flaps his or her tongue, generating physical sound waves that enter your ear, triggering a sequence of physical processes in your brain that ultimately result in the flapping of your own tongue, and so on. In short: the **experience** of assimilating someone's words and formulating a reply is superfluous to the assimilation and the reply, both of which are just intricate mechanical processes.

Besides, if conscious experience arose to abet human language, then why does it also accompany such things as getting our fingers smashed by rocks—things that existed long before human language? The question of consciousness—as I'm defining it here—isn't the question of why we think when we talk, and it isn't the question of why we have **self**-awareness. The question of consciousness is the question of subjective experience **in general**, ranging from pain to anxiety to epiphany; it is the question of sentience (2000, p. 307, parenthetical item and emp. in orig.).

Peter Wilson asked:

But how is self-consciousness possible? What evolutionary conditions in the constitution and environment of the early hominid came together, formulating a problematic that made such consciousness adaptive? We might choose to cite certain suggestions that language is the prerequisite, for it is only with the aid of language that we can find the way to give reality, by articulation to the inchoate intuition of the divided self. But language may play this role only in a mechanical sense, by providing a means of **expressing** and **symbolizing** consciousness (1980, p. 86, emp. in orig.).

"Expressing" and "symbolizing" consciousness are not the same as "explaining" consciousness.

Alwyn Scott, in his book, *Stairway to the Mind: The Controversial New Science of Consciousness*, suggested that "consciousness gives an evolutionary advantage to the species that develops it" (1995, p. 162). But what, exactly, might that advantage be? W.H. Thorpe chose the simplest option of all: "The production of consciousness may have been an evolutionary necessity, in that it may have been the only way in which highly complex living organisms could become fully viable" (1965, p. 493). Adam Zeman, in the review of the subject of consciousness that he wrote for the journal, *Brain*, chose a different tact: "[I]t can be argued, at a conceptual level, that the concept of one's own mind presupposes the concept of other minds" (2001, 124:1281). In an article he wrote for *New Scientist* titled "Nature's Psychologists" (and, later, in his book, *A History of the Mind*), Nicholas Humphrey seized on that thought to provide one example of the type of theories that have been proposed to explain the "evolutionary advantage" of consciousness. He suggested that the purpose of consciousness is to allow "social animals" to model another's behavior on the basis of their insight into another creature's psychological motivation. In other words, our knowledge of our own mental states supplies us with insight into the mental states underlying the actions of others–which then: (a) provides us with the ability to predict what someone else is likely to do; and (b) thereby becomes a major determinant of our own biological success (1978). Or, as Paul Ehrlich asked:

> What could have been the selective advantage that led to the evolution of intense consciousness? This type of consciousness helps us to maneuver in a complicated society of other individuals, each of whom is also intensely conscious. Intense consciousness also allows us to plan without acting out the plans and to consider that other individuals probably also are planning (2000, p. 113).

Not to be outdone, Merlin Donald, in *A Mind So Rare*, offered up his own supposition. "Conscious capacity," he wrote, "may be seen as an evolutionary adaptation in its own right, whose various functions have evolved to optimize or boost cognitive processing" (2001, p. 131). Ah, yes–"optimizing cognitive processing." And how would consciousness (which, as Eccles admitted, is "causally impotent") accomplish that? Then, last, but certainly not least, Ruse weighed in with his guess.

This raises the question of what consciousness actually does. Why should we not just have a nonthinking machine, which does everything? Is consciousness little more than froth on the top of the electronics of the brain? Is consciousness just an epiphenomenon, as philosophers would say? Slowly but positively, brain scientists do feel that they are groping toward some understanding of the virtues of consciousness, over and above the operation of blind automata. It is felt that **consciousness may act as a kind of filter and guide—coordinating all the information thrown up by the brain**. Consciousness helps to prevent the brain from getting overloaded, as happens all too often with computers. Consciousness regulates experience, sifting through the input, using some and rejecting some and storing some... (2001b, p. 198, emp. added).

Thus, consciousness, so we are told: (a) acts as a filter or guide to coordinate all the information thrown up by the brain; (b) prevents the brain from getting overloaded; (c) regulates experience; (d) sifts through input into the brain; and (d) rejects some experience and stores others. Pretty impressive achievement, wouldn't you say, for the nebulous "something" referred to as consciousness that, supposedly, "natural selection had no or little role in producing" (Ruse), "is causally impotent" (Eccles), "is fundamentally unknowable" (McGinn), and "is not a causal agent" (Gregory). Which, in turn, brings us to our next question.

How Did Consciousness Arise?

It is not enough to ask **why** consciousness arose. One also must inquire as to **how** consciousness originated. In *Man: The Promising Primate*, Wilson asked:

[H]ow is it possible for one species, the human, to develop consciousness, and particular self-consciousness, to such a degree that it becomes of critical importance for the individual's sanity and survival? And what is the meaning of this development in and for human evolution? (1980, p. 84).

Human consciousness is so pervasive, and so undeniable, that the mechanism of its existence **must** be explained. But how? One practically can envision Stephen Jay Gould shrugging his shoulders in exasperation, and sighing in frustration, as he admitted: "...[W]e must view the evolution of human consciousness as a lucky accident that occurred only by the fortunate (for us) concatenation of numerous improbabilities" (1984a, p. 64, parenthetical item in orig.). Five years later, he continued in the same vein: "*Homo sapiens* may form only a twig, but if life moves, even fitfully, toward greater complexity and higher mental powers, then the eventual origin of self-conscious intelligence may be implicit in all that came before" (1989, p. 45). After another five years had passed, he wrote:

> *Homo sapiens* did not appear on the earth, just a geologic second ago, because evolutionary theory predicts such an outcome based on themes of progress and increasing neural complexity. Humans arose, rather, as a fortuitous and contingent outcome of thousands of linked events, any one of which could have occurred differently and sent history on an alternative pathway that would not have led to consciousness (1994, 271 [4]:86).

Then, two years later, in his book, *Full House: The Spread of Excellence from Plato to Darwin*, Dr. Gould concluded:

> If one small and odd lineage of fishes had not evolved fins capable of bearing weight on land (though evolved for different reasons in lakes and seas), terrestrial vertebrates would never have arisen. If a large extraterrestrial object—the ultimate random bolt from the blue—had not triggered the extinction of dinosaurs 65 million years ago, mammals would still be small creatures, confined to the nooks and crannies of a dinosaur's world, and incapable of evolving the larger size that brains big enough for self-consciousness require. If a small and tenuous population of protohumans had not survived a hundred slings and arrows of outrageous fortune (and potential extinction) on the savannas of Africa, then *Homo sapiens* would never have emerged to spread

throughout the globe. **We are glorious accidents of an unpredictable process with no drive to complexity, not the expected results of evolutionary principles that yearn to produce a creature capable of understanding the mode of its own necessary construction** (1996a, p. 216, parenthetical items in orig., emp. added).

While it is convenient to surmise that consciousness is a "concatenation of numerous improbabilities," the result of the "contingent outcome of thousands of linked events," or a "glorious accident," such speculation does not explain **how** consciousness arose. So how did it arise?

On occasion (quite often, in fact), evolutionists have been known to criticize creationists for their reliance on what the evolutionists see as "just-so" stories (a phrase from Rudyard Kipling's children's book of the same title, in which fanciful explanations are offered for adaptations, such as the elephant's trunk). But, as the old adage suggests, "the sauce that is good for the goose also is good for the gander." Or, to put it another way, evolutionists are not above weaving their own "just-so" stories—when it suits their purpose. Consider the following examples.

In *A Mind So Rare*, Donald crafted a fascinating "just-so" story about how consciousness might have arisen. Walk with him on his imaginary journey.

> The path to higher conscious function was long and indirect…. We stand at the far end of a long process of evolution. The material origins of consciousness started in specific kinds of nervous systems. Conscious capacity evolved, with its various component systems in parallel, in many species, in a series of slow-moving adaptations of the vertebrate brain, each for its own local reasons. The earliest conscious functions were focused on achieving basic perceptual unity, and more recently evolved ones on gaining a better fix on short-term events in the environment, as well as achieving more effective control over behavior in the intermediate term. The core brain systems of primates remain

the foundation of human conscious capacity, but they have been greatly expanded in the human brain, through the neocortex.

Conscious capacity involves many brain subsystems, some of which evolved independently of one another. However, there is reason to think that in early hominids, all these systems might have changed together, in a fairly synchronized manner, as a sort of evolutionary cluster. When a cluster of traits evolves more or less simultaneously as a piece, it is sometimes called a suite of adaptations. I have called the cluster of skills underlying human conscious capacity, the hominid Executive Suite. [Donald included in the Executive Suite: self-monitoring, divided attention, self-reminding, autocuing, self-recognition, rehearsal and review, whole-body imitation, mindreading, pedagogy, gesture, symbolic invention, and complex skill hierarchies—BH/BT.] **We don't yet have a complete or detailed picture of the Executive Suite**....

Any species aspiring to a high degree of intelligence must acquire symbolic skill. There is something different and powerful about symbolic capacity, and intentional representations. According to our present indications, **only humans have this ability**....

[T]he special nature of human cognition can be approached by comparing ourselves with other primates. Humans are broadly equipped with more powerful mental models than most primates. We also have more communicative ability, more symbolic capacity, and more advanced tool technology than they have. In this sense, there seems to be some hierarchy of primate intelligence, and it probably parallels our global impression of the hierarchy of primate consciousness. The underlying mechanisms of this putative hierarchy should tell a story of conservative, gradualistic change, regardless of what interpretative spin we might wish to place on it....

Down deep, we are still primates and retain the primate kind of mind, which lacks some of the specialized capacities of bats, fishes, birds, cats, and so on and has its own peculiar profile. Moreover, we are a special kind of primate, with a very particular pattern of emotional and social behavior. **This is a deep design feature of being human**, and our representational capacity cannot alter that fundamental constraint. ...Symbols can radically amplify the power of any mind, whatever its design. They can alter awareness as well. Or is it the other way around? **Perhaps symbolic skill is the result, not the cause, of increased conscious capacity. This is the heart of the matter** (pp. 114,115-116,117,138-139, emp. added).

By way of summary, then, what have we "learned" via this scenario? First, "the path to higher conscious function was long and indirect." Second, "any species aspiring to a high degree of intelligence must acquire symbolic skill." Third, unfortunately, "we don't yet have a complete or detailed picture" of how such things as self-recognition, the use of symbolic language, etc. arose. Fourth, we're not sure if such skills caused consciousness, or if consciousness caused such skills.

The "heart of the matter," therefore, is this: there is not a shred of scientific evidence for the classic "just-so" story as told by Donald. It is little more than "pie-in-the-sky, I-hope-so-by-and-by" wishful thinking. But it is hardly the only such "just-so" story now making the rounds. Stephen Jay Gould—effective popularizer of evolution that he was—spun a much more fascinating tale of how he thought consciousness evolved. By his best guess, **human consciousness is rooted in the destruction of the dinosaurs** 65-70 million years ago as the result of a giant asteroid hitting the Earth and driving them to extinction.

Does this strike you as a bit odd? Does it leave you wondering exactly how the dinosaurs' demise could possibly account for, of all things, **human consciousness**? Read on. Another "just-so" story is right around the corner.

> If mammals had arisen late and helped to drive dinosaurs to their doom, then we could legitimately propose a scenario of expected progress. But dinosaurs

remained dominant and probably became extinct only as a quirky result of the most unpredictable of events—a mass dying triggered by extraterrestrial impact. If dinosaurs had not died in this event, they would probably still dominate the domain of large-bodied vertebrates, as they had for so long with such conspicuous success, and mammals would still be small creatures in the interstices of their world. This situation prevailed for a hundred million years; why not for sixty million more? Since dinosaurs were not moving toward markedly larger brains, and since such a prospect may lie outside the capabilities of reptilian deign, we must assume that consciousness would not have evolved on our planet if a cosmic catastrophe had not claimed the dinosaurs as victims. In an entirely literal sense, we owe our existence, as large and reasoning mammals, to our lucky stars (Gould, 1989, p. 318).

The meaning of the extraterrestrial theory for human consciousness as a cosmic accident begins with a basic fact that should be more widely known (but that will surprise most non-professionals, who assume something different): *dinosaurs and mammals evolved at the same time.* Mammals did not arise later, as superior forms that gradually replaced inferior dinosaurs by competition. Mammals existed throughout the 100 million years of dinosaurian domination—and they lived as small, mostly mouse-sized creatures in the ecological interstices of a world ruled by large reptiles. They did not get bigger; they did not get better (or at least their changes did nothing to drive dinosaurs toward extinction). They did nothing to dislodge the incumbents; they bided their time.

Structural or mental inferiority did not drive the dinosaurs to extinction. They were doing well, and showing no sign of ceding domination, right until the extraterrestrial debacle unleashed a set of sudden consequences (as yet to be adequately specified, although the "nuclear winter" scenario of a cold, dark world has been proposed for the same reasons). Some mammals weathered the storm; no dinosaurs did. We have no reason to believe that mammals prevailed as a result of any feature traditionally asserted to prove their superiority—warm-bloodedness, live bearing, large brains, for example. Their "success" might well be attributed to nothing more than their size—for nothing large and terrestrial got through the Cretaceous debacle, while many small creatures survived.

In any case, had the cometary shower (or whatever) not hit, we have no reason to think that dinosaurs, having dominated the earth for 100 million years, would not have held on for another 65 to continue their hegemony today. In such a case, mammals would probably still be mouse-sized creatures living on the fringes —after all, they had done nothing else for 100 million years before. Moreover, dinosaurs were not evolving toward any form of consciousness. In other words, those comets or asteroids were the *sine quibus non* [something absolutely indispensable—BH/BT] of our current existence. **Without the removal of dinosaurs that they engendered, consciousness would not have evolved on our earth** (Gould, 1984a, pp. 65-66, italics and parenthetical items in orig., emp. added).

Little wonder, then, that Dr. Gould concluded in an article ("The Evolution of Life on the Earth") he wrote for the October 1994 issue of *Scientific American*: "*H. sapiens* is but a tiny, late-arising twig on life's enormously arborescent bush—a small bud that would almost surely not appear a second time if we could replant the bush from seed and let it grow again" (271 [4]:91).

As far as Gould and some of his colleagues are concerned, *Homo sapiens* may be nothing but a "tiny twig" or a "small bud." But human consciousness ("our most precious possession," "the greatest of miracles") has defied every attempt by evolutionists to explain either the reason for its existence or the mechanism leading to its development. Further complicating matters is the obvious and undeniable fact that our consciousness/ self-awareness allows us to experience (and express!) what Sir Roger Penrose has referred to as "non-computable elements"

—things like compassion, morality, and many others–that mere neural activity is extremely hard pressed to explain. As Dr. Penrose put it:

> There are some types of words which would seem to involve non-computable elements–for example, judgement, common sense, insight, aesthetic sensibility, compassion, morality.... These seem to me to be things which are not just features of computations.... If there indeed exists some sort of contact with Platonic absolutes which our awareness enables us to achieve, and which cannot be explained in terms of computational behaviour, then **that seems to me to be an important issue** (1997, p. 125, first ellipsis in orig., second ellipsis and emp. added).

An important issue? Talk about understatement! It is difficult enough to try to invent "just-so" stories to explain **why** consciousness arose in the first place, and then to explain **how** it did so. But to try to explain the role that consciousness plays in such "important issues" within humanity as common sense, judgment, aesthetics, compassion, and morality–well, let's just say that Michael Ruse had it right when he observed: "I hardly need say that **all of these suggestions raise as many questions and problems as they answer**. Philosophers and scientists are working hard toward answers and resolutions" (2001b, pp. 199-200, emp. added). Anthony O'Hear, in his book, *Beyond Evolution: Human Nature and the Limits of Evolutionary Explanation,* remarked: "What is crucially at issue here is not how human self-consciousness might have come about, but what its significance is once it has come about" (1997, p. 22).

In a special April 10, 2000 issue of *Time* magazine devoted to the subject of "Visions of Space and Science," Steven Pinker, professor of brain and cognitive sciences at MIT and author of *How the Mind Works,* wrote an article titled "Will the Mind Figure Out How the Brain Works?," in which he concluded:

> Will we ever understand the brain as well as we understand the heart, say, or the kidney? Will mad scientists or dictators have the means to control our

thoughts? Will neurologists scan our brains down to the last synapse and duplicate the wiring in a silicon chip, giving our minds eternal life?

No one can say. The human brain is the most complex object in the known universe, with billions of chattering neurons connected by trillions of synapses. No scientific problem compares to it. (The Human Genome Project, which is trying to read a long molecular sentence composed of billions of letters, is simple by comparison.) Cognitive neuroscience is arming so many brilliant minds with such high technology that it would be foolish to predict that we will never understand how the brain gives rise to the mind. But the problem is so hard that it would be just as foolish to predict that we will.

One challenge is that we are still clueless about how the brain represents the content of our thoughts and feelings (2000, 155[4]:91, parenthetical item in orig., emp. added).

Or, as brain scientist John Beloff admitted in an article titled "The Mind-Brain Problem": "The fact is that, leaving aside mythical and religious cosmologies, **the position of mind in nature remains a total mystery**.... At present there is no agreement even as to what would count here as decisive evidence" (1994, emp. added).

We would like to close this discussion about **how** consciousness arose with the following statements from Bryan Appleyard.

Hard science will fight back at this point by attempting to deny this is a problem at all. Self-consciousness is merely a by-product of evolutionary complexity. Animals develop larger brains as survival mechanisms. Over millions of years these brains attain awesome levels of miniaturization and organization; indeed, they become the most complicated things in the universe. Then, one day, this complexity gives rise to something utterly unprecedented. Perhaps the internal functional explanation is that the brain-machine becomes so complex that it begins to make new connections not directly related to the daily requirements of survival. By some design fluke, a surplus of processing capacity emerges which manifests itself as self-awareness. The higher primates are able to start the thought processes which will lead to the cosmically staggering insight: "I am a higher primate." Perhaps the critical moment comes when, as the biologist Richard Dawkins has suggested, the brain achieves sufficient complexity to be able to contain a model of itself. Or, as Douglas Hofstadter puts it, "The self comes into being at the moment it has the power to reflect itself."

…The reason such explanations feel inadequate, even though, as children of the scientific age, we probably accept them at the back of our minds, is that they are incoherent. **They do not explain self-consciousness, they explain complexity**.

Of course, the hard evolutionist may still respond by claiming that this is a by-product of complexity. The elaborations and anomalies of our language and our awareness are merely a kind of surplus capacity to idle that happens to occur in the brain. We have more neurons than are strictly necessary to gather food or reproduce, so when they are not thus engaged, or even sometimes when they are, they chatter on in endless circular arguments which only *seem* important. In reality, they are trivial—in the words of Peter Atkins they are "special but not significant."

But, again, this is incoherent. How can it be "not significant" that we are able to use and understand the words "not significant"? What meaning can the word "significant" have in such a context? Significant to what? **If self-consciousness is "not significant," then where on earth is significance to be found?** (1992, pp. 194,195-196, italics in orig., emp. added).

We couldn't have said it better ourselves. If human consciousness doesn't rank as being "significant," what does?

EVOLUTIONARY BIAS AND THE ORIGIN OF HUMAN CONSCIOUSNESS

Bias is a difficult thing to admit. It also is a difficult thing to overcome. Some would even say impossible. Donald Johanson, in his book, *Lucy: The Beginnings of Humankind* (which discusses *Australopithecus afarensis*, arguably the world's most famous "hominid" fossil), addressed this subject in an admirably candid manner when he wrote: "There is no such thing as a total lack of bias. I have it; everybody has it." But Dr. Johanson did not stop there. He went on to note: "**The insidious thing about bias is that it does make one deaf to the cries of other evidence**" (Johanson and Edey, 1981, p. 277, emp. added).

Oh, how true. And the veracity of this assessment is especially evident when the bias involves an intractable determination to live without God. Will Durant was a self-proclaimed humanist and avowed atheist, yet he nevertheless wrote: "The greatest question of our time is not communism vs. individualism, not Europe vs. America, not even the East vs. the West; it is whether men can bear to live without God" (1932, p. 23).

The steely resolve "to live without God" has become the mantra of many scientists and philosophers. Sir Julian Huxley, himself an atheist, compared God to the disappearing act performed by the Cheshire cat in *Alice's Adventures in Wonderland* when he wrote: "The supernatural is being swept out of the universe.... God is beginning to resemble not a ruler, but the last fading smile of a cosmic Cheshire cat" (1957, p. 59). To Huxley, and thousands of others like him, "the God argument" has been effectively routed.

Disbelief in God, though, is an *a priori* decision that **is not based on evidence!** Time and again, eminent atheists, agnostics, skeptics, and infidels have made their positions in this regard crystal clear. The widely published comments of the late biochemist and science writer, Isaac Asimov, are an excellent example. In a thought-provoking interview by the editor of *The*

Humanist, Paul Kurtz, Dr. Asimov was asked how he would classify himself. He responded: "Emotionally, I am an atheist. I don't have the evidence to prove that God doesn't exist, but I so strongly suspect he doesn't that I don't want to waste my time" (Asimov, 1982, 2[2]:9).

Once a person comes to the decision that he "strongly suspects" that God does not exist, where does that leave him? With God out of the picture, two facts become prominent—and problematic—very quickly. First, a naturalistic system of origins (i.e., organic evolution) **must** be invoked to explain, not just man's origin, but **everything**! As Huxley went on to say three years after he made the above statement: "The earth was not created; it evolved. So did all the animals and plants that inhabit it, including our human selves, mind and soul as well as brain and body. So did religion" (1960, pp. 252-253).

George Gaylord Simpson wrote that evolution "achieves the aspect of purpose without the intervention of a purposer, and has produced a vast plan without the action of a planner" (1947, p. 489). In a strictly reductionist scheme, the idea that organisms deliberately pursue goals must be rejected, since "purpose" cannot be reduced to the laws of physics. Biologist Alex Novikoff wrote: "Only when purpose was excluded from descriptions of all biological activity…could biological problems be properly formulated and analyzed" (1945, 101:212-213).

Another scientist from Harvard, E.O. Wilson (the "father of sociobiology"), weighed in on this same theme in his book, *On Human Nature,* when he commented on the very first page: "If humankind evolved by Darwinian natural selection, genetic chance and environmental necessity, not God, made the species" (1978, p. 1). Or, as Brown University evolutionist Kenneth Miller put it in his 1999 volume, *Finding Darwin's God:*

> My particular religious beliefs or yours notwithstanding, **it is a fact that in the scientific world of the late twentieth century, the displacement of God by Darwinian forces is almost complete**. This view is not always articulated openly, perhaps for fear of offending the faithful, but the literature of science is

not a good place to keep secrets. Scientific writing, especially on evolution, shows this displacement clearly (p. 15, emp. added).

Second, with God having been "displaced," like it or not, man is on his own. Simpson remarked in his book, *Life of the Past:*

> **Man stands alone in the universe**, a unique product of a long, unconscious, impersonal material process with unique understanding and potentialities. **These he owes to no one but himself, and it is to himself that he is responsible**. He is not the creature of uncontrollable and undeterminable forces, but is his own master. He can and must decide and manage his own destiny (1953, p. 155, emp. added).

Nobel laureate Jacques Monod, in his dismally depressing *magnum opus, Chance and Necessity,* concluded: "Man at least knows he is alone in the unfeeling immensity of the universe, out of which he has emerged only by chance" (1971, p. 180). But Monod's comments are "lighthearted" compared to those of another Nobel laureate, Steven Weinberg. In his book about the origin and fate of the Universe, *The First Three Minutes,* he penned what many believe are some of the most seriously disheartening words imaginable. Read, and weep.

> It is almost irresistible for humans to believe that we have some special relation to the universe, that human life is not just a more-or-less farcical outcome of a chain of accidents reaching back to the first three minutes, but that we were somehow build in from the beginning. As I write this I happen to be in an airplane at 30,000 feet, flying over Wyoming en route home from San Francisco to Boston. Below, the earth looks very soft and comfortable—fluffy clouds here and there, snow turning pink as the sun sets, roads stretching straight across the country from one town to another. **It is very hard to realize that this all is just a tiny part of an overwhelmingly hostile universe**. It is even harder to realize that this present universe has evolved from an unspeakably unfamiliar early condition, and faces a future extinction of end-

less cold or intolerable heat. **The more the universe seems comprehensible, the more it also seems pointless**. But if there is no solace in the fruits of our research, there is at least some consolation in the research itself. Men and women are not content to comfort themselves with tales of gods and giants, or to confine their thoughts to the daily affairs of life; they also build telescopes and satellites and accelerators, and sit at their desks for endless hours working out the meaning of the data they gather. The effort to understand the universe is one of the very few things that lifts human life a little above the level of farce, and gives it some of the grace of tragedy (1977, pp. 154-155, emp. added).

Alas, then, as Richard Leakey and Roger Lewin put it in their book, *Origins:* "There is no law that declares the human animal to be different, as seen in this broad biological perspective, from any other animal" (1977, p. 256). A bleak thought, to be sure–but from an evolutionist's self-imposed view, inescapably true nevertheless.

Perhaps now is the time to ask: **Where does all of this inevitably lead?** Actions have consequences, and beliefs have implications. In a chapter titled "Scientific Humanism" in his book, *The Humanist Alternative,* Paul Kurtz concluded: "To adopt such a scientific approach unreservedly is to accept as **ultimate in all matters of fact and real existence the appeal to the evidence of experience alone–a court subordinate to no higher authority**, to be over-ridden by no prejudice however comfortable" (1973, p. 109, emp. added). That "higher authority" must be avoided at all cost. Herman J. Eckelmann, in an article titled "Some Concluding Thoughts on Evolutionary Belief," echoed an interesting refrain when he asked: "Is it possible that one can have too high an emotional stake in wanting to have a God-less universe?" (1991, p. 345). That "emotional stake" is a driving force behind the refusal to submit to that "higher authority." If you doubt that, then listen to the admission of Harvard geneticist Richard Lewontin.

Our willingness to accept scientific claims against common sense is the key to an understanding of the real struggle between science and the supernatural. We take the side of science *in spite* of the patent absurdity of some of its constructs, *in spite* of its failure to fulfill many of its extravagant promises of health and life, *in spite* of the tolerance of the scientific community for unsubstantiated just-so stories, because **we have a prior commitment, a commitment to naturalism. It is not that the methods and institutions of science somehow compel us to accept a material explanation of the phenomenal world, but, on the contrary, that we are forced by our *a priori* adherence to material causes** to create an apparatus of investigation and a set of concepts that produce material explanations, no matter how counterintuitive, no mater how mystifying to the uninitiated. Moreover, that materialism is absolute, for **we cannot allow a Divine Foot in the door**. The eminent Kant scholar Lewis Beck used to say that anyone who could believe in God could believe in anything. To appeal to an omnipotent deity is to allow that at any moment the regularities of nature may be ruptured, that miracles may happen (1997, p. 31, italics in orig., emp. added).

Or, as Alwyn Scott confessed:

In the realm of science, one's attitude toward what Karl Popper called "the great tradition of materialism" is often used as an index of respectability. Those who turn away from this tradition to consider the nature of consciousness run the risk of being marked as flakes who might also believe in psychokinesis (spoon bending), mental telepathy, clairvoyance, precognition, and the like. **The safest course—especially for the young scientist—is to shun such temptations and concentrate on the data from a particular level of the hierarchy** (1995, p. 167, parenthetical item in orig., emp. added).

WHAT DOES ALL OF THIS HAVE TO DO WITH THE ORIGIN OF *HUMAN* CONSCIOUSNESS?

Once the scientists and philosophers have admitted their bias against God and the supernatural, and therefore have limited themselves to the purely naturalistic explanations offered by organic evolution, they are severely limited in how they can explain human consciousness—what Popper and Eccles called "the greatest of miracles." These individuals desperately desire—in fact, absolutely must have—evolution as an explanation for "whatever exists" (which includes human consciousness). As Sir Francis Crick put it: "The ultimate aim of the modern movement in biology is in fact to explain **all** of biology in terms of physics and chemistry" (1966, p. 10, emp. added). Emil du-Bois-Reymand (1818-1896), the founder of electrochemistry, and Hermann von Helmholtz (1812-1894), the famed German physiologist and physicist who was the first to measure the speed of nerve impulses, agreed: "**All** the activities of living material, including consciousness, are ultimately to be explained in terms of physics and chemistry" (as quoted in Leake, 1964, sec. 4, pp. 5-6, emp. added). Richard Leakey observed:

> This is one of the paradoxes of *Homo sapiens:* we experience the unity and diversity of a mind shaped by eons of life as hunter-gatherers. We experience its unity in the common possession of an awareness of self and a sense of awe at the miracle of life. And we experience its diversity in the different cultures—expressed in language, customs, and religions—that we create and that create us. **We should rejoice at so wondrous a product of evolution** (1994, p. 157, emp. added).

Robert Ornstein wrote in *The Evolution of Consciousness*:

> Our mind did not spring from a designer, nor from a set of ideal and idealized programs…. Instead, **it evolved on the same adaptive basis as the rest**

of biological evolution, using the processes of random generation and selection of what is so generated…. The story of the mind lies in many accidents and many changes of function (1991, pp. 4-5, emp. added).

Ornstein went on to say:

Working in such boundless time, all evolution needs is a tiny and consistent advantage at any point for things to add up…. In millions of years, and with a generation time of five years, there is an immense time for adaptations to tally up in prehumans. And, in living beings who reproduce quickly (in animals, generation times are only three or four years, and in bacteria, almost no time), major changes can occur in only a few thousand years. *E. coli*, the bacterium of choice for research, has a generation cycle of hours. Granted so much time, and selection for advantages, all the **biological miracles have had *plenty* of time and *plenty* of chance to have happened** (p. 28, italics and parenthetical item in orig., emp. added).

Alan Dressler dryly commented in his book, *Voyage to the Great Attractor*: "The universe has invented a way to know itself" (1994, p. 335).

Or has it? Can "biological miracles" occur just because there is supposed to have been "plenty of time and plenty of chance?" Monod wistfully wrote: "Chance alone is the source of every innovation, of all creation in the biosphere…. All forms of life are the product of chance…" (1972, pp. 110,167). Such a view, however, ascribes to "chance" properties that it does not, and cannot, possess. Sproul, Gerstner, and Lindsley addressed this logical fallacy and concluded: "Chance is incapable of creating a single molecule, let alone an entire universe. Why not? Chance is no thing. It is not an entity. It has no being, no power, no force. It can effect nothing for it has no causal power within it" (1984, p. 118).

One of the twentieth century's most eminent evolutionists was French zoologist Pierre-Paul Grassé, "whose knowledge of the living world," according to evolutionary geneticist

Theodosius Dobzhansky, "was encyclopedic" (1975, 29:376). In his classic tome, *Evolution of Living Organisms*, Dr. Grassé addressed the idea of chance being responsible for evolution when he wrote: **"To insist...that life appeared quite by chance and evolved in this fashion is an unfounded supposition which I believe to be wrong and not in accordance with the facts"** (1977, p. 107, emp. added).

Grassé also addressed, as did Ornstein in his quote above, bacterial generation times and their relevance to evolution. In fact, Dr. Grassé discussed the very microorganism, *Escherichia coli,* that Ornstein mentioned—yet drew an entirely different conclusion.

> Bacteria, the study of which has formed a great part of the foundation of genetics and molecular biology, are the organisms which, because of their huge numbers, produce the most mutations.... [B]acteria, despite their great production of intraspecific varieties, exhibit a great fidelity to their species. The bacillus *Escherichia coli,* whose mutants have been studied very carefully, is the best example. The reader will agree that **it is surprising, to say the least, to want to prove evolution and to discover its mechanisms and then to choose as a material for this study a being which practically stabilized a billion years ago** (p. 87, emp. added).

In spite of all this, numerous scientists and philosophers exhibit a dogged determination to explain the incredible nature of human consciousness—a determination that, if we may kindly say so, is itself **incredible**! And they are not the least bit shy about admitting their built-in bias. Colin McGinn put the matter in perspective quite well when he said: **"Resolutely shunning the supernatural,** I think it is undeniable that it must be in virtue of *some* natural property of the brain that organisms are conscious. There just *has* to be some explanation for how brains [interact with] minds" (1993, p. 6, italics in orig., emp. added).

In other words, now that it has been declared (by what almost amounts to divine fiat) that **God** didn't do it, then it's obvious that "something else" must have. There just **has** to be some **naturalistic** explanation for how brains interact with minds! As Gordon Allport summarized the problem: "For two generations, psychologists have tried every conceivable way of accounting for the integration, organization and striving of the human person without having recourse to the postulate of a self" (1955, p. 37).

Whatever that explanation may be, and wherever that "self" may have come from, there is one thing evolutionists know it is **not**–God and the supernatural. Ian Glynn, in his book, *An Anatomy of Thought: The Origin and Machinery of the Mind*, admitted as much when he wrote:

> My own starting position can be summed up in three statements: first, that the only minds whose existence we can be confident of are associated with complex brains of humans and some other animals; second, that we (and other animals with minds) are the product of evolution by natural selection; and, third, that **neither in the origin of life nor in its subsequent evolution has there been any supernatural interference–that is, anything happening contrary to the laws of physics.... If the origin of life can be explained without invoking any supernatural processes, it seems more profitable to look elsewhere for clues to an understanding of the mind** (1999, p. 5, parenthetical item in orig., emp. added).

Scott addressed this same concept.

> What, then, is the essence of consciousness? An answer to this question requires the specification of an "extra ingredient" beyond mere mechanism. Traditionally this ingredient has been called the *soul*, although the behaviorists dealt with the hard problem by denying it. **From the perspective of natural science, both of these approaches are unacceptable** (1995, p. 172, italics in orig., emp. added).

Crick wrote:

> The idea that man has a disembodied soul is as un-
> necessary as the old idea that there was a Life Force.
> This is in head-on contradiction to the religious be-
> liefs of billions of human beings alive today. How will
> such a radical change be received? (1994, p. 261).

The commitment to materialism and naturalism evinced
by such statements is overwhelming. Claude Bernard, the
progenitor of modern physiology, believed that the cause of
all phenomena is **matter**, and that determinism is "the foundation of all scientific progress and criticism" (as quoted in
Kety, 1960, 132:1863). Thomas Huxley reflected this position when he observed: "Thoughts are the expression of molecular changes in the matter of life, which is the source of our
other vital phenomena" (1870b, p. 152). Huxley also said:
"Mind is a function of matter, when that matter has attained a
certain degree of organization" (1871, p. 464). He therefore
concluded: "Thought is as much a function of matter as motion is" (1870a, p. 371). More recently, Franklin M. Harold, in
The Way of the Cell, was exceedingly blunt in his assessment.

> Biochemists insist, rightly, that when one takes cells
> apart one finds nothing but molecules: no forces
> unique to life, no cosmic plan, only molecules whose
> writhings and couplings underlie and explain all that
> the cell does... **I share the commitment to a mate-
> rial conception of life**.... Ever since Descartes, there
> have been mechanistic biologists who see it as their
> task to "reduce" biology to chemistry and physics, for
> instance, to demonstrate that all biological phenom-
> ena can be completely explained in terms of the mo-
> tions of their constituent parts and the forces between
> them. **Biochemists and molecular biologists, in
> particular, commonly believe that such reduction
> is their objective**, though they will not all agree on
> the meaning of the term. Some are satisfied that re-
> duction has effectively been accomplished, thanks to
> the near-universal consensus that all that living things
> do is based on their physical substance, and that **no
> metaphysical agencies or vital forces need be in-
> voked**....

The bedrock premise of this book is that life is a material phenomenon, grounded in chemistry and physics.... **Even the human mind emerges from the activities of the brain and represents a product of evolution**, though these are matters of which we know little, and understand less. I know of no evidence for the existence of vital forces unique to living organisms, and their erratic history gives one no reason to believe that life's journey is directed toward a final destination in pursuit of a plan or purpose. **If life is the creation of some cosmic mind or will, it has taken great care to hide all material traces of its intervention**....

The findings of biologists cut even closer to the bone. They compel us to admit that **we humans, like all other organisms, are transient constellations of jostling molecules, brought forth by a mindless game of chance devoid of plan or intent**. For anyone who takes science seriously, it becomes ever harder to believe that behind the appearances abides a cosmic mind that is even remotely comprehensible to us, or one that has the slightest concern for human welfare, personal or collective.... The universe revealed by science is under no obligation to be meaningful to mankind, and one can make a strong case that it is in fact utterly indifferent to us.... More than a few contemporary scientists believe that a tendency to self-organization is inherent in the physical universe, and that underpins the emergence and progressive evolution of life.... For better or for worse, mankind makes itself.... I do not feel diminished by the discovery that we are all part of a vast biotic enterprise that brought forth consciousness, understanding, and morality from mindless chemistry (2001, pp. 65,67,254,255,256,257, emp. added).

RADICAL MATERIALISM—A "FISHY" THEORY

We are tempted to say, "Methinks thou protesteth too much!" These strained machinations—all of which are being invoked in order to deny any place to God and the supernatural—remind us of the now-famous story told by Sir Arthur Eddington in his book, *The Philosophy of Physical Science*, about the ichthyologist and his "special" net for catching fish.

> Let us suppose that an ichthyologist is exploring the life of the ocean. He casts a net into the water and brings up a fishy assortment. Surveying his catch, he proceeds in the usual manner of a scientist to systematise what it reveals. He arrives at two generalisations: (1) No sea-creature is less than two inches long. (2) All sea-creatures have gills. These are both true of his catch, and he assumes tentatively that they will remain true however often he repeats it. In applying this analogy, the catch stands for the body of knowledge which constitutes physical science, and the net for the sensory and intellectual equipment which we use in obtaining it. The casting of the net corresponds to observation; for **knowledge which has not been or could not be obtained by observation is not admitted into physical science**. An onlooker may object that the first generalisation is wrong. "There are plenty of sea-creatures under two inches long, only your net is not adapted to catch them." The ichthyologist dismisses this objection contemptuously. "Anything uncatchable by my net is *ipso facto* outside the scope of ichthyological knowledge. In short, "what my net can't catch isn't fish." Or—to translate the analogy—"If you are not simply guessing, you are claiming a knowledge of the physical universe discovered in some other way than by the methods of physical science, and admittedly unverifiable by such methods. You are a metaphysician. Bah!" (1958, p. 16, emp. added).

During 1977-1978, Australian electrophysiologist and Nobel laureate Sir John Eccles (who was a personal friend of Sir Arthur Eddington's) was invited to present the prestigious Gifford Lectures at the University of Edinburgh in Scotland. As he began, he commented:

> The tremendous successes of science in the last century have led to the expectation that there will be forthcoming in the near future a complete explanation in

materialist terms of all the fundamental problems confronting us…. When confronted with the frightening assertion by scientists that we are no more than participants in the materialist happenings of chance and necessity, anti-science is a natural reaction. **I believe that this assertion is an arrogant over-statement**, as will appear in lecture after lecture. **In fact, the aim of the whole lecture series is an attack on monist-materialism, which is unfortunately believed in by most scientists with religious-like fervour. You might say that it is the belief of the establishment** (1979, pp. 8-9, emp. added).

Five years later, in his book, *The Wonder of Being Human: Our Brain and Our Mind*, Eccles wrote:

When such troubles arise in the history of thought, it is usual to adopt some belief that "saves" the day. For example, the denial of the reality of mental events, as in radical materialism, is an easy cop-out…. **Radical materialism should have a prominent place in the history of human silliness** (Eccles and Robinson, 1984, p. 17).

We could not agree any more than we do. It is comforting to know that there are men of science as esteemed as Sir John Eccles who are willing to admit as much. It also is comforting to know that there are other individuals of the same stature in science who are willing to step forward and say essentially the same thing. Consider, as just one example, the following.

In November 1982, at the Isthmus Institute in Dallas, Texas, four renowned evolutionists who were Nobel laureates—Sir John Eccles, Ilya Prigogine, Roger Sperry, and Brian Josephson—took part in a series of very frank discussions, narrated by Norman Cousins, the highly esteemed editor of the *Saturday Review* for more than a quarter of a century. Three years later, in 1985, the four Nobel laureates released an absolutely amazing book, *Nobel Prize Conversations,* containing the entire text of those discussions, along with Mr. Cousins' narrative comments. In his "Prelude," Cousins wrote:

Although each represented a different scientific discipline they had one thing in common: each had received the Nobel Prize, each had used the gifts of intelligence they had received in service of human life. The awards they had received in ceremonies in Stockholm's Nobelstiftelsen signified that the scientific community as a whole had come to accept their work not only as valid but as important to mankind. Another element also unites the four Nobel Laureates. **Each of them is concerned about the relation between the human mind and human brain, about the role of human consciousness in an evolving universe, about the interplay between time and mind, about the world as a "work of art" which cannot simply be reduced to neural events within the brain or to immutable mechanisms measured by quantum analysis** (pp. 4-5, emp. added).

Later, we will quote statements made by Roger Sperry and Sir John Eccles in the *Nobel Prize Conversations* book. But for now, we would like to leave the reader with the thought-provoking comments of Brian Josephson. Before we do, however, we would like to offer Mr. Cousins' assessment of what you are about to read. He wrote:

> Dr. Josephson has proposed that **the inclusion of God or Mind in science is not only plausible, but may even be necessary if science is ever to fully understand Nature** or to overcome its difficulties in explaining phenomena like evolution and creativity (p. 95, emp. added).

Now, Josephson's remarks:

> If we want to put God or Mind into science, then we have to say that there is an intelligence behind the scenes, which is creating order, at least leaving things less disordered than they would have been without the intelligence being present. And so we can identify the unobserved order with intelligence....
>
> So just from the fact that scientific work makes no mention of God or Mind, we see that **science and the mentalist revolution are at the present time**

totally separated from each other. But, as you have already said, things are beginning to change and overlapping views are beginning to be found. However, the fact remains that science gets on quite well without God, and perhaps we should look into the reasons why this might be. If we assume God or Mind does exist, then why hasn't this appeared in scientific experiments? I'd like to indicate two facts which may be relevant.

Firstly, science casts the spotlight which it uses to search for knowledge very selectively; in other words **what scientists choose to look at, to try to explain in scientific terms, is rather restricted, rather biased. And the content of science is biased in a materialistic direction.** This applies to almost all the sciences, the physical sciences as well as the biological sciences. The reason is very largely that it is easier to study quantitatively the behavior of matter and the grosser aspects of behavior (both animal and human), than it is to study higher behavior where the influence of God might be significant. So science, in choosing the simpler problems to examine first, tends always to look in directions where theological concepts are not very relevant.

Secondly, even with a particular field, science likes to look at simple phenomena, as these are more easily connected with fundamental laws. Then one tends to say, "We can explain the simple phenomena very well now; eventually, we'll be able to explain the complex phenomena as well." **The gap between simple and complex phenomena is one which scientists tend, just as a matter of faith, to assume (especially if they are of materialistic orientation) will be bridged without invoking any higher being.**

An alternative approach for the scientist is to say, Let's investigate the opposite view, i.e., that **perhaps we should be taking God or Mind into account in science**; what would a science look like which had God in there playing a part, accounting thereby for particular phenomena? There are various ways into this problem, and the way I'm going to take is to say that **if we want to put God or Mind into science, then the primary feature of Mind, the one which is most closely connected with the science we've got, is intelligence** (see Cousins, 1985, pp. 91, 92-93, 94, parenthetical item in orig., emp. added).

How very refreshing! And the fact that such statements come from a Nobel laureate who is an admitted evolutionist, is, to say the very least, surprising. But Dr. Josephson is not alone in such thinking. The eminent British theoretical physicist (and former Master of Queen's College, Cambridge) John Polkinghorne expressed similar thoughts in an article he wrote in 2001 ("Understanding the Universe") for publication in the *Annals of the New York Academy of Sciences.*

> Those of us privileged to be scientists are so excited by the quest to understand the workings of the physical world that we seldom stop to ask ourselves why we are so fortunate. **Human powers of rational comprehension vastly exceed anything that could be simply an evolutionary necessity for survival, or plausibly construed as some sort of collateral spin-off from such a necessity....**
>
> I believe that science is possible because the physical world is a creation and we are, to use an ancient and powerful phrase, creatures "made in the image" of the Creator....
>
> I agree with John Leslie's analysis, presented in his book, *Universes,* that suggests, firstly that it would be irrational just to shrug this off as a happy accident, and secondly that there are two broad categories of possible explanation: either many universes with a vast variety of different natural laws instantiated in them, of which ours is the one that by chance has allowed us to appear within its history; or a single universe that is the way it is because it is not "any old world," but a creation that has been endowed by its Creator with just the circumstances that will allow it to have a fruitful history....

I believe that, while the many-universes hypothesis seems to have only one explanatory piece of work that it can do, there are other kinds of explanations that the thesis of theism can afford, such as granting an understanding of the intelligibility of the universe, and also providing the ground for the widely attested phenomena of religious experience…. My conclusion is to prefer the explanation of Anthropic fruitfulness in terms of a Creator, which strikes me as being more economic and forming part of a cumulative case for theism…. With, for example, Paul Davies in his book *The Mind of God*, **I cannot regard this dawning of consciousness as being just a fortunate accident in the course of an essentially meaningless cosmic history**….

What I have sought to show is that religious believers who see a divine Mind and Purpose behind the universe are not shutting their eyes and irrationally believe impossible things. **We have reason for our beliefs**. They have come to us through that search for motivated understanding that is so congenial to the scientist (950:177,178,179,182, emp. added).

Human powers of rational comprehension do "vastly exceed anything that could be simply an evolutionary necessity." The primary feature of mind, it seems, is intelligence –which we see all around us. Perhaps that is what drove Sir Arthur Eddington himself to say, shortly before he died: "The idea of a universal mind, or Logos, would be, I think, a fairly plausible inference from the present state of scientific theory" (as quoted in Heeren, 1995, p. 233). Or, as John Beloff put it in an article on "The Mind-Brain Problem":

…**[T]he position of mind in nature remains a total mystery. It could be that there exists some sort of a cosmic mind**, perhaps co-equal with the material universe itself, **from which each of our individual minds stems and to which each ultimately returns**. All we can say is that it looks as if a fragment of mind-stuff becomes attached to an individual organism, at or near birth, and thereafter persists with this symbiotic relationship until that organism perishes (1994, emp. added).

Again, we say, how very refreshing. We will have more to say later on this aspect of human consciousness. Now, however, it is appropriate that we examine the idea of whether humans alone possess consciousness, or whether certain members of the animal kingdom possess the same kind of self-awareness.

DO ANIMALS POSSESS CONSCIOUSNESS?

Earlier, we quoted Stephen Jay Gould, who concluded that consciousness has been "vouchsafed only to our species in the history of life on earth" (1997b, p. ix). Is Dr. Gould correct? Or do other creatures possess self-awareness as well? Certainly, the answer to such a question hinges on the definition one assigns to "consciousness." In one of the sections above, we discussed at length the difficulty inherent in attempting to define consciousness. Ervin Laszlo, founder of the General Evolution Research Group, addressed this problem in *Evolution: The Grand Synthesis*, when he observed:

> The first thing to remember is that we cannot investigate the human mind with the methods used to investigate the human brain, or indeed any matter-energy system in the universe. Thoughts, images, feelings, and sensations are "private"; none of us has direct access to the mind of anyone else–not even of his closest friend or relative. Mind can only be investigated through introspection (1987, p. 117).

One way to approach the problem is to define consciousness with the broadest possible stroke and in the simplest possible terms. Previously, we quoted Steven Harnad, editor of *Behavioral and Brain Sciences*, who did exactly that when he defined consciousness as "the capacity to have experiences" (as quoted in Lewin, 1992, pp. 153-154). Penrose followed suit in *The Emperor's New Mind*.

> What evidence do we have that lizards and codfish do *not* possess some low-level form of consciousness? What right do we have to claim, as some might, that

human beings are the only inhabitants of our planet blessed with an actual ability to be "aware"? Are we alone, among the creatures of earth, as things whom it is possible to "be"? I doubt it. Although frogs and lizards, and especially codfish, do not inspire me with a great deal of conviction that there is necessarily "someone there" peering back at me when I look at them, the impression of a "conscious presence" is indeed very strong with me when I look at a dog or a cat or, especially, when an ape or monkey in the zoo looks at me. I do not demand that they feel as I do, nor even that there is much sophistication about what they feel. **I do not ask that they are "self-aware" in any strong sense.... All I ask is that they sometimes** *simply feel!* (1989, p. 383, italics in orig., emp. added).

If these are the sole criteria for defining consciousness—the capacity to "just have experiences" or to "sometimes simply feel"—then animals obviously possess consciousness, since they "have experiences." The problem is that such simple definitions of consciousness are woefully inadequate (we even would go so far as to say that they are, if you will pardon the intended play on words, "simply wrong!"). And, by and large, those in the scientific and philosophical communities have acknowledged as much. Previously, we quoted Robert Ornstein, in his book, *The Evolution of Consciousness*, to that effect: **"Being conscious is being aware of being aware**. It is one step removed from the raw experience of seeing, smelling, acting, moving, and reaction" (1991, pp. 225-226, emp. added).

That "one step" is a mighty **big** step, however! The difference between merely "being aware" (i.e., "just having experiences" or "simply feeling") and actually being "**self**-aware" (i.e., **knowing** that you are having experiences, and **knowing** that you are feeling) is colossal—a fact that seems to have eluded some who wish to imbue "other species" with the trait of consciousness. Marian Dawkins, author of the book, *Through Our Eyes Only? The Search for Animal Consciousness,* is a good example. She wrote:

Our near-certainty about (human) shared experiences is based, amongst other things, on a mixture of the complexity of their behavior, their ability to "think" intelligently and on their being able to demonstrate to us that they have a point of view in which what happens to them *matters* to them. We now know that these attributes—complexity, thinking and minding about the world—are also present in other species. **The conclusion that they, too, are consciously aware is therefore compelling**. The balance of evidence (using Occam's razor to cut us down to the simplest hypothesis) is that they are and it seems positively unscientific to deny it (1993, p. 177, italics and parenthetical item in orig., emp. added).

But we are not talking about other species being "consciously aware." We are talking about them being "consciously **self**-aware." As Laszlo went on to say:

The human mind, however, is not just the subjective side of a two-sided survival mechanism. The mind, as introspection reveals, is also the seat of abstract thought, feeling, imagination, and value. **I not only sense the world, I also interpret my sensations**. Like presumably all human beings, **I have consciousness. I am aware of having sensations and, on successively higher levels of abstraction, I am aware of being aware of having sensations**. Ultimately I, like other members of the human species, learn to abstract from immediate sensations **in ways that lesser species cannot**, and can come to deal with pure *forms* of thought. These include scientific and mathematical concepts, aesthetic constructions, and the abstract meanings of words and concepts. Consciousness is not a mysterious transcendental trait: it is the capacity for internally describing the internal description of the perceived and conceived environment (1987, p. 118, italics in orig., emp. added).

Are other species "self-aware"? Tattersall admitted:

I have already said that nonhuman mammals are far from being automatons, and this is clearly true; but does it necessarily follow that they have a concept of self that would be broadly familiar to us? The answer to this is almost certainly no; but it has to be admitted that the degree to which nonhuman primates may or may not have an internal image of self is a devilishly hard question to approach (2002, p. 63).

Wilson, in *Man: The Promising Primate,* therefore concluded:

It seems to me that human **self-consciousness is something that is "personal" to the human species,** if only in the simple sense that other animals cannot have a consciousness of being human. Anything that is personal to a species cannot have originated or have any meaning in any way other than through self-reference, that is, **the individuals making up the species must think about themselves and must have been in a problematic situation that made thinking about themselves productive and adaptive** (1980, p. 96, emp. added).

Do other species "think about themselves" in "productive and adaptive" ways? Remember: we are not asking if animals possess instinct. Nor are we asking if they can "adapt." We are inquiring as to whether or not they are **self-aware**–to the extent that they actually "think about themselves." Eccles concluded: "It has been well said that an animal knows, but only a man knows that he knows" (1967, p. 10). Nick Carter, in an article titled "Are There Any Insurmountable Obstacles to Descartes' Dualism?," wrote that we might think of animals "as beings that have extension and sensation, but not thought" (2002). In the context, he was speaking of "higher thought"– the ability to think, to think about thinking, and to let others know we are thinking. Humans not only possess such self-awareness and thought capability, but also **the ability to let other humans know that they possess those two things**! As Harvard's Nobel laureate George Wald concluded:

I have all kinds of evidence that other persons are conscious; our mutual communication through speech and writing helps greatly.... There is no way to shore up scientifically one's prejudices about animal consciousness. One is in the same trouble with nonliving devices. Does that garage door resent having to open when the headlights of my car shine on it? I think not. Does a computer that has just beaten a human player at chess feel elated? I think not. But there is nothing one can do about those situations either (1994, p. 128, emp. added).

In their book, *Evolution,* Dobzhansky, et al., followed this same line of reasoning.

In point of fact, **self-awareness is the most immediate and incontrovertible of all realities**. We infer the existence of self-awareness, or mind, in people other than ourselves only by analogy with our own introspective experiences. Therefore, when it comes to the question of whether or not some rudiments of self-awareness may be present among other animals, conclusive evidence is unobtainable. No wonder that competent scientists are far from unanimous in their judgements. Some are willing to ascribe the beginnings of mind to some mammals (apes, monkeys, dogs), or even to all animals with developed nervous systems. Other scientists make mind an exclusively human possession. For example, Teilhard de Chardin, in a now-famous statement, wrote: "**Admittedly the animal knows. But it cannot know that it knows—this is quite certain**...." Human selfawareness obviously differs greatly from any rudiments of mind that may be present in nonhuman animals. **The magnitude of the difference makes it a difference in kind, and not one of degree. Without doubt, the human mind sets our species apart from nonhuman animals**. Unfortunately, what we call the mind is notoriously refractory to scientific study (1977, p. 453, emp. added).

While the mind may be "notoriously refractory to scientific study" (a concept we will discuss at some length later), there are certain things we do know, in addition to those items mentioned above. As Ehrlich confessed (from an evolutionary viewpoint): "...[H]uman beings are also the only animals that seem fully aware of the consciousness of other individuals and thus have been able to develop empathy, the capacity to identify emotionally with others" (2000, p. 111). Nowhere is this more evident than in the human response to death. Dobzhansky concluded: "Self-awareness has, however, brought in its train somber companions—fear, anxiety and death awareness.... Man is burdened by death-awareness. A being who knows that he will die arose from ancestors who did not know" (1967, p. 68).

But consider (to choose just one example) the animal that evolutionists believe is our closest living relative—the chimpanzee. Famed paleoanthropologist Richard Leakey admitted:

> ...[C]himpanzees at best seem puzzled about death.... The chimpanzees' limitation in empathizing with others extends to themselves as individuals: **no one has seen evidence that chimps are aware of their own mortality**, of impending death. But, again, how would we *know*?... Ritual disposal of the dead speaks clearly of an awareness of death, and thus an awareness of self (1994, pp. 153,155, italics. in orig., emp. added).

Dobzhansky, et al., also addressed this same point.

> **Ceremonial burial is evidence of self-awareness because it represents an awareness of death. There is no indication that individuals of any species other than man know that they will inevitably die**.... The adaptive function of death awareness is not as clear. What conceivable advantage could our remote ancestors at the dawn of humanity derive from knowing that they would inevitably die?... It is most probable that **death-awareness arose** originally not because it was adaptively useful by itself, but **because it was a by-product of self-awareness**, which was adaptive (1977, p. 454, emp. added).

The information contained in the two quotations above can be summarized as follows: (1) chimpanzees are unaware of their own mortality, and have no ability to empathize emotionally with others (a peculiarly human trait, according to Ehrlich); (2) in fact, there is no indication that individuals of **any** species other than humans know they will inevitably die; (3)

Only humans carry out elaborate rituals for their dead—an indication that they, unlike animals, are self-aware.

death-awareness arose because it was a product of selfawareness; and (4) ceremonial burial is evidence of selfawareness
because it represents an awareness of death.

Now, note the logical conclusion that inescapably follows.
Death-awareness and ceremonial burial are allegedly evidence of, and products stemming from, self-awareness. But
chimps (our nearest supposed relative), **like all animals**, do
not comprehend the fact that they will one day die, and do
not perform ritualistic burials of their dead. **If understanding death and burying the dead are evidence of self-
awareness, and if no animal understands death or bur-
ies its dead, then no animal is self-aware!**

The scientist who literally "wrote the book" on animal consciousness, Donald R. Griffin, published the first edition of
his now-famous work, *Animal Minds: Beyond Cognition to Consciousness,* in 1992, and the second edition in 2001. In that second edition, he offered the following assessment of animal
consciousness.

Can scientific investigation of animal mentality tell us whether animals are conscious? The short answer is "not yet," because it is very difficult to gather convincing evidence about whatever conscious experiences may occur in animals.... Have scientists proved conclusively that animals are never conscious, perhaps by means of evidence so complex and technical (like quantum mechanics) that ordinary people cannot understand it? No, almost all biologists and psychologists who study animal behavior avoid any such sweeping claim, and they often grant that some animals are probably conscious at times. But they hasten to argue that there is no way to tell whether they are or not, and that for this reason the subject cannot be investigated scientifically.... **Although the available evidence does not prove conclusively that any particular animal is conscious**, it is quite sufficient to open our eyes to an appreciative view of animals in which we attempt to understand what life is like for them....

It is important to distinguish between perceptual and reflective consciousness. The former, called "primary consciousness," includes all sorts of awareness, whereas the latter is a subject of conscious experiences in which the content is conscious experience itself. Reflective consciousness is thinking, or experiencing feelings, about thoughts or feelings themselves, and **it is often held to include self-awareness and to be limited to our species**.... Many behavioral scientists ...believe that it is likely that animals may sometimes experience perceptual consciousness but that reflective consciousness is a unique human attribute....

[R]eflective consciousness...is a form of introspection, thinking about one's thoughts, but with the addition of being able to think about the thoughts of others....

[T]here are in fact several kinds of evidence bearing on the question of animal consciousness.... One type of evidence is especially relevant, and yet it has been almost completely neglected by scientists. This is animal communication. To appreciate its relevance, **we**

need only ask ourselves how we judge whether our human companions are aware of anything or what the content of their conscious experiences may be. Our chief source of evidence comes from human communication....

Because we know far too little to judge with any confidence when animals are or are not conscious, the question of animal consciousness is an open one, awaiting adequate scientific illumination. There is of course no reason to suppose that other animals are capable of the enormous variety of thinking that our species has developed, largely through the use of our magnificent language—especially written language, which allows the dissemination and preservation of knowledge far beyond what can be achieved by direct communication and individual memories. **The principal difference between human and animal consciousness is probably in their** *content* (pp. x,xi,7,8,15, italics and parenthetical item in orig., emp. added).

"The question of animal consciousness," says Dr. Griffin, is an "open one." Admittedly, "reflective consciousness" (which includes, among other things, self-awareness, the process of introspection, and the ability to invent symbolic language—all essential, definitive traits of human consciousness) has eluded every member of the animal kingdom. But, Griffin opined, "the principal difference between human and animal consciousness is probably in their content."

That last statement must surely rank as one of the greatest understatements of all times. "Other than your husband's assassination, Mrs. Lincoln, how did you enjoy the play?" "Except for the difference in their content, what's the difference in human and animal consciousness?" Does anyone besides us see something terribly wrong here? As Tattersall put it:

But comfortable as monkeys may become with mirrors and their properties, it has also been shown that they cannot identify their own reflection in a mirror. ...What do we make of all this? First, it is evident that **there is a qualitative difference among the per-**

ceptions of self exhibited by monkeys, apes, and human beings (2002, p. 65, emp. added).

Key in on Tattersall's reference to monkeys and mirrors, and allow us to explain the significance of such a concept. For more than thirty years, researchers have tried to figure out a way to test—objectively—whether any given animal is "self-aware." In *The Origin of Humankind*, paleoanthropologist Richard Leakey concluded: "An experience as private as consciousness is frustratingly beyond the usual tools of the experimental psychologist. This may be one reason that many researchers have shied away from the notion of mind and consciousness in nonhuman animals" (1994, pp. 149-150). Or, as Griffin noted: "Both reflective consciousness and self-awareness are often held to be uniquely human attributes." Then, in speaking of animals, he asked: "What sorts of evidence might indicate whether or not they think about their own thoughts?" (2001, p. 277).

There is no evidence that animals understand death.

Good question. What "sorts of evidence" could lead scientists and philosophers to conclude that at least some animals possess self-awareness? There have been a number of suggestions offered, such as mind-reading (i.e., the ability to comprehend what another animal has in mind to do in order to alter behavior), divided attention (an ability to concentrate on more than one thing at a time), delayed response (acting later, as if on the "memory" of something), self-recognition (the ability of an animal to recognize itself, as opposed to other animals of its kind), etc.

But it has been self-recognition, for the most part, that has captured the attention of various researchers. In the late 1960s, one of those researchers was Gordon G. Gallup, a psychologist at the State University of New York, Albany. Dr. Gallup devised a test intended to determine an animal's "sense of self"—the mirror test. His idea was that if an animal were able to recognize its own reflection in a mirror as "itself," then it could be duly said to possess an awareness of itself, i.e., consciousness. Gallup's report of the experiment was published in a 1970 article in *Science* (see Gallup, 1970). It has been called "a milestone in our understanding of animal minds" (Leakey, 1994, p. 150). Here is how the test was carried out.

An animal (such as a chimpanzee, an orangutan, or a gorilla) is left in a room to become familiarized with a mirror. After a period time, the animal is gently anesthetized. While it is asleep, a dot is painted on its forehead with paint. The animal then is allowed to wake. After the animal has fully recovered, the mirror is brought back. As Merlin Donald observed in *A Mind So Rare:*

> Most animals will take no notice of the dot and continue to treat the image in the mirror as if it were another animal. But certain ape subjects instantly recognize themselves in the mirror and touch their foreheads as if they knew that (a) the forehead in question was their own and (b) they didn't normally have a dot on it. Monkeys and other mammals do not behave this way. They do not see themselves in the mirror image (2001, p. 141).

In speaking of some of those "ape subjects" (chimpanzees and orangutans), Ian Tattersall remarked:

> Their immediate reaction was to use the mirror as an aid in picking the paint off their faces. Clearly they had recognized themselves, and they were soon pulling faces and exploring their persons using the unfamil-

iar opportunity. Interestingly, several gorillas tested did not seem to recognize themselves, although one, the famous Koko, a sign language star, definitely does recognize her own reflection (2002, pp. 63-64).

Mirror self-recognition has been extensively studied and discussed since the Gallup experiment, as reviewed in the book, *Self-awareness in Animals and Humans: Developmental Perspectives*, edited by Parker, Mitchell, and Boccia (1994). What, then, should we make of all this? Or perhaps a more appropriate question is: What have **researchers** made of all this? First, as Leakey admitted, "…psychologists wondered how widespread self-recognition would prove to be. Not very, is the answer. Orangutans passed the mirror test, but, surprisingly, gorillas did not" (p. 150). Harvard's Griffin admitted:

> It is difficult to be certain whether the failure of most animals to recognize mirror images as representations of their own bodies demonstrates that they are incapable of self-awareness, as Gallup claims, or whether they fail for some other reason to correlate the appearance and movements of the mirror image with those of their own bodies (pp. 275-276).

Yet, while Griffin acknowledged that when the mirror-test results are in, it still is "difficult to be certain" about whether animals who pass the test are self-aware, he nevertheless went on to say: "On balance, it seems most likely that mirror self-recognition as indicated by the Gallup-type experiment does strongly indicate self-awareness" (p. 276). Donald commented: "A loose hierarchy emerges from these considerations. Bits and pieces of conscious capacity appear in different species. Even perception, short-term memory, flexibility of mind, and mindreading skill might be stronger in one species and weaker in another." However, humans, he concluded, "have more of everything. We might be called superconscious. But other species have many component features of our conscious capacity" (p. 130). But are those "component features" enough to justify animals being thought of as possessing consciousness?

Conceding the obvious–that some of the experimental sub-jects did appear to recognize themselves in the mirror–Tat-tersall inquired:

> [T]he fact that most apes recognize their own reflec-tions in mirrors surely is significant at some level, es-pecially when we realize that monkeys do not.... So far so good, perhaps; **but does the ability to recog-nize oneself in a mirror convincingly demon-strate that one has a *concept* of self**? This is a tough issue, but most cognitive scientists would, I think, argue that without such a concept individuals would lack any means of interpreting the reflected image, and would thus be unable to recognize themselves. **Nonetheless, even if we accept this, where does it leave us**? It seems equally likely that recognizing one's reflection is only a part–maybe even, just one small consequence –of what we human beings are familiar with as the concept of self (2002, pp. 63-64, italics in orig., emp. added).

Dr. Tattersall has raised several important points. First, does the ability to recognize oneself in a mirror "convincingly dem-onstrate that one has a **concept** of self?" Second, if we answer yes to such a question "where does that leave us?" And third, is it possible that "recognizing one's reflection **is** 'only a part' –maybe even just one small consequences–of what we hu-man beings are familiar with as the concept of self"?

In an assessment that we will use again later in our section on the theory of consciousness known as "functionalism," Robert Wesson observed:

> Self-awareness is a special quality of the mind. A com-puter may be able to analyze difficult problems, but we do not suppose that it is self-aware, that is, has a mind. **Self-awareness is different from information pro-cessing**; even when confused and unable to think clear-ly, one may be vividly aware of one's self and one's con-fusion. **The essence of mind is less data processing than will, intention, imagination, discovery, and feeling** (1997, p. 277, emp. added).

Dr. Wesson is correct. Self-awareness **is** different from mere information processing. The chimpanzee or orangutan with a spot of paint on its forehead may be able to process the information that tells the animal it has a spot of paint on its forehead. But does that mean the chimpanzee or orangutan possesses intention, imagination, discovery, feeling, and all the other things that we normally associate with consciousness and/or self-awareness? Hardly. Listen to Dennett's assessment.

> We human beings do many intelligent things unthinkingly. We brush our teeth, tie our shoes, drive our cars, and even answers questions without thinking. **But most of these activities of ours are different, for we _can_ think about them in ways that other creatures can't think about their unthinking but intelligent activities**....
>
> Please imagine, in some detail, a man in a white lab coat climbing hand over hand up a rope while holding a red plastic bucket in his teeth. An easy mental task for you. Could a chimpanzee perform the same task? I wonder. I chose the elements—man, rope, climbing, bucket, teeth—as familiar objects in the perceptual and behavioral word of a laboratory chimp. I'm sure that such a chimp can not only perceive such things but see them _as_ a man, a rope, a bucket, and so forth. In some minimal sense, then, I grant that the chimp has a _concept_ of a man, a rope, a bucket (but does not have concepts, presumably, of a lobster, or a limerick, or a lawyer). **My question is: What can a chimp do with its concepts**? ... Can a chimp _call to mind_ the elements of a solution when these elements are not present to provide the chimp with visible reminders of themselves?...
>
> **What makes a mind powerful—indeed, what makes a mind conscious—is not what it is made of, or how big it is, but what it can do**. Can it concentrate? Can it be distracted? Can it recall earlier events? Can it keep track of several different things at once? Which features of its own current activities can it notice or monitor?...

[T]he dog cannot consider its concept. It cannot ask itself whether it knows what cats are; it cannot wonder whether cats are animals; it cannot attempt to distinguish the essence of cat (by its lights) from the mere accidents. Concepts are not things in the dog's world in the way that cats are. Concepts *are* things in our world... (1996, pp. 154-155,156-157,158,159, italics in orig., emp. added).

What sets human consciousness apart from animals, with their "bits and pieces" or "component features of conscious capacity" is, as Dennett correctly observed, **what the human mind can do**! Earlier, we quoted O'Hear, who assessed the situation quite succinctly when he commented that a "self-conscious person"

does not simply have beliefs or dispositions, does not simply engage in practices of various sorts, does not just respond to or suffer the world. He or she is aware that he or she has beliefs, practices, dispositions, and the rest. It is this awareness of myself as a subject of experience, as a holder of beliefs, and an engager in practices which constitutes my self-consciousness. **A conscious animal might be a knower...but only a self-conscious being knows that he is a knower** (1997, p. 24, emp. added).

When Griffin asked, "Can scientific investigation of animal mentality tell us whether animals are conscious?," and answered, "not yet" (2001, p. x), he fairly well summed up most researchers' opinion of the matter. While he personally believes that "the weight of the evidence" suggests that many animal species do possess "perceptual consciousness," he nevertheless was willing to admit: "But it remains an open question" (p. 277). And it is safe to say that "the researchers" are badly split on whether or not even "advanced mammals" (like, for example, chimpanzees and orangutans) can justifiably be said to possess self-awareness. For example, three contributors to a 1997 symposium volume (*Animal Consciousness and Animal Ethics*) argued that many animals do have conscious experiences of some sort. But just as many (or more) other contributors disagreed (see Dol, et al., 1997).

In the book he wrote that contained lengthy interviews with a variety of scientists and philosophers on consciousness (*Complexity: Life at the Edge of Chaos*), Roger Lewin asked Tufts University philosopher Daniel Dennett (the author of *Consciousness Explained*): "So you're denying this kind of consciousness to all animals but humans?" Dr. Dennett responded: "I am." Lewin then remarked: "No animal without language experiences a sense of self, argued Dan, not in the way that humans experience self" (Lewin, 1992, p. 157).

But **why** is all of this so? W.H. Thorpe was constrained to say: "I find it very difficult to imagine a highly organized consciousness which could be of real use to the animal in its everyday life **without a fairly elaborate mechanism behind it**" (1965, p. 498, emp. added). Our point exactly. Now, whence came that mechanism?

THE BRAIN, THE MIND, AND HUMAN CONSCIOUSNESS

We suspect that it hardly will come as any great shock for us to observe that, "somehow," brains, minds, and consciousness are viewed as "going together." Brains are "mysteriously" linked to minds. Ehrlich commented: "[W]hen we think of brains, we ordinarily think of minds, just as when people think of legs they think of walking and running…" (2000, p. 109). True enough. And, as philosopher Colin McGinn (quoted earlier) opined: "There just **has** to be some explanation for how brains [interact with] minds" (1993, p. 6, emp. in orig.).

But minds, just as "mysteriously," are linked to consciousness. When we think of minds, we also think of consciousness, a fact that physicist Freeman Dyson of Princeton's Institute for Advanced Study discussed in his semi-autobiographical book, *Disturbing the Universe*.

> **It is remarkable that mind enters into our awareness of nature on two separate levels**. At the high-

est level, the level of human consciousness, our minds are somehow directly aware of the complicated flow of electrical and chemical patterns in our brains. At the lowest level, the level of single atoms and electrons, the mind of an observer is again involved in the description of events…. But I, as a physicist, cannot help suspecting that there is a logical connection between the two ways in which mind appears in my universe. I cannot help thinking that our awareness of our own brains has something to do with the process which we call "observation" in atomic physics. That is to say, **I think our consciousness is not just a passive epiphenomenon carried along by the chemical events in our brains, but is an active agent** forcing the molecular complexes to make choices between one quantum state and another. In other words, mind is already inherent in every electron, and the processes of human consciousness differ only in degree but not in kind from the processes of choice between quantum states which we call "chance" when they are made by electrons (1979, p. 249, emp. added).

The undeniable fact that brains are linked to minds, and that minds are linked to consciousness, has produced a true conundrum for evolutionists. As science writer James Trefil asked: "How can we go from a purely physical-chemical system such as the brain to something nonphysical such as our mental experience? What, in other words, is the connection between the firing of neuron 1,472,999,321 and my **experience** of seeing blue?" (1997, p. 180, emp. in orig.). In an "invited review" on the subject of consciousness that he was asked to write for the journal, *Brain*, Zeman commented on what he referred to as "the current fascination with consciousness," and suggested that it "reflects the mounting intellectual pressure to explain how 'vital activity' in the brain generates a 'mental element' with rich subjective content" (2001, 124: 1284).

There is indeed "mounting intellectual pressure" to explain the brain's "vital activity," which somehow generates the "mental element" we know as consciousness. After all, consciousness, we are assured, is "our most precious possession." Surely, that alone would serve to justify a serious and sustained investigation into the "rich subjective content" of human self-awareness.

MATERIALISM, SUPERNATURALISM, AND THE BRAIN/MIND CONNECTION

Truth be told, however, from an evolutionary perspective, the investigation is extremely self-delimiting. After all, evolution, by definition, is a naturalistic process. George Gaylord Simpson once noted: "Evolution is a **fully natural process**, inherent in the physical properties of the universe, by which life arose in the first place and by which all living things, past or present, have since developed, divergently and progressively" (1960, 131:969, emp. added). If evolution is accepted as the correct explanation of human origins, and if evolution is a "fully natural process," then whatever exists **must** be the result of purely naturalistic processes. In short, to paraphrase McGinn, "there just **has** to be" some **naturalistic** explanation for how the brain produces the mind, and for how the mind, in turn, produces consciousness. As Christopher Wills wrote in his volume, *Children of Prometheus:* "[T]he human brain is the most remarkable product of evolution to be found among the Earth's living organisms" (1998, pp. 228-229). Ehrlich similarly concluded: "Evolution is the key to the mind" (p. 109)

As you might expect, whatever the evolutionary explanation turns out to be for how the brain gave rise to the mind, and how the mind then gave rise to consciousness, **material causes ultimately were responsible; nothing supernatural was involved!** As Heinberg noted:

But if the existence of purpose in organisms is problematic for the purely mechanistic explanation of life —and for the more general philosophy of *materialism*, which holds that all observable phenomena are explainable as the results of material causes—consciousness is doubly so.... Understandably, **reductionist and materialist science—which is at war with theistic philosophies and features a non-physical God at the center of cosmos and creation—has therefore sought to find purely physical, chemical explanations for consciousness in humans and other creatures** (1999, p. 68, italics in orig., emp. added).

It should not surprise us, then, to see evolutionist Andrew Brown, writing in *The Darwin Wars*, state: "All working biologists agree that intelligence, curiosity, free will and so on are produced by the normal, law-bound mechanical processes of the world" (1999, p. 154). James Trefil observed in *101 Things You Don't Know about Science and No One Else Does Either:* "Let me define materialism as the belief that the brain is a physical system governed by knowable laws of nature, and that **every phenomenon (including mental phenomena) can ultimately be explained in this way**" (1997, pp. 187-188, parenthetical item in orig., emp. added). Elbert remarked in *Are Souls Real?:*

The brain is all that is needed for consciousness.... Modern knowledge of the brain and **consciousness supports the idea that consciousness results from the operation of the central nervous system, especially the brain**. Nothing else seems to be needed to generate consciousness.... In my opinion, there is **no good reason to believe that the mind needs a supernatural explanation** (2000, pp. 222,249, 255, emp. in orig.).

Donald Griffin (of animal-consciousness fame) was equally blunt in his assessment.

I will take it for granted that behavior and consciousness (human and nonhuman) result entirely from events that occur in their central nervous systems. In other words, **I will proceed on the basis of emergent materialism,** and assume that subjective consciousness is an activity of central nervous systems, which are of course part of the physical universe. Just what sort of neural activity leads to consciousness remains a challenging mystery,...but **there is no need to call upon immaterial, vitalistic, or supernatural processes to explain how some fraction of human or animal brain activity results in conscious, subjective thoughts and feelings** (2001, p. 5, parenthetical item in orig., emp. added).

Neurophysiologist and Nobel laureate Ragnar Granit, in an article on "Reflections on the Evolution of the Mind and Environment," admitted: "Like so many other biologists, I think of mind or conscious awareness as an emergent property in the evolution of life. This implies that it exists *in nuce* [necessarily—BH/BT] in properties of matter, just as does the insulin molecule or the double helix containing DNA" (1982, p. 97).

Richard Gregory, in his discussion on "Consciousness" in *The Encyclopaedia of Ignorance,* suggested that when it comes to the appeal to the supernatural, "there is no such evidence **between** brains, and no evidence **within** brains, for non-physical causes" (1977, p. 277, emp. in orig.). Francis Crick, in *The Astonishing Hypothesis,* provided what may well be the most complete and well-thought-out statement of the scientific materialists' view of the human brain ever to be put into print.

> You, your joys and your sorrows, your memories and your ambitions, your sense of personal identity and free will, are in fact no more than the behavior of a vast assembly of nerve cells and their associated molecules. As Lewis Carroll's Alice might have phrased it: "You are nothing but a packet of neurons" (1994, p. 3).

Or, as Robert Wesson put it in *Beyond Natural Selection:* "The mind is no more independent of the body than living creatures are independent of their physiology" (1997, p. 277). E.O.

Wilson intoned: "Virtually all contemporary scientists and philosophers expert on the subject agree that the mind, which comprises consciousness and rational process, is the brain at work" (1998, p. 98).

THE CONCEPT OF MIND

Evolutionists speak effusively of an individual cell as containing "previously unimagined complexity and dynamism" (Koch, 1997, 385:207), and the brain (which is composed of between **10 and 100 billion** cells!) as being "the most developed and complex system known to science" (Davies, 1992, 14[5]:4). Whence has come the "amazing complexity" that careens through the human body—from the individual cells to the master organ, the brain? And what part does it play in regard to the human mind and human consciousness?

On the one hand, evolutionists freely admit that, even at the cellular level, there is an "unimagined complexity and dynamism." Yet on the other hand, they expect us to believe that, ultimately, this has resulted from a disorganized bunch of macromolecules fortuitously coming together in a "just-so" fashion to produce not only the cell's (and the organism's) incredible intricacy, but also the human mind and its accompanying self-awareness. In fact, Daniel Dennett addressed this very point in *Kinds of Minds*. Speaking specifically about humanity's rise from macromolecules to cells to complete organisms that possess both minds and consciousness, he wrote:

> **These impersonal, unreflective, robotic, mindless little scraps of molecular machinery are the ultimate basis of all the agency, and hence meaning, and hence consciousness, in the world**. It is rare for such a solid and uncontroversial scientific fact to have such potent implications for structuring all subsequent debate about something as controversial and mysterious as minds, so let's pause to remind ourselves of these implications.

There is no longer any serious informed doubt about this: we are the direct descendants of these self-replicating robots. We are mammals, and all mammals have descended from reptilian ancestors whose ancestors were fish whose ancestors were marine creatures rather like worms, who descended in turn from simpler multicelled creatures several hundred million years ago, who descended from single-celled creatures who descended from self-replicating macromolecules, about three billion years ago. There is just one family tree, on which all living things that have ever lived on this planet can be found—not just animals, but plants and algae and bacteria as well. You share a common ancestor with every chimpanzee, every worm, every blade of grass, every redwood tree. **Among our progenitors, then, were macromolecules**.

To some people, all this seems shocking and unlikely, I realize, but I suspect that they haven't noticed how desperate the alternatives are (1996, pp. 22-23, emp. added)

The "alternatives" mentioned by Dennett are any concepts which suggest that something other than strict materialism may be at work (concepts that he, as a self-professed atheistic evolutionist, absolutely abhors). "So," said Dennett, "let's see what story can be told with the conservative resources of science. **Maybe the idea that our minds evolved from simpler minds is not so bad after all**" (p. 24, emp. added).

Notice the progression allegedly involved in all of this. Macromolecules evolved into single-celled creatures, which evolved into multi-celled creatures, which eventually evolved into creatures with "simpler minds," which then evolved into —humans. And at the conclusion of that laborious and time-consuming process, how did the human mind turn out? Apparently, not very well, as Robert Ornstein forthrightly concluded:

The mind is a squadron of simpletons. It is not unified, it is not rational, it is not well designed—or designed at all. **It just happened**, an accumulation of innovations of the organisms that lived before us. The mind evolved, through countless animals and through countless worlds. Our mind did not spring from a designer, nor from a set of ideal and idealized programs.... Like the rest of biological evolution, the human mind is a collage of adaptations (the propensity to do the right thing) to different situations. Our thought is a pack of fixed routines—simpletons. We need them.... The mind is the way it is because the world is the way it is. The evolved systems organize the mind to mesh with the world.

This complicated internal system should have forewarned us that the mind isn't designed to be understood as we might a software routine. **It is, basically, just another organ** to help a person operate in the world, to stay out of trouble, to eat, sleep, and reproduce. **So why should human beings ever have evolved the ability to know what their mental system is doing, any more than we know what our pancreas is doing? We have not done so. Our natural view of our mental state is deeply distorted** (1991, pp. 2,4,7,11, parenthetical item in orig., emp. added).

Now, let's see if we understand all of this correctly? Non-living macromolecules gave rise to living cells, which then gave rise to organisms with "simpler minds," which then evolved into humans with minds that are "not unified, not rational, and not well designed," but instead are composed of "a squadron of simpletons." Admittedly, there is a "complicated internal system" with a "previously unimagined complexity and dynamism" that permits humans (and humans alone!) to possess self-awareness, use symbolic language, and be aware of the fact that they one day will die. But, in the end, the human mind "did not spring from a designer," and is "basically, just another organ."

The real truth of the matter is, while evolutionists fall all over themselves to avoid any possible hint that the human mind may have a supernatural origin (what Dennett referred to as a "desperate alternative"), they nevertheless cannot offer an adequate explanation for the concept of mind, or how it could have arisen from "chemical and electrical signals that give rise to such complex effects as cognition and consciousness." Renowned physiologist Sir Charles Sherrington remarked in his book, *Man on His Nature:* "A radical distinction has therefore arisen between life and mind. The former is an affair of chemistry and physics; the latter escapes chemistry and physics" (1975, p. 230). Max Delbrück, the father of molecular genetics and a Nobel laureate, found even more deeply puzzling the matter of how human rationality could have evolved out of "natural" occurrences. He wrote:

> Why, then, do the formal operations of the mind carry us so much further? Were those abilities not also matters of biological evolution? If they, too, evolved to let us get along in the cave, how can it be that they permit us to obtain deep insights into cosmology, elementary particles, molecular genetics, number theory? To this question I have no answer (1978, 47:353; cf. also Delbrück, 1986, p. 280).

E.O. Wilson noted in his book, *Consilience:* "But even as mind-body dualism is being completely abandoned at long last, in the 1990s, **scientists remain unsure about the precise basis of mind**" (1998, p. 99, emp. added). Nobel laureate Roger Sperry commented in a similar vein:

> One can agree that the scientific evidence speaks against any preplanned purposive design of a supernatural intelligence. At the same time the evidence shows that **the great bulk of the evolving web of creation is governed by a complex pattern of great intricacy** with many mutually reinforcing directive, purposive constraints at higher levels, particularly. **The "grand orderly design" is, in a sense, all the more remarkable for having been self-developed**.
>
> The point is that human nature and these **higher kinds of controls in nature** don't reduce any more to physical and chemical mechanisms, but **have to**

be reckoned with now in their own form, in their own right. Vital, mental, social and other higher forces**, once evolved, become just as real as the evolved forces of molecules and atoms and **must be given their due, over and above the elementary physical components** (as quoted in Cousins, 1985, pp. 85-86,87, emp. added).

In an interview ("You Have to be Obsessive") in the February 17, 2003 issue of *Time* magazine, the cover-story article of which was intended to celebrate the fiftieth anniversary of James Watson and Francis Crick's discovery of the structure of DNA, Dr. Watson commented:

We have more frontiers [in biology—BH/BT] now than when I was getting started. **How the mind works, for example, is still a mystery**. We understand the hardware, but we don't have a clue about the operating system. There are enough questions to keep people occupied for the next hundred years (161[7]:52, emp. added).

Writing on the subject, "What is Mind?," in the on-line journal, *Brain & Mind* (for which she serves as editor), Silvia Cardoso asked:

But...what about the mind?... [A] few neuroscientists, such as the Nobel Prize recipient Sir John Eccles, asserted that the mind is distinct from the body. But most of them now believe that all aspects of mind, which are often equated with consciousness, are likely to be explained in a more materialistic way as the behavior of neuronal cells. In the opinion of the famous neurophysiologist José Maria Delgado [1969, p. 30]: "It is preferable to consider the mind as a functional entity devoid of metaphysical or religious implications *per se* and related only to the existence of a brain and to the reception of sensory inputs" (1997/1998).

Yet Cardoso admitted:

Mind is a definition which tries to rescue the essence of man. **The essence of a person arises from the existence of mental functions** which permit him or her to think and to perceive, to love and to hate, to learn and to remember, to solve problems, to communicate through speech and writing, to create and to destroy civilizations. These expressions are closely related with brain functioning. Therefore, without the brain, the mind cannot exist, without the behavioral manifestation, the mind cannot be expressed (1997/1998, emp. added).

Daniel Dennett, in *Kinds of Minds,* wrote:

A naked human mind—without paper and pencil, without speaking, comparing notes, making sketches —is first of all something we have never seen. Every human mind you've ever looked at—including most especially your own, which you look at "from the inside"—is a product not just of natural selection but of cultural redesign of enormous proportions. **It's easy enough to see why a mind seems miraculous, when one has no sense of all the components and how they got made** (1996, pp. 153-154, emp. added).

Trefil asked:

The mind is…well, what is it, exactly? Formal definitions usually mention something like "the sum of mental activities," but that doesn't tell us very much. On the other hand, we all have had the experience of mind. Close your eyes and think of an episode from your childhood. You probably can conjure up a fairly detailed visual image of some setting, maybe even some sounds and smells. **You have these images "in mind," but where, exactly, are they**? They obviously don't correspond to any sensory input into your brain right now, even though they must involve the firing of neurons somewhere… (1996, pp. 217218, first ellipsis in orig., emp. added).

But can "mind" be reduced simply to "the firing of neurons"? In addressing this very issue, E.O. Wilson wrote:

I have spoken so far about the physical processes that produce the mind. Now, to come to the heart of the matter, what *is* the mind? Brain scientists understandably dance around this question. Wisely, they rarely commit themselves to a single declarative definition. Most believe that the fundamental properties of the elements responsible for mind—neurons, neurotransmitters, and hormones—are reasonably well known. **What is lacking is a sufficient grasp of the emergent, holistic properties of the neuron circuits, and of cognition, the way the circuits process information to create perception and knowledge**.... Who or what within the brain monitors all this activity? No one. Nothing. The scenarios are not seen by some other part of the brain. They just *are*.... Consciousness is the massive coupled aggregates of such participating circuits. The mind is a self-organizing republic of scenarios that individually germinate, grow, evolve, disappear, and occasionally linger to spawn additional thought and physical activity (1998, pp. 109,110, italics in orig., emp. added).

The last part of Dr. Wilson's quote is another terrific example of a "just-so" story. But notice what he admits is "lacking" in regard to explaining mind and/or consciousness—"a sufficient grasp of the emergent, holistic properties of the neuron circuits, and of cognition, the way the circuits process information to create perception and knowledge." Physicist Erwin Schrödinger correctly pointed out, in fact:

Not every nervous process, nay by no means every cerebral process, is accompanied by consciousness. Many of them are not, even though physiologically and biologically they are very much like the "conscious" ones, both in frequently consisting of afferent impulses [conveying nerve impulses to the central nervous system—BH/BT] followed by efferent ones [conveying nerve impulses away from the central nervous system—BH/BT]... (1967, p. 101, emp. added).

In an article he authored on "Brain, Mind and Behavior," Malcolm Jeeves recognized what he called the "take-home message" in regard to the brain-mind problem.

Nevertheless, the same take-home message emerged from all of these studies, whether human or animal, namely, the remarkable localization of function in the brain and the specificity of the neural substrate underlying mental events. **As each advance occurred, mind and brain were seen to be ever more tightly linked together** (1998, p. 81, emp. added).

Evidence of the fact that the "mind and brain" are, in fact, "tightly linked together" came to the forefront between May 1973 and February 1974 when three teams of American astronauts participated in prolonged orbital flights known as the Skylab Program. During this exercise, astronauts spent 84 days in space—longer than ever previously attempted. The flights were designed to enable ground-based specialists to monitor the health of people in space. One of NASA's principal discoveries was that, on the day the astronauts were due to return to Earth (and thus, admittedly, a day that they would have been under a great deal of stress), the astronauts' immune systems were visibly affected. Important processes in the immune system (such as white-cell transformation) were abnormally depressed. Remember: the astronauts' environment had not changed. The "matter" that surrounded them had not changed. Yet their mental states had changed dramatically. This provided additional evidence which documented that the mind could have a physical effect on the body. But how can the mind do that if it is merely a brain made up of neuronal circuits?

Brain researcher and Nobel laureate Roger Sperry spent his entire adult career trying to get "a sufficient grasp" of the "brain/mind problem." It was from that perspective that he admitted:

I have not been inclined to look particularly at the little molecules of the brain or even at its big macro-molecules in this connection. **It has always seemed rather improbable that even a whole brain cell has what it takes to sense, to perceive, to feel or to think on its own** (1977, p. 424, emp. added).

Roger Lewin of Harvard spoke to this when he said:

> **The magic of it all is that while no single neuron is conscious, the human brain as a whole is....** How does it do it? How are simple electrical signals across individual cell membranes transformed into cascades of cognition? How are billions of individual neurons assembled into a brain, seat of the mind? (1992, p. 163, emp. added).

One of the overriding questions in regard to the so-called brain/mind problem, as Dr. Lewin noted, is how a single cell (i.e., a neuron) that **is not conscious** somehow **becomes conscious**. As Dennett put it:

> Each cell—a tiny agent that can perform a limited number of tasks—is about as mindless as a virus. Can it be that enough of these dumb homunculi—little men—are put together the result will be a real, conscious person, with a genuine mind? According to modern science, there is no other way of making a real person (1996, p. 23).

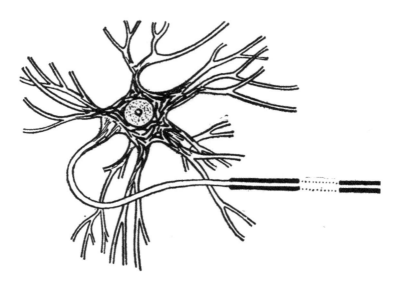

Is human consciousness held within single neurons?

He is absolutely right. According to modern science, "mind" does not, and cannot, arise out of the "mindlessness" of "just" brain cells. Gordon Rattray Taylor, in *The Natural History of the Mind*, presented and discussed the medical evidence concerning consciousness, and concluded: **"Consciousness thus cannot be a property of neurones as such"** (1979, p. 75, emp. added; "neurones" is the British spelling for neurons). Susan Greenfield, writing in 2002 on "Mind, Brain and Consciousness" for the *British Journal of Psychiatry*, concluded:

> **Within each macro brain region there is no single isolated complete function**.... So brain regions are bit players on the brain stage, and not autonomous units.... We can no more attribute autonomous functions to the most basic level of brain function—genes —than we can to the most macro—the brain regions. In both cases there is very little room for manoeuvre and therefore **it is hard to see how personalisation of the brain—the mind—might develop** (181:91, emp. added).

[As odd as it may sound, some researchers, in order to avoid the problem of how the mind could develop consciousness, have opted for exactly the opposite—that consciousness developed the mind! In his book, *Enchanted Looms: Conscious Networks in Brains and Computers,* Rodney Cotterill boldly suggested: **"I believe...that it is the mind that is the product of consciousness**. I believe, moreover, that it is the sheer abundance of experience mediated by consciousness that fools us into misunderstanding the nature of this fundamental attribute" (1998, p. 10, emp. added).]

While we were carrying out the research for this book, we stumbled across one of the most concise, yet profound, discussions on these points that we have ever seen. Although it was penned eight decades ago, it appears as fresh and current as if it had been written yesterday. In his 1923 book, *Life: Its Origin and Nature*, Hereward Carrington made the following observations.

There can be no doubt that the majority of the bodily activities can be accounted for on purely physical and chemical lines, and there are many scientists today who contend that *every* activity of the body can thus be accounted for. The body and its activities are regarded as a physico-chemical mechanism. On this view, the activities of the mind and consciousness are the production of brain-action, in the same way that other activities of the body result from their functioning of certain specific organs and *their* activities. This is the materialistic conception.

Certainly, the *matter* of the brain cannot in itself "think." There is no more reason why a certain specific nervous structure should give rise to active consciousness, than that any other complex living material should do so. The question is: Does consciousness somehow *arise* from the flow of the nervous currents within the brain? Materialistic science says that the activities of the mind are somehow synonymous with these nervous currents. Yet there are other nervous currents traveling about all over the body, which do not give rise to self-consciousness. Why is it that they should do so in the special organ of thought, known as the brain?

[Thomas Henry] Huxley attempted to account for consciousness by assuming that it somehow followed along with, or resulted from, certain specific brain activities, and that, just as the shadow of a horse accompanies the horse, so thoughts and mental activities of all kinds accompany the nervous currents, which play to-and-fro in the higher centers of the cerebral cortex. He coined the term "epiphenomenon" to express or signify this by-product, so to say, of brain activity. **The difficulty with this theory is that, for us, the important thing is the shadow and not the horse! And it is also difficult to explain why such a mere by-product should ever have come into being in the process of evolution. Furthermore the specific character of the relationship between these two (mind and brain) is not in the**

**least explained by this formula. It merely states
the facts. The primary question still remains: How
can a particular thought (apparently a non-material thing) and a particular brain-change (a material thing) be related one to another?** (pp. 45,
49-50, italics and parenthetical items in orig., emp.
and bracketed item added).

Talk about "cutting to the chase" (and eighty years ago at that!).
Carrington was right to ask: "How can a particular thought
(apparently a non-material thing) and a particular brain-
change (a material thing) be related one to another?" Should
the fact that eighty years have passed, and neuroscience still
cannot answer these types of questions, tell us something?

Is it possible that the problem lies with evolutionary theory? We are convinced that it does. If one begins with the
wrong assumption, one inevitably will reach the wrong conclusion. The eminent biologist Paul Weiss elucidated this principle, from the standpoint of attempting to understand living
organisms, when he wrote:

> Maybe our concept of our nervous system is equally
> inadequate and insufficient, because so long as you
> use only electrical instruments, you get only electrical
> answers; if you use chemical detectors, you get chemi-
> cal answers; and if you determine numerical and ge-
> ometrical values, you get numerical and geometrical
> answers. **So perhaps we have not yet found the
> particular kind of instrument that tells us the next
> unknown** (as quoted in Smythies, 1969, p. 252, emp.
> added; NOTE: Weiss' comment is included in a dis-
> cussion of a paper by J.R. Smythies, "Some Aspects
> of Consciousness," in *Beyond Reductionism*, edited by
> Arthur Koestler and J.R. Smythies).

After reading Dr. Weiss' assessment, Arthur C. Custance commented in his book, *The Mysterious Matter of Mind:* "Obviously,
we shall not even try to **invent** this particular kind of instru-
ment of research so long as we accept the monistic view of mind
as really only the outworking of brain…" (1980, p. 23, emp. in
orig.). "Modern science" begins with the wrong assumption

(evolution), looks in the wrong place (the brain alone), and is using the wrong equipment (a materialistic viewpoint). As Eccles and Robinson put it:

> The theories of the brain-mind relationship that are today held by most philosophers and neuroscientists are purely materialistic in the sense that the brain is given complete mastery! The existence of mind or consciousness is not denied except by radical materialists, but it is relegated to the passive role of mental experiences accompanying some types of brain action, as in epiphenomenalism… (1984, p. 34).

Sperry was quite blunt in his forceful criticism of such materialism. "When reductionist doctrine tried to tell us that there are no vital forces, just as it also had long taught that there are no mental forces, **materialist science was simply wrong**" (as quoted in Cousins, 1985, p. 77, emp. added). Or, as Eccles and Robinson went on to note:

> Finally, the most telling criticism of all materialist theories of the mind is against its key postulate that the happenings in the neural machinery of the brain provide *a necessary and sufficient explanation of the totality both of the performance and of the conscious experience of a human being….* Our opposition to materialism, therefore, has been on exclusively metaphysical and scientific grounds and is not to be read as a veiled *apologia* for religion…. **The history of humanity establishes that there are human attributes—moral, intellectual, and aesthetic attributes—that cannot be explained solely in terms of material composition and organization of the brain** (1984, pp. 37, 169, italics in orig., emp. added).

It is our contention that consciousness is one of the "human attributes" that "cannot be explained solely in terms of material composition and organization of the brain." As evidence, we now would like to examine the various theories of how human consciousness arose.

8

THE EVOLUTION OF CONSCIOUSNESS [PART II]

THEORIES OF THE ORIGIN OF HUMAN CONSCIOUSNESS

In his 1997-1998 Gifford Lectures at the University of Edinburgh, Holmes Rolston said to his audience: "Humans do seem to be an exceptional species" (1999, p. 164). Yes, we do! And one of the things that makes us "exceptional" is the reality of our self-consciousness. Evolutionists acknowledge, to use Michael Ruse's words, that "consciousness is a real thing." Zeman, in commenting on the fact that human self-awareness is intuitive, discussed just how "real" it is.

> The first intuition is that consciousness is a robust phenomenon which deserves to be explained rather than being explained away. Sensory experiences like those of colour, sound or pain, the simplest and most vivid instances of consciousness, are phenomena which any full description of the world must reckon with. Indeed, experiences of this kind are arguably our point of departure in gaining knowledge of the world. Consciousness, in this sense, is the "sea in which we swim."

> The second intuition is that consciousness is bound up with our physical being. This thought is pre-scientific: everyone knows that fatigue, alcohol, knocks on the head and countless other physical events can modify the state and contents of consciousness. But science has fleshed out the thought...[and] suggests

that consciousness is rooted in the brain, and that the structure of consciousness is mirrored by the structure of a set of neural processes. It has become reasonable to suppose that every distinction drawn in experience will be reflected in distinctive patterns of neural activity.

The third intuition is that **consciousness makes a difference**. It seems self-evident that much of our behaviour is explained by mental events; if we could not see or hear or touch, if we could not experience pain or pleasure, if we lacked conscious desires and intentions, we would not and could not behave as we do. If this is true it is natural to suggest that consciousness is a biological capacity which evolved in the service of action (2001, 124:1282, emp. added).

But consciousness is more than merely "a real thing." It is **important**—because **"it makes a difference!"** As we noted earlier, Stephen Jay Gould called it the "most god-awfully potent evolutionary invention ever developed." Johanson and Edgar somewhat blushingly observed that it "adds layers of richness to our lives" (1996, p. 107). Laszlo referred to it as "perhaps the most remarkable of all the phenomena of the lived and experienced world." Donald Griffin admitted:

> **The effectiveness of conscious thinking** and guiding behavioral choices on the basis of emotional "feels" about what is liked or disliked may well be so great that this core function **is one of the most important activities of which central nervous systems are capable**.... Although much of our behavior takes place without any awareness, and this includes most of our physiological functions and the details of such fairly complex actions as coordinated locomotion, **the small fraction of which we *are* aware is certainly important** (2001, pp. 3,4-5,13, italics in orig., emp. added).

Such comments provide powerful testimony to the ultimate importance of human consciousness. Robert Jahn and Brenda Dunne, in the chapter they co-authored ("The Spiritual

Substance of Science") for the book, *New Metaphysical Foundations of Modern Science,* commented on the significance of the role of consciousness when they wrote:

> In our age, however, as science and its derivative technologies press forward into increasingly abstract and probabilistic domains of quantum and relativistic mechanics, **the role of spirit or consciousness**—whether divine or human, individual or collective—in the structure and operation of the physical world inescapably returns to more pragmatic and theoretical relevance, and **can no longer casually be set aside if the goal is a truly comprehensive understanding of nature** (1994, p. 157, emp. added).

Indeed, the role of consciousness can "no longer casually be set aside." What Popper and Eccles unhesitatingly called "the greatest of miracles—the emergence of full consciousness," **must somehow be explained**. Even though, as Wald (quoted earlier) admitted, "the problem of consciousness tends to embarrass biologists," it nevertheless finally seems to be getting its fair due in "polite discourse." Eccles himself commented: "...[T]here are now signs that the conscious self or psyche can be referred to in 'polite' scientific discourse without evoking an outrage verging on obscenity!" (1992, p. 234).

Let us, then, enter into a "polite scientific discourse" about the conscious self. And as we begin, let us do so by noting that, as Eccles and Robinson said about humans, "we are not 'basically' or 'fundamentally or 'at root' zygotes; we are **persons**, the most extraordinary production of all" (1984, p. 51, emp. in orig.). Admitting that fact has serious implications. Eccles and Robinson continued:

> There is in all of this a chilling neglect of what can only be called a moral point of view.... What is the moral point of view, and how is it related to human happiness?... Without being specific at this point, we may say that **the moral point of view begins with man's awareness of the fact of his own transcendence; the recognition that human persons are different from and rise above those utterly material events comprised in the purely physical cosmos**.

Even if a citizen has had special training in science, he is still conditioned in his daily perceptions by a pervasive *metaphysics* that imposes a definite character on the full range of cognitive, emotional, social, and aesthetic processes–**the processes that are brought to bear on the serious matter of life** (pp. vii,viii, italics in orig., emp. added).

Human persons undeniably "are different from, and rise above those utterly material events comprised in the purely material cosmos." Dobzhansky and his co-authors freely admitted: "Without doubt, the human mind sets our species apart from nonhuman animals" (1977, p. 453). Yes, it does–far apart! The question is: **Why?** How does the General Theory of Evolution account for the origin of the emergence of full consciousness–"the greatest of miracles"? It is our intent here to answer that question. We would like to present and discuss a veritable plethora of theories that has been proposed in what we believe are failed attempts to explain the origin of human consciousness.

THE "HARD PROBLEM" OF HUMAN CONSCIOUSNESS

At the outset, let us point out that not everyone within the evolutionary community believes that consciousness **can** be explained. That is the very position that David Chalmers has taken. [James Trefil refers to those who say that the problem of consciousness never will be solved as "Mysterians" (1997, p. 185).] E.O. Wilson wrote concerning Chalmers' views:

The Australian philosopher David Chalmers recently put the matter in perspective by contrasting the "easy problems" of general consciousness with the "hard problem" of subjective experience…. The hard problem is more elusive: how physical processes in the brain addressed in the easy problems give rise to subjective feeling. What exactly does it mean when we say we **experience** a color such as red or blue? Or experience, in Chalmers' words, "the ineffable sound of a distant oboe, the agony of an intense pain, the sparkle of happiness or the meditative quality of a moment lost in thought? All are part of what I am calling consciousness. It is these phenomena that compose the real mystery of the mind" (1998, pp. 115-116, emp. in orig.).

This "hard problem" may be, in fact, **so** hard that it is unsolvable. As Griffin noted:

> The lack of definitive evidence revealing just what neural processes produce consciousness has led Chalmers (1996) to designate the question of how brains produce subjective awareness as the "hard problem." **He and others claim that it is such a difficult problem that normal scientific investigation is unable, in principle, to solve it,** and that consciousness must be something basically distinct from the rest of the physical universe (2001, p. 13, emp. added).

In short, Chalmers' philosophical resolution of this "hard problem" is to offer a new way of thinking, which he calls **naturalistic dualism**. In essence, this is the idea that there exists both a physical realm with its own set of well-established laws, and a "consciousness" realm with its own set of "psychophysical" laws—laws, by the way, that have yet to be discovered (see Wyller, 1996, p. 218). Thus, when it comes to explaining human consciousness, science is impotent—at least for the time being. Alwyn Scott remarked along these lines:

> In the last few decades, however, science has made some progress in gathering objective information about a phenomenon that is thought by many to be ineffable. Once off limits to serious researchers, consciousness is again becoming an acceptable subject of scientific inquiry. It has benefited from medical technology to analyze the brain—positron emission tomography is but one example—and still more insights come from physics, chemistry, biology, neuroscience, psychology, and even sociology and philosophy. The evidence, bit by bit, is derived from ex-

periments and theories testing elements of the experience of consciousness…. **Yet here, as with the efforts of ancient sages, no comprehensive understanding of consciousness has arisen from the scientific Balkanization of the subject**. The research has not yet been synthesized into one overarching understanding. The experience of consciousness is richer; its explanation, by necessity, must be more complex. **Consciousness cannot, alas, be reduced to the response to an inkblot or the activity of a set of neurons** (1995, pp. 1-2, emp. added).

"Failure is not an Option"

Darwinians realize, of course, that evolution is not "just" a theory, but also a cosmogony—i.e., an entire world view. Dobzhansky acknowledged as much when he wrote in *Science:*

Evolution comprises all the states of development of the universe; the cosmic, biological, and human or cultural developments. Attempts to restrict the concept of evolution to biology are gratuitous. Life is a product of the evolution of inorganic matter, and man is a product of the evolution of life (1967, 155:409).

Because evolution is so pervasive, whatever is **here** must be explained by evolution; there can be no exceptions—not even human self-awareness. James Trefil conceded this point:

No matter how my brain works, no matter how much interplay there is between my brain and my body, one single fact remains. For whatever reason, by whatever process, I am aware of a self that looks out at the world from somewhere inside my skull. I would suggest to you that this is not simply an observation, but the central datum with which every theory of consciousness has to grapple. **In the end, the theory has to explain how to go from a collection of firing neurons to this essential perception** (1997, p. 181, emp. added).

Yes, it certainly does! **Not** explaining consciousness is **not** an option. And so, evolutionists have no choice but to "buckle down," "put their collective noses to the grindstone," "burn the midnight oil," and come up with a believable explanation for the origin of consciousness. Even though, to use Bryan Appleyard's summary of the problem, "hard, deterministic science's view of man is that he is a curious accident" and that "self-consciousness is a problem," it is "not of a different order from other problems…" (1992, p. 191). In short, yes, it's a problem. And it's a serious problem—of considerable magnitude. But we'll figure it out. To use Trefil's words, even though consciousness is produced by "mechanisms we still haven't worked out, **we will do so!**" (1996, p, 218, emp. added). And so, the journey begins.

THEORIES OF HUMAN CONSCIOUSNESS

Speaking in broad strokes, there are two main approaches to what most scientists and philosophers refer to as the "mind-body problem." In *The Natural History of the Mind*, Gordon Taylor assessed them as follows:

> It will be useful to remind you here that there are two main philosophical positions about the Mind/Body problem, as it is called. They are known as the **dualist** and **monist**, terms I shall not be able to avoid using. Dualists maintain that the brain and the mind are two distinct beings; monists assert that they are only one thing seen from two different angles, so to speak. Dualists are generally divided into three clans: those who think the body creates mental effects as a byproduct but is not affected by mind (a view known as epiphenomenalism); those who think the two interact; and those who claim that the two move in parallel by pure coincidence, a view not many people take seriously. Monists are also split into those who deny that mental events exist at all…and those who claim that mental events are just physical events described in another language…. None of these views, I may as well warn you, stands up to inspection (1979, pp. 2021, parenthetical item in orig., emp. added).

We would like to discuss these two broad groups, and their subdivisions, in some detail. Then, as we bring this discussion on consciousness to a close, we want to offer a third alternative that **does** "stand up to inspection."

Dualism

The concept known as **dualism** is attributed to the seventeenth-century French physician/mathematician/philosopher René Descartes (1596-1650), who probably is most famous for his well-known statement, "I think, therefore I am." Interestingly, however, the idea for dualism did not originate with Descartes (although he is the one who generally receives credit for it). Some twelve hundred years earlier, Augustine, in his *City of God* (11.26), had written:

> Without any delusive representation of images and phantasms, I am most certain that I am, and that I know and delight in this. In respect of these truths, I am not afraid of the arguments of the Academicians, who say, "What if you are deceived?" For if I am deceived, I am. For he who is not, cannot be deceived; and if I am deceived, by this same token I am (see Custance, 1980, p. 28).

In the end, however, it was Descartes who "resolved to take myself as an object of study and to employ all the powers of my mind in choosing the paths I should follow" (as quoted in Fincher, 1984, p. 16). The paths Descartes chose, eventually designated him as the father of the mind/body theory of interactionism. In his book, *Discourse on Method and the Meditations* (1642), Descartes suggested that the mind was every bit as real as matter, yet was entirely separate from matter—and therefore from the brain as well. In Descartes' language, the mind was *res cogitans* (thinking substances), as opposed to the brain, which was *res extensa* (material or physical substances). Descartes even thought he had located the "seat" of consciousness in the brain—the pineal gland. Wyller summarized Descartes' views as follows:

> René Descartes is generally considered to be the originator of the modern mind-body problem. He argued that the essence of physical bodies is their extension in space, while the mind is a substance which does not extend in space, but which **thinks**. He believed that mind states and physical states are mutually in-

teractive—through the pineal gland in the brain. Thus arose the Cartesian mind-body dualism that still influences modern scientific thinking in this field (1996, p. 213, emp. in orig.).

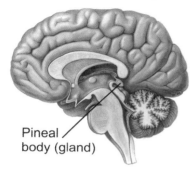

Pineal body (gland)

Figure 1 – Descartes taught that the seat of consciousness was centered in the pineal gland. LifeART image copyright © (2003) Lippincott, Williams & Wilkins. All rights reserved. Used by permission.

It is something of a mild understatement to suggest that dualism "still influences modern scientific thinking in this field." In his classic 1949 book, *The Concept of Mind*, philosopher Gilbert Ryle (whom we shall discuss more in greater detail shortly) referred to dualism as "the official doctrine" (p. 11). In commenting on that phrase, Australian physicist and mathematician Paul Davies inquired in his book, *God and the New Physics:*

What are the features of the dualistic theory of the mind? The "official doctrine" goes something like this. The human being consists of two distinct, separate kinds of things: the body and the soul, or mind. The body acts as a sort of host or receptacle for the mind, or perhaps even as a prison from which liberation may be sought through spiritual advancement or death. The mind is coupled to the body through the brain, which it uses (via the bodily senses) to acquire and store information about the world. It also uses the brain as a means to exercise its volitions, by acting on the world in the fashion described earlier in this chapter. However, the mind (or soul) is not located inside the brain, or any other part of the body; or indeed anywhere in space at all.... An important feature of this picture is that the mind is a thing; perhaps even more specifically, a substance. Not a physical substance, but a tenuous, elusive, aetherial sort of substance, the stuff that thoughts and dreams are made of, free and independent or ordinary ponderous matter (1983, p. 79, parenthetical items in orig.).

Trefil summed it up like this:

One way of looking at this question (which is almost certainly wrong) is to imagine that somewhere in the brain is an "I" who is watching the final products of the processing of signals by neurons. The essence of this view is that there is something in "mind" that transcends (or at least is distinct from) the workings of the physical brain. The seventeenth-century French philosopher and mathematician René Descartes advocated such a view of mind/body dualism, so the hypothetical place where mental images are viewed is often referred to as the "Cartesian Theater" (1996, pp. 217-218, parenthetical items in orig.).

[The phrase "Cartesian Theater" was invented by Daniel Dennett when he wrote: "As we shall soon see, the exclusive attention to specific subsystems of the mind/brain often causes a sort of theoretical myopia that prevents theorists from seeing that their models still presuppose that somewhere, conveniently hidden in the obscure 'center' of the mind/brain, there is a Cartesian Theater, a place where 'it all comes together' and consciousness happens. This may seem like a good idea, an inevitable idea, but until we see, in some detail, why it is not, the Cartesian Theater will continue to attract crowds of theorists transfixed by an illusion" (1991, p. 39).]

Earlier, we mentioned a fascinating book, *Nobel Prize Conversations,* which included the text of a series of "conversations" that occurred in November 1982, at the Isthmus Institute in Dallas, Texas, among four Nobel laureates: Sir John Eccles, Ilya Prigogine, Roger Sperry, and Brian Josephson. Norman Cousins was the esteemed moderator for those conversations. After listening to Drs. Eccles and Sperry discuss their research (which we will discuss below) documenting that the mind exerts a significant influence on the brain, Cousins was constrained to say that when we see evidence such as that produced by the scientific research of Nobel laureates like Sperry and Eccles

> ...that mind is in charge of brain, we spontaneously recognize their conviction as something we've always known or at least suspected. What grips us as we listen to these men is not only the elegance of their demonstrations, nor the sheerly rational force of their arguments, but their everydayness.... **We find ourselves agreeing with Sperry and Eccles because what they say seems "right"** (1985, pp. 39-40, emp. added).

As Trefil put it: "There is a sense in which something like Descartes' procedure remains valid for the question of human consciousness" (1997, p. 181). Perhaps that explains, at least in part, why, as Trefil went on to note, "[t]his so-called mind-body dualism has played a major role in thinking about mental activity ever since Descartes" (p. 181).

But that is not all that Dr. Trefil had to say. He also commented: "Philosophers have, in fact, written long and detailed critiques of the Cartesian approach to the world" (p. 181). Later, we will return to the idea behind Trefil's comment that "there is a sense in which something like Descartes' procedure remains valid for the question of human consciousness," because he is absolutely correct in such an assessment. For now, however, we would like to concentrate on his statement that "philosophers have, in fact, written long and detailed critiques of the Cartesian approach to the world."

Yes, they certainly have. And so have their counterparts in the scientific community. In his exhaustive review on "consciousness" for the journal *Brain*, Zeman stated that "there is a deep dissatisfaction with the Cartesian separation of body and mind" (2001, 124:1264). True enough. But, as Adrian admitted: "...[A]greement in rejecting dualism has not been coupled with agreement in accepting anything else" (1965, p. 239). The question, then, is **why** is there such a "deep dissatisfaction"?

Simply put, there is "deep satisfaction" with the Cartesian view that body and mind are separate because: (a) such a concept is deemed "unscientific"; (b) it does not "square" with evolutionary concepts; and (c) still worse (at least in the eyes of many), it has "theological overtones." Canadian anthropologist Arthur C. Custance addressed these matters in *The Mysterious Matter of Mind*.

> Most of the important thinkers who followed Descartes rejected interactionism. It was not a testable hypothesis. **Above all, it introduced the supernatural into the picture and thus removed the concept from the scientific laboratory into the theological seminary**.... What emerged was a determination to reduce everything to physics and chemistry, or perhaps more precisely to physics and mathematics... (1980, p. 31, emp. added).

Harvard's Kirtley Mather was a bit more blunt when he wrote in *The Permissive Universe:*

> Enough is now known about human nature to validate the concept that each human being is an indivisible unity composed of body, mind, and spirit... I know of no scientifically verifiable data that would support the idea that the human soul is a separate entity inserted from above or without into the human body and residing therein during a person's lifetime.... Equating thus the human soul with the spiritual aspects of the life of man, it follows that **the soul, like the body or the mind, is a product of evolutionary processes**... (1986, p. 174, emp. added).

As Sperry put it:

> [A] central requirement imposed by science would seem to be a relinquishment of dualist concepts in conformance with the explanation of mind in monist-mentalist terms. Such a shift from various dualistic, other worldly beliefs to a monistic, this-world faith, would mean that our planet should no longer be conceived, or treated, as merely a way-station to something better beyond. This present world and life would thus in each case, acquire an added relative value and meaning (as quoted in Cousins, 1985, pp. 159-160).

Or, to use Mather's words: "The conclusion is inescapable. Mankind's destiny is that of an earth-bound creature. Salvation must be sought here on this terrestrial planet" (p. 157). Zeman therefore concluded:

> The suggestion that conscious events are identical with the corresponding neural events offers a reductionist and materialist, or physicalist, solution to the mind-body problem.... **Why should consciousness be an exception to the stream of successful reductions of phenomena once considered to be beyond the reach of science?** (124:1282, emp. added).

A few paragraphs prior to this one, we mentioned the 1949 book, *The Concept of Mind,* by British philosopher Gilbert Ryle. That book played a critical role in what many today view as the final debunking of Cartesian dualism. Ryle stated clearly that his goal was to expunge once and for all the "official doctrine" of what he called "the dogma of the ghost in the machine" (pp. 15-16). In fact, he was the one who invented that now-famous phrase.

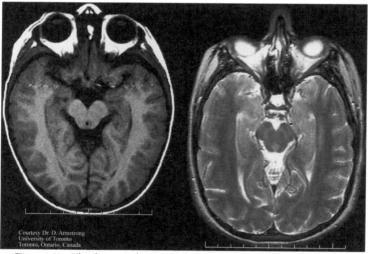

Courtesy Dr. D. Armstrong
University of Toronto
Toronto, Ontario, Canada

Figure 2 — The human brain. Is there a "ghost in the machine?" LifeART image copyright © (2003) Lippincott, Williams & Wilkins. All rights reserved. Used by permission.

The vaunted and venerable *Encyclopaedia Britannica*, in its assessment of Descartes, offered the following concise commentary.

> The strongest 20th-century attack on Cartesian dualism was launched by the British analytic philosopher Gilbert Ryle in *The Concept of Mind* (1949), where he exposes what he describes as the fallacy of the ghost in the machine. He argues that the mind—the ghost—is simply the intelligent behaviour of the body. Like many contemporary analytic philosophers, Ryle maintains that metaphysical questions about being and reality are nonsense because they include reference to empirically unverifiable entities. **His position**, like that of the Australian philosopher J.J.C. Smart, **is ultimately materialist: The mind is the brain**. The American pragmatist Richard Rorty in *Philosophy and the Mirror of Nature* (1979) argues that the Cartesian demand for certain knowledge by way of representative ideas is a holdover from the mistaken quest for God. **Rorty says that philosophy in the Cartesian tradition is the 20th century's substitute for theology and should, like God, be gently laid to rest** ("Descartes and Cartesianism," 1997, 15:559, emp. added).

Roger Lewin, in his discussion of human consciousness in *Complexity: Life at the Edge of Chaos,* suggested that "Cartesian dualism dominated philosophical thinking for three centuries until the British philosopher Gilbert Ryle effectively demolished it" (1992, p. 157). Ryle's vicious attack upon Cartesian dualism was only the first of many to follow, leading E.O. Wilson to conclude: "Virtually all contemporary scientists and philosophers expert on the subject agree that the mind, which comprises consciousness and rational process, is the brain at work. They have rejected the mind-brain dualism of René Descartes..." (1998, p. 98). Or, as Michael Lemonick chirped in the January 20, 2003 issue of *Time* magazine: "Descartes was dead wrong" (2003b, 161[3]:63).

Monism

Was Descartes "dead wrong"? We do not believe that he was. And we will have more to say on that shortly. But for now, we would like to examine monistic theories of consciousness. As we begin, perhaps a definition of "monism" is in order. The *American Heritage Dictionary* defines monism as:

> the view in metaphysics that reality is a unified whole and that all existing things can be ascribed to or described by a single concept or system; the doctrine that mind and matter are formed from, or reducible to, the same ultimate substance or principle of being.

Webster's Unabridged Dictionary goes farther.

> That doctrine which refers all phenomena to a single ultimate constituent or agent–the opposite of dualism. The doctrine has been held in **three generic forms**: (1) matter and its phenomena have been explained as a modification of mind, involving an idealistic monism; (2) mind has been explained by and resolved into matter, giving a materialistic monism; or (3) matter, mind, and their phenomena have been held to be manifestations or modifications of some one substance, or a supposed "unknown something" of some evolutionists, which is capable of an objective and subjective aspect (emp. added).

In speaking about the concept of monism, Ruse offered this assessment:

> On the other hand, there are the monists. Most famously, there was the seventeenth-century Dutch philosopher Benedict Spinoza. He argued that when thinking of consciousness, there is no reason to think that one is considering a separate substance. **Consciousness, in some way, is simply a manifestation of the physical world**. Spinoza and his modern-day followers do not want to say that consciousness does not exist, or that it is simply material substance in a traditional way. Consciousness is obviously not round, or red, or hard, or anything like that. Rather, consciousness in some sense is emergent from or an aspect of

material substances. **In other words, the notion of material substance has to be extended, from red and round and hard, to include consciousness** (2001b, pp. 199-200, emp. added).

According to this view, the human brain is considered to be an electrochemical machine. The mind and the brain are one, with the mind being merely an extension of the physical mechanisms of the brain (and being entirely dependent upon those mechanisms for its existence/expression). The pillar upon which modern neural science is founded—materialistic monism—contends that **all** behavior is a reflection of brain function. Thus, according to this view, everything that a person says, thinks, and does can be accounted for by certain physical actions within the brain. The "mind"—such as it is—therefore is reduced to a range of functions carried out by the physical matter within the brain. This reductive perspective allows evolutionists to then declare that matter is all that exists, and that the human brain and mind evolved from lower animals, so that humans have no "spiritual" component. There is, so it has been said, no "ghost in the machine."

Today, "for the most part, materialism, the philosophical alternative to dualism, dominates modern thinking about consciousness" (Lewin, 1992, p. 157). Yes, it certainly does. British physiologist Lord E.D. Adrian, in the chapter he wrote on "Consciousness" for the book, *Brain and Conscious Experience,* admitted: "…[B]y the beginning of the century it was becoming more respectable for psychologists to use some kind of monism as a working hypothesis and even to be whole-hearted behaviorists" (1965, p. 239). The late, eminent British electrophysiologist, Sir John Eccles, writing in his book, *The Human Psyche,* commented:

The dominant theories of the brain-mind relationship that are today held by neuroscientists are purely materialistic in the sense that the brain is given complete mastery. The existence of mind or consciousness is not denied, but it is relegated to the passive role of mental experiences accompanying some types of brain action, as in psychoneural identity, but with absolutely no effective action on the brain. The complex neural machinery of the brain functions in its determined materialistic fashion regardless of any consciousness that may accompany it. The "common sense" experiences that we can control our actions to some extent or that we can express our thoughts in language are alleged to be illusory. Actually, it is rare for this to be stated so baldly, but despite all the sophisticated cover-up the situation is exactly as stated. **An effective causality is denied to the self-conscious mind *per se*** (1992, p. 17, italics in orig., emp. added).

Dr. Eccles' assessment is correct, and provides a satisfactory springboard from which we can begin an investigation into the "the dominant theories of the brain-mind relationship."

Psychical Monism

We would like to discuss psychical monism first, in order to quickly dispense with it. This doctrine contends that **consciousness is the only reality**–i.e., **the material world only "appears" to be there**. Thoughts are causally connected, but physical events are not necessarily so. (This doctrine is the exact inverse of epiphenomenalism, which we shall discuss shortly.) As Carrington pointed out eighty years ago:

> The contention of this theory is that nothing exists save states of consciousness in the individual. Neither the material world nor other minds exist (save in the mind of the individual). In refutation of this theory, it may be pointed out that, if brain changes are thus caused by, or are the outer expression of, thought–why not muscular changes, and in fact all physical phenomena throughout the world everywhere–for we cannot rationally draw the line of distinction here. Such is the logical outcome of the theory…. While many philosophers are inclined to accept this view, it may be stated that the **physical scientists are naturally repelled by it, and so is common sense** (1923, pp. 52,53, emp. added).

Common sense is indeed "repelled" by psychical monism —more popularly known as solipsism—which, according to the *Cambridge International Dictionary of English,* is "the theory or view that the self is the only reality." Carrington correctly concluded: "This doctrine is so opposed to common sense and daily experience that it is unnecessary to dwell upon it" (p. 53). Agreed.

Radical Materialism (Functionalism)

Currently, there exists a small-but-vocal group of philosophers that parades under the title of the "radical materialists." Previously, we quoted from Eccles and Robinson, who noted: "The existence of mind or consciousness is not denied **except by radical materialists**..." (1984, p. 34, emp. added). According to Eccles, in radical materialism, "there is a denial or repudiation of the existence of mental events. They are simply illusory. The brain-mind problem is a non-problem" (1992, pp. 17-18). In a fascinating article ("The Mind-Brain Problem") that he wrote for publication on-line, John Beloff addressed the concept of radical materialism and those of the past who have defended it.

> Our third solution, which denies that there **are** any distinct mental or subjective events that need explaining, is a purely twentieth century development and it stems from four quite different sources that have very little connection with one another. The first, in point of time, arose among psychologists of the first decades of this century who sought to make psychology the study of behaviour, human or animal, and, in doing so to discredit introspection that was previously taken to be the distinctive technique of psychology as a science. We may call this "Watsonian Behaviourism and its offshoots." The second, in point of time, arose within Anglo-American philosophy and I shall call it "Linguistic Behaviourism." Its classic statement is to be found in Gilbert Ryle's *The Concept of Mind* (1949). The third was likewise a product of AngloAmerican philosophy (if that can be stretched to include Australia

where some of its most vocal proponents taught philosophy), and we could call it "Strict Materialism," i.e. the doctrine that there are no private sense-data, only brain-events and their associated behaviours. D.M. Armstrong's *A Materialist Theory of Mind* (1968) may be cited as a classic text (1994, parenthetical item and emp. in orig.).

Today, it is unlikely that anyone is better known for defending the concept of "radical materialism" in a more formidable fashion than philosopher Daniel C. Dennett of Tufts University in Boston, whose reverence for Ryle's work is utterly unabashed, and who has written a slew of books on human consciousness (1984, 1987, 1991, 1996, 1998), including one titled *Consciousness Explained* (1991). Speaking of that book and its author, Andrew Brown wrote in *The Darwin Wars:*

> It is difficult to think of anyone else who would have the self-confidence to write a book called simply *Consciousness Explained*, or the nerve, once it was finished, to publish the contents under that title. It's a wonderful book; but it doesn't explain consciousness. **The heart of Dennett's position seems to be that consciousness itself is a misleading category, and that the only way to make sense of it is to redefine all one's terms in terms of externally visible states and behaviours**. Carried to extremes—the normal destination of Dennett's ideas—this leads him to assert such things as that thermostats have beliefs.... He has devoted his life to exorcising the ghost from the machine (1999, pp. 153,154, emp. added).

Paul Ehrlich went on record as stating: "In *Consciousness Explained*, he takes an interesting cut at the problem, but he does not 'explain' consciousness to my satisfaction" (2000, p. 112). Nor did he explain it to anyone else's. In his 1994 book, *How the Self Controls Its Brain*, Sir John Eccles quoted Dennett's statement from page 21 of *Consciousness Explained*, "human consciousness is just about the last surviving mystery," and then wryly commented: "It is still a mystery at the end of his 468-page book" (p. 31). In a review of Daniel Dennett's 2003 book, *Freedom Evolves*, that he authored for the March 2, 2003 issue of the *New York Times*, Galen Strawson (professor of philosophy at the University of Reading in England, and author of *Freedom and Belief*) commented:

> In the last several years the philosopher Daniel C. Dennett has published two very large, interesting and influential books. The first, *Consciousness Explained* (1991), aimed to account for all the phenomena of consciousness within the general theoretical framework set by current physics. It failed, of course, and came to be affectionately known as *Consciousness Ignored...* (2003).

Dennett has indeed "devoted his life to exorcising the ghost from the machine." Speaking of himself, and others of his ilk, he wrote:

> For other, more theoretically daring researchers, there is a new object of study, the mind/brain. This newly popular coinage nicely expresses the prevailing materialism of these researchers, who happily admit to the world and to themselves that what makes the brain particularly fascinating and baffling is that somehow or other it **is** the mind (1991, pp. 38-39, emp. in orig.).

As one might expect, the radical materialism espoused by Dennett has not gone down well with those who believe that consciousness **does** exist, and that it **does** matter. Even among some of his evolutionist colleagues, his ideas have drawn considerable (and substantial) criticism. In assessing Dennett's work, Trefil wrote:

> One group of thinkers argues, in essence, that the problem of consciousness either cannot or should not be addressed. In its simplest form, this position holds that there is no problem of consciousness at all—that once you understand what the neurons are doing, there's nothing else to explain. Perhaps the most influential of these is the philosopher Daniel Dennett in *Consciousness Explained....*

> The problem comes when Dennett approaches the problem of consciousness. The first time I read his book, I became confused because about halfway through I began to think, "Hey—this guy doesn't think that consciousness exists."

This seemed to me to be such a bizarre view that I actually read the book several times, and when that failed to persuade me otherwise I still worried that I was missing something. I'm sure Dennett would deny that this is a proper interpretation of his work, but other scholars (most notably John Searle in the *New York Review of Books*) seem to have come to the same conclusion....

Until you have explained how I come to that central conclusion about my own existence, you have not solved the problem of consciousness. **You certainly won't solve the problem by denying that consciousness exists**. For me, reading Dennett's book was a little like reading a detailed discussion on the workings of a transmission, only to be told that there is no such thing as a car (1997, pp. 182,183,184, parenthetical comment in orig., emp. added).

[Strawson, in his review of Dennett's *Freedom Evolves*, wrote rather bluntly: "Dennett continues to deny the existence of consciousness, and continues to deny that he is denying it" (2003, emp. added). Eccles, in *How the Self Controls Its Brain*, concluded: "Dennett...discounts a unique Self which is central to our experience. Dennett wants to get rid of the Cartesian Theater, but all he seems to finish with is emptiness" (1994, p. 33).]

Two aspects of radical materialism are closely associated with Dennett. The first is what he refers to as "the intentional stance," which, not coincidentally, happens to be the title of one of his books (1987). Dennett's definition in that book was this: "The intentional stance is the strategy of prediction and explanation that attributes beliefs, desires, and other 'intentional' states to systems—living and nonliving" (p. 495). Griffin, in *Animal Consciousness*, investigated Dennett's position, and concluded:

The contemporary philosopher Daniel Dennett has advocated what he calls "the intentional stance" when analyzing not only human and animal cognition but also many examples of self-regulating inanimate mechanisms.... His insistence on including such simple devices as thermostats in this extended category of intentional systems **leads him to deny any special status to conscious mental experiences**.... **Dennett appears to be arguing that if a neurophysiological mechanism were shown to organize and guide a particular behavior pattern, this would rule out the possibility that any conscious mental experiences might accompany or influence such behavior**....

Dennett prefers a theoretical framework that encompasses the whole range of systems from thermostats to scientists and philosophers. Yet he applies terms that ordinarily refer to conscious mental states, such as *belief* and *desire* even to thermostats. This amounts to a sort of semantic piracy in which the meaning of widely used terms is distorted by extension in order to paper over a fundamental problem—namely, the question whether conscious mental experiences occur in other species (2001, p. 263, italics in orig., emp. added).

Griffin, of course, is renowned in his own right for his work with animal consciousness—which is why he raised the issue of how Dennett's work questions "whether conscious mental experiences occur **in other species**." But Dennett's position does not question consciousness solely "in other species." It is most notorious for calling into question whether consciousness occurs in **humans**.

The second aspect of radical materialism closely associated with Dennett is the concept of "functionalism." This view ultimately arises from Dennett's strong ties to the artificial intelligence (AI) community. Beloff summarized the functionalist position as follows.

Functionalism differs from previous materialist theories of mind by insisting that mental events need not be identified exclusively with brain events; if computing machinery made from wires, transistors, etc. can serve the **same functions** as our brain in mediating between inputs and outputs, then mental events may be predicated of **any** such system that possessed the necessary information-processing capacities. Functionalism was a late twentieth-century doctrine that obviously owed its existence to the rise of Artificial Intelligence. Its most compendious exposition today is a book with the question-begging title, *Consciousness Explained,* by Daniel C. Dennett (1994, emp. in orig.).

In reviewing Dennett's position, Johanson and Edgar explained that he

> ...argues that consciousness can be understood from the metaphor of a computer. He views the mind as the software to the brain's hardware, a program that writes a narrative of our experience, edited and compiled from the multiple drafts of information streaming into the brain. In this view, the present moment of sensation is insignificant compared to the subsequent mental reflection and contemplation, from which meaning arises. Consciousness—the mind—is simply a product of the brain... (1996, p. 107).

As Scott put it, this is the view that "the essential aspects of mental dynamics will eventually be expressed as a formula and represented on a system constructed from integrated computer circuits" (1995, p. 2).

What are the implications of Dennett's brand of functionalism in regard to things such as the mind/soul? Davies addressed those implications when he wrote:

> Functionalists recognize that the essential ingredient of mind is not the hardware—the stuff your brain is made of, or the physical processes that it employs—but the software—the organization of the stuff, or the "program." They do not deny that the brain is a machine, and that neurons fire purely for electrical reasons—**there are no mental causes of physical processes**. Yet they still appeal to causal relations between mental states: very crudely, thoughts cause thoughts, notwithstanding the fact that, at the hardware level, the causal links are already forged....

Functionalism solves at a stroke most of the traditional queries about the soul. What stuff is the soul made of? The question is as meaningless as asking what stuff citizenship is made of or Wednesdays are made of. The soul is a holistic concept. It is not made of stuff at all. Where is the soul located? Nowhere. To talk of the soul as being in a place is as misconceived as trying to locate the number seven, or Beethoven's fifth symphony. Such concepts are not in space at all (1983, pp. 85,86, emp. added).

If all of this strikes you as a bit odd, let us reassure you: you are not alone. In fact, even Daniel Dennett, the current high priest of functionalism, has admitted that his ideas generally do not go down terribly well. Beloff went on to note:

[M]aterialists and behaviourists are not stupid. They are as much aware as we are that what they are saying is outrageous, in the sense of defying something deep rooted in our thought and language, it is just that they are undeterred. Dennett, at the outset of his lengthy treatise, warns us that his efforts at "demystification" as he calls it, will be viewed by many as an "act of intellectual vandalism." But, if we cannot formally refute the materialism or functionalism…, neither can its proponents persuade us to deny or overlook that red patch that refuses to go away. In dismissing the third solution from further consideration, I can do no better than John Searle (*The Rediscovery of the Mind*, 1992, p. 8) when he says, **"if your theory results in the view that consciousness does not exist, you have simply produced a *reductio ad absurdum* of your theory"** (1994, emp. added).

We agree. Suggesting that consciousness (a.k.a., self-awareness) does not exist **is absurd!** [That fact, nevertheless, has not kept some from actually denying that consciousness exists. Lawrence Kubie wrote in *Brain Mechanisms and Consciousness: A Symposium:* "Although we cannot get along without the concept of consciousness, actually there is no such thing" (1956, p. 446).] In *Beyond Natural Selection,* Wesson concluded:

Self-awareness is a special quality of the mind.... Self-awareness is different from information processing; even when confused and unable to think clearly, one may be vividly aware of one's self and one's confusion. The essence of mind is less data processing than will, intention, imagination, discovery, and feeling. If some kinds of thinking can be initiated by a computer, others cannot (1997, p. 277).

Earlier, we gave the first part of the quote below by Roger Lewin. Now we would like to present the last portion of the quote in this context.

To say that the brain is a computer is a truism, because, unquestionably, what goes on in there is computation. But so far, no man-made computer matches the human brain, either in capacity or design.... Can a computer think? And, ultimately, can a computer generate a level of consciousness that Dan Dennett or Nick Humphrey, or anyone else, has in mind? (1992, p. 160).

Good questions, those. And we all know the answers to them, do we not?

One last item bears mentioning in regard to radical materialism. It has a counterpart in psychology—behaviorism. Paul Davies commented on this fact when he wrote:

The materialist believes that mental states and operations are nothing but physical states and operations. In the field of psychology, **materialism becomes what is known as behaviourism, which proclaims that all humans behave in a purely mechanical way in response to external stimuli** (1983, p. 82, emp. added).

According to behaviorists, only the brain exists, and mind is just an "off-shoot" of it (referred to as an "epiphenomenon"—discussed below). In the discipline of behaviorism, "mind has no independent existence and the question of the origin of mind is entirely secondary to the question of the origin and nature of brain tissue" (Custance, 1980, p. 21).

But such a position presents its own set of problems. Writing under the title of "Consciousness" for *The Encyclopaedia of Ignorance,* Richard Gregory discussed some of them.

> Psychology has traditionally sought "laws of mind" to explain behaviour. There are many terms, such as "motivation," "fear," "hunger," and "shame," which it is quite difficult to conceive as having simple physiological correlates. One can well imagine that the physical state of lack of food is monitored, and signaled to brain regions which activates food-seeking behaviour; and we might describe this in an animal, or another person, to include a sensation like our feeling of hunger. It is more difficult to conceive a physiological state for shame, or guilt, or pride.... **The issue is important. It raises the question of how physiology is related to psychology, and whether consciousness can be affected or controlled apart from physiological changes** (1977, pp. 278-279, emp. added).

Behaviorism has fallen onto hard times of late—and for several good reasons, among which are the ones summarized below by Beloff, who referred to behaviorism as "methodologically misleading, philosophically false, and ideologically pernicious." And that was the kindest thing he had to say! Read on.

> My first charge against Behaviourism is that it commits what Aldous Huxley once called "The Original Sin of the Intellect: Oversimplification." In other words it offers us a picture of man in which the most important dimension of existence has been left out, and in which the highlights have been placed on what is, in fact, extraneous. I believe that to accept this shallow travesty as a revelation of truth is to coarsen one's sensibilities and to close one's mind to just those aspects of reality which should evoke our deepest feelings of wonder or reverence.
>
> Secondly, I regard behaviourism as incompatible with any genuine morality.... We defined behaviourism in the previous chapter as the doctrine that everything that can be said about Mind can, in principle, be said in terms of behaviour, whether actual or potential....

Our conclusions were that it was methodologically misleading, philosophically false and ideologically pernicious. But in the end, **perhaps its most glaring fault is simply a certain unmistakable *silliness* which qualifies it, surely, as one of the oddest intellectual aberrations of the twentieth century** (1962, pp. 47,48,49, italics in orig., emp. added).

In his 1994 book, *How the Self Controls Its Brain*, Sir John Eccles threw down the gauntlet in what he termed a "challenge to all materialists" (p. x). He expressed sharp criticism of, among others, Sir Francis Crick and his collaborator, Christof Koch, when he referred to their work as "science fiction of a blatant kind" (p. 30). But he reserved his harshest criticism for Daniel Dennett's brand of radical materialism when he referred to functionalism as an "impoverished and empty theory" (p. 33). Why characterize functionalism in such terminology? In John Searle's uncompromising words: "... the deeper objection can be put quite simply: the theory has left out the mind" (as quoted in Zeman, 2001, 124:1283).

Panpsychism

In his classic work, *Lay Sermons, Addresses, and Reviews*, Thomas H. Huxley had a chapter titled "On the Physical Basis of Life." Within that chapter was this sentence: "Thoughts are the expression of molecular changes in the matter of life, which is the source of our other vital phenomena" (1870b, p. 152). Lord Adrian concluded:

> ...[N]ow we can add that there is no need to invoke extraphysical factors to account for any of the public activities of the brain.... Consciousness is a logical construction.... It arises when unconscious processes are integrated; its base line in the individual and in the animal kingdom is arbitrary (1965, pp. 239-240, 246).

This is the essence of the view known as panpsychism. When Gregory asked: "What is the relation between consciousness and the matter or functions of the brain?" (1977, p. 274), he hit at the very heart of panpsychism, which is the view that "some primordial consciousness attaches to all matter, presumably even to atoms and subatomic particles" (Eccles and Robinson, 1984, p. 37). As Eccles and Robinson remarked in regard to the radical materialism that we discussed above:

> The alternative is to espouse panpsychism. All types of panpsychists evade the problems by proposing that **there is a protoconsciousness in all matter**, even in elementary particles! According to panpsychism, the evolutionary development of brain is associated merely with an amplification and refinement of what was already there as a property of all matter. It merely is exhibited more effectively in the complex organizations of the brains of higher animals (p. 14).

Huxley put it like this: "Mind is a function of matter, when that matter has attained a certain degree of organization" (1871, p. 464). But, there is a caveat. To quote Eccles, while "it is asserted that all matter has an inside mental or protopsychical state, **since this state is an integral part of matter, it can have no action on it**" (1992, p. 17, emp. added).

In other words, consciousness **does** exist—everywhere, all the time, in every material thing. In the case of human beings, it "just happened" to come together in a "certain degree of organization" that permitted consciousness to be expressed, and then generated self-awareness as the end result.

However, after all is said and done, as Rupert Sheldrake correctly noted: "The conscious self [has]...a reality which is not merely derivative from matter" (1981, p. 203). Paul Davies commented: "We still have no clue how mind and matter are related, or what process led to the emergence of mind from matter in the first place" (1995). With some understatement, Zeman confessed: "...[W]e have no clear understanding of what kind of property could render physical events intrinsically mental" (2001, 124:1284). Not surprisingly, then, Eccles and Robinson concluded: "[Panpsychism] finds no support whatsoever in physics" (1984, p. 37).

Epiphenomenalism

The careful reader will have noticed that, from time to time during our discussion of the concept of consciousness, the terms "epiphenomenon," "epiphenomena," or "epiphenomenalism" have appeared. We purposely postponed any discussion of epiphenomenalism until this point, because it is best considered under the subject of the monist-materialist views that we are discussing here.

Epiphenomenalism, according to Eccles, is the view that "mental states exist in relation to some material happenings, but causally are completely irrelevant" (1992, pp. 17). The *Merriam-Webster Dictionary* defines epiphenomenon as "a secondary phenomenon accompanying another and caused by it." For example, pathologists frequently use the word to refer to the secondary symptoms of a disease. So, when Eccles says that epiphenomenalism suggests that mental states exist, but "causally are completely irrelevant," his point is that, like in a disease, **the symptom does not cause anything, but is itself caused by something else**. That, in essence, is how epiphenomenalism works. Shadworth Hodgson, in his book, *The Theory of Practice* (1870), proposed that conscious mental events were caused by physical changes in the nervous system, but could not themselves cause physical changes. As one author put it: "Like the whistle of a railway engine (which does not affect the engine), or the chime of a clock (which does not affect the clock), they were caused by (and accompanied) physical events, but they did not themselves act as causal agents. In a slightly later terminology, they were **epiphenomena**…" (Glynn, 1999, p. 8, parenthetical items and emp. in orig.).

The man who referred to himself as "Darwin's bulldog," Thomas Henry Huxley (1825-1895), coined the term "epiphenomenalism" in an article he authored for the *Fortnightly Review* in 1874. The time was ripe for him to originate such a concept because, as Beloff explained

> …the view that prevailed among scientists of the late
> 19th century was to look for the causes of our behav-

iour in the brain alone…. For the epiphenomenalist, the brain was a machine, like everything else in nature, and the mind no more than a passive reflection of its activity (1994).

Huxley, therefore,

> proposed that as the noise of the babbling brook is only a by-product of the rushing water, so the mind, though distinct from the brain, is nevertheless only a by-product of it. The brain therefore causes the mind as the brook causes the babbling, but the mind cannot have any influence on the brain any more than the babbling can have any influence on the brook. This was termed epiphenomenalism (Custance, 1980, p. 23).

Today, from the perspective of the reductionist-materialist, epiphenomenalism is as good an explanation as any, since "so far as we can tell, mental activity is always associated with nervous activity" (Glynn, 1999, p. 9). Griffin wrote:

> Conscious thinking may well be a **core function** of central nervous systems…. The fact that we are consciously aware of only a small fraction of what goes on in our brains has led many scientists to conclude that consciousness is an epiphenomenon or trivial by-product of neural functioning (2001, p. 3, emp. in orig.).

Richard Lewontin and the late Stephen Jay Gould argued that language, consciousness, and, in fact, most of our other distinctively human mental capacities are merely "side effects" of the fact that our brain grew big for "other reasons" (reasons, they say, by the way, that cannot be reconstructed). According to Lewontin, our extraordinary human abilities are "epiphenomena of all those loose brain connections with nothing to do" (as quoted in Schwartz, 1999).

Referring to human consciousness as a "trivial by-product" or a "side effect" seems to be the height of folly (if not conceit). Being asked to think of self-awareness as a "symptom" of a "disease" (i.e., the brain) isn't much better. And, apparently, we are not the only ones who think so. In *The Wonder of Being Human: Our Brain and Our Mind*, Eccles and Robinson referred to the concept of epiphenomenalism as "gibberish."

> The epiphenomenalist's causal theory should not be confused with the ordinary causal laws of the physical sciences. The latter are confined to the manner in which force and matter are distributed in time and space. But with epiphenomenalism we are faced with a radically different entity—a *mental* entity—taken to be nonmaterial and nonphysical. **If it exists at all, then by definition it cannot be composed of or reduced to material elements or combinations thereof**. To say that it "arises" from these is, alas, gibberish (1984, p. 55, italics in orig., emp. added).

But why is this the case? The two authors continued:

> On the epiphenomenalist's assumption, there are two entities—the mental and material—having real existence. Furthermore, the former is alleged to be caused by the latter, in just the way that entirely material causes result in entirely material effects. But note that in any purely physical interaction, it is never **necessary** that event A cause event B; it is merely contingently the case, given the composition and laws of the physical world, that events of type A happen to cause or faithfully lead to events of type B. Accordingly, to argue that brain states, in a natural-causal fashion, produce mental states is to admit that it could be otherwise. **All purely natural phenomena could be other than they are**. Thus, the epiphenomenalist, to the extent that he endorses a causal theory of brain-mind relationships, can never establish that the brain is **necessary** in order that there be mind. There is nothing logically contradictory in the claim that there are minds without brain and brains without minds…. Once it is granted that there are genuinely mental (nonphysical) events, it follows that an exhaustive inventory of the **physical** universe and its laws must be incomplete as an inventory of real exis-

tents, because mental events are left out. If there can be mind in addition to matter, there can be mind without matter (p. 55, emp. in orig.).

Whew! No epiphenomenalist would willingly want to go **that far**, we can assure you. Mind without matter? Eccles and Robinson are absolutely correct, of course: "To argue that brain states…produce mental states is to admit that it could be otherwise." And it gets progressively worse for the epiphenomenalist, as Ian Glynn pointed out in his book, *An Anatomy of Thought: The Origin and Machinery of the Mind.*

> **[I]f mental events are epiphenomena, they cannot have any survival value**. Darwin's struggle for existence is a struggle in the physical world, and if mental events cannot cause physical effects they cannot affect the outcome in that struggle. **But if they cannot affect the outcome–if they have no survival value–why should we have evolved brains that make them possible?**… That they make conscious thought possible is not relevant, for thought that merely accompanies behaviour without influencing it will be ignored by natural selection….
>
> **Even if the notion that mental events are epiphenomena is true, it leaves unexplained what most needs explaining. Why should particular physical changes in our nervous systems cause feelings or thoughts? Even epiphenomena need to be accounted for**. The smoke from the engine may not move the train, but its presence is not a mystery. There's no smoke without fire, we are told, and we are confident of locating the fire in the engine's firebox…. So despite its promising start, the notion that mental events are epiphenomena has not got us out of the difficulties that a combination of common-sense and physics got us into (1999, pp. 10,11-12, emp. added).

It seems that we keep returning to that phrase "common sense." And rightly so! Would that there were **more** of it in discussions by philosophers and scientists regarding the subject of human consciousness. Things that are counter-intuitive may just be…**wrong**–as Beloff concluded:

There are, however, at least three good reasons for doubting the epiphenomenalist thesis. In the first place, it is profoundly counter-intuitive; in the second place its implications lead to absurd conclusions; in the third place there exist certain anomalous mental phenomena which are inexplicable given the known properties of the brain.

As if this were not enough, we must note that epiphenomenalism necessarily sacrifices the concept of "free-will," a concept which permeates so profoundly all talk of "justice," "merit" and "morality." For, clearly, the commission of a crime is as much the outcome of impersonal brain processes as is altruistic behaviour. Hitler is no more blameworthy for his misdeeds than he is for his reflexes, both ultimately being products of his brain, essentially just a complex electrochemical machine (1994).

Depriving humans of free will is no small matter. In speaking of the implications of philosopher John Searle's work, Rodney Cotterill remarked:

Searle also stresses the importance of **intentionality**, by which he means that mental states are usually related to, or directed toward, external situations and circumstances…. One aspect of intentionality concerns *choice*, irrespective of whether this implies the exercise of free will. **Even if choices were not really free, the fact that we are able to handle it would still warrant contemplation.** Searle's point is well taken…. **Searle has identified one of the defining characteristics of the higher organism** (1998, p. 320, italics in orig., emp. added).

Free will **is** "one of the defining characteristics of higher organisms." And it does exist—sort of.

Sort of? Apparently so. Writing on "Problems Outstanding in the Evolution of Brain Function" in *The Encyclopaedia of Ignorance,* brain scientist and Nobel laureate Roger Sperry wrote:

> Unlike "mind," "consciousness," and "instinct," "free will" has made no comeback in behavioral science in recent years. Most behavioral scientists would refuse to list free will among our problems outstanding, or at least as an unanswered problem.... **Every advance in the science of behavior**, whether it has come from the psychiatrist's couch, from microelectrode recording, from brain-splitting, or from the running of cannibalistic flatworms, **seems only to reinforce that old suspicion that free will is just an illusion. The more we learn about the brain and behavior, the more deterministic, lawful, and causal it appears** (1977, p. 432, emp. added).

And so, with one fell swoop of the pen, we are asked to believe that free will is "just an illusion." It appears that the best the evolutionists can do is to suggest that "in the abstract there may be no free will," but "in practice," there really is. Paul Ehrlich has suggested exactly that—in those very words.

> That enormous complexity of our brains can also, in a way, explain humanity's famed "free will." ...Thus, although in the abstract there may be no free will, in practice the brains of human beings evolved so that intentional individuals can make real choices and can make them within a context of ethical alternatives.... Natural selection has endowed us with the capacity to figure out a course of action in virtually any situation, "accepting" the possibility that a chosen course may prove unfortunate (2000, pp. 124,125).

[After reading a quotation like the one above from Ehrlich, we cannot help but wonder if the people who write such things ever read them?!]

But what is the **origin** of human free will? Steven Pinker is convinced that the explanation is "all in the circuits." In an article he authored ("Are Your Genes to Blame?") for the January 20, 2003 issue of *Time* magazine, he testified:

> As we increase our knowledge of how the genome works, many beliefs about ourselves will indeed have to be rethought. But the worst fears of the genophobes

are misplaced. It is easy to exaggerate the significance of behavioral genetics for our lives. For one thing, genes cannot pull the strings of behavior directly. Behavior is caused by the activity of the brain, and the most genes can do is affect its wiring, size, shape and sensitivity to hormones and other molecules. Among the brain circuits laid down by genes are the ones that reflect on memories, current circumstances and the anticipated consequences of various courses of action and that select behavior accordingly—in an intricate and not entirely predictable way. **These circuits are what we call "free will," and providing them with information about the likely consequences of behavioral options is what we call "holding people responsible."** All normal people have this circuitry, and that is why the existence of genes with effects on behavior should not be allowed to erode responsibility in the legal system or in everyday life (161[3]:99, emp. added).

Not everyone is willing to buy into such a hypothesis, however. As Paul Davies asked: "Where is there room in the deterministic predictive laws of electrical circuitry for **free will**?" (1983, p. 74, emp. in orig.). Or, in the words of Daniel Dennett:

> If the concept of consciousness were to "fall to science," what would happen to our sense of moral agency and free will? If conscious experience were "reduced" somehow to mere matter in motion, what would happen to our appreciation of love and pain and dreams and joy? If conscious human beings were "just" animated material objects, how could anything we do to them be right or wrong? (1991, pp. 24-25).

Sir John Eccles, though by his own admission a committed Darwinian (see Eccles, 1967, p. 7; 1977, p. 98), argued strongly (from his own research into the relationship between mental intentions and neural events) in behalf of free will—what he called "the freedom to know and freedom to act" (see Cousins, 1985, p. 152). As Eccles himself stated:

> If we can establish that we have freedom to bring about simple movements at will, then more complex social and moral situations must also in part at least be open to control by a voluntary decision, i.e., of mental thought processes. Thus we have opened the way to the consideration of personal freedom and moral responsibility (as quoted in Cousins, p. 154).

There is one thing epiphenomenalism does **not** do—and that is to "open the way to the consideration of personal freedom and moral responsibility." To quote E.O. Wilson:

> And old impasse nonetheless remains. **If the mind is bound by the laws of physics**, and if it can conceivably be read like calligraphy, **how can there be free will**? I do not mean free will in the trivial sense, the ability to choose one's thoughts and behavior free of the will of others and the rest of the world all around. I mean, instead, **freedom from the constraints imposed by the physiochemical states of one's own body and mind** (1998, p. 119, emp. added).

Good question. If the mind is "bound by the laws of physics," then "how can there be free will?" Little wonder that Herbert Feigl lamented: "Scientific psychology, as the well-known saying goes, having first lost its soul, later its consciousness, seems finally to lose its mind altogether" (1967, p. 3).

The truth of the matter is, however, that: "If consciousness has a biological function at all, it must ultimately be manifest in behaviour" (Zeman, 2001, 124:1280). Yet, as Eccles and Robinson rightly remarked: "Observable **behavior** is not a reliable guide to comprehending the psychological dimension of life.... Morally we are possessed of 'oughts,' which, as we have argued, have absolutely no material or physical reference" (1984, pp. 52,169, emp. in orig.). Enough said.

Identity Theory

Earlier in this discussion, we quoted Gordon Taylor, who mentioned that monists are "split into those who deny that mental events exist at all...and **those who claim that mental events are just physical events described in another**

language. This last position [is] known as identity theory" (1979, pp. 20-21, emp. added). Herbert Feigl, one of identity theory's most ardent defenders (in his 1967 book, *The "Mental" and the "Physical"*), described the concept in this manner:

> I think that it is precisely one of the advantages of the identity theory that **it removes the duality of two sets of correlated events**, and replaces it by the much less puzzling duality of **two ways of knowing the same event**—one direct, the other indirect (p. 106, emp. added).

Confused? We are not surprised. In our judgment, identity theory is not exactly an easy concept to comprehend. Doubt that? Listen to the following definition offered by Feigl, who began by stating that "it will be advisable first to state my thesis quite succinctly," and then offered the following "succinct" summary:

> The raw feels of direct experience as we "have" them, are empirically identifiable with the referents of certain specifiable concepts of molar behavior theory, and these in turn are empirically identifiable with the referents of some neurophysiological concepts.... **The identity thesis which I wish to clarify and to defend asserts that the states of direct experience which conscious human beings "live through," and those which we confidently ascribe to some of the higher animals, are identical with certain aspects of the neural processes in those organisms.** ...[I]dentity theory regards sentience...[as] the basic reality (1967, pp. 78,79,107, emp. added).

Now, doesn't that clear up any confusion you may have experienced?!

In short, identity theory (a.k.a., "phenomenalistic parallelism") suggests that while sentience itself is indeed "the basic reality," whatever hints of consciousness that an organism (including a human) might experience are, in fact, the end result of "neural processes." Brain and consciousness (or mind and body) are but two different expressions of one underlying reality—just as the convex and concave surfaces of a sphere are but two expressions of an underlying reality. As Ruse described it:

> [M]ost Darwinians who think about these sorts of things are inclined to some kind of monism, or (as it is often known today) to some kind of **identity theory**. They think that **body and mind are manifestations of the same thing**, and that as selection works on one it affects the other, and as it works on the other it affects the former (2001b, pp. 199-200, parenthetical item in orig., emp. added).

The key phrase here, of course, is that "body and mind are manifestations of the same thing." And so, "mental" events are just "physical" events" described in another language. Eccles offered this synopsis:

> Mental states exist as an inner aspect of some material structures that in present formulations are restricted to brain structures such as nerve cells. This postulated "identity" may appear to give an effective action, just as the "identical" nerve cells have an effective action. However, **the result of the transaction is that the purely material events of neural action are themselves *sufficient* for all brain-mind responses** (1992, pp. 17-18, italics in orig., emp. added).

However, seventeen years earlier in a chapter he had authored on "The Brain-Mind Problem as a Frontier of Science" for the 1975 Nobel Conference, Eccles had debunked such a view.

> Most brain scientists and philosophers evade this confrontation across such a horrendous frontier by espousing some variety of psychoneural parallelism. The conscious experiences are regarded as merely being a spin-off from the neural events, every neural event being postulated by its very nature to have an associated conscious experience. This simple variety of parallelism is certainly mistaken, because the great majority of neural activities in the brain do not give rise to conscious experiences. Parallellism also is unable

to account for the experience that thought can give rise to action, as in the so-called voluntary movements, which must mean that cognitive events can effect changes in the patterns of impulse discharges of cerebral neurons. An even more pervasive experience is that we can, at will, set in train neural machinery to recall conscious memories from the data banks in our brains, and then judge the correctness of the recalls.

The most telling criticism against parallelism can be mounted against its key postulate that the happenings in the neural machinery of the brain provide **a necessary and sufficient explanation of the totality both of the performance and of the conscious experience of a human being** (1977, pp. 75-76, emp. in orig.).

Furthermore, four years prior to that, Dr. Eccles had pointed out that, in identity theory,

...it is postulated that all neuronal activity in the cerebrum comes through to consciousness somehow or other and is all expressed there. An often-used analogy is that neuronal activity and conscious states represent two different views of the same thing, one as seen by an external observer, the other as an inner experience by the "owner" of the brain. **This proposed identification, at least in its present form, is refuted by the discovery that after commissurotomy, none of the neuronal events in the minor hemisphere is recognized by the conscious subject** (1973, pp. 218-219, emp. added).

[A commissurotomy is a procedure wherein the corpus callosum (the great tract of approximately 200 million nerve fibers that links the brain's two hemispheres) is surgically severed, thereby disconnecting the two hemispheres from each other. Connections of the hemispheres to lower brain regions (known as the basal ganglia or midbrain) remain intact, and the person on whom the surgery has been performed remains relatively unaffected (see Eccles, 1989, pp. 205-210).] Dr. Eccles' point is well taken. If certain neuronal events no longer are recognized by the "owner" of the brain, yet that "owner" still is conscious, the consciousness is something more than simply "neuronal events." In the book that Dr. Eccles edited on *Brain and Conscious Experience,* he concluded: "There can be much complex functional activity going on in the fully organized human brain and yet it does not reach consciousness. **I think it is very important to appreciate that it is not just complex nerve structure that gives consciousness**" (1965, p. 499, emp. added).

John Searle, in *The Rediscovery of the Mind* (1992), argued that mental phenomena are caused by neurophysiological processes in the brain, and are themselves features of the brain. He referred to this point of view as "biological naturalism," and suggested that "mental processes are as much a part of our biological natural history as digestion, mitosis, meiosis, or enzyme secretion" (see Scott, 1995, p. 132). Beloff, in his discussion of identity theory, expressed serious doubts about its explicatory value.

> Thus the so-called "mind-brain identity" theory, associated with Herbert Feigl in the United States and with Bertrand Russell in Britain, which flourished during the 1950s, insisted that the mental events we associate with consciousness just *are* the relevant brain events but viewed, as it were, from the inside rather than the outside. Whether such a formulation is even tenable, I am still very doubtful; **it begs the question as to whether two entities that have entirely different properties could, ontologically, be regarded as one and the same** (1994, italics in orig., emp. added).

But surely that is just the point! How can two entities that have completely different properties be regarded as "one and the same"? Is it not obvious that identity theory fails to account for the important **qualitative** properties of consciousness—the features that we experience in the first person as an "I" or a "me." Identity theory cannot begin to explain what Eccles referred as "the certainty of my inner core of unique individuality" (1992, p. 240).

Nonreductive Materialism/Emergent Materialism

Without doubt, one of the most vocal supporters of monistic materialism is Sir Francis Crick, who suggested in his 1994 book, *The Astonishing Hypothesis*, that, eventually, **everything** will be explicable in terms of the neural pathways in the brain —a claim that he correctly identified in the title of his book as "astonishing!" During the twentieth century, refinements of monistic-materialistic concepts appeared under the name of **nonreductive materialism**. The British philosopher C.D. Broad and certain of his contemporaries held the view that the brain is the seat of all mental capacities, but they simultaneously maintained that while "mental states" **emerge from** the physical substratum of the brain, those mental states are not **reducible to** the brain. This view came to be called **emergent materialism** (see Wyller, 1996, p. 215). In the words of Jerome Elbert:

> The chemistry of living and nonliving matter is the same. The differences between living and nonliving matter are found in the elaborate and intricately organized structure of living matter. Living matter is the highly refined product of billions of years of testing and modification of self-reproducing structures. Living matter is a completely natural and beautifully organized product of Earth's unusually favorable environment.... **Emergent properties of matter [are] described as properties that emerge from matter when special circumstances apply to it, such as the organization of the matter into large numbers of similar units that can interact with each other. Consciousness may be the most challenging example of such an emergent property**. It gives matter a radically new property that is acquired only under very special conditions. Think of what a tiny fraction of the solar system's matter is conscious! (2000, pp. 215,243, emp. in orig.).

Scott concurred: "Thus, I suggest, consciousness is an **emergent** phenomenon, one born of many discrete events fusing together as a single experience" (1995, p. 3, emp. in orig.).

One of the best-known advocates of emergentism is philosopher John Searle. In opposition to the pure reductionists, Searle argues that first-person mental experiences ("I am in pain") cannot be reduced to mere neural firings, for in so doing, important first-person features like subjectivity are lost. In opposition to the dualists, however, Searle suggests that the strict dichotomy between mental and physical properties should be discarded. Mental properties are simply "one kind of property" that physical things can possess. **Pain and other mental phenomena are just features of the brain (and perhaps the rest of the central nervous system)** [see Searle, 1984, p. 19]. Consciousness, therefore, is simply a higher-order feature of the brain. Searle denies that consciousness transcends the physical, or that it possesses causal powers that cannot be explained by the interactions of the brain's neurons. According to this view, as Reichenbach and Anderson pointed out, "consciousness has no life of its own apart from that in which it is realized. But because of this, Searle's emergentist view leaves no room for free moral agency" (1995, p. 286). Such an assessment is correct, as Searle himself admitted:

> **As long as we accept this conception of how nature works, then it doesn't seem that there is any scope for the freedom of the will** because on this conception the mind can only affect nature in so far as it is a part of nature. But if so, then like the rest of nature, its features are determined at the basic micro-level of physics (1984, p. 93, emp. added).

Consciousness, then, according to this theory, is viewed as something that has "emerged from" the neural pathways of the brain, but, in and of itself, is not reducible to those neural pathways.

Another well-known advocate of the nonreductive physicalist viewpoint is Roger Sperry who, like Francis Crick and John Eccles, won the Nobel Prize in Physiology or Medicine. Dr. Sperry, however, adopted a view diametrically opposed to that of Crick's monist-materialism, yet was unwilling to accept the form of dualism advocated by Eccles. He concluded:

> **Consciousness is conceived to be a dynamic emergent property of brain activity, neither identical with nor reducible to, the neural events of which it is mainly composed**.... Consciousness exerts potential causal effects on the interplay of cerebral operations.... In the position of top command at the highest levels in the hierarchy of brain organization, the subjective properties were seen to exert control over the biophysical and chemical activities at subordinate levels (as quoted in Jeeves, 1998, p. 88, emp. added).

Sperry's concept is what is referred to as a "top-down view" (like that of Dr. Eccles) where mental events are given ontological priority. But, unlike Eccles, Sperry is adamant about avoiding any hint of dualism. Thus, while the emergent materialists may claim that mental states emerge from the physical substratum of the brain without being reducible to the brain, the fact remains, as Ernst Mayr noted, "emergentism is a thoroughly materialistic philosophy" (1982, p. 64). Yes, it is.

The nonreductive physicalist view regards mental activity and correlated brain activity as "inner" and "outer" aspects of one complex set of events, which together constitute "conscious human agency." As Jeeves explained:

> The irreducible duality of human nature is on this view seen as **duality of aspects rather than duality of substance**.... It does not mean that the mind is a mere epiphenomenon of the physical activity of the brain. We may think of the way the mind "determines" brain activity as analogous to the relation between the software and the hardware of our computers. According to this view, we regard mental activity as *embodied in* brain activity rather than as being *identical with* brain activity (p. 89, italics in orig., emp. added).

Sperry, in a chapter ("Holding Course Amidst Shifting Paradigms") he authored for the book, *New Metaphysical Foundations of Modern Science,* discussed the concepts behind emergent materialism. He began by noting that, in emergent materialism, "the traditional difference between the physical and the mental (as subjectively perceived) is deliberately retained, but with these previously separate, dual realms not inextricably merged..." (1994, p. 110, parenthetical item in orig.). In Sperry's view, conscious or mental phenomena are "dynamic, emergent phenomena (or configurational) properties of the living brain in action" (as quoted in Cousins, 1985, p. 66, parenthetical item in orig.). In commenting on this, Cousins remarked:

> This seems to imply that the source of mental intentions is the brain itself in living action—but that once these emergent mental properties appear, they have causal control potency over the "lower" activities of the brain at the subnuclear, nuclear and molecular levels. **Mind emerges from brain, then takes charge as chief or director in the complex chain of command within the brain**. In Sperry's view, there is no need to appeal to any source outside the living brain in order to explain the origin and existence of mental phenomena (1985, pp. 66-67, emp. added).

Cousins is correct. Sperry himself stated:

> One can agree that the scientific evidence speaks against any preplanned purposive design of a supernatural intelligence. At the same time the evidence shows that the great bulk of the evolving web of creation is governed by a complex pattern of great intricacy with many mutually reinforcing directive, purposive constraints at higher levels, particularly. The "grand orderly design" is, in a sense, all the more remarkable for having been self-developed (as quoted in Cousins, 1985, p. 87).

[W.H. Thorpe wrote in a similar vein: "The most important biological discovery of recent years is the discovery that the processes of life are directed by programmes...[and] that life is not merely programmed activity but **self-programmed activity**" (1977, p. 3, emp. added).] But Sperry did not end there. Rather, he went on to comment:

In my view, **mental phenomena as dynamic emergent properties of physical brain states become inextricably interfused with, and thus inseparable from, their physiologic substrates**…. [I]t still seems to me a mistake overall to abandon the age-old common-sense distinction between mind and matter, the mental and the physical. This basic common distinction long preceded the varied philosophic jargon and scientific terminology. **The highly distinctive specialness of conscious states with their subjective qualities does not go away just because they are taken to be emergent properties of physical brain processes** (pp. 109-110,111, emp. added).

With all due respect, Dr. Sperry (distinguished scientist and Nobel laureate that he is) appears to "want it both ways." He believes that it is a mistake to abandon the distinction between the physical and the mental, and admits that consciousness endows a "highly distinctive specialness" that does not disappear just because someone (like him) claims that it is merely an "emergent property of physical brain processes." Yet he wants to believe that "the scientific evidence speaks against any preplanned purposive design of a supernatural intelligence" and that "there is no need to appeal to any source outside the living brain in order to explain the origin and existence of mental phenomena." Richard Heinberg contradicted Sperry with common sense facts of nature when he commented:

Darwin added an essential historical dimension to the discussion: Not only are all living organisms composed **solely** of insensate matter obeying physical laws, but they have been assembled over eons of time into their present functional combinations by a process that is random and purposeless….

However, the idea that organisms have no inner sense of purpose is contradicted by our own human experience. We each make plans, formulate goals, and pursue strategies routinely. And there is every indication that other creatures do the same, if perhaps not as consciously. The evidence is so persuasive that many biologists who otherwise subscribe to a reductionist-mechanist view are nevertheless forced to acknowledge some capacity of inner purpose on the part of organisms (1999, pp. 65,67-68, emp. in orig.).

Medawar and Medawar, in their textbook, *The Life Sciences: Current Ideas of Biology*, wrote in agreement: "Purposiveness is one of the distinguishing characteristics of living things. **Of course** birds build nests in order to house their young, and equally obviously, the enlargement of a second kidney when the first is removed comes about to allow one kidney to do the work formerly done by two" (1977, pp. 11-12, emp. in orig.). Cell biologist Edmund Sinnot remarked:

> Life is not aimless, nor are its actions at random. They are regulatory and either maintain a goal already achieved or move toward one which is yet to be realized.... [Every living thing exhibits] activity which tends toward a realization of a developmental pattern or goal. ...Such teleology [purpose], far from being unscientific, is implicit in the very nature of the organism (1961, p. 41, bracketed items added).

Evolutionist Sir John Eccles strongly disagreed with his Nobel Prize-winning evolutionist colleague, Roger Sperry, when he wrote:

> Great display is made by all varieties of materialists that their brain-mind theory is in accord with natural law as it now is. However, this claim is invalidated by two most weighty considerations. Firstly, **nowhere in the laws of physics or in the laws of the derivative sciences, chemistry and biology, is there any reference to consciousness or mind**.... Regardless of the complexity of electrical, chemical or biological machinery, there is no statement in the "natural laws" that there is an emergence of this strange nonmaterial entity, consciousness or mind. This is not to affirm that consciousness does not emerge in the evolutionary process, but merely to state that **its emergence is not reconcilable with the natural laws as at present understood** (1992, pp. 19-20, emp. added).

Sperry may **want** emergent materialism to be true, but, as Eccles so eloquently pointed out, such "is not reconcilable with the natural laws as at present understood."

Dualist-Interactionism

When we began our examination of theories of human consciousness, we quoted Gordon Taylor, who assessed a number of the theories of the mind, and then stated: "None of these views, I may as well warn you, stands up to inspection" (1979, pp. 20-21, emp. added). Our comment at the time was: "As we bring this discussion on consciousness to a close, we want to offer a third alternative that **does** 'stand up to inspection.'" We now have reached that point.

Earlier, we quoted from Adam Zeman who, in his review, "Consciousness," for the journal *Brain*, mentioned that "the current fascination with consciousness reflects the mounting intellectual pressure to explain how 'vital activity' in the brain generates a 'mental element,' with rich subjective content" (2001, 124:1284). In other words, the pressure is on to answer the question: **Whence comes consciousness**?

Surely, by now it is evident from our review that all of the monist-materialistic concepts have failed miserably to offer any cogent, consistent, and adequate theory about the origin of human consciousness. Acknowledgment of that fact prompts the question: "Why, then, do so many scientists and philosophers cling to the monist-materialist viewpoint?"

We are convinced that the monist-materialistic view has remained so deeply ingrained because the only legitimate alternative—some form of dualism—postulates a supernatural origin for human self-awareness! And we cannot do better to prove our point than to quote from Daniel Dennett.

> The prevailing wisdom, variously expressed and argued for, is *materialism*: there is only one sort of stuff, namely *matter*—the physical stuff of physics, chemistry, and physiology—and the mind is somehow nothing but a physical phenomenon. In short, the mind is the brain. According to the materialists, we can (in prin-

ciple) account for every mental phenomenon using the same physical principles, laws, and raw materials that suffice to explain radioactivity, continental drift, photosynthesis, reproduction, nutrition, and growth. **It is one of the main burdens of this book to explain consciousness without ever giving in to the siren song of dualism**....

The standard objection to dualism was all too familiar to Descartes himself in the seventeenth century, and it is fair to say that neither he nor any subsequent dualist has ever overcome it convincingly. If mind and body are distinct things or substances, they nevertheless must interact; the bodily sense organs, via the brain, must inform the mind, must send to it or present it with perceptions or ideas or data of some sort, and then the mind, having thought things over, must direct the body in appropriate action. Hence the view is often called Cartesian interactionism or interactionist dualism....

It is surely no accident that the few dualists to avow their views openly have all candidly and comfortably announced that they have no theory whatever of how the mind works—something, they insist, that is quite beyond human ken. There is the lurking suspicion that the most attractive feature of mind stuff is its promise of being so mysterious that it keeps science at bay forever. **This fundamentally unscientific stance of dualism is, to my mind, its most disqualifying feature, and is the reason why in this book I adopt the apparently dogmatic rule that dualism is to be avoided at all costs**. It is not that I think I can give a knock-down proof that dualism, in all its forms, is false or incoherent, but that, given the way dualism wallows in mystery, **accepting dualism is giving up** (1991, pp. 33,34,37, italics and parenthetical item in orig., emp. added).

In Dennett's view, **monistic-materialism must rule!** Period. The acceptance of something—anything—outside of science is unthinkable, and represents what Nobel laureate Jacques Monod referred to as "animism" (belief in spirits). In his book, *Chance and Necessity*, Monod addressed this matter in very blunt terms.

Animism established a covenant between nature and man, a profound alliance outside of which seems to stretch only terrifying solitude. Must we break this tie because the postulate of objectivity requires it? [Monod answers "Yes!"–BH/BT]

...[A]ll these systems rooted in animism exist outside objective knowledge, outside truth, and are strangers and fundamentally *hostile* to science, which they are willing to use but do not respect or cherish. The divorce is so great, **the lie so flagrant, that it can only obsess and lacerate anyone who has some culture or intelligence**, or is moved by that moral questioning which is the source of all creativity. It is an affliction, that is to say, for all those who bear or will bear the responsibility for the way in which society and culture will evolve....

The ancient covenant is in pieces; **man knows at last that he is alone in the universe's unfeeling immensity, out of which he emerged only by chance**. His destiny is nowhere spelled out, nor is his duty. The kingdom above or the darkness below; it is for him to choose (1972, pp. 31,171-172,180, italics in orig., emp. added).

Animism, says Monod, is a "lie so flagrant, that it can only obsess and lacerate anyone who has some culture or intelligence." Why does he write in such terrifyingly angry words about a belief in something other than the monist-materialist viewpoint? Perhaps Carrington answered that question best when he wrote that in animism

...we have the world-old notion of mind or soul, and body, existing as separate entities, influencing each other. Mind is here supposed to influence matter, and utilize it for the purposes of its manifestation. Were such a theory true, it would of course enable us to accept not only the reality of psychic phenomena but **the persistence of individual human consciousness after death. The main objection to this doctrine is that it postulates a form of *dualism*, which is very obnoxious to many minds!** It is possible,

however, that such a doctrine may one day be forced
upon us by the gradually increasing evidence furnished us by psychical research (1923, p. 53, italics
in orig., emp. added).

Those of the monist-materialist bent know full well what
the implications would be if they were to allow (or, perish the
thought, accept) any form of dualism. As Custance asked:
"[H]ow can we account for 'mind' if it did not originate in the
physical world?" (1980, p. 20). Let us answer that by quoting
two of Monod's evolutionist colleagues—Eccles and Robinson.

> It is not in doubt that each human recognizes its own
> uniqueness.... **Since materialist solutions fail to
> account for our experienced uniqueness, we are
> constrained to attribute the uniqueness of the
> psyche or soul to a supernatural creation**. To give
> the explanation in theological terms: Each soul is a
> Divine creation, which is "attached" to the growing
> fetus at some point between conception and birth. It
> is the certainty of the inner core of unique individual-
> ity that necessitates the "Divine creation." **We sub-
> mit that no other explanation is tenable** (1984, p.
> 43, emp. added).

Strong stuff, that. But equally strong was their out-and-out con-
demnation of the monist-materialist viewpoint.

> [T]he denial of the reality of mental events, as in radi-
> cal materialism, is an easy cop-out.... **Radical mate-
> rialism should have a prominent place in the his-
> tory of human silliness. We regard promissory
> materialism as a superstition without a rational
> foundation**. The more we discover about the brain,
> the more clearly do we distinguish between the brain
> events and the mental phenomena, and the more won-
> derful do both the brain events and the mental phe-
> nomena become. **Promissory materialism is sim-
> ply a religious belief held by dogmatic material-
> ists...who often confuse their religion with their
> science** (1984, pp. 17,36, emp. added).

So what is the alternative? Darwin's contemporary, Alfred Russel Wallace, addressed that question in 1903 when he wrote (at the age of 80) his classic work, *Man's Place in Nature: A Study of the Results of Scientific Research in Relation to the Unity or Plurality of Worlds.*

> The other body and probably much larger would be represented by **those who, holding that mind is essentially superior to matter and distinct from it, cannot believe that life, consciousness, mind are products of matter**. They hold that the marvelous complexity of forces, which appear to control matter, if not actually to constitute it, **are and must be mind products** (as quoted in Wyller, 1996, p. 231, emp. added).

Neurologist Wilder Penfield wrote:

> Or, if one chooses the second, the dualistic alternative, the mind must be viewed as a basic **element** in itself. One might, then, call it a **medium**, an **essence**, a **soma**. That is to say, it has a **continuing existence**. On this basis, one must assume that although the mind is silent when it no longer has its special connection to the brain, it exists in the silent intervals, and takes over control when the highest brain-mechanism does go into action (1975, p. 81, emp. in orig.).

More recently, James Trefil conceded: "Nonetheless, **there is a sense in which something like Descartes' procedure remains valid for the question of human consciousness**" (1997, p. 181, emp. added). Paul Davies wrote: "…[P]hysics, which led the way for all other sciences, is now moving towards a more accommodating view of mind…" (1983, p. 8). He is correct. In fact, speaking of Cartesian dualism, Custance maintained:

> The theory cannot be disproved so long as there are mental phenomena whose neural correlates remain unknown. That there *are* mental phenomena cannot be doubted for reasons which are logically compulsive and were adopted (though not invented) by Descartes; they cannot be doubted because the very act

of doubting them establishes their reality. **The reality of conscious existence is confirmed each time it is denied**…. Most of the important thinkers who followed Descartes rejected interactionism…. **But slowly, as the evidence has accumulated, it appears that the monistic view is showing signs of insufficiency and a new dualism is in the making** (1980, pp. 30,31, italics and parenthetical items in orig., emp. added).

Custance, too, is correct. There is now a "new dualism in the making." In speaking of the evolutionary emergence of self-consciousness, for example, various writers (e.g., Lack, 1961, p. 128; Lorenz, 1971, 2:170) have even broached the subject of the "unbridgeable gap or gulf between soul and body." Carl Gustav Jung summed up this idea of a separate mind/body interaction when he said: "I simply believe that some part of the human Self or Soul is not subject to the laws of space and time" (as quoted in Davies, 1983, p. 72). Lord Adrian tartly snorted: "…[T]he gulf between mental and material can scarcely be called self-evident." Then he quietly admitted:

> Yet for many of us there is still the one thing which does seem to lie outside that tidy and familiar framework. That thing is ourself, our ego, the I who does the perceiving and the thinking and acting, the person who is aware of his identity and his surroundings. As soon as we let ourselves contemplate our own place in the picture we seem to be stepping outside the boundaries of natural science (1965, pp. 239,240).

Or, as Eccles concluded: "It is my thesis that we have to recognize that **the unique selfhood is the result of a supernatural creation of what in the religious sense is called a soul**" (1982, p. 97, emp. added).

Notice, too, what Carrington conceded: "It is possible, however, that such a doctrine may one day be forced upon us by the gradually increasing evidence furnished us by psychical research" (1923, p. 53). Even Zeman, seventy-eight years later in his exhaustive, peer-reviewed article on consciousness, admitted that "a number of commentators believe that some version of this...'dual-aspect' theory holds out the greatest promise of an eventual solution to the philosophical conundrum of consciousness" (2001, 124:1284, emp. added). Roger Lewin conceded:

> [F]or the most part, materialism, the philosophical alternative to dualism, dominates modern thinking about consciousness.... True, Cartesian **dualism is not completely dead**, as evidenced in the views of Sir John Eccles, one of this century's greatest neurologists... (1992, p. 157, emp. added).

In an article—"Scientists in Search of the Soul"—that he wrote for *Science Digest,* John Gliedman admitted:

> From Berkeley to Paris and from London to Princeton, prominent scientists from fields as diverse as neurophysiology and quantum physics are coming out of the closet and **admitting they believe in the possibility, at least, of such unscientific entities as the immortal human spirit and divine creation** (1982, 90[7]:77, emp. added).

One of the scientists discussed at some length by Mr. Gliedman was Sir John Eccles of Great Britain. Daniel Dennett wrote in his book, *Consciousness Explained*: "Ever since Gilbert Ryle's classic attack (1949) on what he called Descartes' 'dogma of the ghost in the machine,' dualists have been on the defensive" (1991, p. 33). **Not any more!** Allow us to introduce you to Sir John Eccles—the man Roger Lewin called "one of this century's greatest neurologists."

Dr. Eccles, until his death in 1997 at the age of 94, was one of the world's most eminent electrophysiologists. He graduated from Oxford (where he matriculated on a Rhodes scholarship under the man he called "the greatest neuroscientist of the age, Sir Charles Sherrington"–Eccles, 1994, p. 13) in 1929 with a D.Phil. (the British equivalent of an American Ph.D.), was a professor of physiology at Australian National University from 1952-1966, was knighted by Queen Elizabeth II in 1958, and five years later in 1963 won the Nobel Prize in Physiology or Medicine (shared with Alan L. Hodgkin and Andrew F. Huxley) for his research on the biophysical properties of synaptic transmission. Gliedman, in his 1982 article on "Scientists in Search of the Soul," had this to say about Dr. Eccles:

> At age 79, Sir John Eccles is not going "gentle into the night." Still trim and vigorous, the great physiologist has declared war on the past 300 years of scientific speculation about man's nature.
>
> Winner of the 1963 Nobel Prize in Physiology or Medicine for his pioneering research on the synapse–the point at which nerve cells communicate with the brain **–Eccles strongly defends the ancient religious belief that human beings consist of a mysterious compound of physical and intangible spirit.**
>
> Each of us embodies a nonmaterial thinking and perceiving self that "entered" our physical brain sometime during embryological development or very early childhood, says the man who helped lay the cornerstones of modern neurophysiology. This "ghost in the machine" is responsible for everything that makes us distinctly human: conscious self-awareness, free will, personal identity, creativity and even emotions such as love, fear, and hate. **Our nonmaterial self controls its "liaison brain" the way a driver steers a car or a programmer directs a computer. Man's ghostly spiritual presence, says Eccles, exerts just the whisper of a physical influence on the computerlike brain, enough to encourage some neurons to fire and others to remain silent**. Boldly advancing what for most scientists is the greatest heresy of all, Eccles also asserts that our nonmaterial self survives the death of the physical brain (90[7]:77, emp. added).

While there are many other things we could say about Dr. Eccles and the various honors and awards that were bestowed upon him during his lengthy and impressive professional career, these are enough to convince the reader of his qualifications to speak on the subjects that he is about to address. [The reader who is interested in learning more about Dr. Eccles might wish to visit the following Web sites: (1) http://www.asap.unimelb.edu.au/bsparcs/biogs/P000382b.htm; (2) http://www.nobel.se.medicine/laureates/1963/index.html. We also strongly recommend his 1994 book, *How the Self Controls Its Brain*, which was written in what was to be the twilight of a magnificent career that spanned seven decades. Note especially chapter two, which he titled simply "My Story."]

Anyone familiar with neurophysiology or neurobiology knows the name of Sir John Eccles. [One of us (BH) studied Dr. Eccles' works while earning a Ph.D. in neurobiology.] But for those who might not be familiar with this amazing gentleman, we would like to introduce Dr. Eccles via the following quotation, which comes from a chapter ("The Collapse of Modern Atheism") that Norman Geisler authored for the book, *The Intellectuals Speak Out About God* (which, by the way, also contained a chapter by Dr. Eccles). Geisler wrote:

> The extreme form of materialism believes that mind (or soul) *is* matter. More modern forms believe mind is *reducible to* matter or *dependent on* it. **However, from a scientific perspective much has happened in our generation to lay bare the clay feet of materialism. Most noteworthy among this is the Nobel Prize winning work of Sir John Eccles. His work on the brain demonstrated that the mind or intention is more than physical. He has shown that the supplementary motor area of the brain is fired by mere *intention* to do something, without the motor cortex of the brain (which controls muscle movements) operating.** So, in effect, the mind is to the brain what an archivist is to a library. The former is not reducible to the latter (1984, pp. 140-141, italics and parenthetical item in orig., emp. added).

Eccles, and his lifelong friend, Sir Karl Popper, the famed British philosopher of science, viewed the mind as a distinctly non-material entity. But neither did so for religious reasons. Dr. Eccles was a committed Darwinian evolutionist (as was

Popper). Rather, they believed what they did about the human mind because of their research! Speaking specifically of human self-consciousness, Eccles wrote:

> It is dependent on the existence of a sufficient number of such critically poised neurons, and, consequently, only in such conditions are willing and perceiving possible. However, it is not necessary for the whole cortex to be in this special dynamic state.... On the basis of this concept [activity of the cortex] we can face up anew to the extraordinary problems inherent in a strong dualism—interaction of brain and conscious mind, brain receiving from conscious mind in a willed action and in turn transmitting to mind in conscious experiences. **...Let us be quite clear that for each of us the primary reality is our consciousness—everything else is derivative and has a second order reality**. We have tremendous intellectual tasks in our efforts to understand baffling problems that lie right at the center of our being (1966, pp. 312, 327, bracketed item and emp. added).

Dr. Eccles spent his entire adult life studying the brain-mind problem, and concluded that the two were entirely separate. In the book from which we quoted above (*Nobel Conversations*), Norman Cousins, who moderated a series of conversations among four Nobel laureates, including Dr. Eccles, made the following statement: "Nor was Sir John Eccles claiming too much when **he insisted that the action of non-material mind on material brain has been not merely postulated but scientifically demonstrated**" (1985, p. 68, emp. added). Eccles himself, in his book, *The Understanding of the Brain*, wrote:

> When I postulated many years ago, following Sherrington [Sir Charles Sherrington, Nobel laureate and Eccles' mentor—BH/BT], that there was a special area of the brain in liaison with consciousness, I certainly did not imagine that any definitive experimental test could be applied in a few years. But now we have this distinction between the dominant hemisphere in liaison with the conscious self, and the minor hemisphere with no such liaison (1973, p. 214).

Before we proceed, we would like to add this one note. On March 15, 1952, the *British Medical Journal* ran an obituary notice for Sir Charles Sherrington. That notice read as follows:

> The death on March 4, 1952 of Sir Charles Sherrington at the age of 94 marked the passing of the man of genius who laid the foundations of our knowledge of the functioning of the brain and spinal cord. His classic work *Integrative Action of the Nervous System,* published in 1906, is still a source of inspiration to physiologists all over the world. It was reprinted as recently as 1947 for the first post-war (World War II) International Congress on Physiology. His work did for neurology what the atomic theory did for chemistry. It is still as refreshing as it was in 1906, and it has needed no revision.

How embarrassing it must be for evolutionists to have to admit that this "genius" who "laid the foundation of our knowledge of the functioning of the brain and spinal cord" told one of his prized students, Sir John Eccles, just prior to his (Sherrington's) death: "**For me now, the only reality is the human soul**" (as quoted in Popper and Eccles, 1977 p. 558, emp. added). What an amazing statement from the man who constructed many of the pillars on which modern neuroanatomy now stands! Cousins continued:

> Until quite recently, science assumed that to attribute to non-material forces such as mental intentions any kind of "causal" potency or control is to lapse into primitive mysticism or vague religious feeling…. **Eccles is the one who showed that the mental acts of intention *initiate* the burst of discharges in a nerve's brain cell**. He has tried to re-enfranchise the human mind, to get science to recognize thinking as a more comprehensive human activity than the mere operation of neural mechanisms….
>
> In any event it is clear that both you [Eccles–BH/BT] and Dr. [Roger] Sperry are upholding a "mentalist revolution" in science. Strictly orthodox materialists may doubt such a revolution and label it an atavistic

throwback to "prescientific" perceptions of nature which believed that non-material reality could act on the material. **But in fact, both of you have reached your conclusions through the rigorous discipline of the laboratory. If you are persuaded that mental realities initiate and direct biochemical reactions in the brain, it is scientific experimentation, not philosophical speculation, that has convinced you** (1985, pp. 56,21,57, italics in orig., emp. added).

What, precisely, is the relationship between mind and brain? Eccles answered as follows.

How can the mental act of intention activate across the mind-brain frontier those particular SMA [supplementary motor area–BH/BT] neurons in the appropriate code for activating the motor programs that bring about intended voluntary movements? The answer is that, **despite the so-called "insuperable" difficulty of having a non-material mind act on a material brain, it has been demonstrated to occur by a mental intention–no doubt to the great discomfiture of all materialists and physicalists** (as quoted in Cousins, 1985, pp. 55-56, emp. in orig.).

As I indicated earlier in this Conversation, what may be called "mental intentions," with their ability to initiate a burst of discharges in a nerve cell, are not confined strictly to the human species. I alluded to the work of Robert Porter and Cobie Brinkman, whose laboratory monkeys initiated voluntary movements by pulling levers to obtain food. It was found that with this voluntary act, performed by simians, **many of the nerve cells of the SMA began to discharge well before the cells in the motor cortex** and indeed before any other nerve cells of the brain, except for a small focus in the premotor cortex, which is just anterior to the motor cortex....

[These examples] show that mental intentions truly exist and that they initiate the burst of discharges in a nerve cell that leads to voluntary movement.... **[W]e have discovered that mental intentions act upon the SMA in a highly selective, discriminating**

manner. In a fashion which is not yet fully understood, mental intentions are able to activate across the mind-brain frontier those *particular* SMA neurons that are coded for initiating the specialized motor programs that cause voluntary movements. As I remarked earlier, this may present an "insuperable" difficulty for some scientists of materialist bent, **but the fact remains, and is demonstrated by research, that non-material mind acts on material brain** (pp. 61-62,85-86, italics in orig., emp. added).

In *The Wonder of Being Human: Our Brain and Our Mind*, Eccles and Robinson discussed the research of three groups of scientists (Robert Porter and Cobie Brinkman, Nils Lassen and Per Roland, and Hans Kornhüber and Luder Deecke), all of whom produced startling and undeniable evidence that **a "mental intention" preceded an actual neuronal firing—thereby establishing that the mind is not the same thing as the brain, but is a separate entity altogether** (1984, pp. 156-164). As Eccles and Robinson concluded:

> But it is impressive that many of the samples of several hundred SMA nerve cells were firing probably about one-tenth of a second **before** the earliest discharge of the pyramidal cells down to the spinal cord. ...Thus there is strong support for the hypothesis that the SMA is the sole recipient area of the brain for mental intentions that lead to voluntary movements (pp. 157,160, emp. in orig.).

Interestingly, Eccles was not the first to document this type of independence in regard to the mind's action on the brain, as he himself conceded:

> Remarkable series of experiments in the last few years have transformed our understanding of the cerebral events concerned with the initiation of a voluntary movement. It can now be stated that the first brain reactions caused by the **intention to move** are in nerve cells of the **supplementary motor area** (SMA). It is right at the top of the brain, mostly on the medial surface. This area was recognized by the renowned neu-

rosurgeon Wilder Penfield when he was stimulating the exposed human brain in the search for epileptic "foci" (regions of aberrant activity associated with epileptic seizures) [Eccles and Robinson, 1984, p. 156, parenthetical items and emp. in orig.].

In 1961, Canadian neurosurgeon Wilder Penfield reported a dramatic demonstration of the reality of active mind at work. He observed **mind acting independently of the brain** under controlled experimental conditions that were reproducible at will (see Penfield, 1961; 1975; Custance, 1980, p. 19). Dr. Penfield's patient suffered from epilepsy, and had one hemisphere of his temporal lobe exposed from a previous surgery. Penfield reported:

> When the neurosurgeon applies an electrode to the motor area of the patient's cerebral cortex causing the opposite hand to move, and when he asks the patient why he moved the hand, the response is: "I didn't do it. You made me do it." ...It may be said that the patient thinks of himself as having an existence separate from his body. Once when I warned a patient of my intention to stimulate the motor area of the cortex, and challenged him to keep his hand from moving when the electrode was applied, he seized it with the other hand and struggled to hold it still. Thus one hand, under the control of the right hemisphere driven by an electrode, and the other hand, which he controlled through the left hemisphere, were caused to struggle against each other. **Behind the "brain action" of one hemisphere was the patient's mind**. Behind the action of the other hemisphere was the electrode (as quoted in Koestler, 1967, pp. 203-204, emp. added).

Penfield went on to conclude:

> But what is it that calls upon these mechanisms, choosing one rather than another? Is it another mechanism or is there in the mind something of different essence? To declare that these two are one does not make them so. But it does block the progress of research (p. 204).

Upon closing his surgical practice, Dr. Penfield wrote:

> Throughout my own scientific career, I, like the other scientists, have struggled to prove that the brain accounts for the mind. But now, perhaps, the time has come when we may profitably consider the evidence as it stands, and ask the question: Do brain-mechanisms account for the mind? **Can the mind be explained by what is now known about the brain? If not, which is more reasonable of the two possible hypotheses: that man's being is based on one element, or on two?** (1975, p. xiii, emp. added).

Penfield's final observations caused him to reflect as follows:

> This is the correct scientific approach for a neurophysiologist: to try to prove that the brain explains the mind and that mind is no more than a function of the brain. But during this time of analysis, **I found no suggestion of action by a brain-mind mechanism that accounts for mind-action**....
>
> In the end I conclude that there is **no good evidence**, in spite of new methods, such as the employment of stimulating electrodes, the study of conscious patients, and the analysis of epileptic attacks, **that the brain alone can carry out the work that the mind does. I conclude that it is easier to rationalize man's being on the basis of two elements than on the basis of one** (1975, pp. 104,114, emp. added).

These are the words of a man who studied the brain for decades, and who collected and analyzed the data firsthand. In *The Mystery of the Mind,* Penfield concluded that the mind might very well be **"a distinct and different essence"** (p. 62, emp. added). We agree wholeheartedly. A.O. Gomes, in his chapter, "The Brain-Consciousness Problem in Contemporary Scientific Research" for the book, *Brain and Conscious Experience,* wrote:

> ...[R]esearch is frequently conducted as if the whole occurrences under study were ultimately nothing more than the transformations of some physiological events into others; the mental phenomena involved

are either ignored or given only a secondary importance…. How can physical sense receptors affect
sense? **How can a reaction in the brain condition
a reaction in the mind?** How can the (often quoted!)
"enchanted loom" of nerve impulses in the brain, which
always weaves meaningful, but never abiding, patterns
—how can this "loom" evoke such rich mental experiences as the vision of everything we see, all the
sounds we hear, all the bodily sensations we may ever
become aware of? (1965, pp. 448, 446, parenthetical
item in orig., emp. added).

In the book containing the Nobel laureate conversations on
these matters, Cousins commented: **"The question naturally
arises: where do mental intentions come from, what is
their source, their origin?"** (1985, pp. 66-67, emp. added).
These "mental intentions" are truly important, as Tattersall
admitted when he wrote:

Everybody can agree that a major aspect of consciousness is the ability to form intentions; and nobody will
dispute that human beings spend much of their lives
in this activity, however hollow those intentions may
eventually turn out to be (2002, p. 58).

So how did Eccles answer the question of where these mental intentions originate? He responded: "In contrast to these
materialist or parallelist theories are the dualist-interaction
theories. **The essential feature of these theories is that
mind and brain are independent entities…**" (Eccles and
Robinson, 1984, p. 35, emp. added). By way of summary, here
is Dr. Eccles' view:

A brief outline of the hypothesis may be given as follows. The self-conscious mind is actively engaged in
reading out from the multitude of active centers at
the highest level of brain activity, namely, the liaison
modules that are largely in the dominant cerebral
hemisphere. The self-conscious mind selects from
these modules according to attention and interest,
and from moment to moment integrates its selection
to give unity even to the most transient experiences.

Furthermore, the self-conscious mind acts upon these neural centers modifying the dynamic spatiotemporal patterns of the neural events. **Thus it is proposed that the self-conscious mind exercises a superior interpretative and controlling role upon the neural events**…. A key component of the hypothesis is that the unity of conscious experience is provided by the self-conscious mind and not by the neural machinery of the liaison areas of the cerebral hemisphere. …The present hypothesis regards the neuronal machinery as a multiplex of radiating and receiving structures: **the experienced unity comes, not from a neurophysiological synthesis, but from the proposed integrating character of the self-conscious mind** (1982, pp. 244-245, emp. added).

It was the concept of the "self-conscious mind" to which Dr. Eccles devoted his life's research, and on which he spoke and wrote so often. In his invited lecture at the 1975 Nobel Conference, he reminded his fellow Nobel laureates:

There is the continual experience that the self-conscious mind can **effectively** act on the brain events. This is most overtly seen in voluntary action, but throughout our waking life we are deliberately evoking brain events when we try to recall a memory or to recapture a word or phrase or to express a thought or to establish a new memory…. This hypothesis gives a prime role to the action of the self-conscious mind, an action of choice and searching and discovering and integrating…. **A key component of the hypothesis is that the unity of conscious experience is provided by the self-conscious mind and not by the neural machinery of the liaison areas of the cerebral hemisphere**…. Furthermore, **the active role of the self-conscious mind is extended in our hypothesis to effect changes in the neuronal events**. Thus not only does it read out selectively from the ongoing activities of the neuronal machinery, but **it also modifies these activities** (1977, pp. 81,82,83, emp. in orig.).

Dr. Eccles then concluded by saying:

> **There must be a partial independence of the self-conscious mind from the brain events with which it interacts.** For example, if a decision is to be freely made it must be initiated in the self-conscious mind and then communicated to the brain for executive action. This sequence is even more necessary in the exercise of creative imagination, where *flashes of insight become expressions by triggering appropriate brain actions* (p. 87, italics in orig., emp. added).

How, then, would Dr. Eccles categorize himself? He certainly does not fit the description of a monist-materialist. Is he then a strict dualist? Does he consider himself a vitalist? What position does he take as a result of his fascinating, Nobel Prize-winning discoveries? In his book, *The Human Mystery*, he quelled any suspicions.

> If I should be asked to express my philosophical position, I would have to admit that I am an animist on Monod's definition. As a dualist I believe in the reality of the world of mind or spirit as well as in the reality of the material world. Furthermore I am a finalist in the sense of believing that there is some Design in the processes of biological evolution that has eventually led to us self-conscious beings with our unique individuality; and we are able to contemplate and we can attempt to understand the grandeur and wonder of nature, as I will attempt to do in these lectures. But I am not a vitalist in the generally accepted sense of that term. I believe that all of the happenings in living cells will be found to be in accord with physics and chemistry, much of which has yet to be discovered. Yet, as I have already stated, I believe with Polanyi that **there is a hierarchic structure with emergence of higher levels that could not have been predicted from the operations going on at a lower level.** For example the emergence of life could not have been predicted even with a complete knowledge of all happenings in a prebiotic world, nor could the emergence of self-consciousness have been predicted (1979, pp. 9-10, emp. added).

Eventually, Sir John came to refer to himself as a "dualist-interactionist" (as did Sir Karl Popper). Eccles calmly admitted:

> **As a dualist-interactionist, I believe that my experienced uniqueness lies not in the uniqueness of my brain, but in my psyche**. It is built up from the tissue of memories of the most intimate kind from my earliest recollection onwards to the present.... It is important to disclaim a solipsistic solution of the uniqueness of the self. Our direct experiences are of course subjective, being derived solely from our brain and self. The existences of other selves *are established* by intersubjective communication (1992, p. 237, italics in orig., emp. added).

Popper and Eccles presented their views in their massive 600-page book published in 1977, *The Self and Its Brain: An Argument for Interactionism,* which became an overnight sensation, and ultimately a classic in its field. In his portion of that volume, Popper wrote:

> **But the human consciousness of self transcends, I suggest, all purely biological thought**.... [O]nly a human being capable of speech can reflect upon himself. I think that every organism has a programme. **But I also think that only a human being can be conscious of parts of this programme, and revise them critically** (Popper and Eccles, 1977, p. 144, emp. added).

Four years before that book's publication, Eccles went on record as stating:

> I was a dualist, now I am a **trialist**! Cartesian dualism has become unfashionable with many people. They embrace monism in order to escape the enigma of brain-mind interaction with its perplexing problems. But Sir Karl Popper and I are interactionists, and what is more, **trialist interactionists**! (1973, p. 189, emp. in orig.).

[NOTE: The term "trialist" as employed by Dr. Eccles is not to be confused with the word "trialism" that John Cottingham uses in his attempt to provide what he believes is "a more realistic category" in which to put animals—as creatures that have extension and sensation, but not thought (see Carter, 2002).]

In the section that he wrote for *The Self and Its Brain*, Popper discussed his view (shared by Eccles) that reality should be seen as having three different aspects, which he subsequently labeled as World I, World II, and World III. World I is the objective world of **physical entities**. World II is the subjective psychic **inner reality** of each human being. World III is the world of **human culture** (i.e., the world of ideas). Popper and Eccles both agreed that **"the self-conscious mind is an independent entity to be superimposed upon the neural machinery"**—a superimposition that can lead to a variety of interactions in the brain as it moves between Worlds I, II, and III. Continuous subjective interactions exist between World I and World II, as well as cultural interactions affecting both World I and World II. As Reichenbach and Anderson summarized it:

> Events in World 1 affect World 2, and vice versa, not by any physical interaction, since the mental is non-physical, but through transfer of information. That is, there is a constant information flow between the brain and the mind. The brain is the liaison between the world of our mental experience and the world of our motor and bodily events. Thus, in voluntary movement, **mental intentions initiate a sequence by transferring information to the brain**. Eccles locates the point of interaction between mental intention and the body in the nerve cells of the supplementary motor area (SMA), located at the top of the brain. He notes experiments in which nerve cells in the SMA discharged before cells responsible for motor activity. From this he concludes that mental intentions act on cells in the SMA, which contain an "inventory of all learned motor programs" [Eccles and Robinson, 1984, p. 161] (1995, pp. 281-281, emp. added).

Dr. Eccles himself performed numerous experiments in which nerve cells in the SMA discharged—solely as a result of mental intention—**before** the cells responsible for motor activity. He discussed on numerous occasions the scientific evidence substantiating that the mind is a separate entity from the brain —evidence that he had gathered through a lifetime of study on the brain-mind problem (see Eccles, 1973, 1979; 1982; 1984; 1989, 1992, 1994). Eccles stated: **"We are a combination of two things or entities: our brains on the one hand, and our conscious selves on the other"** (1984, p. 33, emp. added).

Could Popper and Eccles be onto something here? Could there be a "world," within each human, containing a "psychic inner reality"? Jay Tolson, in an article ("The Ghost Hunters") that he penned for the December 16, 2002 issue of *U.S. News & World Report,* used humans' ability to employ symbolic language (in a way that no animal can) to inquire about "a person beneath the personality."

> Using language at its most refined limit—irony—shows how we often mean something more or other than what we say. **Might that not be a tantalizing glimpse of a self beyond the mere representation of the self, a person beneath the personality? A ghost in the machine, after all?** (133[23]:46, emp. added).

Even Paul Davies was constrained to ask:

> Can the mind somehow reach into the physical world of electrons and atoms, brain cells and nerves, and create electrical forces? Does mind really act on matter in defiance of the fundamental principles of physics? **Are there, indeed, two causes of movement in the material world: one due to ordinary physical processes and the other due to mental processes?**… The only minds of which we have direct experience are those associated with brains (and arguably computers). Yet nobody seriously suggests that God, or departed souls, have a brain. **Does the notion of a disembodied mind, let alone a mind**

completely decoupled from the physical universe, make any sense? (1983, pp. 75,72, parenthetical item in orig., emp. added).

While the committed monist-materialist would answer "no" to every one of Dr. Davies' questions, our research answers "yes" to each of them. With the available scientific evidence (from reputable scientists such as Penfield, Eccles, and others) which documents that mind **does** interact with matter (the brain), what other conclusion could one possibly reach? As Eccles himself put it:

A purely materialist explanation would seem to suffice with the conscious experiences as a derivative from brain functioning. However, **it is a mistake to think that the brain does everything and that our conscious experiences are simply a reflection of brain activities,** which is a common philosophical view. If that were so, our conscious selves would be no more than passive spectators of the performances carried out by the neuronal machinery of the brain. Our beliefs that we can really make decisions and that we have some control over our actions would be nothing but illusions. There are of course all sorts of subtle cover-ups by philosophers from such a stark exposition, but they do not face up to the issue. In fact all people, even materialist philosophers, behave as if they had at least some responsibility for their own actions.

These considerations lead me to the alternative hypothesis of dualist-interactionism. **It is really the commonsense view, namely that we are a combination of two things or entities: our brains on the one hand; and our conscious selves on the other** (1982, pp. 87,88, emp. added).

Even Feigl admitted:

Vitalists or interactionists...hold that biological concepts and laws are not reducible to the laws of physics, and hence—*a fortiori*—that psychological concepts and laws are likewise irreducible.... The upshot of this longish discussion on the difference between the scientific and the philosophical components of the mind-body problem is this: **If interactionism or any genuine emergence hypotheses are sensibly formulated, they have empirical content and entail incisive limitations of the scope of physical determinism** (1967, pp. 7,18, emp. added).

But did he accept the evidence then available for interactionism? As a defender of the materialistic "identity theory," no, he did not. He demurred, suggesting that "someday," a better explanation would come along.

> Whatever role the self may play in the determination of human conduct, it may yet very well be explained by a more or less stable structure of dispositions due to some constitutionally inherited, maturationally and environmentally modified, and continually modulated structure of the organism (especially the nervous and endocrine systems) [pp. 7,18,19, parenthetical item in orig.].

Then, not long after Feigl wrote that interactionism hypotheses, if "sensibly formulated," could have "empirical content," Sir John Eccles came along and "sensibly formulated" his dualist-interactionist theory—and then provided the "empirical content" to go along with it.

And where does such "empirical content" lead? Davies inquired: "Does the notion of a disembodied mind, let alone a mind completely decoupled from the physical universe, make any sense?" We respond that it most certainly does. Eccles, Penfield, and others have shown conclusively that **mind exists independently of matter**.

The thought, then, of a "universal mind" that stands behind this Universe no longer sounds quite so far-fetched. In fact, Harvard's Nobel laureate, George Wald, in the chapter he wrote ("The Cosmology of Life and Mind") for *New Metaphysical Foundations of Modern Science,* addressed this very theme.

> I had already for some time taken it as a foregone conclusion that the mind—consciousness—could not be located. It is essentially absurd to think of locating a phe-

nomenon that yields no physical signals, the presence or absence of which, outside of humans their like, cannot be identified.

But further than that, mind is not only not locatable, it **has no location**. It is not a **thing** in space and time, not measurable; hence, as I said at the beginning of this chapter, not assimilable as science. And yet it is not to be dismissed as an epiphenomenon: it is the foundation, the condition that makes science possible....

A few years ago it occurred to me that these seemingly very disparate problems might be brought together. And this could happen through the hypothesis that **mind**, rather than being a very late development in the evolution of living things, restricted to organisms with the most complex nervous systems— all of which I had believed to be true—**has been there always. And that this universe is life-breeding because the pervasive presence of mind had guided it to be so** (1994, pp. 128,129, emp. added).

Dr. Wald is in good company in sensing what he called "the pervasive presence of mind." The late, distinguished astronomer from Great Britain, Sir Arthur Eddington, admitted: "The idea of a universal mind, or Logos, would be, I think, a fairly plausible inference from the present state of scientific theory" (as quoted in Heeren, 1995, p. 233). Over seventy years ago, physicist Sir James Jeans wrote:

Today there is a wide measure of agreement which on the physical side of science approaches almost unanimity, that the stream of knowledge is heading towards a non-mechanical reality: the Universe begins to look more like a great thought than a great machine. **Mind no longer looks like an accidental intruder into the realm of matter; we are beginning to suspect that we ought rather to hail it as the Creator and governor of the realm of matter....** We discover that the Universe shows evidence of a designing or controlling Power that has something in common with our own minds (1930, emp. added).

In a discussion about the origin of the genetic code in their college biology text, *The New Biology*, Robert Augros and George Stanciu asked:

> What cause is responsible for the origin of the genetic code and directs it to produce animal and plant species? It cannot be matter because of itself matter has no inclination to these forms, any more than it has to the form Poseidon or the form of a microchip or any other artifact. **There must be a cause apart from matter that is able to shape and direct matter. Is there anything in our experience like this? Yes, there is: our own mind**s. The statue's form originates in the mind of the artist, who then subsequently shapes matter, in the appropriate way.... **For the same reasons there must be a mind that directs and shapes matter in organic forms** (1987, p. 191, emp. added).

Or, to quote NASA astronomer Robert Jastrow: "That there are what I, or anyone would call supernatural forces at work is now, I think, a scientifically proven fact" (1982, p. 18).

Physicist Freeman Dyson addressed the idea of a "universal soul" in his semi-autobiographical book, *Disturbing the Universe.*

> We had earlier found two levels on which mind manifests itself in the description of nature. On the level of subatomic physics, the observer is inextricably involved in the definition of the objects of his observations. On the level of direct human experience, **we are aware of our own minds**, and we find it convenient to believe that other human beings and animals have minds not altogether unlike our own. Now we have found a third level to add to these two. **The peculiar harmony between the structure of the universe and the needs of life and intelligence is a third manifestation of the importance of mind in the scheme of things**. This is as far as we can go as scientists. We have evidence that mind is important on three levels. We have no evidence for any deeper unifying hypothesis that would tie these three levels to-

gether. As individuals, some of us may be willing to go further. **Some of us may be willing to entertain the hypothesis that there exists a universal mind or world soul which underlies the manifestations of mind that we observe**. If we take this hypothesis seriously, we are, according to Monod's definition, animists. The existence of a world soul is a question that belongs to religion and not to science (1979, pp. 251-252, emp. added).

Nine years later, in an article he authored ("Mankind's Place in the Cosmos") for *U.S. News and World Report,* Dyson went even farther:

The mind, I believe, exists in some very real sense in the universe. But is it primary or an accidental consequence of something else? The prevailing view among biologists seems to be that the mind arose accidentally out of molecules of DNA or something. I find that very unlikely. **It seems more reasonable to think that mind was a primary part of nature from the beginning and we are simply manifestations of it at the present stage of history** (1988, p. 72, emp. added).

In his article, "The Mind-Brain Problem," John Beloff made a startling admission.

The fact is that, leaving aside mythical and religious cosmologies, the position of mind in nature remains a total mystery. **It could be that there exists some sort of a cosmic mind**, perhaps co-equal with the material universe itself, **from which each of our individual minds stems and to which each ultimately returns**. All we can say is that it looks as if a fragment of mind-stuff becomes attached to an individual organism, at or near birth, and thereafter persists with this symbiotic relationship until that organism perishes (1994, emp. added).

Then, with an even bolder tact, Arne Wyller dared to ask in his book, *The Creating Consciousness:* "**What if there existed a mind before people**…perhaps a consciousness we will one day find in another part of the Universe, perhaps a universal consciousness field: **The Planetary Mind**" (1996, p. 223, emp. added).

Just think. "What if" there existed a mind before people—a "universal/planetary/cosmic Mind Who could "attach a fragment of mind-stuff" to an individual organism at birth? Just think! As Richard Heinberg remarked in *Cloning the Buddha: The Moral Impact of Biotechnology*:

> But at least the spiritual view leaves open the door for the possibility that our explanations for biological phenomena are still incomplete in some fundamental way. To prematurely close that door might be a profound error. If we think we have essentially the whole picture of what life is and how it works, when in reality we have only a part of that picture; if our working philosophy systematically excludes certain kinds of evidence and certain kinds of explanations; and further, if we act on our philosophy in ways that have global repercussions, then we could be getting ourselves into serious trouble indeed. A spiritual perspective, even in its weakest and most generalized form, would hold that **present material explanations for biological and psychological realities are necessary but not sufficient. Something else must be taken into account** (1999, pp. 74-75, emp. added).

CONCLUSION

That "something else" of which Heinberg wrote has intrigued almost everyone who has worked on the brain-mind problem—some to a greater degree than others. In his book, *The Large, the Small and the Human Brain*, British mathematical physicist Sir Roger Penrose remarked:

> **It seems to me that there is a fundamental problem with the idea that mentality arises out of physicality**—that is something which philosophers worry about for very good reasons. The things we talk about in physics are matter, physical things, mas-

sive objects, particles, space, time, energy and so on. How could our feelings, our perception of redness, or of happiness have anything to do with physics? **I regard that as a mystery** (1997, p. 94, emp. added).

So do thousands (maybe even millions!) of others. As Dennett admitted:

> It does seem as if the happenings that *are* my conscious thoughts and experiences cannot be brain happenings, but must be *something else*, or something cause or produced by brain happenings, no doubt, but something in addition, made of different stuff, located in a different space.... **Mind stuff...has some remarkable properties...but it is extremely resistant to definition**....
>
> Since we don't have the faintest idea (yet) what properties mind stuff has, we cannot even guess (yet) how it might be affected by physical processes emanating somehow from the brain, so let's...concentrate on the return signals, the directives from mind to brain. These, *ex hypothesi,* are not physical; they are not light waves or sound waves or cosmic rays or streams of subatomic particles. No physical energy or mass is associated with them. How, then, do they get to make a difference to what happens in the brain cells they must affect, if the mind is to have any influence over the body?... How can mind stuff *both* elude all physical measurements and control the body? (1991, pp. 27, 28,34,35, italics and parenthetical items in orig., emp. added).

Good questions. Pity, isn't it, that monistic materialists like Dennett cannot answer them?

One thing is certain, however: the **fact** of our self-awareness—of our consciousness—is both self-evident and undeniable. The belief in an "inner self," a "personal psyche," or a "soul" is well nigh universal. Dennett also noted:

> The idea that a *self* (or a person, or, for that matter, a soul) is distinct from a brain or a body is deeply rooted in our ways of speaking, and hence in our ways of thinking.... **It is quite natural to think of "the self**

and its brain" as two distinct things, with different properties, no matter how closely they depend on each other. If the self is distinct from the brain, it seems that it must be made of mind stuff. In Latin, a thinking thing is *res cogitans*…. So the conscious mind is not just the place where the witnessed color and smells are, and not just the thinking thing. It is where the appreciating happens. It is the ultimate arbiter of why anything matters. Perhaps this even follows somehow from the fact that the conscious mind is also supposed to be the source of our intentional actions (1991, pp. 29,31, italics and parenthetical item in orig., emp. added).

Jerome Elbert wrote in agreement: "The soul belief is so basic in our culture that, through ordinary communications, most of us come to believe that a network of neurons cannot, by itself, generate our thoughts and awareness of the world" (2000, p. 217). How very true.

Materialism certainly has not disproved the existence of our oh-so-vital "inner self." Nor will it ever. Steven Goldberg, in his book, *Seduced by Science,* was correct when he explained:

> **Modern science certainly does not claim that it can prove the nonexistence of the soul**. On the contrary, the dominant philosophical assumption of most twentieth-century scientists has been precisely the opposite: science deals with falsifiable propositions, that is, propositions that can be demonstrated wrong in an empirical test…. [S]cience simply does not speak to the validity of other systems, such as metaphysics, pure mathematics, or logic (1999, p. 18, emp. added).

Eccles, in his Gifford Lectures (presented at the University of Edinburgh in 1977-1978), warned:

> We must not claim to be self-sufficient. **If we espouse the philosophy of monist-materialism, there is no base on which we can build a meaning for life or for the values**. We would be creatures of chance and circumstance. All would be determined by our inheritance and our conditioning. Our feeling of free-

dom and of responsibility would be but an illusion. As against that I will present my belief that **there is a great mystery in our existence and in our experiences of life that is not explicable in materialist terms**... (1979, p. 10, emp. added).

After one has rightly rejected monistic materialism, what, then, is left? As Eccles and Robinson noted:

> We reject materialism because, as we have seen, it doesn't **explain** our concepts but denies them. It is at this point that we, as noble and rational beings, can give vent to the urgings of faith; not faith as the veil of ignorance, sloth, or fear, but faith as a state of mind vindicated by the efforts of reason and common sense (1984, p. 173, emp. in orig.).

How refreshing—to see a man of the stature of Sir John Eccles speak of faith "vindicated by the efforts of reason and common sense." Roger Sperry went on to say: "More than ever there is need today to raise our sights to higher values above those of material self-interest, economic gain, politics, production power, daily needs for personal subsistence, etc, to higher, more long term, more god-like priorities" (1985, pp. 158-159). German physicist Max Planck, in his *Scientific Autobiography and Other Papers* (1950), wrote:

> Religion and natural science do not exclude each other, as many contemporaries of ours would have us believe or fear; they mutually supplement and condition each other. The most immediate proof of the compatibility of religion and natural science, even under the most thorough critical scrutiny, is the historic fact that the very greatest natural scientists of all times—men such as Kepler, Newton, Leibniz—were permeated by a most profound religious attitude. Religion and natural science are fighting a joint battle in an incessant, never-relaxing crusade against skepticism and against dogmatism, against disbelief and against superstition, and the rallying cry in this crusade has always been, and always will be: "On to God!" (as quoted in Eccles, 1992, p. 247).

Sadly, however, the perception persists that "faith" has somehow "lost out" to science—an idea that Dr. Eccles worked feverishly during his lifetime to dispel.

> There is a pervasive belief that religion and science are antagonistic, and that religion has been mortally defeated. This is a mistake based upon ignorance and/or prejudice. Yet atheistic materialism is the in-thing for all "tough-minded" materialists. It is surprising that this fallacious belief has been propagated despite the fact that some of the greatest scientists of this century have recognized the necessity for a religious attitude to life and to science (1992, p. 244).

In the end, Eccles was compelled to admit:

> We have to be open to some deep dramatic significance in this earthly life of ours that may be revealed after the transformation of death. We can ask: What does this life mean? We find ourselves here in this wonderfully rich and vivid conscious experience and it goes on through life; but is that the end? This self-conscious mind of ours has this mysterious relationship with the brain and as a consequence achieves experiences of human love and friendship, of the wonderful natural beauties and of the intellectual excitement and joy given by appreciation and understanding of our cultural heritages. Is this present life all to finish in death, or can we have hope that there will be further meaning to be discovered?…

> Man has lost his way ideologically in this age. It is what has been called the predicament of mankind. I think that science has gone too far in breaking down man's belief in his spiritual greatness…and has given him the belief that he is merely an insignificant animal that has arisen by chance and necessity in an insignificant planet lost in the great cosmic immensity….

> I think the principal trouble with mankind today is that the intellectual leaders are too arrogant in their self-sufficiency. We must realize the great unknowns in the material makeup and operation of our brains, in the relationship of brain to mind and in our creative imag-

ination. When we think of these unknowns as well as the unknown of how we come to be in the first place, we should be much more humble. The unimaginable future that could be ours would be the fulfillment of this, our present life, and we should be prepared to accept its possibility as the greatest gift. In the acceptance of this wonderful gift of life and of death, we have to be prepared not for the inevitability of some other existence, but we can hope for the possibility of it....

This whole cosmos is not just running on and running down for no meaning. In the context of Natural Theology, I come to the belief that we are creatures with some supernatural meaning that is as yet ill defined. We cannot think more than that we are all part of some great design...

Each of us can have the belief of acting in some unimaginable supernatural drama. We should give all we can in order to play our part. Then we wait with serenity and joy for the future revelations of whatever is in store after death (1992, pp. 251-252).

Twenty-five years earlier, Dr. Eccles had been even more specific. He wrote, incredibly:

The arguments presented by [American biologist H.S.] Jennings **preclude me from believing that my experiencing self has an existence that merely is derivative from my brain** with its biological origin, and with its development under instructions derived from my genetic inheritance. If we follow Jennings, as I do, in his arguments and inferences, **we come to the religious concept of the soul and its special creation by God**.... I cannot believe that this wonderful divine gift of a conscious existence has no further future, no possibility of another existence under some other, unimaginable conditions (1967, p. 24, emp. added).

Biblical teaching regarding man acknowledges that he is composed of two distinct parts—the physical and the spiritual. We get an introduction to the origin of the **physical** portion as early as Genesis 2:7 when the text states: "Jehovah God formed man of the dust of the ground, and breathed into his nostrils the breath of life; and man became a living soul (*nephesh chayyah*)." It is important to recognize both what this passage is discussing and what it is not. Genesis 2:7 **is** teaching that man was given **physical life**; it is **not** teaching that man was instilled with an **immortal nature**. The immediate (as well as the remote) context is important to a clear understanding of the intent of Moses' statement. Both the King James and American Standard Versions translate *nephesh chayyah* as "living soul." The Revised Standard Version, New American Standard Version, New International Version, and the New Jerusalem Bible all translate the phrase as "living being." The New English Bible translates it as "living creature."

The variety of terms employed in our English translations has caused some confusion as to the exact meaning of the phrase "living soul" or "living being." Some have suggested, for example, that Genesis 2:7 is speaking specifically of man's receiving his immortal soul and/or spirit. This is not the case, however, as a closer examination of the immediate and remote contexts clearly indicates. For example, the apostle Paul quoted Genesis 2:7 in 1 Corinthians 15:44-45 when he wrote: "If there is a **natural body**, there is also a **spiritual body**. So also it is written, 'The first man Adam became a living soul.' The last Adam became a life-giving spirit." The comparison/contrast offered by the apostle between the first Adam's "natural body" and the last Adam (Christ) as a "life-giving spirit" is absolutely critical to an understanding of Paul's central message (and the theme of the great "resurrection chapter" of the Bible, 1 Corinthians 15), and must not be overlooked in any examination of Moses' statement in Genesis 2:7.

There are six additional places in the Old Testament where similar phraseology is employed, and in each case the text obviously is speaking of members of the animal kingdom. In Genesis 1:24, God said: "Let the earth bring forth living creatures (*nephesh chayyah*) after their kind." Genesis 1:30 records that God provided plants as food "to every beast of the earth, and to every bird of the air, and to everything that creeps on the earth, everything that has the breath of life (*nishmath chayyah*)." When the Genesis Flood covered the Earth, God made a rainbow covenant with Noah and with every living creature (*nephesh chayyah*) that was in the ark with Him (Genesis 9:12). God pledged that He would remember the covenant that He made with every "living creature" (*nephesh chayyah*; Genesis 9:12), and therefore He never again would destroy the Earth by such a Flood. The rainbow, He stated, would serve as a reminder of that "everlasting covenant" between God and every living creature (*nephesh chayyah,* Genesis 9:15). The final occurrence of the phrase is found in Ezekiel's description of the river flowing from the temple in which every living creature (*nephesh chayyah*) that swarms will live (47:9).

Additionally, the Bible declares: "For that which befalleth the sons of men befalleth beasts; even one thing befalleth them: as the one dieth, so dieth the other; yea, they have all one breath; and man hath no preeminence above the beasts" (Ecclesiastes 3:19). Does this mean, therefore, that man possesses only a material nature and has no immortal soul/spirit? No, it does not! In speaking to this very point, Jack P. Lewis wrote:

> It would seem that arguments which try to present the distinctiveness of man from the term "living soul" are actually based on the phenomena of variety in translation of the KJV and have no validity in fact. Had the translators rendered all seven occurrences by the same term, we would have been aware of the fact that both men and animals are described by it. To make this observation is not at all to affirm that the Old Testament is materialistic. We are concerned at this time only with the biblical usage of one term. Neither is it to deny a distinction in biblical thought between men and other animals when one takes in consideration the whole Old Testament view. Man may perish like the animals, but he is different from them. Even here in Genesis in the creation account, God is not said to breathe into the animals the breath of life;

animals are made male and female; there is no separate account of the making of the female animal; they are not said to be in God's image and likeness; they are not given dominion. Man is the crown of God's creation (1988, p. 7).

When Dr. Lewis suggested that "man may perish like the animals," he captured the essence of the passage in Ecclesiastes 3:19. It is true that both men and beasts ultimately die, and that in this regard man "hath no preeminence above the beasts." Yet while both creatures are referred to as *nephesh chayyah*, the Scriptures make it clear that God did something special in reference to man. Genesis 1:26-27 records: "And God said, 'Let us make man **in our image, after our likeness**....' And God created man in his own image, in the image of God created he him; male and female created he them." Nowhere does the Bible state or imply that animals are created in the image of God. What is it, then, that makes man different from the animals?

The answer, of course, lies in the fact that man possesses an immortal nature. Animals do not. God Himself is a spirit (John 4:24). And a spirit "hath not flesh and bones" (Luke 24:39). In some fashion, God has placed within man a portion of His own essence—in the sense that man possesses a spirit that never will die. The Old Testament prophet, Zechariah, spoke of Jehovah, Who "stretcheth forth the heavens, and layeth the foundation of the earth, and formeth the spirit (*ruach*) of man within him" (12:1). The Hebrew word for "formeth," *yatsar*, is defined as to form, fashion, or shape (as in a potter working with clay; Harris, et al., 1980, 1:396). The same word is used in Genesis 2:7, thereby indicating that both man's physical body and his spiritual nature were formed, shaped, molded, or fashioned by God. The authors of the *Theological Wordbook of the Old Testament* noted:

> The participial form meaning "potter" is applied to God in Isa. 64:7 where mankind is the work of his hand. When applied to the objects of God's creative

work, the emphasis of the word is on the forming or structuring of these phenomena. The word speaks to the **mode of creation** of these phenomena only insofar as the act of shaping or forming an object may also imply the **initiation of that object** (Harris, et al., 1:396, emp. added).

As the Creator, God "initiates" the object we know as man's immortal nature (i.e., his soul or spirit). Solomon, writing in the book of Ecclesiastes, noted that "the dust returneth to the earth as it was, and the spirit returneth unto **God who gave it**" (12:7, emp. added). Man's physical body was formed of the physical dust of the Earth. Would it not follow, then, that his spiritual portion would be formed from that which is spiritual? When the writer of Hebrews referred to God as "the Father of our spirits" (12:9), he revealed the spiritual source of the soul —God.

9

THE PROBLEM OF SKIN COLOR AND BLOOD TYPES

Humans come in a rainbow of colors: sandy yellows, reddish-tans, creamy whites, pale pinks. And who among us is not curious about the skin colors, hair textures, bodily structures and facial features associated with racial background. Why do many Africans have deep black skin, while that of most Europeans is pale pink? Why do the eyes of most "white" people and "black" people look pretty much alike, but differ so much from the eyes of Orientals? Why do some races have kinky hair, while others have straight hair? Why do some races grow to over 7 feet tall (e.g., African Watusis), while others are less than 5 feet (e.g., African Pygmies)? The answers to some of these questions, and others, may often be found in a study of the origin of various races.

Currently, society recognizes three or four major "races" of humans, as the word race generally is defined: (a) Caucasoid; (b) Mongoloid; (c) Negroid; and (d) Australoid. Generally speaking, the Australoids are considered a subgroup of the Caucasoids, simply because the two groups have so many features in common, despite the fact that Australoids possess dark skin (the Australoid group often is known as the Australian Aboriginal Group).

But consider the conundrum evolutionists face in explaining why humans have mostly naked skin that comes in a variety of sandy yellows, reddish-tans, silky browns, creamy whites, and pale pinks. We are the only "primates" (their classification, not ours) that remain hairless and that exhibit this rainbow of colors. Yet, these colors also cause many of us to stop and ask: "How could so many different colors have originated from Adam and Eve?"

Like Rudyard Kipling, in his *Just So* stories, we could weave all sorts of yarns to explain why different peoples are the way they are. We could spin one tale about how the Scandinavians became tall, and still another story about how they became light-skinned. For instance, researchers used to believe that the Pygmy people of southern Africa were short because food was scarce—until additional scientific studies showed normal levels of growth hormone, but revealed a genetic defect that prevents the Pygmies' bodies from using the hormone to its fullest extent (Fackelmann, 1989). Did nature select this mutation because it offered survival advantages, or did this characteristic arise as a result of random variation?

The answer is not at all obvious, because we know so many exceptions to the rules of natural selection. The fact is, for most variations that endow human populations with their distinctive characteristics, it is difficult to know **what** forces of selection (if any) have been at work. Take the Japanese, for instance. Their teenagers are considerably taller than their grandparents ever were. The difference, as it turns out, is a matter of a vastly improved diet, not genetics. For hundreds of years, the people of Japan have survived without nature's "selecting" mutations for smaller stature. So how do we know for sure that a scarce food supply was responsible for the survival of growth-limiting changes in the Pygmy?

The list of such just-so stories is endless. Why are the Inuit relatively short and bulky? The answer in the past has been that such a stature helps them retain heat. Why are some people in Africa relatively tall and slender? The answer in the past has been that such a stature helps them lose heat. Yet, in each case, we could list a dozen exceptions. What about those tall peoples who have survived quite well in cold areas, like the Dutch? And what about those short peoples who have done just fine in hot areas, like the Pygmies?

If Africans have less hair to keep them cooler, as some have suggested (Folger, 1993), then how have Asians—with relatively little body hair—fared so well in cold climates? Asians also have an epicanthic fold—an extra layer of skin on the upper eyelid. We could invent an anecdotal account about their eyes adapting to the winds of the Mongolian steppes and/or the bright glare of snow. But if we did, would this be enough? Are variations in the structure of the eyelid a matter of life and death? Were individuals who had this epicanthic fold much more likely to survive than those who lacked it?

The goal for such a traditional Darwinian approach, of course, is to answer the following question: How does a particular trait enhance survival value, or enable the production of more offspring? One anthropology textbook emphasized the "pervasiveness of adaptation in the microevolution [small-scale differentiation—BH/BT] of man" (Keesing and Keesing, 1971, p. 51). Yet, as we will show in this chapter, this turns out to be more of a hope than a statement substantiated by the actual evidence.

An article in the October 2002 issue of *Scientific American* claims to hold the answer to this complex puzzle. The authors believe that human skin color has continued to evolve—in an effort to get "just the right color." The claim is: "Throughout the world, human skin color has evolved to be **dark enough** to prevent sunlight from destroying the nutrient folate **but light enough** to foster the production of vitamin D" (Jablonski and Chaplin, 2002, 287[4]:75, emp. added). The skin on chimpanzees and apes is light because it is covered and protected by the abundance of hair on their bodies. As such, evolutionists like Jablonski and Chaplin believe the first humans had light skin. [Other evolutionists, however, believe exactly the opposite, and suggest that humans "started out" black and "became" white. Jones addressed this point when he wrote: "Although a change in skin colour is the most striking event in human evolution, nobody really knows why melanin was lost as people emerged from Africa" (1996, p. 195). Jones certainly got it right when he admitted: "The theory of evolution is infinitely flexible" (p. 184).]

According to Jablonski and Chaplin's theory, we were forced to give up our hair in order to cool our growing brains (maybe this explains why many humans today find themselves "folliclely challenged!"). Once rid of the body hair, evolutionists proclaim, humans then were subjected to the damaging effects of sunlight, especially UV rays. To combat this problem, evolutionists contend, humans began producing more melanin, the dark-pigmented molecule that serves the dual purpose of physically and chemically filtering out harmful UV rays. The *Scientific American* report also points out (p. 76) that the melanin may have played a role in preserving folate—a compound important in preventing neural-tube defects such as spina bifida.

The article informs readers that "the earliest members of *Homo sapiens*, or modern humans, evolved in Africa between 120,000 and 100,000 years ago and had darkly pigmented skin adapted to the condition of UV radiation and heat that existed near the equator" (p. 79). This dark skin became problematic, however, when humans began to venture out of this tropical region. With less sunlight available, humans were unable to produce vitamin D in sufficient quantities, and were subject to various diseases such as **rickets and osteomalacia**. Thus, people who settled in regions without as much sunlight were then forced to undergo further evolution in order to produce a lighter skin color. [For those of you keeping track, here's a quick summary: We lost body hair to cool our growing brains. Our pink skin and folate levels were in danger of UV radiation, so we evolved lots of melanin and became dark skinned. But some humans traveled to areas where there was not as much sunlight, thus they were required to evolve lighter skin.] **Humans therefore evolved skin dark enough to prevent sunlight from destroying the nutrient folate, but light enough to foster vitamin D production.** Seems like an awful lot of "evolving" to solve a puzzle that creationists solved a long time ago—with much less evolving. Equally troubling is the fact that we see all colors on the Earth today. If there were one skin color that was ideal—protecting folate, while permitting the production of vitamin D—then why do we see so many color variations today?

So, how, exactly, has natural selection worked to preserve dark and light skin coloring? The traditional explanation, as shown above, makes what seems to be at first glance a reasonable link between the strong sunlight of the tropics and the protective powers of melanin. Natural selection, so the argument goes, favored the survival of dark-skinned people in equatorial areas. If light-skinned people lived in the tropics, they would suffer from higher rates of skin cancer.

Then what prevented Africans from migrating to higher latitudes? The answer, we are told, lies in vitamin D. To make this important substance, humans need exposure to ultraviolet light. [It is true that exposure to sunlight stimulates the production of vitamin D in significant quantities. To quote Jones: "Ultraviolet light, though, is not all bad. When it penetrates the skin, it makes vitamin D; far more than comes from even a well balanced diet" (1996, p. 194).] If people in higher latitudes were too dark, their skin would not be able to make enough vitamin D. A shortage of vitamin D results in rickets, which has a severe effect on bone development. So everything works out perfectly: light people get a little melanin to avoid rickets; and dark people get a lot of melanin to avoid skin cancer. One thing is certain, however: whatever explanation is proffered, some sort of evolutionary process **must** be responsible for lighter and darker strains of humans (see Wills, 1994, p. 80).

The story seems less plausible, however, when we try to imagine exactly how such a selection process might have worked. Yes, skin cancer is deadly. And yes, it is something that afflicts lighter-skinned people who spend a lot of time in strong sunlight. People of European ancestry living in the sunny climes of Australia, New Zealand, and Hawaii do suffer the highest rates of skin cancer in the world.

But as we look backwards in human history, we have to face the fact that the danger of dying from basal cell carcinomas and melanomas hardly would compare to the tragedies represented by childhood diseases, plagues, strife, starvation, and natural hazards. It is difficult to imagine that in a mixed population of light- and dark-skinned people living near the tropics, evolution selected the traits for dark skin because **cancer** gradually eliminated their lighter-skinned neighbors.

On the other hand, unlike the skin-cancer scenario, the ability to produce sufficient vitamin D represents a definite survival advantage. But exposure to the Sun is not an absolute requirement. Oils from various fish—cod, halibut, sardines, salmon, and mackerel—are a rich source of vitamin D (Sackheim and Lehman, 1994, p. 516). Not surprisingly, such fish figure prominently in the diets of Scandinavians and the Inuit. With the right foods, they have been able to overcome the disadvantage of living in areas where the Sun is weaker, and in which the cold climate dictates many layers of protective clothing, both of which are factors that would prevent them from manufacturing adequate levels of vitamin D.

Still, all of this does not begin to explain why Africans remained in tropical zones. They could have moved northward, and endured (as many European children did) dastardly doses of cod liver oil. Today, thanks to the availability of vitamin supplements, and the fact that vitamin D is added routinely to food products (like milk), people of African descent can survive in England and Canada without a high incidence of rickets. When we look to the original population of the Americas, the story blurs completely. People of brownish complexion live across every climatic zone—from Alaska in the north, to Tierra del Fuego in the south. Apparently, no mechanism has been at work to sort skin color by latitude.

There are numerous other problems with the climatic theory of skin color (see Diamond, 1992, pp. 114-117), and still, we have barely touched on the rich storehouse of human variety. Perhaps apparently neutral characteristics will turn out to have some survival advantage (Patterson, 1999, pp. 40-44). For example, researchers have found a correlation between ABO blood groups and resistance (or susceptibility) to different diseases. Further, blood groups seem to have a strong geographic distribution. We may discover that a particular blood type became concentrated in a region where it offered a slightly better chance of survival. On this point, however, all we have so far is another Kiplingesque just-so type story. No doubt, natural selection has had some impact on human history, but it seems largely inadequate to explain a good portion of the variations that exist between different human populations.

WHAT IS A "RACE"?

A human race most often is defined as a group of people with certain features in common that distinguish them from other groups of people. While the Bible recognizes only one race—the human race—society has categorized at least four major races. As we mentioned earlier, those four are as follows: (1) Causcasoid; (2) Mongoloid; (3) Negroid; and (4) Australoid. These designations represent the entire spectrum of human skin colors based upon the amount of melanin that is contained in the skin. If someone were to attempt a breakdown by percentages of people worldwide, the groups would look like this:

Caucasoid	55% (of world's population)
Mongoloid	33%
Negroid	8%
Australoid	4%

It is interesting to note that these races are distributed around the globe throughout over 100 or more nations of significance, and speak more than 3,000 tribal languages and dialects. As we examine the various groups of people around the world—from the Inuit to the !Kung, from the Swedish to the Greek, and from the Indian to the Watusi—we witness an astounding array of skin color, hair type, stature, and facial features. Then, in addition to all that physical diversity, we must add differences in culture and language. Thanks to incredible technological advances, humans have lived (if only for a short time) at the South Pole, on the top of Mount Everest, and even beyond Earth itself. Well before the advent of modern science, we have occupied the remotest islands, the driest deserts, and the coldest steppes. It is difficult to imagine any other creature that has been so successful at colonizing so many different parts of this planet (giving the cockroach its due, of course).

Yet, for all these differences, we constitute a single biological species. Men and women with familial and cultural ties on different continents can meet, marry, and have families of their own—a fact that frustrates any attempt to parcel the world's populations into distinct subspecies or well-defined races. We witness immense diversity because we are able to detect patterns and distinguish among individuals of our own kind. This discriminating discernment of the human form is something that we cannot ignore, and is something that results in a variety of psychological responses (such as physical attraction and group identity). Nevertheless, at the biological level, such variation reflects only minute differences in our genetic code. We view a few of these in our physical appearance, but find many more only at the cellular or molecular level. One person may possess resistance to a particular disease, while another is unable to digest milk as an adult. Whether on the inside or the outside, the combination of many subtle differences makes each human stand out as an individual within a group, while our similarities identify us with humanity as a whole. As British evolutionist Steve Jones put it in his book, *In the Blood: God, Genes and Destiny*, "…[T]he essence of race lies on the surface. The genes involved, and many others, show that *Homo sapiens* is, compared to other mammals, very uniform from place to place" (1996, p. 183).

Speaking in broad terms, research on racial differences has led scientists to at least three major conclusions. First, there are many more differences among people than just hair texture, skin color, and facial features. Dozens of other variations have been found to exist. Consider, for example, these examples.

(a) Apocrine glands, which produce scents that we commonly refer to as body odor, vary widely among the races. Asians have an extremely low distribution of apocrines (Koreans are among the least odor-producing people on Earth—50% of them have no apocrine glands at all). Blacks have an extremely high distribution of apocrines. Whites fall midway between the two.

(b) Ear wax among races is quite different. One of the most accurate ways to distinguish Asians from blacks and whites is to check for differences in earwax. Asians produce dry, crumbly earwax. Blacks and whites produce moist, adhesive earwax.

(c) Metabolism rates can differ significantly among races. The higher the metabolic rate, the higher the threshold for sensing cold. The Eskimo's metabolic rate is 15-30% higher than that of a European. Equatorial people have the lowest metabolism of all because fewer calories are needed to keep their bodies warm.

There are many other differences that could be discussed—teeth, brain size, blood-flow rates, body shape, etc.

Second, research has shown that in many instances the success of a race's survival has been aided by its genetic variability. While the evolutionist would equate this with chance processes operating in the sphere of "survival of the fittest," creationists see it as just one more example of God's beneficent design. He has given us such variability, genetically speaking, that we can successfully adapt as the need arises. More will be said about this later.

Third, despite the human species' wealth of built-in variation, and despite our constant references to "race," no one has ever been able to suggest a truly reliable way to distinguish one race from another. While it is possible to classify a great many people on the basis of certain physical characteristics, there are no known features, or groups of features, that will do the job in all cases.

Some have suggested that skin color be the criterion. Yet, this provides innumerable difficulties because, while most Africans from south of the Sahara and their descendants around the world have skin that is darker than that of most Europeans, there are millions of people in India, whom many anthropologists classify as members of the Caucasoid race, who have darker skins than most American Negroes. And some Africans, living in the sub-Saharan regions, have skin coloration that is no darker than that of some Spaniards, Italians, Greeks, or Lebanese.

Some have suggested that **stature** be the criterion for a race. African Pygmies, because of their short height, have been considered racially distinct from other dark-skinned Africans, for example. Yet if stature is then to become a (or the) racial criterion, would not it be necessary to include in the same race both the tall African Watusis and Scandinavians of similar stature? Yet no one recommends such.

Still others have suggested that a variety of **appearance features** become the criterion for race determination. For example, most people are familiar with the almond shaped eye of the Oriental. The little web of skin that is so characteristic in Oriental eyes is said to be a distinguishing feature of the Mongoloid race. Yet, if one were to accept that argument, how, then, could it be argued that the American Indian, who lacks this epicanthic fold, is also Mongoloid (which is the case)? Other so-called distinguishing features fare no better. Such features as hair color, eye color, hair form, the shapes of noses and lips, and many of the other traits often set forth as typical "markers" of one race or another are all too often found distributed throughout many races. Among the tall people of the world there are those who exhibit every skin color imaginable —from black to white and everything in between. Among black people of the world there are some who possess kinky hair, some who possess straight or wavy hair, and again, many in between. Among the broad-nosed, full-lipped people of the world, it is true that there are many with dark skins, but there are likewise many with light skins, and many in between.

And the situation worsens. The world is filled with populations that just seem to defy classification. Consider some of these well-known examples: (a) the Bushmen of southern Africa appear to be as much Mongoloid as Negroid; (b) the Negritos of the South Pacific do look Negroid, but are far-removed from Africa and have no known links to that continent; (c) the Ainu of Japan are a hairy aboriginal type of people who appear to the naked eye to be more Caucasoid than anything else; (d) the aborigines of Australia sometimes look Negroid, but often have straight or wavy hair and are occasionally blond as children.

To accommodate this immense diversity, many different classification systems have been proposed. Some have suggested as many as two- or three-dozen races. But none has ever been able to accomplish its task of successfully defining just how, in the end, a race should be accurately determined.

WHY SO MANY RACIAL CHARACTERISTICS?

Why are there so many different racial characteristics? What is their origin? And how long did it take for all this to occur?

It will come as no great surprise to learn that, once again, the evolutionists' explanations fall far afield from those offered by creationists. Listen, first, to the proposed evolutionary explanation, offered by Boyce Rensberger in the January/February 1981 issue of *Science Digest:*

> To understand the origin and proliferation of human differences, one must first know how Darwinian evolution works. Evolution is a two-step process. Step one is mutation: somehow a gene in the ovary or testes of an individual is altered, changing the molecular configuration that stores instructions for forming a new individual. The children who inherit that gene will be different in some way from their ancestors. Step two is selection: for a racial difference, or any other evolutionary change to arise, it must survive and be passed through several generations. If the mutation confers

some disadvantage, the individual dies, often during embryonic development. But if the change is beneficial in some way, the individual should have a better chance of thriving than relatives lacking the advantage. If a new trait is beneficial, it will bring reproductive success to its bearer. After several generations of multiplication, bearers of the new trait may begin to outnumber nonbearers. Darwin called this natural selection to distinguish it from the artificial selection exercised by animal breeders (89[1]:56).

Since racial differentiation is dependent upon genetic mutations, and (as every evolutionist knows full well) since mutations occur rarely, it is plainly obvious that the production of races in an evolution-based continuum will be a painfully slow process—thus, the assumption that a lot of time is required to explain human variation, since evolution works at a steady-but-slow pace. Charles Darwin, of course, accepted this as a matter of principle; but not all evolutionists agree. A few bold dissenters, citing examples from the fossil record, believe that species arise on Earth during brief moments of intense change, rather than by slow accumulation of new features (e.g., Eldredge, 1985, pp. 21-22). So, too, we are told, within human populations, distinct groups might possibly arise during momentous natural events. Add to that the fact that more and more evolutionists are expressing concern about the so-called "molecular clock," which was supposed to express the rate at which genetic differences have accumulated in two related species. Such a calculation, however, depends on knowing the date of a putative presumed common ancestor—something on which not everyone agrees (nor is there always agreement on whether the two species are, in fact, closely related). In any case, evolutionists assume that humans diverged from each other at about the same rate that we diverged from our supposed closest relative—chimpanzees. Yet, interestingly, a closer look at families of **known** lineage has revealed mutation rates that are almost **twenty times higher** than previous estimates (see Gibbons, 1998a). The upshot is this: we cannot trust the intuition of Darwinists' regarding the time it "might" take to produce the differences we see in human populations. The rate may be slow—or not. It may be steady—or not. And, undoubtedly, other (perhaps even unknown) factors have had their own part to play in all of this as well.

Consider the creationist alternative. Biologists determine species (among other ways) by including in a species all individuals that are capable of interbreeding to produce fertile offspring. There is only one species of man on Earth—*Homo sapiens*. That, on the face of it, is an interesting fact. Anthropologists and biologists place all races in existence today into a single species, which points to the fact that the differences between human races are not really all that great. Members of all races can intermarry and produce fertile offspring.

It also is interesting to note that these "differences" **within** the groups are just as pronounced as differences **among** the groups. Negroid people range in color from black to sallow; Mongoloid people range from yellow to white to bronze-brown; Caucasoids range from pink (as in England) to dark brown (as in Southern India). These skin colors—to which most people refer when they speak of a "race" of people—are caused by the brown pigment in the skin known as melanin. Unfortunately, "melanin has been much disregarded by biologists because it is hard to study and because, at first sight, its function is obvious. It is found in all kinds of creatures and comes in several different varieties" (Jones, 1996, p. 185). Melanin actually is the molecule at the end of a long, biochemical pathway that, along its way, produces chemicals involved in nerve transmission. It is manufactured in special cells known as "melanocytes." Each melanocyte produces small granules (known as melanosomes) that pass into the other cells of the skin. [Black-skinned people have no more melanocytes than white-skinned people, but the melanocytes that are present are much more active.] Melanin, as it turns out, "has remarkable and unexpected properties" that allows it to wield "an influence far greater than once appeared possible" (Jones, p. 188).

The more melanin a person has, the darker the skin will be as an adult. Conversely, the less melanin in the skin, the lighter the skin will be as an adult. A person whose skin possesses **no** melanin is referred to as an **albino**, and cannot produce body pigment. Such a person's pinkish-white color is caused by blood vessels showing through the colorless skin. The claim that there are many different skin colors in the world is not altogether accurate. The **apparent** differences in color are simply differences in the amount of the melanin found in the skin, not differences in the type of color. There is only one coloring agent for the human race; the shade of color simply depends upon how much melanin a person possesses.

Melanin does far more than simply provide the body with pigmentation. Its most important role is in protecting the body by absorbing ultraviolet (UV) radiation from sunlight that falls on the skin. UV radiation can damage the skin and produce skin cancer if not filtered out by the melanin. People who have large amounts of melanin in their skin generally are very resistant to the effects of UV radiation. People with only small amounts of melanin may suffer badly if exposed to too much UV light. The energy of the UV light penetrates deeper into their skin, and can cause damage to the skin tissues. As Jones has pointed out:

> Ultraviolet light is powerful stuff, as anyone who has watched their carpets fade knows. Melanin is good at keeping it out. People without much melanin are at high risk of skin cancer.... Whites with light skins are at eight times greater risk than are those with dark. Thirty times more sun is needed to cause sunburn (the prime cause of skin cancer) in blacks than in whites (parenthetical item in orig., p. 192).

There are at least three factors to be considered, from a creationist point of view, in any attempt to explain the origin of what we today call races: (a) the origin of man; (b) the known historical and/or biblical facts regarding man; and (c) the nature of the areas to which man migrated. Here are some pertinent facts bearing on each of these points.

First, the biblical record makes it abundantly clear that God created man. As a part of the whole creation, man was pronounced "very good." Thus, man did not "evolve" his skin color. God gave him the best possible combination of skin color genes. The writer of Acts observed that God "made of one every nation of man to dwell on all the face of the earth" (17:26). This fits perfectly with both recorded history and current scientific facts—man always has been man. Adam was the first man (1 Corinthians 15:45). And, through Eve, all living would come (Genesis 3:20). This becomes critical in determining the origin of racial characteristics.

Second, we do know that historically, and biblically, the line of human descent passed through Adam and Eve and their descendants to Noah and his family. However, whatever genetic material had been dispersed into the human race prior to the global Flood was severely limited by the destruction of that Flood.

Third, after the Flood, the Tower of Babel incident occurred. Men refused to obey God and cover the Earth. So, God confused their languages, and as a natural result, men migrated to various parts of the globe where they could be with others who spoke their language. This migration, as will be discussed shortly, had a part to play in producing various racial characteristics.

THE ORIGIN OF MAN'S "COLORS"

Most people, when they speak of a "race," refer to the racial characteristic of skin coloration. For the purpose of the present discussion, we will limit our discussion, for the most part, to the origin of such a characteristic (being careful to do so only in an accommodative sense). In humans, skin color is caused by melanin. Around 1913, Charles Davenport observed that humans carried two genes for color, and that each gene consisted of "black" or "white" alleles (one allele from the mother, and one from the father, for each gene). Jones put it like this: "The genetics of skin pigment is simple. Blacks and whites differ by just one gene, present in two forms. One makes pigment, the other does not" (p. 187). Hence, our coloration depends on the number of black and white alleles we received from our parents. Davenport noted (correctly) that children inherited these genes independently of other characteristics, such as straight versus curly hair (which explains why albino Nigerians look different from albino Scots).

These genes reside in the nucleus of every cell in our body, along with copies of all the other genes we inherited from our parents. However, color genes express themselves in only one place—the melanocytes. These are specialized skin cells that have a monopoly on melanin production. Each melanocyte is an incredibly complex chemical factory, transforming raw materials into granules of melanin, which it delivers to neighboring cells.

We also now know there is more to the production of skin color than simply turning genes on or off to make black, white, and a variety of shades in between. We all possess the essential ingredients for making melanin; all of us **could** be black or brown (the exception, of course, being albinos, whose bodies produce no melanin at all). Actual coloration varies according to the pigment package delivered by the melanocytes. The end product depends not only on slight genetic differences, but also on certain environmental stimuli (such as exposure to strong ultraviolet radiation). The story does not end there, however. Skin also includes keratin—a fibrous protein that contributes to the toughness of the skin, and which grows to form nails and hair. Because this substance has a relatively high concentration of sulfur, it adds a yellow hue to our palette of skin colors. Asians (especially from the Far East) happen to have an extra-thick layer of keratin which, when combined with melanin, contributes to the yellow-brown color of their skin.

While geneticists today believe that almost half a dozen genes may have at least some effect on pigmentation (Wills, 1994, pp. 78-79), pigment production appears to be controlled in large part by two pairs of genes. Geneticists refer to them using the letter designations **Aa** and **Bb**, where the capital letters represent dominant genes and the small letters represent recessive genes. **A** and **B**, being dominant, produce melanin very well. Being recessive, **a** and **b** produce melanin to a lesser degree.

If Adam and Eve were both **AABB**, they could have produced only children that were the darkest Negroid coloration possible, and they themselves would likewise have been Negroid. That, in all likelihood, would have produced a world composed only of Negroid people. But, as has already been noted, the Negroid race composes less than 10% of the world's population, so by a process of elimination, this choice can be ruled out.

If Adam and Eve had both been **aabb**, they could have had only children that were **aabb**, and which were the lightest Caucasoid possible. Then, the world would contain no other groupings. But it does. So, this option also is ruled out by a process of elimination.

The real question is this: Is there a mechanism by which the racial characteristics which we see today could have originated with one human couple—in the short, few thousand year or so history of the Earth?

The answer is a resounding yes! If Adam and Eve had been "heterozygous" (**AaBb**; two dominant, two recessive genes), they would have been middle-brown in color. And, from them —in one generation—racial differences easily could have occurred.

A person born **AABB** carries genes for the darkest Negroid coloration possible, and since all genes are dominant, has no genes for lightness. If that person married another person who likewise carried all dominant genes, and moved to an area where no intermarriage with people of different colors occurred, the offspring resulting from this marriage would then carry the same dominant genes. These offspring will have "lost" the ability to be "white." Conversely, if a person who is

aabb, and hence the lightest Caucasoid possible, marries another person who likewise carries all recessive genes, and moves into an area where no intermarriage with people of other colors occurs, henceforward this union will produce only offspring of the lightest possible Caucasoid coloration. The offspring so produced have "lost" the ability to be "black." They no longer have the genes necessary to produce enough melanin for the black color. Observe the following skin-color possibilities that can occur in a single generation.

AaBb — AaBb

	AB	Ab	aB	ab
AB	AA BB	AA Bb	Aa BB	Aa Bb
Ab	AA Bb	Aa bb	Aa Bb	Aa Bb
aB	Aa BB	Aa Bb	aa BB	aa Bb
ab	Aa Bb	Aa bb	aa Bb	aa bb

From these possibilities, one obtains the following:

> 1 — Darkest Negroid
> 4 — Dark
> 6 — Medium skin
> 4 — Light
> 1 — Lightest Caucasoid

Thus, starting with two parents who were heterozygous (i.e., middle-brown in color), extreme racial colors (black and white, to name only two examples) could be produced in such a way that races would have permanently different colors. Of course, it is also possible to produce a middle-brown race that will have a fixed middle-brown color. If the original middle-brown parents produce offspring of either **AAbb** (or **aaBB**), and these offspring marry only their own kind (avoiding intermarriage with those not of their own genetic makeup), their descendants will be a fixed middle-brown color.

The whole process is "put into reverse," however, when people from different colored races intermarry. Different combinations of genes (i.e., different from those originally carried by the two parents) occur, and the offspring thus begin to show a rainbow effect of skin colors, ranging from black to white.

Is it likely that people of various colorations intermarried? The preponderance of so many colorations in the world is evidence aplenty that they did. Interestingly, even evolutionists agree on this point. Rensberger remarked:

> Race mixing has not only been a fact of human history but is, in this day of unprecedented global mobility, taking place at a more rapid rate than ever. It is not farfetched to envision the day when, generations hence, the entire "complexion" of major population centers will be different. Meanwhile, **we can see such changes taking place before our eyes**, for they are a part of everyday reality (1981, 89[1]:54, emp. added).

Francisco Ayala of the University of California has observed that if the process started out with a couple that had only a 6.7% heterozygosity (which is the average in modern humans), the different combinations possible would be 1×10^{2017} before the couple would have one child identical to another (1978, p. 63)! It is quite likely that Adam and Eve were heterozygous. Otherwise, their descendants would have lacked variation. However, one might suggest that Adam and Eve began with all dominant (or all recessive) sets of genes, but that changes occurred after the Creation as the result of mutations. Indeed, many of the genetic differences, and many of the genetic disorders, no doubt have arisen since the first couple was removed from that original, pristine environment. Thus, the possibility that some heterozygosity is a product of mutations cannot be ruled out.

OTHER FACTORS

There can be little doubt that racial characteristics existed before the Flood, at least to some degree. But once the Flood had come and gone, drastically altering both the Earth and man's environment, and once the Tower of Babel incident had occurred, man found himself migrating to new (and different environments). To what extent did these factors influence racial characteristics? One scientist has observed:

> Studies on the relationship between skin colour and health or diet in a given environment suggest the following influences: after Babel, those who went to colder climates but had darker skin could suffer from vitamin D deficiency such as rickets (for example, the Neanderthals). Since the skin produces vitamin D from sunlight, any person with a darker skin is worse off in a cold region since there is less sunlight. A dark skin is more sunlight resistant and therefore can produce less vitamin D. Such a colder environment, because of the available sunlight and the available diet, would tend to favour those who inherited fairer skins. Dark-skinned people in such an area would therefore tend to be less healthy and would have fewer children. Gradually the number black people in any group that went to a cold region would be outnumbered by the white. Likewise those who went to more sunny or hotter regions with darker skins would survive better (that is, get less skin cancer). In this case the fairer persons would dwindle from the population and a black race would result.

> It is reasonable to suggest that Noah and his family possessed genes for both dark and light—dark enough to protect them, yet light enough to ensure sufficient vitamin D. It is unlikely that in the world before the Flood there would have been extremes of heat or cold,

so that a balanced skin colour was most suitable. This balance would be in the middle-brown range. After Babel, when the genes for darkness or lightness were separated out into different groups, the environment played a part in favouring certain heredity groups in certain areas. This is not to say that the environment produced dark skin or light skin. We know this has not been the case because there are a certain number of dark-skinned races, such as the Pygmies, who live in the dark jungles and are not exposed to much sunlight; the Eskimos, who are dark skinned yet live in very cold sunless regions; and the white Europeans who have moved to hot areas and stayed a white race, for example the Australians. These people demonstrate that the genes governing skin colour which they inherited are more important factors than any effect the environment can have. The final ratio of dark to light genes in any one group however, is commonly a most useful balance for surviving in that environment. People did not gain their light or dark skins merely as an adaptation to the environment in the evolutionary sense of an organism developing something new to cope with a new environment. All the basic factors of skin colour were present in the first created man. Adam was designed to cope by having the best ability to produce vitamin D and the best protection from any radiation. He was most probably middle-brown in colour, and indeed most of the world's population still is (Mackay, 1984, 6[4]:9-10).

Besides environment, other physical characteristics play a part in what we call racial characteristics. For example, the yellowish color in Mongoloid races is due to the extra thickening of the keratin layer in the skin, which causes the sunlight to be reflected from the skin. The normal brown color produced by the melanin is "altered," and the end result is a yellow brown. Or, consider the Mongoloid eye as opposed to the Caucasoid eye. The Caucasoid eye has only one layer of fat; the Mongoloid eye has a double fold of fat, producing an "almond" appearance.

But why are certain racial features as they are? Oftentimes, we simply do not know. Evolutionists fare no better. Nobody knows, for example, **why** Orientals have epicanthic eye folds or flatter facial profiles. The thin lips of Caucasoids and most Mongoloids have no known advantages over the full lips of Negroid races. Why should middle-aged and older Caucasoid men go bald so much more frequently than the men of other races? Why does the skin of Bushmen wrinkle so heavily in the middle and later years? Or why does the skin of Negroids resist wrinkling so well? These are questions for which we currently possess no answers.

One possible answer to varying racial characteristics, however, is a phenomenon known as the "founder effect." We witness this most often in small, isolated communities that have an unusually high incidence of rare, inherited disorders (Diamond, 1988, p. 12). Using genealogical detective work, medical researchers trace their patients' ancestries to a single couple (or a very small group) of close relatives—"the founders." This appears to be the case with French Canadians, particularly those of eastern Quebec, whose ancestors emigrated from the Perche region of France in the seventeenth century. Small pioneering groups, together with early marriages, large families, and geographical isolation, created a pronounced founder effect. One study discovered that a middling **15%** of the settlers contributed **90%** of the genetic characteristics in individuals who suffered from one or more of five genetic disorders (Heyer and Tremblay, 1995).

As discomfiting as it may be, in reality, it is only natural that much of our information on founder effects should come from the study of debilitating, and often fatal, diseases. If medical researchers can isolate a faulty gene that is responsible for a particular problem, then this may suggest a specific treatment or cure. Also, genetic testing can tell prospective parents whether they might pass on these mutations to their children. And genetic counseling can help such prospective parents decide if they even want to have children in the first place.

Fortunately, however, the historical records also include some cases of the founder effect that were not related directly to diseases. In an article on "The Origin of Peoples," Trevor Major described one such instance as follows.

> In a now-classic study, H. Bentley Glass (1953) found that the Dunkers—a community of German Baptist Brethren in Pennsylvania's Franklin County—are, in most respects, very similar to other people of European descent. Their religious customs require them to dress a certain way, and marry within the community, but otherwise their physical appearance is not unusual. Although there have been some outside marriages, most of the surviving members are descended from fifty families that emigrated from Germany in the early 1700s. Glass found that the frequencies of blood types and other genetic traits among the Dunkers differ from the frequencies of these features between U.S. and German populations. It seems unlikely that any selective forces were in operation to favor the survival of Dunkers with blood group A, for instance. Therefore, Glass concluded, the founding population of Dunkers included, purely by chance, an unusually high proportion of people with blood group A (1998, 18:12).

As it turns out, the founder effect is a small part of a much broader concept known as genetic drift, which occurs anytime the frequency of a genetic trait changes within a population. If, in the case of the founder effect, the emigrating group possessed a set of unique or rare traits, then those specific traits would be that much more difficult to locate among the people who had stayed behind. In other words, there will be a "drift" **away** from those characteristics. Furthermore, in some cases, a highly prolific individual or family may skew the genes of a relatively diverse population, and this may occur in combination with some other form of genetic drift, such as the founder effect. As Major went on to note:

> For example, groups of Ashkenazic Jews moved eastward out of Germany in the 17th century, and were isolated culturally from the surrounding population.

Several rare inherited disorders, such as Tay-Sachs disease, afflict this group at high rates. Evolutionists have thought this to be a sign of natural selection at work. Perhaps the population hung on to these genes because they offered some survival advantage, such as resistance to tuberculosis and other maladies of the crowded ghettos in which they lived (Diamond, 1991). However, Neil Risch believes otherwise, at least in the case of idiopathic torsion dystonia, which occurs at a rate of one in three thousand among the Ashkenazim today (Glausiusz, 1995). First, migration patterns favor genetic drift via the founder effect in these people. And second, historical records show that wealthier couples had more children. If a mutation arose in one of these families, as Risch infers from the genetic data, then it could become more frequent in later generations. This is a matter of misfortune, not adaptation (18:12-13).

There is another form of genetic drift known as a "population bottleneck," which is the most striking. Typically, these bottlenecks occur when catastrophes such as natural disasters, epidemics, or wars decimate all but a small remnant of the original population. For instance, a tornado could destroy an entire village, except for a fortunate few. Those survivors would bequeath their genetic characteristics to subsequent generations. If there were a high degree of relatedness among the survivors, then their descendants might appear quite distinct from neighboring peoples. Of course, the Bible shows the Flood of Noah to be the greatest bottleneck of all time. According to the Genesis account, all of us must trace our ancestry to Noah's three sons and their wives.

One last effect upon racial characteristics may well be mate selection (see Diamond, 1992, pp. 99-109). More often than not (although, admittedly, not always), we marry someone who speaks the same language as we do, who belongs to the same cultural, religious, social, and political group, and who may even possess the same color skin or racial characteristics that we possess. The inadvertent result is a barrier, obvious or otherwise, that may exist between two neighboring peoples, or even between groups who live exist in close proximity.

What is the bottom line? In reference to the human race, Daniel E. Koshland made the following admission: "Such dilemmas make us confront another reality. At the present time the way in which mutation and selection (survival of the fittest) has worked over evolutionary time no longer seems to apply to *Homo sapiens*" (2002, 295:2216, parenthetical item in orig.). What we do know is that the races were produced in a very short time span, and that the racial variations we see today are merely an expression of the original genetic endowment of Adam and Eve as carried through to us by Noah. No "evolutionary process" was able, or needed, to produce them.

DIFFERENCES BETWEEN HUMAN AND ANIMAL BLOOD TYPES

Blood has been called the liquid of life. With it, lives that have been ravaged by traumatic injuries can be saved, while on the opposite end of the spectrum, sustained blood loss typically results in death. It is via this crimson fluid that oxygen is transported throughout the human body. On average, human adults possess approximately five liters of this vital liquid, which travels through more than 50,000 miles of convoluted arteries, arterioles, veins, venules, and capillaries. The total volume of blood represents only 8-9% of the total weight of a human. However, this small percentage does not reflect the major role blood plays in properly maintaining all the organs in the body. Even organs that play an active role in the circulatory system —such as the heart that is responsible for pumping blood, or the endocrine system that secretes hormones and salts into the vascular system—are themselves dependent on it. Evolutionists have a difficult time explaining how the heart could have evolved to serve as a blood "pump," since the heart itself requires oxygenated blood.

"Blood is thicker than water" is the cry from society in defense of the actions of family members. From a strictly physiological perspective, this is true. Blood has a viscosity that ranges between 4.5 and 5.5, while water has a viscosity of 1. But what else do we really know about this iron-rich fluid that flows just below the skin's surface? Evolutionists tout the idea that the blood running through the human circulatory system is similar in nature to the blood coursing through the veins of fish, bears, and birds. Is it just another product of evolution as many would have us believe? Does the fact that humans possess **four** blood types, prove that we could not all have descended from Adam and Eve? The Lord said to Moses:

> For the life of the flesh is in the blood: and I have given it to you upon the altar to make an atonement for your souls: for it is the blood that maketh an atonement for the soul (Leviticus 17:11).

It is our hope that this study will help you learn more about this precious liquid that was selected by God Himself to wash away man's sins.

COMPONENTS OF HUMAN BLOOD

The study of blood is called hematology. Blood is one of the few substances in the human body that is not "fixed" in place. Tissues (such as nerves, muscles, and organs) have a specific function and are limited in movement. Blood, however, is not limited to any one part of the body. Its job is to provide these "fixed" tissues with nourishment and then carry off waste products. Blood itself is composed of a cellular portion referred to as **formed elements**, and a fluid portion designated as **plasma**. The formed elements constitute approximately 45% of the total volume of blood, and are comprised of erythrocytes, leukocytes, and platelets. Plasma is a straw-colored liquid that consists primarily of water and dissolved solutes. Approximately 90% of plasma is water, 9% is protein material, 0.9% is salts, and 0.9% is sugar, urea, etc.

Erythrocytes (also known as red blood cells—see illustration on next page) are the most common of the formed elements. These cells provide oxygen to tissues, and assist in recovering carbon dioxide (a waste product). In humans, red blood cells are anucleated (i.e., they are devoid of nuclei), while birds, amphibians, and other animals have red blood cells that are nucleated—something else evolutionists have a difficult time explaining. Some animals produce these cells intravascularly (i.e., in the blood stream), whereas humans and some animals produce them extravascularly (in the bone marrow or other hematopoietic tissue). All cells require a nucleus for replication and maturation. Even red blood cells have a nucleus during their very early stages of development. However, in humans the production of red blood cells occurs in the bone mar-

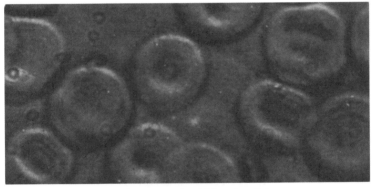

Erythrocytes (red blood cells)

row, and thus we do not normally see these nucleated cells in the circulation (although they occasionally are found in newborns). As the red blood cell matures and is ready to leave the bone marrow, it expels its nucleus. The reason for anucleated red blood cells in humans is best explained by understanding the blood cell's specific function. In humans, the smallest blood vessels (capillaries) often are so narrow that nucleated red blood cells would have a difficult time passing through them. Even an anucleated red blood cell is larger (8µm) than capillaries (2-3µm). However, without the nucleus present, the red blood cell is flexible, and is able to fold over on itself. The anucleated red blood cell's shape (a biconcave disc) can best accomplish this feat.

Red blood cells contain **hemoglobin**, which carries oxygen to every cell in the body. Hemoglobin is a complex protein that has two chains (referred to as alpha and beta). An evolutionary origin of hemoglobin would require a minimum of 120 mutations to convert an alpha to a beta. At least 34 of those changes require changeovers in 2 or 3 nucleotides. Yet, if a single nucleotide change occurred through mutation, the result would ruin the blood and kill the organism.

The formed element portion of blood also possesses **platelets** and **leukocytes**. Platelets are much smaller than red blood cells, and serve to stop blood loss from wounds (hemostasis). Leukocytes serve as the primary line of defense in the vascular system. Two categories, granulocytes and lymphoid cells, circulate throughout the blood stream in an effort to identify and combat foreign pathogens such as bacteria, viruses, etc.

Adding to this complexity are the numerous salts that are required in blood. These salts are primarily basic ions, such as sodium, potassium, phosphate, and magnesium that help maintain a steady pH value for the blood. These bicarbonate ions remove carbon dioxide from the tissues and help maintain a slightly alkaline pH of 7.4. During traumatic injuries or surgeries, a great deal of attention is given to the pH of the blood significant decrease or loss of this alkalinity can cause rapid and violent breathing, with death likely to occur at a pH of 7.0 or below. Conversely, if the pH of the blood is allowed to go beyond 7.6, it also can prove fatal.

Evolutionists assert that life evolved from the sea, and are quick to point out the sodium chloride and other salts found in blood probably originated from the sea. However, on average, the concentration of sodium chloride (salt) in seawater is 2.7% (0.8% other salts, some of which are not present in blood and would not benefit the cardiovascular system). If evolutionists took the time to do the math, they would find that the Baltic Sea—one of the "fresher" large bodies of water—still is much too salty to have played any physiological part in the evolution of blood.

DIFFERENT BLOOD TYPES

Human blood is categorized into four different types: A, B, AB, and O. But **why** that is the case—from an evolutionary viewpoint—is an enigma. As evolutionist Steve Jones admitted: "What blood groups are actually for, nobody really knows" (1996, p. 179). Each letter designates the type of antigen, or protein, found on the surface of the red blood cells. [For example, the surface of red blood cells for type B blood would have antigens known as B-antigens.]

Through blood testing, we can determine a person's blood type, and identify the so-called ABO antigens. Most of us, for example know what our own blood type is in the ABO system—e.g., O-negative, AB-negative, B-positive (the positive or negative refers to the Rhesus factor, which is another type of antigen on the surface of red blood cells).

Blood typing is critical when blood transfusions become necessary during illness, surgery, or other such situations. Persons with type O blood are so-called universal donors, and can donate blood to people with types A, B, AB, or O. However, a person with AB blood type can give blood only to persons with AB blood type.

Blood Type	Percent of Population	Possible Recipients
O+	37%	O+, A+, B+, AB+
O-	6%	Anyone
A+	34%	A+, AB+
A-	6%	A+, A-, AB+, AB-
B+	10%	B+, AB+
B-	2%	B+, B-, AB+, AB-
AB+	4%	AB+
AB-	1%	AB+, AB-

THE ADAM AND EVE ISSUE

Admittedly, humans possess four blood types, which at first glance appears to be a strong victory for evolutionists and a gargantuan hurdle for creationists. However, the variations that we see in blood types fit easily into the biblical account, once we understand the possibilities. From the four phenotypic blood groups (A, B, AB, and O), there are six possible genotypes: AA, AO, BB, BO, AB, OO. No medical difference exists between AA, and AO; both are considered type "A," and behave the same. In a similar manner, there is no significance to BB or BO; they are classified as type "B."

Types "A" and "B" are said to be codominant. That is, they take precedence over "O" if it also is present. This means that they both are dominant to type "O," but equal to each other. Thus, if a mother has type AO blood, the A is dominant, and she can be described as having type A blood even though the O also is present (think of O as being the silent partner). So if a mother and father are types AO and BO, then the blood type of their offspring can be, A, B, AB, or O.

In the case of Adam and Eve, if Adam was type AO and Eve was type BO, then all four blood types would be possible in their offspring (see chart below). Any resulting children would have a 25% chance of being A, B, O, or AB. Thus each child would have 25% chance of being any of the four blood types.

25%	AB
25%	BO
25%	AO
25%	OO

So, obviously, Adam and Eve can easily account for the four different blood types we see today. In addition, there were **eight** members of Noah's family aboard the ark when God destroyed all other living creatures via the global flood. Those eight individuals would have had no problem passing on all four blood types through their family lines.

HUMANS, ANIMALS, AND BLOOD

When God created all living creatures, He did so knowing that we all would have different needs. With those needs came different requirements. Paul, writing to the Christians in Corinth, stated: "All flesh is not the same flesh: but there is one kind of flesh of men, another flesh of beasts, another of fishes, and another of birds" (1 Corinthians 15:39). Evolutionists will find no comfort in knowing that human blood is vastly different from that of animals. Human blood does not need to be specialized for long periods of hibernation (like the blood of North American bears). Additionally, a human's oxygen needs are different from fish and birds, and consequently the composition of our blood varies as well. Scientists categorize animals into two broad classes—warm-blooded and cold-blooded —according to how the animals regulate their internal temperatures. Yet evolutionists would have us believe that blood from all living creatures shares a common origin.

WHAT ABOUT BLOOD TYPES OF OTHER ANIMALS?

The red blood cells of all non-mammalian vertebrates (i.e., fish, amphibians, reptiles, and birds) are nucleated, flattened, and ellipsoidal. If, in fact, humans evolved from a common ancestor several million years ago, then it would make sense that blood cells would be similar in all animals. This is far from the case, however.

Chimpanzees have blood types A and minimal O, but **never B**. Gorillas have blood types B and minimal O, but **never A**. Plus, there is no blood type AB in either of these primates, while some humans do possess AB type blood. Currently, **eight** blood groups are commonly found in dogs, and are categorized under what is known as the dog erythrocyte antigen (DEA) system. The table on the next page outlines the eight common blood groups of the DEA system used in the United States.

New Nomenclature	Old Nomenclature	Incidence
DEA-1.1	A_1	40
DEA-1.2	A_2	20
DEA-3	B	5
DEA-4	C	98
DEA-5	D	25
DEA-6	F	98
DEA-7	Tr	45
DEA-8	He	40

So, while humans have blood types A,B, and O, dogs possess eight different types. And since we know that blood types are inherited, the question arises, "Whence did dogs inherit these additional blood types?" Furthermore, consider that cats have 11 blood types, and **cows are reported to** have almost 800 different blood types! Evolving 800 different blood types is no small feat, considering man has yet to evolve even one. Additionally, evolutionists must answer the question, "Why don't **all** living things have blood?" If a true circulatory system is the most energy-efficient method of distributing oxygen and food, and is the best mechanism for cleansing organisms, then why do plants not employ a similar system?

WHAT ABOUT HIBERNATION?

While we all enjoy a good night's sleep, how many of us sleep for several weeks at a time? Hibernating animals have an element in their blood known as Hibernation Inducement Trigger (HIT). Research suggests that it is some kind of opiate chemically related to morphine. As the days get shorter, as the temperature changes, and as food becomes scarce, HIT triggers hibernation. Exactly how and why it happens remains a mystery, but we do know that humans do not possess HIT in their blood.

WHAT ABOUT BIRDS?

Birds have a circulatory system that is very similar to a mammal's. Bird blood is similar to ours in that it contains both red cells and leukocytes. **However, unlike humans, a bird's red blood cells are nucleated!** This, of course, poses the question of which was the original blood cell—the nucleated one or the anucleated one? Additionally, birds' oxygen requirements are much greater than those of humans, and therefore the composition of birds' blood is different from humans'.

WHAT ABOUT FISH?

Is your blood ready for a good **long** swim? Most of us rarely consider the complexity involved in living in an aquatic environment where even blood is different. Fish blood is thicker than human blood, and has a lower pressure, because it is pumped by a heart with only two chambers. Consequently, the flow of blood through a fish's body is slow. Because the blood flows slowly through the gills where it takes on oxygen, and because water contains less oxygen than air, fish blood is not as rich in oxygen as human blood. Also, as a result of the slow flow of blood through the gills, the blood cools and approaches the temperature of the water surrounding the fish. If human blood were to do the same, there would be a race to the death—either death by hypothermia, or death from a lack of oxygen.

CONCLUSION

When you take into account such things as: (a) the **inherited** nature of human blood; (b) its osmolality (osmolality is a measurement of the concentration of solutes per liter of solution); (c) the specific amounts of ions, proteins, and organic molecules it contains; (d) the fact that it must be kept at a specific volume; and (d) the fact that it must be maintained at a specific pH, it quickly becomes apparent that there must have been a designer behind this incredible life-giving liquid.

Additionally, the bloodletting (for sin) of every lamb under the Old Covenant could not do what the blood of one sinless Lamb of God could do in taking away the sins of the entire world (Exodus 12:12; 1 Corinthians 5:7). The writer of the book of Hebrews expressed it this way: "For it is not possible that the blood of bulls and of goats should take away sins" (Hebrews 10:4). The blood of Jesus Christ—shed on the cross at Calvary—was red just like yours and mine, but it paid a debt that cannot be repaid. Could all four blood types have come from Adam and Eve? Definitely! The only question that remains in regard to Adam and Eve is, which one was type "A" and which one was type "B."

10

CONCLUSION

There are numerous ways in which mankind bears God's image. For example, only human beings have a yearning to know a **cause** for things. Only humans are concerned with their **origin**, their present **purpose**, and their **destiny**. No animal—regardless of how "close" to humans certain evolutionists think that animal may be—ever pondered such things. Also, only human beings contemplate death, practice funeral rituals, and bury their dead. God has indeed "placed eternity" in our hearts (Ecclesiastes 3:11). Human civilizations from time immemorial have believed in life after death, and therefore have attempted to make some plans for it. One look at the Egyptian pyramids is evidence aplenty of this fact. Additionally, only humans are historical beings. We record past events, recount them, discuss them, and even learn from them. And so on.

The Bible paints a picture of man as a being that stands on a different level from all other creatures upon the Earth. He towers high above all earthly creation because of the phenomenal powers and attributes that God Almighty has freely given him. No other living being was given the capacities and capabilities, the potential and the dignity, that God instilled in each man and woman. Humankind is the peak, the pinnacle, the crown, the apex of God's creation. And what a difference that should make in our lives. As Poe and Davis put it:

> Whether people are an aspect of God or creatures of God has profound implications for human existence on earth. If people are the result of the creative activity of God based on God's intentional, self-conscious decision to make people, then creation results from

the purpose of God. People have a purpose, and this purpose emerges from the Creator-creature relationship. If, on the other hand, people are aspects of a... unity of which all things are a part, but which lacks self-consciousness, then life has no purpose. It merely exists (2000, p. 128).

Whether or not we are created in the image and likeness of God does indeed have "profound implications for human existence." Anthropologist Jonathan Marks made the following statement in his book, *What It Means to be 98% Chimpanzee*: **"The question of who and what you are is not trivial"** (emp. added). The context in which he made that statement, however, is as important as the statement itself. Here, from his book, are the comments immediately preceding that sentence:

> Science gives us authoritative ideas about kinship, which force us to reconceptualize our place in the order of things, which is by that very fact disorienting. But it doesn't stick around to explain it to us, to reintegrate us, to give new meaning to our existence. That's the problem with Darwinian theory, of course. It tells us our ancestors were kin to apes, the products of eons of ordinary biological processes of survival and reproduction, and not merely zapped into existence in the Garden of Eden, **but it doesn't tell us what that means or what to do about it**. It just walks away from the wreckage (2002, p. 222, emp. in orig.).

What "wreckage," exactly, is Dr. Marks talking about? Let Richard Dawkins, the renowned evolutionist of Oxford University, answer. In the 1989 edition of his highly acclaimed 1976 book, *The Selfish Gene*, Dawkins wrote: **"My own feeling is that a human society based simply on the gene's laws of universal ruthless selfishness would be a very nasty society in which to live**. But unfortunately, however much we may deplore something, it does not stop it being true" (pp. 2,3). Six years later, in his book, *River Out of Eden*, he continued in the same vein:

> [I]f the universe were just electrons and selfish genes, meaningless tragedies...are exactly what we should expect, along with equally meaningless **good** fortune. Such a universe would be neither evil nor good in its intention. It would manifest no intentions of any kind. In a universe of electrons and selfish genes, blind physical forces and genetic replication, some people are going to get hurt, other people are going to get lucky, and you won t find any rhyme or reason in it, nor any justice. The universe that we observe has precisely the properties we should expect if there is, at bottom, no design, no purpose, no evil and no good, nothing but pitiless indifference (1995, pp. 132-133, emp. in orig.).

Nobel laureate Steven Weinberg referred to a similar "pitiless indifference" in his classic book on the origin of the Universe, *The First Three Minutes*, when he lamented:

> It is almost irresistible for humans to believe that we have some special relation to the universe, that human life is not just a more-or-less farcical outcome of a chain of accidents reaching back to the first three minutes, but that we were somehow built in from the beginning. ...It is very hard to realize that this all is just a tiny part of an overwhelmingly hostile universe...[which] has evolved from an unspeakably unfamiliar early condition, and faces a future extinction of endless cold or intolerable heat. **The more the universe seems comprehensible, the more it also seems pointless** (1977, pp. 150,155, emp. added).

The "Darwinian wreckage" that has been foisted on humanity has caused untold sorrow. If we teach people that they have **descended** from animals, why would it surprise us that they then **act** like animals? If we convince people that they live in a "pointless" universe where their lives are filled with "pitiless indifference," why should we be at all surprised when they **spend** their lives in a fruitless search for an ever-elusive happiness, and **end** their lives (sometimes intentionally!) in complete and utter despair?

Man did not evolve from an "imageless" lower creation. Rather, God created him with the unique abilities we have discussed in this book. While in some aspects, man is very different from the infinite God Who created him, the passages of Scripture that speak of the *imago Dei* reveal his likeness to Him. Thus, we are justified in concluding that man was created "**to be and do on a finite level what God was and did on an infinite level**" (Morey, 1984, p. 37, emp. added). How very thrilling, and yet how extremely humbling, to know that we alone bear God's image! And yes, what a profound difference such knowledge should make in our lives!

REFERENCES

Ackerman, Jennifer (2001), *Chance in the House of Fate* (Boston, MA: Houghton Mifflin).

Adrian, E.D. (1965), "Consciousness," *Brain and Conscious Experience* (Rome, Italy: Pontifica Academia Scientarium), pp. 238-248. [This book is the written papers, and the written record of the oral discussions that took place concerning those papers, from a symposium held at the Vatican during the week of September 28-October 4, 1964.]

Aitchison, Jean (2000), *The Seeds of Speech: Language Origin and Evolution* (Cambridge, England: Cambridge University Press).

Alberts, Bruce, Dennis Bray, Julian Lewis, Martin Raff, Keith Roberts, and James D. Watson (1994), *Molecular Biology of The Cell* (New York: Garland Publishing), third edition.

Allan, John (1989), *The Human Difference* (Oxford, England: Lion).

Allport, Gordon (1955), *Becoming* (New Haven, CT: Yale University Press).

Anderson, Ian (1983), *New Scientist*, 98:373.

Anderson, S., A.T. Bankier, B.G. Barrell M.H. de Bruijn, A.R. Coulson, et al. (1981), "Sequence and Organization of the Human Mitochondrial Genome," *Nature*, 290:457-465, April 9.

Andrews, Peter and Christopher Stringer (1993), "The Primates' Progress," *The Book of Life*, ed. Stephen Jay Gould (New York: W.W. Norton).

"Animals Talk" (2002), [On-line], URL: http://www.global psychics.com/lp/Animalstalk/menu.htm.

Anthroquest [The Leakey Foundation News], (1991), 43:13, spring.

Appleyard, Bryan (1992), *Understanding the Present: Science and the Soul of Modern Man* (New York: Doubleday).

Asfaw, Berhane, W.H. Gilbert, et al. (2002), "Remains of *Homo erectus* from Bouri, Middle Awash, Ethiopia," *Nature,* 416: 317-320, March 21.

Ashman, Tia-Lynn (2000), "A Prescription for Gender Study in the Next Century," *American Journal of Botany*, 87:147-149, January.

Asimov, Isaac (1970), "In the Game of Energy and Thermodynamics You Can't Even Break Even," *Smithsonian Institute Journal,* pp. 4-10, June.

Asimov, Isaac (1982), "Interview with Isaac Asimov on Science and the Bible," Paul Kurtz, Interviewer, *Free Inquiry*, 2[2]:6-10, Spring.

Augros Robert and George Stanciu (1987), *The New Biology* (Boston, MA: New Science Library).

"*Australopithecus anamensis*," (2003), [On-line], URL: http://archae ologyinfo.com/australopithecusanamensis.htm.

Awadalla Philip, Adam Eyre-Walker, and John Maynard Smith (1999), "Linkage Disequilibrium and Recombination in Hominid Mitochondrial DNA," *Science*, 286:2524-2525, December 24.

Ayala, Francisco J. (1978), "The Mechanisms of Evolution," *Scientific American*, 239[3]:56-69, September.

Barbulescu, Madalina, Geoffrey Turner, Mei Su, Rachel Kim, Michael I. Jensen-Seaman, Amos S. Deinard, Kenneth K. Kidd, and Jack Lentz (2001), "A HERV-K Provirus in Chimpanzees, Bonobos, and Gorillas, but not Humans," *Current Biology*, 11:779-783.

Bartelmez, George W. (1926), "Human Structure and Development," *The Nature and the World of Man*, ed. H.H. Newman (Garden City, NY: Garden City Publishing), pp. 440-470.

BBC News (2000), "Ancestors Walked on Knuckles," [On-line], URL: http://bric.postech.ac.kr/science/97now/01_2now/010222c.html.

Begun, David (2001), "Early Hominid Sows Division," [On-line], URL: http://bric.postech.ac.kr/science/97now/01_2now/010222c.html.

Bell, Graham. (1982), *The Masterpiece of Nature: The Evolution and Genetics of Sexuality* (Berkeley, CA: University of California Press).

Beloff, John (1962), *The Existence of Mind* (London: MacGibbon and Kee).

Beloff, John (1994), "The Mind-Brain Problem," [On-line], URL: http://moebius.psy.ed.ac.uk/~dualism/papers/brains.html, emp. in orig. [NOTE: This article was published originally in *The Journal of Scientific Exploration* (1994), Vol. 8, No. 4.]

Berger, Lee R. (2001), "Is It Time to Revise the System of Scientific Naming?," [On-line], URL: http://news.nationalgeographic.com/news/2001/12/1204_hominin_id.html, December 4.

Bergman, Jerry (1996), "The Enigma of Sex and Evolution," *Creation Research Society Quarterly*, 33:217-223, December.

Bernstein, H., F.A. Hopf, and R.E. Michod (1989), "The Evolution of Sex: DNA Repair Hypothesis," *The Sociobiology of Sexual and Reproductive Strategies*, ed. C. Rasa and E. Voland (London: Chapman and Hall).

Blanchard, John (2000), *Does God Believe in Atheists?* (Auburn, MA: Evangelical Press).

Bonner, John Tyler (1958), "The Relation of Spore Formation to Recombination," *American Naturalist*, 92:193-200.

Bower, Bruce (1989), "A Walk Back Through Evolution," *Science News*, 135:251, April 22.

Breasted, James Henry (1930), *The Edwin Smith Surgical Papyrus* (Chicago, IL: Chicago Press), 2 volumes.

Britten, Roy J. (2002), "Divergence between Samples of Chimpanzee and Human DNA Sequences is 5%, Counting Intels," *Proceedings of the National Academy of Sciences*, 99:13633-136 35, October 15.

Brown, Andrew (1999), *The Darwin Wars* (London: Simon & Schuster).

Brunet M., F. Guy, D. Pilbeam, H.T. Mackay, et al. (2002), "A New Hominid from the Upper Miocene of Chad, Central Africa," *Nature*, 418:145-151, July 11.

Butzer, Karl W. (1974), "Paleoecology of South African Australopithecines: Taung Revisited," *Current Anthropology*, 15: 4, December.

Cann, Rebecca L., Mark Stoneking, and Allan C. Wilson (1987), "Mitochondrial DNA and Human Evolution," *Nature*, 325:31-36, January 1.

Cardoso, Silvia H. (1997-1998), "What is Mind?," *Brain & Mind*, [On-line], URL: http://www.epub.org.br/cm/n04/editori4 _i.htm, No. 4, December (1997)-February (1998).

Carrington, Hereward (1923), *Life: Its Origin and Nature* (Girard, KS: Haldeman-Julius).

Carter, Nick (2002), "Are There Any Insurmountable Obstacles to Descartes' Dualism?," [On-line], URL: www.revise.it/ reviseit/EssayLab/Undergraduate/Philosophy/e44.htm.

Cartwright, John (2000), *Evolution and Human Behavior* (London: Macmillan).

Cavalieri, Paola and Peter Singer (1993), *The Great Ape Project* (London: Fourth Estate).

Cavalli-Sforza, Luigi Luca (2000), *Genes, Peoples, and Languages* (New York: North Point Press).

Chalmers, David J. (1995), "Absent Qualia, Fading Qualia, Dancing Qualia," *Conscious Experience*, ed. Thomas Metzinger (Schoningh: Imprint Academic), pp. 309-328.

Chalmers David J. (1996), *The Conscious Mind* (Oxford, England: Oxford University Press).

Chalmers, John (2002), "Seven Million-Year-Old Skull Just a Female Gorilla," *Sydney [Australia] Morning Herald*, [Online], URL: http://www.smh.com/au/articles/2002/07/13/1026185124750.htm, July 14.

Cherfas, Jeremy (1983), "Trees Have Made Man Upright," *New Scientist*, 93:172-178, January 20.

Chomsky, Noam (1972), *Language and the Mind* (New York: Harcourt, Brace, Jovanovich).

Chomsky, Noam (1980), *Rules and Representations* (New York: Columbia University Press).

Clark, W. LeGros (1958), "Bones of Contention," *Ideas of Human Evolution*, ed. C. Howells (Cambridge, MA: Harvard University Press), pp. 357-360.

Coffing, K., C. Feibel, M. Leakey, and A. Walker (1994), "Four-million-year-old Hominids from East Lake Turkana, Kenya," *American Journal of Physical Anthropology*, 93:55-65.

Coghlan, Andy (2002), "Human-chimp DNA Difference Trebled," [On-line], URL: http://www.newscientist.com/news/news.jsp?id=ns99992833, September 23.

Corballis, Michael C. (2002), *From Hand to Mouth: The Origins of Language* (Princeton, NJ: Princeton University Press).

Cotterill, Rodney (1998), *Enchanted Looms: Conscious Networks in Brains and Computers* (Cambridge, England: Cambridge University Press).

Cousins, Norman (1985), "Commentary," in *Nobel Prize Conversations* (Dallas, TX: Saybrook). [This book is a record of conversations that occurred in November, 1982 at the Isthmus Institute in Dallas, Texas, among four Nobel laureates: Sir John Eccles, Ilya Prigogine, Roger Sperry, and Brian Josephson.]

Crick, Francis (1966), *Of Molecules and Men* (Seattle, WA: University of Washington Press).

Crick, Francis (1981), *Life Itself: Its Origin and Nature* (New York: Simon and Schuster).

Crick, Francis (1994), *The Astonishing Hypothesis: The Scientific Search for the Soul* (New York: Simon & Schuster).

Crook, J.H. (1972), "Sexual Selection, Dimorphism, and Social Organization in the Primates," *Sexual Selection and the Descent of Man: 1871-1971*, ed. B. Campbell (New York: Aldine).

Crow, J.F. (1988), "The Importance of Recombination," *The Evolution of Sex: An Examination of Current Ideas*, ed. Michod and Levin (Sunderland, MA: Sinauer Associates) pp. 56-73.

Custance, Arthur C. (1980), *The Mysterious Matter of Mind* (Grand Rapids, MI: Zondervan).

Daley, Janet (1996), "Interview" in *Daily Telegraph* (London), May 1.

Dalton, Rex (2003), "Flat-faced Man in Family Feud," *Nature Science Update*, [On-line] URL: http://www.nature.com/nsu/030324/030324-10.html, March 28.

Daniel, Kavitha S. (2002), "Human Cloning Project Claims Progress," [On-line], URL: http://www.gulfnews.com/Articles/news.asp?ArticleID=46275.

Dart, Raymond A. (1925), "*Australopithecus africanus*: The Man-Ape of South Africa," *Nature*, 115:195-199.

Darwin, Charles (1871), *The Descent of Man* (New York: Modern Library reprint).

Darwin, Charles (1956 edition), *The Origin of Species* (London: J.M. Dent & Sons).

Davies, Paul (1983), *God and the New Physics* (New York: Simon & Schuster).

Davies, Paul (1992), "The Mind of God," *Omni*, 14[5]:4, February.

Davies, Paul (1995), "Physics and the Mind of God," [On-line], URL: http://print.firstthings.com/ftissues/ft9508/articles/davies.html. [This is the address Dr. Davies presented from Westminster Abbey in 1995 when he was awarded the Templeton Prize for progress in religion. It was printed originally in *First Things*, 55:31-35, August-September.]

Davies, Paul and Phillip Addams (1998), *More Big Questions* (Sydney, Australia: ABC Books).

Dawkins, Marian (1993), *Through Our Eyes Only? The Search for Animal Consciousness* (Oxford, England: Blackwell).

Dawkins, Richard (1976), *The Selfish Gene* (Oxford, England: Oxford University Press).

Dawkins, Richard (1986), *The Blind Watchmaker* (New York: W.W. Norton).

Dawkins, Richard (1989), *The Selfish Gene* (Oxford, England: Oxford University Press), second edition.

Dawkins, Richard (1995), *River Out of Eden: A Darwinian View of Life* (New York: Basic Books).

Deacon, Terrance (1997), *The Symbolic Species: The Co-Evolution of Language and the Brain* (New York: W.W. Norton).

Deacon, Terrence W. (1999), "Impressions of Ancestral Brains," in *Cambridge Encyclopedia of Human Evolution*, ed. Steve Jones, Robert Martin, and David Pilbeam (New York: Cambridge University Press).

Delbrück, Max (1978), "Mind from Matter?," *American Scholar*, 43:339-353.

Delbrück, Max (1986), *Mind from Matter? An Essay on Evolutionary Epistemology* (Palo Alto, CA: Blackwell Scientific).

Delgado, José Maria (1969), "Mind and Soul," *Physical Control of the Mind* (New York: Harper & Row).

Dennett, Daniel C. (1984), *Elbow Room* (Cambridge, MA: Bradford).

Dennett, Daniel C. (1987), *The Intentional Stance* (Cambridge, MA: MIT Press).

Dennett, Daniel C. (1991), *Consciousness Explained* (Boston, MA: Little, Brown).

Dennett, Daniel C. (1995), *Darwin's Dangerous Idea* (New York: Simon & Schuster).

Dennett, Daniel C. (1996), *Kinds of Minds* (New York: Basic Books).

Dennett, Daniel C. (1998), *Brainchildren* (New York: Penguin).

Dennis, Carina (2003), "Error Reports Threaten to Unravel Databases of Mitochondrial DNA," *Nature*, 421:773-774, February 20.

"Descartes and Cartesianism" (1997), *Encyclopaedia Britannica* (Chicago, IL: Encyclopaedia Britannica, Inc.), pp. 553-560.

Diamond, Jared (1988), "Founding Fathers and Mothers," *Natural History*, 97[6]:10-15, June.

Diamond, Jared (1991), "Curse and Blessing of the Ghetto," *Discover*, 12[3]:60-61, March.

Diamond, Jared (1992), *The Third Chimpanzee* (New York: Harper Collins).

Diamond, Jared (1997), *Why is Sex Fun?* (New York: Basic Books).

Dickerson, R.E. (1978), "Chemical Evolution and the Origin of Life," *Scientific American*, 239[3]:70-86, September.

Dobzhansky, Theodosius (1967), "Changing Man," *Science*, 155:409-415, January 27.

Dobzhansky, Theodosius (1975), "Darwin or 'Oriented' Evolution?," *Evolution*, 29:376).

Dobzhansky, Theodosius, F.J. Ayala, G.L. Stebbins, and J.W. Valentine (1977), *Evolution* (San Francisco, CA: W.H. Freeman).

Dol, M., et al., (1997), *Animal Consciousness and Animal Ethics* (Assen, The Netherlands: Van Gorcum).

Donald, Merlin (2001), *A Mind So Rare* (New York: W.W. Norton).

Dose, Klaus (1988), "The Origin of Life: More Questions than Answers," *Interdisciplinary Science Reviews*, 13[4]:348.

Dressler, Alan (1994), *Voyage to the Great Attractor* (New York: Knopf).

Duarte, Cidalia, Joao Mauricio, et al. (1999), "The Early Upper Paleolithic Human Skeleton from the Abrigo do Lagar Veho (Portugal) and Modern Human Emergence in Iberia," *Proceedings of the National Academy of Science*, 96:7604-7609, June.

Duncan, Ronald and Miranda Weston-Smith, eds. (1977), *The Encyclopaedia of Ignorance* (Oxford, England: Pergamon).

Durant, Will, ed. (1932), *On the Meaning of Life* (New York: Long and Smith).

Dyson, Freeman (1979), *Disturbing the Universe* (New York: Harper & Row).

Dyson, Freeman (1988), "Mankind's Place in the Cosmos," *U.S. News and World Report,* p. 72, April 18.

Eccles, John C., ed. (1966), *Brain and Conscious Experience* (Rome, Italy: Pontifica Academia Scientarium). [This book is the written papers, and the written record of the oral discussions that took place concerning those papers, from a symposium held at the Vatican during the week of September 28-October 4, 1964.]

Eccles, John C. (1967), "Evolution and the Conscious Self," *The Human Mind: A Discussion at the [1967] Nobel Conference*, ed. John D. Roslansky (Amsterdam: North-Holland Publishing Co.).

Eccles, John C. (1970), *Facing Reality* (New York: Springer-Verlag).

Eccles, John C. (1973), *The Understanding of the Brain* (New York: McGraw-Hill).

Eccles, John C. (1977), "The Brain-Mind Problem as a Frontier of Science," *The Future of Science: 1975 Nobel Conference*, ed. Timothy C.L. Robinson (New York: John Wiley & Sons), pp. 73-104.

Eccles, John C. (1979), *The Human Mystery* (London: Routledge). [This book is the text of the Gifford Lectures presented by Dr. Eccles at the University of Edinburgh in 1977-1978.]

Eccles, John C. (1982), *Mind & Brain: The Many-faceted Problems* (Washington, D.C.: Paragon House).

Eccles, John C. (1989), *Evolution of the Brain: Creation of the Self* (London: Routledge).

Eccles, John C. (1992), *The Human Psyche* (London: Routledge).

Eccles, John C. (1994), *How the Self Controls Its Brain* (New York: Springer-Verlag).

Eccles, John C. and Daniel N. Robinson (1984), *The Wonder of Being Human: Our Brain and Our Mind* (New York: The Free Press).

Eccles, John C., Roger Sperry, Ilya Prigogine, and Brian Josephson (1985), *Nobel Prize Conversations* (Dallas, TX: Saybrook). [This book is a record of conversations that occurred in November, 1982 at the Isthmus Institute in Dallas, Texas, among four Nobel laureates: Sir John Eccles, Ilya Prigogine, Roger Sperry, and Brian Josephson.]

Eckelmann, Herman J. (1991), "Some Concluding Thoughts on Evolutionary Belief," *Evidence for Faith: Deciding the God Question*, ed. John W. Montgomery (Dallas, TX: Word).

Eckhardt, Robert (1972), "Population Genetics and Human Origins," *Scientific American*, 225:94-101, January.

Eddington, A.S. (1958), *The Philosophy of Physical Science* (Ann Arbor, MI: University of Michigan Press).

Edelman G.M (1992), *Bright Air, Brilliant Fire* (London: Penguin).

"Eggs Fertilised without Sperm," (2002), [On-line], URL: http://news.bbc.co.uk/1/hi/health/1431489.stm.

Ehrlich, Paul R. (2000), *Human Natures: Genes, Cultures, and the Human Prospect* (Washington, D.C.: Island Press).

Eiseley, Loren (1957), *The Immense Journey* (New York: Random House).

Elbert, Jerome W. (2000), *Are Souls Real?* (Amherst, NY: Prometheus).

Eldredge, Niles (1985), *Time Frames: The Evolution of Punctuated Equilibria* (Princeton, NJ: Princeton University Press).

Eldredge Niles and Joel Cracraft (1980), *Phylogenetic Patterns and the Evolutionary Process: Method and Theory in Comparative Biology*, (New York: Columbia University Press).

Elgin, Suzette H. (1973), *What is Linguistics?* (Englewood Cliffs, NJ: Prentice Hall).

"Ethiopian Fossil Skull Indicates *Homo erectus* was Single, Widespread Species 1 Million Years Ago" (2002), [On-line], URL: http://www.eurekalert.org/pub_releases/2002-03-uoc−efs031802.php.

Fackelmann, K.A. (1989), "Pygmy Paradox Prompts a Short Answer," *Science News*, 136[2]:22, July 8.

Feigl, Herbert (1967), *The "Mental" and the "Physical"* (Minneapolis, MN: University of Minnesota Press).

Fincher, Jack (1984), *The Human Body−The Brain: Mystery of Matter and Mind,* ed. Roy B. Pinchot (New York: Torstar Books).

Fix, William R. (1984), *The Bone Peddlers: Selling Evolution* (New York: Macmillan).

Flanagan O.J. (1992), *Consciousness Reconsidered* (Cambridge, MA: MIT Press).

Fodor, Jerry A. (1992), "The Big Idea: Can There be a Science of Mind?," *Times Literary Supplement*, July 3.

Folger, Tim (1993), "The Naked and the Bipedal," *Discover*, 14[1]:34-35, November.

Folger, Tim and Shanti Menon (1997), "...Or Much Like Us?," *Discover*, 18[1]:33, January.

Forster, Peter (2003), "To Err is Human," *Annals of Human Genetics*, 67:2-4, January.

Fox, Maggie (2000), "Man's Early Ancestors Were Knuckle Walkers," *San Diego Union Tribune*, Quest Section, March 29.

Fujiyama, Asao, Hidemi Watanabe, et al., (2002), "Construction and Analysis of a Human-Chimpanzee Comparative Clone Map," *Science*, 295:131-134, January 4.

Fuller, Harry J. and Oswald Tippo (1961), *College Botany* (New York: Holt, Rinehart, Winston).

Gallup, G.G. Jr. (1970), "Chimpanzees: Self-recognition," *Science*, 167:86-87.

Gardner, Eldon J. (1968), *Principles of Genetics* (New York: John Wiley and Sons).

Geisler, Norman (1984), "The Collapse of Modern Atheism," *The Intellectuals Speak Out About God*, ed. Roy A. Varghese (Chicago, IL: Regnery), pp. 129-152.

Ghiselin, Michael T. (1988), "The Evolution of Sex: A History of Competing Points of View," *The Evolution of Sex: An Examination of Current Ideas*, ed. Michod and Levin (Sunderland, MA: Sinauer).

Gibbons, Ann (1996), "*Homo erectus* in Java: A 250,000-year Anachronism," *Science*, 274:1841-1842, December 13.

Gibbons, Ann (1998a), "Calibrating the Mitochondrial Clock," *Science*, 279:28-29, January 2.

Gibbons, Ann (1998b), "Solving the Brain's Energy Crisis," *Science*, 280:1345-1347, May 29.

Gibbons, Ann (2001), "The Riddle of Coexistence," *Science*, 291:1725-1729, March 2.

Gish, Duane T. (no date), *Latest Research on the Origin of Man* [a cassette tape] (San Diego, CA: Creation Science Research Center).

Gish, Duane T., (1985), *Evolution: the Challenge of the Fossil Record* (El Cajon, CA: Creation-Life).

Gish, Duane T. (1995), *Evolution: The Fossils Still Say No!* (El Cajon, CA: Institute for Creation Research).

Gitt, Werner (1999), *The Wonder of Man* (Bielefeld, Germany: Christliche Literatur-Verbreitung E.V.).

Glass, H. Bentley (1953), "The Genetics of the Dunkers," *Scientific American*, August. Reprinted in *Human Variation and Origins* (San Francisco, CA: W.H. Freeman), pp. 200-204.

Glausiusz, Josie (1995), "Unfortunate Drift," *Discover*, 16[6]:34-35, June.

Gliedman, John (1982), "Scientists in Search of the Soul," *Science Digest*, 90[7]:77-79,105, July.

Glynn, Ian (1999), *An Anatomy of Thought: The Origin and Machinery of the Mind* (New York: Oxford University Press).

Goldberg, Steven (1999), *Seduced by Science* (New York: New York University Press).

Gomes, A.O. (1965), "The Brain-Consciousness Problem in Contemporary Scientific Research," *Brain and Conscious Experience* (Rome, Italy: Pontifica Academia Scientarium), pp. 446-469. [This book is the written papers, and the written record of the oral discussions that took place concerning those papers, from a symposium held at the Vatican during the week of September 28-October 4, 1964.]

Gould, Stephen Jay (1977a), *Ever Since Darwin* (New York: W.W. Norton).

Gould, Stephen Jay (1977b), "Evolution's Erratic Pace," *Natural History*, 86[5]:12-16, May.

Gould, Stephen Jay (1984a), "Challenges to Neo-Darwinism and Their Meaning for a Revised View of Human Consciousness," The Tanner Lectures on Human Values, [On-line], URL: http://www.tannerlectures.utah.edu/lectures/gould 8 5.pdf. [NOTE: Dr. Gould presented these lectures on April 30 and May 1, 1984, at Clare Hall, Cambridge University.]

Gould, Stephen Jay (1984b), "Is a New and General Theory of Evolution Emerging?," speech given at Hobart College February 14, 1980; as quoted in Luther Sunderland (1984), *Darwin's Enigma* (San Diego, CA: Master Books).

Gould, Stephen Jay (1989), *Wonderful Life: The Burgess Shale and the Nature of History* (New York: W.W. Norton).

Gould, Stephen Jay (1994), "The Evolution of Life on the Earth," *Scientific American*, 271[4]:85-91, October.

Gould, Stephen Jay (1995), "The Pattern of Life's History," [On-line], URL: http://www.edge.org/3rd_culture/gould/gould_p3.html. This essay was the second chapter in *The Third Culture*, ed. John Brockman (New York: Simon & Schuster).

Gould, Stephen Jay (1996a), *Full House: The Spread of Excellence from Plato to Darwin* (New York: Three Rivers Press).

Gould, Stephen Jay (1996b), "The Tallest Tale," *Natural History*, 105[5]:18-23,54,56-57, May.

Gould, Stephen Jay (1997a), "Evolution: The Pleasures of Pluralism," *New York Review of Books*, 44[11]:47-52, June 26.

Gould, Stephen Jay (1997b), "Foreword: The Positive Power of Skepticism," *Why People Believe Weird Things*, Michael Shermer (New York: W.H. Freeman).

Gould, Stephen Jay and Richard C. Lewontin (1979), "The Spandrels of San Marco and the Panglossian Paradigm: A Critique of the Adaptationist Programme," *Proceedings of the Royal Society of London*, Series B, 205:581-598.

Gould, Stephen Jay and Elisabeth S. Vrba (1982), "Exaptation —A Missing Term in the Science of Form," *Paleobiology,* 8[1]: 4-15.

Granit, Ragnar (1982), "Reflections on the Evolution of the Mind and Environment," *Mind in Nature: Nobel Conference XVII,* ed. Richard Q. Elvee (San Francisco, CA: Harper and Row).

Grassé, Pierre-Paul (1977), *Evolution of Living Organisms* (New York: Academic Press).

Green, D.E. and R.F. Goldberger (1967), *Molecular Insights into the Living Process* (New York: Academic Press).

Greenfield, Susan (2002), "Mind, Brain and Consciousness," *British Journal of Psychiatry,* 181:91-93.

Gregory, Richard L. (1977), "Consciousness," *The Encyclopaedia of Ignorance,* ed. Ronald Duncan and Miranda Weston-Smith (Oxford, England: Pergamon), pp. 273-281.

Gregory, W.K. (1927), "*Hesperopithecus* Apparently not an Ape nor a Man," *Science,* 66:579-581, December.

Gribbin, John and Jeremy Cherfas (1982), *The Monkey Puzzle* (New York: Pantheon).

Griffin, Donald R. (2001), *Animal Minds: Beyond Cognition to Consciousness* (Chicago, IL: University of Chicago Press), revised edition.

Haile-Selassie, Yohannes (2001), "Late Miocene Hominids from the Middle Awash, Ethiopia," *Nature,* 412:178-181, July 12.

Haney, Daniel (2002), "Humans: More Genes than Thought?," [On-line], URL: http://www.msnbc.com/news/6185458.asp, August 23.

Harold, Franklin M. (2001), *The Way of the Cell* (Oxford, England: Oxford University Press).

Harris, R.L., G.L. Archer Jr., and B.K. Waltke (1980), *Theological Wordbook of the Old Testament* (Chicago, IL: Moody).

Hausler, Martin and Peter Schmid (1995), "Comparison of the Pelvis of Sts 14 and AL 288-1: Implications for Birth and Sexual Dimorphism in Australopithecines," *Journal of Human Evolution*, 29:363-383.

Heeren, Fred (1995), *Show Me God* (Wheeling, IL: Searchlight Publications).

Heinberg, Richard (1999), *Cloning the Buddha: The Moral Impact of Biotechnology* (Wheaton, IL: Quest Books).

Heyer, E. and M. Tremblay (1995), "Variability of the Genetic Contribution of Quebec Population Founders Associated to Some Deleterious Genes," *American Journal of Human Genetics,* 56[4]:970-978.

Highfield, Roger (2002), "Spermless Fertilization," *New Zealand Herald* [July 1], [On-line], URL: http://www.dhushara.com/book/upd2/jul01/scans1/egge.htm.

Hinshelwood, Cyril (1965), "Discussion," *Brain and Conscious Experience* (Rome, Italy: Pontifica Academia Scientarium). [Dr. Hinshelwood's comments formed part of a group discussion concerning a paper ("Ethology and Consciousness") presented by W.H. Thorpe at a symposium held at the Vatican during the week of September 28-October 4, 1964; see Eccles, 1966, pp. pp. 470-505.]

Hodgson, Shadworth (1870), *The Theory of Practice* (London: Longmans, Green, Reader, and Dyer).

Hofstadter, Douglas R. (1980), *Godel, Escher, Bach: An Eternal Golden Braid* (New York: Vintage Books).

Holloway, R.L. (1976), "Paleoneurological Evidence for Language Origins," *Origins and Evolution of Language and Speech*, ed. S.R. Harnad, D. Horst, and J. Lancaster, *Annals of New York Academy of Science*, 280:330-348.

Horgan, John (1995), "A Sign is Born," *Scientific American,* 273[6]:18-19, December.

Horgan, John (1996), *The End of Science* (Reading, MA: Addison-Wesley).

Houston, Alasdair (1990), "Matching, Maximizing and Melioration as Alternative Descriptions of Behaviour," *From Animals to Animats*, ed. J.A. Meyer and S. Wilson (Cambridge, MA: MIT Press), pp. 498-509.

Hoyle, Fred and Chandra Wickramasinghe (1993), *Our Place in the Cosmos* (London: J.M. Dent).

Howe, George (1971), "Evolution and the Problem of Man," *Scientific Studies in Special Creation*, ed. Walter E. Lammerts (Grand Rapids, MI: Baker), pp. 206-228.

Hublin, J.J., F. Spoor, M. Braun, F. Zonneveld, and S. Condemi (1996), "A Late Neanderthal Associated with Upper Palaeolithic Artifacts," *Nature,* 381:224-226, May 16.

Hull, David (1965), "The Effect of Essentialism on Taxonomy—Two Thousand Years of Stasis [Part II]," *British Journal for the Philosophy of Science*, 16[61]:1–18.

"Human Genome Report Press Release" (2003), International Consortium Completes Human Genome Project, [Online], URL: http://www.ornl.gov/TechResources/Human_Genome/project/50yr.html, April 14.

"Human Origins" (1997), *Discover*, 18[4]:19, April.

Humphrey, Nicholas (1978), "Nature's Psychologists, *New Scientist,* 78:900-903.

Hunt, Dave (1996), *In Defense of the Faith* (Eugene, OR: Harvest House).

Hurley S.L. (1998), *Consciousness in Action* (Cambridge, MA: Harvard University Press).

Huxley, Julian (1957), *Religion Without Revelation* (New York: Mentor Books).

Huxley, Julian (1960), "The Evolutionary Vision," *Issues in Evolution* [Volume 3 of *Evolution After Darwin*, ed. Sol Tax], (Chicago, IL: University of Chicago Press).

Huxley, Thomas H., (1870a), "Descartes," *Lay Sermons, Addresses, and Reviews* (London: D. Appleton).

Huxley, Thomas H. (1870b), "On the Physical Basis of Life," *Lay Sermons, Addresses, and Reviews* (London: D. Appleton).

Huxley, Thomas H. (1871), "Mr. Darwin's Critics," *Contemporary Review*, November.

"Italian Cloning Scientist Says Three Cloned Embryos Implanted" (2002), [On-line], URL: http://www.lifesite.net/ldn/2002/apr/02042404.html.

Ivanhoe, F. (1970), "Was Virchow Right About Neanderthal?" *Nature*, 227:577-579, August 8.

Jablonski, Nina G. and George Chaplin (2002), "Skin Deep," *Scientific American*, 287[4]:74-81, October.

Jacobson, Homer (1955), "Information, Reproduction, and the Origin of Life," *American Scientist*, 43:119-127, January.

Jahn, Robert G. and Brenda J. Dunne (1994), "The Spiritual Substance of Science," *New Metaphysical Foundations of Modern Science*, ed. Willis Harman and Jane Clark (Sausalito, CA: Institute of Noetic Sciences), pp. 157-177.

Jasper H.H., L. Descarries, V.F. Castelucci, and S. Rossignol, eds. (1998), *Consciousness at the Frontiers of Neuroscience* (Philadelphia, PA: Lippincott-Raven), pp. 75-94.

Jastrow, Robert (1981), *The Enchanted Loom: Mind in the Universe* (New York: Simon and Schuster).

Jastrow, Robert (1982), "A Scientist Caught Between Two Faiths," Interview with Bill Durbin, *Christianity Today*, August 6.

Jeans, James (1930), *The [London] Times*, November 5.

Jeeves, Malcolm (1998), "Brain, Mind and Behavior," *Whatever Happened to the Soul: Scientific and Theological Portraits of Human Nature*, ed. Warren S. Brown, Nancey Murphy, and H.N. Malony (Minneapolis, MN: Fortress Press), pp. 73-98.

Jennings, H.S. (1930), *The Biological Basis of Human Nature* (New York: W.W. Norton).

Johanson, Donald C. (1996), "Face-to-Face with Lucy's Family," *National Geographic,* 189[3]:96-117, March.

Johanson, Donald C. and Blake Edgar (1996), *From Lucy to Language* (New York: Nevraumont).

Johanson, Donald C. and Maitland Edey (1981), *Lucy: The Beginnings of Humankind* (New York: Simon & Schuster).

Johanson, Donald, Lenora Johanson, and Blake Edgar, (1994) *Ancestors: In Search of Human Origins* (New York: Villard Books).

Johanson, Donald C. and Tim D. White (1979), "A Systematic Assessment of Early African Hominids," *Science,* 203: 321-330, January 26.

Johanson, Donald C., Tim D. White, and Yves Coppens (1978), "A New Species of the Genus *Australopithecus* (Primates: *Hominidae*) from the Pliocene of Eastern Africa," *Kirtlandia,* 28:2-14.

Jones, Steve (1993), *The Language of Genes* (New York: Doubleday).

Jones, Steve (1996), *In the Blood: God, Genes, and Destiny* (London: HarperCollins).

Jones, Steve, Robert Martin, and David Pilbeam, eds. (1992), *Cambridge Encyclopedia of Human Evolution* (New York: Cambridge University Press).

Kahn, Patricia and Ann Gibbons (1997), "DNA from an Extinct Human," *Science,* 277:176-178, July 11.

Kandel, Eric R. (1991), "Nerve Cells and Behavior," *Principles of Neural Science,* ed. Eric R. Kandel, James H. Schwartz, and Thomas M. Jessell (New York: Elsevier), third edition.

Keesing, Roger M. and Felix M. Keesing (1971), *New Perspectives in Cultural Anthropology* (New York: Holt, Rinehart and Winston).

Kety, S.S. (1960), "A Biologist Examines the Mind and Behavior," *Science,* 132:1863.

Kimbel, William, Donald C. Johanson, and Yoel Rak (1994), "The First Skull and Other New Discoveries of *Australopithecus afarensis* at Hadar, Ethiopia," *Nature,* 368:449-451, March 31.

King, Mary-Claire and A.C. Wilson (1975), "Evolution at Two Levels in Humans and Chimpanzees," *Science,* 188:107-116, April 11.

Kitcher, Philip (1982), *Abusing Science: The Case Against Creationism* (Massachusetts: MIT Press).

Klein, Richard (1989), *The Human Career: Human Biological and Cultural Origins* (Chicago, IL: University of Chicago Press).

Koch, Christof (1997), "Computation and the Single Neuron," *Nature,* 385:207-210, January 16.

Koestler Arthur (1967), *Ghost in the Machine* (London: Hutchinson).

Koestler, Arthur (1978), *Janus: A Summing Up* (New York: Vintage Books).

Koshland, Daniel E. Jr., (2002), "The Seven Pillars of Life," *Science,* 295:2215-2216, March 22.

Krings, M.A. Stone, R.W. Krainitzki, M. Stoneking, and S. Pääbo (1997), "Neanderthal DNA sequences and the Origin of Modern Humans" *Cell,* 90:19-30, July 11.

Kubie, Lawrence S. (1956), *Brain Mechanisms and Consciousness: A Symposium,* ed. Edgar D. Adrian, Frederick Brenner, and Herbert H. Jasper (Oxford, England: Blackwell).

Kurtz, Paul (1973), "Scientific Humanism," *The Humanist Alternative,* ed. Paul Kurtz (Buffalo, New York: Prometheus).

Lack, D. (1961), *Evolutionary Theory and Christian Belief: The Unresolved Conflict* (London: Metheun).

Langone, John (1980), *Like, Love, Lust* (London: Little Brown).

Laszlo, Ervin (1987), *Evolution: The Grand Synthesis* (Boston, MA: New Science Library).

Leake, Chauncey D. (1964), "Perspectives in Adaptation: Historical Background," *Handbook of Physiology* (Washington, D.C.: American Physiological Society).

Leakey, Louis S.B. (1960), "Finding the World's Earliest Man," *National Geographic,* 118[3]:420-435, September.

Leakey, Louis S.B. (1966), "*Homo habilis, Homo erectus,* and *Australopithecus,*" *Nature,* 209:1280-1281.

Leakey, Louis S.B., P.V. Tobias, and J.R. Napier (1964), "A New Species of the Genus *Homo* from Olduvai Gorge, *Nature,* 202:7-9, April 4.

Leakey, Mary D. (1971), *Olduvai Gorge* (Cambridge, England: Cambridge University Press).

Leakey, Mary D. (1979), "Footprints in the Ashes of Time," *National Geographic,* 155:446-457, April.

Leakey, Mary D. (1984), *Disclosing the Past* (New York: Doubleday).

Leakey, Meave, C. Feibel, I. McDougall, and A. Walker (1995), "New Four-million-year-old Species from Kanapoi and Allia Bay, Kenya," *Nature,* 376:565-571, August 17.

Leakey, Meave, et al. (2001), "New Hominin Genus from Eastern Africa Shows Diverse Middle Pliocene Lineages," *Nature,* 410:433-440, March 22.

Leakey, Richard (1973a), "Evidence for an Advanced Plio-Pleistocene Hominid from East Rudolf, Kenya," *Nature,* 242: 447-450, April 13.

Leakey, Richard (1973b), "Skull 1470," *National Geographic,* 143 [6]:819-829, June.

Leakey, Richard (1994), *The Origin of Humankind* (New York: Basic).

Leakey Richard and Roger Lewin (1977), *Origins* (New York: E.P. Dutton).

Leakey, Richard and Roger Lewin (1978), *People of the Lake* (New York: E.P. Dutton).

Leakey, Richard and Roger Lewin (1992), *Origins Reconsidered: In Search of What Makes Us Human* (New York: Doubleday).

"Leakey's New Skull Changes our Pedigree and Lengthens our Past" (1972), *Science News,* 102:324. November 18.

Lemonick, Michael D. (1987), "Everyone's Genealogical Mother," *Time,* p. 66, January 26.

Lemonick, Michael D. (1994), "How Man Began," *Time,* 143 [11]:80-87, March 14.

Lemonick, Michael D. (2003a), "The Power of Mood," *Time,* 161[3]:64-69, January 20.

Lemonick, Michael D. (2003b), "Your Mind, Your Body," *Time,* 161[3]:63, January 20.

Lemonick, Michael D. and Andrea Dorfman (1999), "Up from the Apes," *Time,* 154[8]:50-58, August 23.

Lemonick, Michael D. and Andrea Dorfman (2001), "One Giant Step for Mankind," *Time,* 158[3]:54-61, July 23.

Lewin, Roger (1987), "The Unmasking of Mitochondrial Eve," *Science,* 238:24-26, October 2.

Lewin, Roger (1992), *Complexity: Life at the Edge of Chaos* (New York: Macmillan).

Lewis, C.S. (1960), *Studies in Words* (Cambridge, England: Cambridge University Press).

Lewis, Jack P. (1988), "Living Soul," *Exegesis of Difficult Passages* (Searcy, AR: Resource Publications).

Lewontin, Richard (1995), *Human Diversity* (Scientific American Library: New York).

Lewontin, Richard (1997), "Billions and Billions of Demons," *The New York Review,* January 9.

Lieberman, Philip (1997), "Peak Capacity," *The Sciences,* 37:27, November/December.

Lieberman, Philip (1998), *Eve Spoke: Human Language and Human Evolution* (New York: W.W. Norton).

Libet B. (1996), "Neural Processes in the Production of Conscious Experience," *The Science of Consciousness*, ed. M. Velmans (London: Routledge), pp. 96-117.

Lipson, H.S. (1980), "A Physicist Looks at Evolution," *Physics Bulletin*, 31:138, May.

Lloyd, D. (1989), *Simple Minds* (Cambridge, MA: MIT Press).

Lorenz, K. (1971), *Studies in Animal and Human Behavior* (London: Meuthen).

Lubenow, Marvin (1992), *Bones of Contention* (Grand Rapids, MI: Baker).

Lubenow, Marvin (1998), "Recovery of Neandertal mtDNA: An Evaluation," *CEN Technical Journal*, 12[1]:87-97.

Lyons, Eric and Bert Thompson (2002a), "In the 'Image and Likeness of God' [Part I]," *Reason & Revelation*, 22:17-23, March.

Lyons, Eric and Bert Thompson (2002b), "In the 'Image and Likeness of God' [Part II]," *Reason & Revelation*, 22:25-31, April.

MacKay, David (1965), "Discussion," *Brain and Conscious Experience* (Rome, Italy: Pontifica Academia Scientarium). [Dr. MacKay's comments formed part of a group discussion concerning a paper ("Ethology and Consciousness") presented by W.H. Thorpe at a symposium held at the Vatican during the week of September 28-October 4, 1964; see Eccles, 1965, pp. 470-505.]

Mackay, John (1984), "The Origin of the Races," *Creation Ex Nihilo*, 6[4]:6-12, May.

Maddox, John (1993), "The Kinship of Apes and People," *Nature*, 364:185, July 15.

Maddox, John (1994), "The Genesis Code by Numbers," *Nature,* 367:111, January 13.

Maddox, John (1998), *What Remains to be Discovered* (New York: The Free Press).

Major, Trevor J. (1994), "Chimp Speak," *Resources* (in *Reason & Revelation*), 14[3]:1, March.

Major, Trevor J. (1995), "Do Animals Possess the Same Kind of Intelligence as Human Beings?," *Reason & Revelation*, 15:87-88, November.

Major, Trevor J. (1996), "Human Evolution: The Molecular and Fossil Evidence—Part I," *Reason & Revelation*, 16:73-77, October.

Major, Trevor J. (1998), "The Origin of Peoples," *Reason & Revelation*, 18:9-14, February.

Malakoff, David (2001), "Will a Smaller Genome Complicate the Patent Chase,?" *Science*, 291:1194, February 16.

Margulis, Lynn and Dorion Sagan (1995), *What is Life?* (Berkeley, CA: University of California Press).

Margulis, Lynn and Dorion Sagan (1997), *Slanted Truths: Essays on Gaia, Symbiosis, and Evolution* (New York: Springer-Verlag).

Marks, Jonathan (2000), "98% Alike? (What Similarity to Apes Tells Us about Our Understanding of Genetics)," *The Chronicle of Higher Education*, May 12.

Marks, Jonathan (2002), *What It Means to be 98% Chimpanzee* (Berkeley, CA: University of California Press).

Mather, Kirtley F. (1986), *The Permissive Universe* (Albuquerque, NM: University of New Mexico Press).

Matthews, Stephen, Bernard Comrie, and Marcia Polinsky, eds. (1996), *Atlas of Languages: The Origin and Development of Languages Throughout the World* (New York: Facts on File, Inc.).

Maynard-Smith, John (1971), "What Use is Sex?," *Journal of Theoretical Biology*, 30:319-335.

Maynard-Smith, John (1986), *The Problems of Biology* (Oxford, England: Oxford University Press).

Mayr, Ernst (1965), *Animal Species and Evolution* (Boston: Harvard University Press).

Mayr, Ernst (1982), *The Growth of Biological Thought* (Cambridge, MA: Harvard University Press).

Mayr, Ernst (2001), *What Evolution Is* (New York: Basic Books).

McCall, William (2001), "It's Old, Unusual–Is It Us?," *Tallahassee Democrat*, pp. 3A-4A, March 22.

McCrone, John (1991), *The Ape That Spoke: Language and the Evolution of the Human Mind* (New York: William Morrow and Company).

McGinn, Colin (1991), *The Problem of Consciousness* (Oxford, England: Basil Blackwell).

McGinn, Colin (1993), *The Problem of Consciousness: Essays Towards a Resolution* (Malden, MA: Blackwell).

McKee, Jennifer (2002), "Fossil May Shed Light on Human Evolution," *Albuquerque Journal,* March 21.

Medawar, P.B. and J. Medawar (1977), *The Life Sciences: Current Ideas of Biology* (New York: Harper & Row).

Melnick, D. and G. Hoelzer (1992), "What in the Study of Primate Evolution is mtDNA Good For?," *American Journal of Physical Anthropology.*

Menton, David (1988), "The Scientific Evidence for the Origin of Man," [On-line], URL: http://www.evolusham.com /a_9.htm.

Metzinger T., ed. (1995), *Conscious Experience* (Schoningh: Imprint Academic).

Miller, Kenneth R. (1999), *Finding Darwin's God: A Scientist's Search for Common Ground Between God and Evolution* (New York: Cliff Street Books)

Milner, A.D. and M.D. Rugg (1992), *The Neuropsychology of Consciousness* (London: Academic Press).

Monod, Jacques (1971), *Chance and Necessity*, trans. A. Wainhouse (New York: Knopf).

Monod, Jacques (1972), *Chance and Necessity* (London: Collins).

Montagu, Ashley (1957), *Man: His First Million Years* (Yonkers, New York: World Publishers).

Moore, John N. (1983), *How to Teach Origins Without ACLU Interference* (Milford, MI: Mott Media).

Moore, Keith L. and T.V.N. Persaud (1993), *The Developing Human* (Philadelphia, PA: W.B. Saunders).

Morey, Robert A. (1984), *Death and the Afterlife* (Minneapolis, MN: Bethany House).

Morgan, Elaine (1989), *The Aquatic Ape: A Theory of Human Evolution* (London: Souvenir Press).

Morris, Andrew A. M., and Robert N. Lightowlers (2000), "Can Paternal mtDNA be Inherited?," *The Lancet*, 355:1290-1291, April 15.

Morris, John D. (2002), "There They Go Again!," *Acts and Facts*, 31[9]:1-2, September.

Morris, Richard (2001), *The Evolutionists: The Struggle for Darwin's Soul* (New York: W.H. Freeman).

Mountain, J.L., A.A. Lin, A.M. Bowcock, and L. Cavalli-Sforza (1993), "Evolution of Modern Humans: Evidence from Nuclear DNA Polymorphisms," *The Origin of Modern Humans and the Impact of Chronometric Dating*, ed. M.J. Aitken, C.B. Stringer, and P.A. Mellars (Princeton, NJ: Princeton University Press).

Muchmore, Elaine A., Sandra Diaz, and Ajit Varki (1998), "A Structural Difference Between the Cell Surfaces of Humans and the Great Apes," *American Journal of Physical Anthropology*, 107[2]:187-198, October.

Murphy, Nancey (1998), "Nonreductive Physicalism: Philosophical Issues," *What Ever Happened to the Soul?: Scientific and Theological Portraits of Human Nature*, ed. Warren S. Brown, Nancey Murphy, and H. Newton Malony (Minneapolis, MN: Fortress Press), pp. 127-148.

"Neanderthal Noisemaker" (1996), *Science News,* 150:328, November 16.

Netter, Frank H (1994), *Atlas of Human Anatomy* (Summit, NJ: Ciba-Geigy Corporation).

Nottebohm, F. (1980), "Testosterone Triggers Growth of Brain Vocal Control Nuclei in Adult Female Canaries," *Brain Research,* 189:429-436.

Novikoff, Alex (1945), "The Concept of Integrative Levels of Biology," *Science,* 101:212-213, March 2.

Nowak, Martin A. and David C. Krakauer (1999), "The Evolution of Language," *Proceedings of the National Academy of Science,* 96:8028-8033, July 6.

Nowak, Martin A., N.L. Komarova, and P. Niyogi (2001), "Evolution of Universal Grammar," *Science,* 291:114-118, January 5.

Nuland, Sherwin B. (1997), *The Wisdom of the Body* (New York: Knopf).

O'Hear, Anthony (1997), *Beyond Evolution: Human Nature and the Limits of Evolutionary Explanation* (New York: Oxford University Press).

Oliwenstein, Lori (1995), "Lucy's Walk," *Discover,* 16[1]:42, January.

Oller, J.W. and Omdahl, J.L. (1997), "Origin of the Human Language Capacity: In Whose Image?," *The Creation Hypothesis,* ed. J.P. Moreland (Downers Grove, IL: InterVarsity Press).

Onion, Amanda (2002), "New Face in the Family," [On-line], URL: http://abcnews.go.com/sections/scitech/DaileyNews/hominid020710.html, July 10.

Orgel, Leslie (1982), "Darwinism at the Very Beginning of Life," *New Scientist,* 94:149-152, April 15.

Ornstein, Robert (1991), *The Evolution of Consciousness* (New York: Prentice Hall Press).

Ornstein, Robert and Richard F. Thompson (1984), *The Amazing Brain* (Boston, MA: Houghton Mifflin).

Oxnard, Charles E. (1975), "The Place of the Australopithecines in Human Evolution: Grounds for Doubt?," *Nature,* 258:389-395, December.

Oxnard, Charles E. (1981), *Homo,* 30:243.

Palmer, Douglas (2002), "One Great Leap for Mankind," *New Scientist,* 173[2334]:50, March 16.

Parker, S.T., P.W. Mitchell, and M.L. Boccia, eds. (1994), *Self-awareness in Animals and Humans: Developmental Perspectives* (New York: Cambridge University Press).

Parsons, Thomas J., et al. (1997), "A High Observed Substitution Rate in the Human Mitochondrial DNA Control Region," *Nature Genetics,* 15:363.

Partridge, T.C. (1973), "Geomorphological Dating of Cave Openings at Makapansagat, Sterkfontein, Swartkrans, and Taung," *Nature,* 246:75-79, November 9.

Patterson, Colin (1999), *Evolution* (Ithaca, NY: Cornell University Press).

Pearson, Helen (2003a), "Human Fertility Experiment Prompts Wrath," *Nature,* Science Update, [On-line], URL: http://www.nature.com/nsu/031013/031013-4.html.

Pearson, Helen (2003b), "Human Genome Done and Dusted," *Nature Science Update,* [On-line], URL: http://www.nature.com/nsu/030414/030414-1.html.

Peck, Joel (2003), "Keeping Up with Evolution," [book review of *Encyclopedia of Evolution*, ed. Mark Pagel, Oxford University Press, 2002] *Nature,* 421:895, February 27.

Penfield, Wilder (1961), "The Physiological Basis of the Mind." *Man and Civilization: Control of the Mind,* ed. S.M. Farber and R.H.L. Wilson (New York: McGraw-Hill), pp. 3-17.

Penfield, Wilder (1975), *The Mystery of the Mind: A Critical Study of Consciousness and the Human Brain* (Princeton, NJ: Princeton University Press).

Pennisi, Elizabeth (2001), "The Human Genome," *Science,* 291: 1177-1180, February 16.

Pennisi, Elizabeth (2002), "Jumbled DNA Separates Chimps and Humans," *Science,* 298:719-721, October 25.

Penrose, Roger (1989), *The Emperor's New Mind: Concerning Computers, Minds, and the Laws of Physics* (New York: Oxford University Press).

Penrose Roger (1994), *Shadows of the Mind* (Oxford, England: Oxford University Press).

Penrose, Roger (1997), *The Large, the Small and the Human Brain* (Cambridge, England: Cambridge University Press).

Pilbeam, David (1968), *Advancement of Science,* 24:368.

Pilbeam, David (1982), "New Hominoid Skull Material from the Miocene of Pakistan," *Nature,* 295:232-234, January.

Pilbeam, David and Elwyn Simons (1971), "A Gorilla-Sized Ape from the Miocene of India," *Science,* 173:23, July.

Pinker, Steven (1994), *The Language Instinct* (New York: William Morrow).

Pinker, Steven (1997a), *How the Mind Works* (New York: W.W. Norton).

Pinker, Steven (1997b), "Interview," *Sunday Telegraph* (London).

Pinker, Steven (2000), "Will the Mind Figure Out How the Brain Works?," *Time*, 155[14]:90-91, April 10.

Pinker, Steven (2003), "Are Your Genes to Blame?," *Time*, 161 [3]:99-100, January 20.

Planck, Max (1950), *Scientific Autobiography and Other Papers* (London: Williams and Norgate).

Poe, Harry Lee and Jimmy H. Davis (2000), *Science and Faith* (Nashville, TN: Broadman and Holman).

Polkinghorne, John (1986), *One World: The Interaction of Science and Theology* (Princeton, NJ: Princeton University Press).

Polkinghorne, John (2001), "Understanding the Universe," *Annals of the New York Academy of Sciences*, 950:175-182.

Popper, Karl R. (1972), *Objective Knowledge: An Evolutionary Approach* (Oxford, England: Oxford University Press).

Popper, Karl R. and John C. Eccles (1977), *The Self and Its Brain* (Berlin: Springer-Verlag).

Poundstone, William (1999), *Carl Sagan: A Life in the Cosmos* (New York: Henry Holt and Co.).

Profet, Margie (1993), "Menstruation as a Defense Against Pathogens Transported by Sperm," *Quarterly Review of Biology*, 68:355-386.

Provine, William (1998), "Evolution: Free Will and Punishment and Meaning in Life," [On-line], URL: http://fp.bio .utk.edu/darwin/1998/slides_view/default.html.

Ratzsch, Del (2000), *Science and Its Limits: The Natural Sciences in Christian Perspective* (Downers Grove, IL: InterVarsity Press).

Raup, David (1981), Letter to the editor, *Science*, 13:289, July 17.

Reader, John (1981), "Whatever Happen to *Zinjanthropus?*," *New Scientist*, 89:802, March 26.

Reichenbach, Bruce and V. Elving Anderson (1995), *On Behalf of God* (Grand Rapids, MI: Eerdmans).

ReMine, Walter James (1993), *The Biotic Message: Evolution Versus Message Theory* (Saint Paul, MN: St. Paul Science).

Rennie, John (2002), "15 Answers to Creationist Nonsense," *Scientific American*, 287[1]:78-85, July.

Rensberger, Boyce (1981), "Racial Odyssey," *Science Digest*, 89[1]:50-57,134-136, January/February.

Richmond, Brian G. and David S. Strait (2000), "Evidence that Humans Evolved from a Knuckle-Walking Ancestor," *Nature*, 404:382-385, March 23.

Ridley, Mark (2001), *The Cooperative Gene* (New York: The Free Press).

Ridley, Matt (1993), *The Red Queen* (London: Viking).

Rifkin, Jeremy (1983), *Algeny* (New York: Viking Press).

Roach, John (2003), "Oldest *Homo sapiens* Fossils Found, Experts Say," *National Geographic*, [On-line] URL: http://news.nationalgeographic.com/news/2003/06/0611_030611_earliesthuman.html.

Robbins, Louise (1979), *Science News*, 115:196-197.

Rodriguez-Trelles, Francisco, Rosa Tarrio, and Francisco J. Ayala (2001), "Erratic Overdispersion of Three Molecular Clocks: GPDH, SOD, and XDH," *Proceedings of the National Academy of Sciences*, 98:11405-11410, September 25.

Rodriguez-Trelles, Francisco, Rosa Tarrio, and Francisco J. Ayala (2002), "A Methodological Bias Toward Overestimation of Molecular Evolutionary Time Scales," *Proceedings of the National Academy of Sciences*, 99:8112-8115, June 11.

Rolston, Holmes (1999), *Genes, Genesis and God* (Cambridge, England: Cambridge University Press).

Rose S., ed. (1998), *From Brains to Consciousness?* (Princeton, NJ: Princeton University Press).

Ross, Phillip E. (1991), "Hard Words," *Scientific American*, 264 [4]:138-147, April.

Rudin, Norah (1997), *Dictionary of Modern Biology* (Hauppauge, NY: Barrons).

Ruse, Michael (1995), *Evolutionary Naturalism* (Routledge: London).

Ruse, Michael (2001a), *Can a Darwinian Be a Christian?* (New York: Cambridge University Press).

Ruse, Michael (2001b), *The Evolution Wars* (New Brunswick, NJ: Rutgers University Press).

Ryle, Gilbert (1949), *The Concept of Mind* (New York: Barnes and Noble).

Sackheim, George I. and Dennis D. Lehman (1994), *Chemistry for the Health Sciences* (New York: Macmillan).

Savage-Rumbaugh, Sue and Roger Lewin (1994), "Ape at the Brink," *Discover*, 15[9]:90-96,98, September.

Schecter, Julie (1984), "How Did Sex Come About?," *Bioscience*, 34:680-681, December.

Schrödinger, Erwin (1967), *What is Life? & Mind and Matter* (Cambridge, England: Cambridge University Press).

Schutzenberger, Marcel-Paul (1996), "The Miracles of Darwinism," *Origins & Design*, 17[2]:10-15, Spring.

Schwabe, Christian (1986), "On the Validity of Molecular Evolution," *Trends in Biochemical Sciences*, 11:280-283, July.

Schwartz, James (1999), "Oh My Darwin! Who's the Fittest Evolutionary Thinker of Them All?," [On-line], URL: http://www.arn.org/docs2/news/ohmydarwin1199.htm.

Schwartz, Marianne and John Vissing (2002), "Paternal Inheritance of Mitochondrial DNA," *New England Journal of Medicine*, 347:576-580, August 22.

Scott, Alwyn (1995), *Stairway to the Mind: The Controversial New Science of Consciousness* (New York: Springer-Verlag).

Scott, Andrew (1985), "Update on Genesis," *New Scientist,* 106:30-33, May 2.

Searle, John (1984), *Minds, Brain and Science* (Cambridge, MA: Harvard University Press).

Searle, John (1992), *The Rediscovery of the Mind* (Cambridge, MA: MIT Press).

Sheldrake, Rupert (1981), *A New Science of Life: The Hypothesis of Formative Causation* (Los Angeles, CA: Tarcher).

Sheppard, P.M. (1963), "Evolution in Bisexually Reproducing Organisms," *Evolution as a Process*, ed. J. Huxley, A.C. Hardy, and E.B. Ford (New York: Collier), pp. 237-256.

Sherrington, Charles S. (1975), *Man on His Nature* (Cambridge, England: Cambridge University Press).

Shouse, Ben (2002), "Revisiting the Numbers: Human Genes and Whales," *Science,* 295:1457, February 22.

Shreeve, James (1996), "New Skeleton Gives Path from Trees to Ground an Odd Turn," *Science,* 272:654, May 3.

Simoni, L., F. Calafell, D. Pettener, J. Bertranpetit, and G. Barbujani (2000), "Geographic Patterns of mtDNA Diversity in Europe," *American Journal of Human Genetics,* 66:262-278, January.

Simpson, George Gaylord (1947), "The Problem of Plan and Purpose in Nature," *Scientific Monthly*, pp. 481-489.

Simpson, George Gaylord (1953), *Life of the Past* (New Haven, CT: Yale University Press).

Simpson, George Gaylord (1960), "The World into Which Darwin Led Us," *Science,* 131:966-974, April 1.

Simpson, George Gaylord (1964), *This View of Life* (Harcourt, Brace, & World: New York).

Simpson, George Gaylord (1966), "The Biological Nature of Man," *Science,* 152:467-477, April 22.

Simpson, George Gaylord (1967), *The Meaning of Evolution* (New Haven, CT: Yale University Press).

Sinnott, Edmund W. (1961), *Cell and Psyche: The Biology of Purpose* (New York: Harper & Row).

Sinnott, Edmund W., L.C. Dunn, and Theodosius Dobzhansky (1958), *Principles of Genetics* (Columbus, OH: McGraw Hill) fifth edition.

Skoyles, John R. and Dorion Sagan (2002), *Up from Dragons* (New York: McGraw-Hill).

Smythies, J.R. (1969), "Some Aspects of Consciousness," *Beyond Reductionism*, ed. Arthur Koestler and J.R. Smythies (London: Hutchinson).

Snelling, Andrew (1990), *The Revised Quote Book* (Sunnybank, Brisbane, Australia: Creation Science Foundation).

Sperry, Roger W. (1966), "Mind, Brain, and Humanist Values," *Bulletin of the Atomic Scientists*, September.

Sperry, Roger W. (1977), "Problems Outstanding in the Evolution of Brain Function," *The Encyclopaedia of Ignorance*, ed. Ronald Duncan and Miranda Weston-Smith (Oxford, England: Pergamon), pp. 423-433.

Sperry, Roger (1994), "Holding Course Amidst Shifting Paradigms," *New Metaphysical Foundations of Modern Science*, ed. Willis Harman and Jane Clark (Sausalito, CA: Institute of Noetic Sciences), pp. 97-121.

Spoor, Fred, Bernard Wood, and Frans Zonneveld (1994), "Implications of Early Hominid Labyrinthine Morphology for Evolution of Human Bipedal Locomotion," *Nature*, 369:645-648, June, 23.

Sproul, R.C., John Gerstner, and Arthur Lindsley (1984), *Classical Apologetics* (Grand Rapids, MI: Zondervan).

Stannard, Russell (2000), *The God Experiment: Can Science Prove the Existence of God?* (Mahway, NJ: Paulist Press).

Stern, Jack T. Jr. and Randall L. Susman (1983), "The Loco-motor Anatomy of *Australopithecus afarensis,*" *Journal of Physical Anthropology,* 60:279-317.

Strauss, Evelyn (1999a), "Can Mitochondrial Clocks Keep Time?," *Science,* 283:1435-1438, March 5.

Strauss, Evelyn (1999b), "mtDNA Shows Signs of Paternal Influence," *Science,* 286:2436, December 24.

Strawson, Galen (2003), *Freedom Evolves:* Evolution Explains It All for You," *New York Times,* [On-line], URL: http://www. nytimes.com/2003/03/02/books/review/002STRAWT. html, March 2. [This article is a review of Daniel Dennett's 2003 book, *Freedom Evolves.* Strawson is a professor of philosophy at the University of Reading in England, and author of *Freedom and Belief.*]

Strickberger, Monroe W. (2000), *Evolution* (Boston, MA: Jones and Bartlett), third edition.

Stringer, Andrew and Clive Gamble (1993), *In Search of Neanderthals* (New York: Thames and Hudson).

Stringer, C.B. and P. Andrews (1988), "Genetic and Fossil Evidence for the Origin of Modern Humans," *Science,* 239: 1263-1268, March 11.

Stringer, Chris (2003), "Out of Africa," *Nature,* 423:692, June 12.

Sunderland, Luther D. (1988), *Darwin's Enigma: Fossils and Other Problems* (El Cajon, CA: Master Books).

Susman, Randall L. (1994), "Fossil Evidence for Early Hominid Tool Use," *Science,* 265:1570-1573, September 9.

Sutherland, Stuart (1989), "Consciousness," *The Macmillan Dictionary of Psychology* (London: Macmillan).

Swisher, C.C. III, W.J. Rink, S.C. Anton, H.P. Schwarcz, et al. (1996), "Latest *Homo erectus* of Java: Potential Contemporaneity with *Homo sapiens* in Southeast Asia," *Science,* 274: 1870-1874, December 13.

Sykes, Bryan (1999), *The Human Inheritance: Genes, Language, and Evolution* (London: Oxford University Press).

Tattersall, Ian (1992), "The Many Faces of *Homo habilis*," *Evolutionary Anthropology*, 1[1]:34-36.

Tattersall, Ian (1998), *Becoming Human* (San Diego, CA: Harcourt Brace).

Tattersall, Ian (2002), *The Monkey in the Mirror: Essays on the Science of What Makes Us Human* (New York: Harcourt).

Tattersall, Ian, Eric Dolson, and John van Couvering, eds. (1988), *Encyclopedia of Human Evolution and Prehistory* (New York: Garland Publishing).

Taylor, Gordon Rattray (1979), *The Natural History of the Mind* (New York: E.P. Dutton).

Thomas, Lewis (1979), *The Medusa and the Snail* (New York: Viking).

Thomas, Lewis (1980),"On Science and Uncertainty," *Discover*, 1:59, October.

Thompson, Bert (2002), *Rock-Solid Faith: How to Sustain It* (Montgomery, AL: Apologetics Press).

Thorpe, W.H. (1965), "Ethology and Consciousness," *Brain and Conscious Experience*, ed. John C. Eccles (Rome, Italy: Pontifica Academia Scientarium), pp. 470-505. [This book is the written papers, and the written record of the oral discussions that took place concerning those papers, from a symposium held at the Vatican during the week of September 28-October 4, 1964.]

Thorpe, W.H. (1977), "The Frontiers of Biology," *Mind in Nature*, ed. John Cobb and David Griffin (Washington, D.C.: University Press of America).

Tierney, John, Lynda Wright, and Karen Springen (1988), "The Search for Adam and Eve," *Newsweek*, pp. 46-52, January 11.

"Tiny Worm Challenges Evolution" (no date), [On-line], URL: http://www.cs.unc.edu/~plaisted/ce/worm.html.

Toder, R. F. Grutzner, T. Haaf, and E. Bausch (2001), "Species-Specific Evolution of Repeated DNA sequences in Great Apes," *Chromosome Research*, 9:431-435.

Tolson, Jay (2002), "The Ghost Hunters," *U.S. News & World Report*, 133[23]:44-45, December 16.

Trefil, James (1996), *101 Things You Don't Know about Science and No One Else Does Either* (Boston, MA: Houghton Mifflin).

Trefil, James (1997), *Are We Unique? A Scientist Explores the Unparalleled Intelligence of the Human Mind* (New York: John Wiley & Sons).

Trinkaus, Erik (1978), "Hard Times Among the Neandertals," *Natural History*, 87[10]:58-63, December.

Tudge, Colin (2000), *The Impact of the Gene: From Mendel's Peas to Designer Babies* (New York: Hill and Wang).

Tuttle, Russell (1989), "The Pattern of Little Feet" [abstract], *American Journal of Physical Anthropology*, 78[2]:316, February.

Tuttle, Russell (1990), "The Pitted Pattern of Laetoli Feet," *Natural History*, pp. 60-65, March.

Twain, Mark (1883), *Life on the Mississippi* (Boston, MA: J.R. Osgood).

Van De Graaf, M. Kent and Stuart Ira Fox (1989), *Concepts of Human Anatomy and Physiology* (Dubuque, IA: William C. Brown).

Van Valen, Leigh (1973), "A New Evolutionary Law," *Evolutionary Theory*, 1:1-30.

Velmans M., ed. (1996), *The Science of Consciousness* (London: Routledge).

Velmans M. (2000), *Understanding Consciousness* (London: Routledge).

Vigilant, Linda, Mark Stoneking, Henry Harpending, Kristen Hawkes, and Allan C. Wilson (1991), "African Populations and the Evolution of Human Mitochondrial DNA," *Science*, 253:1503-1507, September 27.

Wakeford, Tom (2001), *Liaisons of Life* (New York: John Wiley & Sons).

Wald, George (1994), "The Cosmology of Life and Mind," *New Metaphysical Foundations of Modern Science*, ed. Willis Harman and Jane Clark (Sausalito, CA: Institute of Noetic Sciences), pp. 123-131.

Walker, Allan, R.E. Leakey, J.M. Harris, and F.H. Brown (1986), "2.5-Myr *Australopithecus boisei* from West of Lake Turkana, Kenya," *Nature*, 322:517-522, August 7.

Wallace, Robert A. (1975), *Biology: The World of Life* (Pacific Palisades, CA: Goodyear).

Ward, Peter (2001), *Future Evolution* (New York: Henry Holt).

Ward, Peter D. and Donald Brownlee (2000), *Rare Earth* (New York: Springer-Verlag).

Watson, James (2003), "You have to be Obsessive," Interview in *Time* magazine, 161[7]:52, February 17.

Watson, Lyall (1982), "The Water People," *Science Digest*, 90 [5]:44, May.

Weaver, Kenneth F. (1985), "The Search for Our Ancestors," *National Geographic*, 168[5]:560-623, November.

Weinberg, Steven (1977), *The First Three Minutes* (New York: Basic Books).

Weiskrantz, L. (1997), *Consciousness Lost and Found* (Oxford, England: Oxford University Press).

Weiss, Joseph (1990), "Unconscious Mental Functioning," *Scientific American*, March.

Wesson, Robert (1997), *Beyond Natural Selection* (Cambridge, MA: MIT Press).

White, Tim (2003), "Early Hominids–Diversity or Distortion?," *Science*, 299:1994-1995,1997, March 28.

White, Tim, G. Suwa, and B. Asfaw (1994), "*Australopithecus ramidus*, a New Species of Early Hominid from Aramis, Ethiopia," *Nature*, 371:306-312, September 22.

White, Tim, G. Suwa, and B. Asfaw (1995), "*Australopithecus ramidus*, a New Species of Early Hominid from Aramis, Ethiopia," [Corrigendum], *Nature*, 375:88, May 4.

White, Tim D., Berhane Asfaw, David DeGusta, Henry Gilbert, Gary D. Richards, Gen Suwa, and F. Clark Howell (2003), "Pleistocene *Homo sapiens* from Middle Awash, Ethiopia," *Nature*, 423:742-747, June 12.

Whittaker, R.H. (1959), "On the Broad Classification of Organisms," *Quarterly Review of Biology*, 34:210-226.

"Whose Ape Is It, Anyway?" (1984), *Science News*, 125:361, June 9.

Wieland, Carl (1999), "Towering Change," *Creation Ex Nihilo,* 22[1]:22-26, December-February, 2000.

Wilford, John N. (2002), "Skulls Found n Africa and Europe Challenge Theories of Human Origins," [On-line], URL: http://www.nytimes.com/2002/08/06/science/06SKUL.html?tntemail1.

Williams, George C. (1975), *Sex and Evolution* [in the *Monographs in Population Biology* series] (Princeton, NJ: Princeton University Press).

Williams, George C. (1977), *Sex and Evolution* (Princeton, NJ: Princeton University Press).

Williams, R. Sanders (2002), "Another Surprise from the Mitochondrial Genome," *New England Journal of Medicine*, 347: 609-611, August 22.

Wills, Christopher (1994), "The Skin We're In," *Discover*, 15 [11]:76-81, November.

Wills, Christopher (1998), *Children of Prometheus: The Accelerating Pace of Human Evolution* (Reading, MA: Perseus Books).

Wilson, Edward O. (1978), *On Human Nature* (Cambridge, MA: Harvard University Press).

Wilson, Edward O. (1998), *Consilience* (New York: Knopf).

Wilson, Peter J. (1980), *Man, The Promising Primate* (New Haven: Yale University Press).

Wise, Kurt (1994), "*Australopithecus ramidus* and the Fossil Record," *CEN Technical Journal,* 8[2]:160-165).

Wong, Kate (1998), "Ancestral Quandary," *Scientific American,* 278[1]:32, January.

Wright, Robert (2000), *Nonzero: The Logic of Human Destiny* (New York: Pantheon).

Wyller, Arne A. (1996), *The Creating Consciousness: Science as the Language of God* (Denver, CO: Murray and Beck).

Wysong, R.L. (1976), *The Creation-Evolution Controversy* (Midland, MI: Inquiry Press).

Zacharias, Ravi (1990), *A Shattered Visage* (Brentwood, TN: Wolgemuth & Hyatt).

Zeman, Adam (2001), "Consciousness," *Brain,* 124[7]:1263-1289, July.

Zhang, John, Guanglun Zhuang, Yong Zeng, Carlo Acosta, Yimin Shu, and Jamie Grifo (2003), "Pregnancy Derived from Human Nuclear Transfer" (Abstract), *Fertility and Sterility,* 80:[supplement 3]:S56, September.

Zihlman, Adrienne (1984), "Pygmy Chimps, People, and the Pundits," *New Scientist,* 104:349-40, November 15.

Zimmer, Carl (2000), *Parasite Rex* (New York: The Free Press).

Zimmer, Carl (2001), *Evolution* (New York: Harper Collins).

Zuckerkandl, Emile (1963), "Perspectives in Molecular Anthropology," *Classification and Human Evolution,* ed. S.L. Washburn (Chicago, IL: Aldine).

Zuckerman, Solly (1970), *Beyond the Ivory Tower* (New York: Taplinger).

SUBJECT INDEX

A

Aegyptopithecus zeuxis–16, 18,20
Afar Depression–27
AL 288-1–42,47-49,56
albino–442,444
animism–394
anti-pathogen hypothesis–169
Ardipithecus ramidus–27,29, 35
Ardipithecus ramidus kadabba–29-31,33
asexual reproduction–142-143,147-148,153,159,162
Australopithecus–9,15-16,24, 36,54,57,64,74-75,96
  Australopithecus afarensis– 3,28,33,36,41-45,50-53,55,57,60,66-67,73, 296
  Australopithecus africanus– 7,44,51,57-63,69,73, 226
  Australopithecus anamensis– 28-29,36,38
  Australopithecus boisei– 57,61-63

  Australopithecus garhi–38
  Australopithecus robustus– 61-63
  Australopithecus ramidus (see *Ardipithecus ramidus*)

B

binomial nomenclature–4
blastula–238
brain size–283
Broca's area–190-191

C

Cartesian approach–357
Cartesian dualism (see dualism)
Cartesian Theater–356,367
chimp DNA (see DNA)
chromosomal counts–103
chromosomes–103-105, 159,163
  double homologous–164
  sex chromosomes–164
  X chromosome–164
  Y chromosome–164
cloning–178,180

tree of life—167
trialist—411
triune brain—240
Tugen Hills—26
twelve cranial nerves—242

U

ultraviolet radiation—442
universal language—188-189

V

vitamin D—86-87,431-434,
448-449

W

Washoe—197,200
Wernicke's area—190
written language—222

X

X chromosomes (see
chromosomes)

Y

Y chromosome (see
chromosomes)

Z

Zinjanthropus boisei (see
Australopithecus boisei)

NAME INDEX

A

Adrian, E.D.–273-274, 362,398
Antinori, Severino–178
Aristotle–212-213
Asimov, Isaac–216,296-297
Awadalla, Philip–125

B

Bell, Graham–137,162, 252-253
Berger, Lee R.–8,10,57
Bergman, Jerry–142,149
Britten, Roy–107-108
Broca, Paul–190
Broom, Robert–57,61
Brunet, Michel–93-94

C

Cann, Rebecca–111,113, 115
Cardoso, Silvia–337
Carrington, Hereward–342,344,363-364, 395,398
Cavalli-Sforza, Luigi–130,132,154
Cave, A.J.E.–86

Chalmers, David–271, 350-351
Chaplin, George–431-432
Chomsky, Noam–189,197-198,205
Clark, W. Legros–283
Copeland, Herbert F.–5
Corballis, Michael–185
Crick, Francis–99-100,220, 233,249,265,272,301, 332,337,373,387-388

D

Damasio, Antonio–264
Dart, Raymond–57,61,63
Darwin, Charles–11,440
Dawkins, Richard–ix,29, 159,221,282,464
Dawkins, Marian–314
Dax, Mark–190
Delbrück, Max–336
Dennett, Daniel–218,232, 271,325-326,328,333-334,338,341,356,365-371, 373,381,393-394,399,420
Descartes, René–214-215, 354,356,358,360-361, 394,397-398

Poundstone, William—240
Prigogine, Ilya—308,356
Profet, Margie—169

R

Rennie, John—92
Richmond, Brian—50
Robinson, Daniel—236,247,
256,259,274,308,345,349,
364,374,377-378,382,396,
405,408,412,422
Robinson, John T.—57
Ruse, Michael—134,227,
234,237,254,273,275,281,
285-286,293,361,384

S

de Sade, Marquis—236
Sagan, Carl—ix,240
Sagan, Dorion—138-139,142,
146,156,158,195-197,236
Schmid, Peter—46-49
Schwartz, Karleve V.—6
Searle, John—367,370,379,
386-388
Senut, Brigitte—26,95
Shakespeare, William—213
Sherrington, Charles—336,
399,402-403
Simons, Elwyn—19,23-24,39
Simpson, George Gaylord—
ix,10,37,205,297-298,330
Skoyles, John R.—195-197

Smith-Woodward, Arthur—
89,91-92
Sperry, Roger—245,281,
308-309,336,340,345,
356-357,379,388-393,
403,422
Spoor, Fred—16,54
Stoneking, Mark—111
Strait, David—50
Strassmann, Beverly—169
Strauss, Evelyn—117-118

T

Thomas, Lewis—158,202
Trefil, James—217,240,277,
329,331,338,350,352,
356-357,366,397

V

da Vinci, Leonardo—213
Voltaire—223
Vrba, Elisabeth—225,279-
280

W

Wald, George—316,349,
415-416
Walker, Alan—53-54,60
Watson, James—99-100,337
Watson, Lyall—13
Weinberg, Steven—ix,298,
465
Weismann, August—161